# Behavior and Adaptation in Late Life

# Behavior and Adaptation in Late Life

BY 17 AUTHORS

EDITED BY

## Ewald W. Busse, M.D.

*J. P. Gibbons Professor and Chairman,*
*Department of Psychiatry, Duke University*
*School of Medicine; Director, Center for the Study*
*of Aging and Human Development,*
*Duke University*

AND

## Eric Pfeiffer, M.D.

*Associate Professor of Psychiatry,*
*Department of Psychiatry, Duke University*
*School of Medicine*

LITTLE, BROWN AND COMPANY
BOSTON

PUBLISHED IN GREAT BRITAIN
BY J. & A. CHURCHILL LTD., LONDON
BRITISH STANDARD BOOK NO. 7000 0169 7

PRINTED IN THE UNITED STATES OF AMERICA

# Contributing Authors

KURT W. BACK, Ph.D.
*Professor of Sociology,*
*Department of Sociology and Anthropology, Duke University;*
*Professor of Medical Sociology, Department of Psychiatry,*
*Duke University School of Medicine, Durham, N.C.*

EWALD W. BUSSE, M.D., D.Sc.
*J. P. Gibbons Professor and Chairman,*
*Department of Psychiatry, Duke University School of Medicine;*
*Director, Center for the Study of Aging and Human Development,*
*Duke University, Durham, N.C.*

CARL EISDORFER, M.D., Ph.D.
*Professor of Medical Psychology,*
*and Professor of Psychiatry, Department of Psychiatry,*
*Duke University School of Medicine, Durham, N.C.*

E. HARVEY ESTES, JR., M.D.
*Professor and Chairman, Department of Community Health Sciences,*
*Duke University School of Medicine,*
*Durham, N.C.*

ALVIN I. GOLDFARB, M.D.
*Associate Clinical Professor of Psychiatry,*
*Mt. Sinai Medical School, New York City;*
*Associate Attending Psychiatrist in charge of Geriatrics,*
*Mt. Sinai Hospital, New York City*

DOROTHY K. HEYMAN, M.S.W.
*Research Social Worker, Department of Psychiatry,*
*Duke University School of Medicine,*
*Durham, N.C.*

FRANCES C. JEFFERS, M.A.
*Research Associate, Center for the Study of Aging and Human Development,*
*and Research Social Worker and Counselor,*
*Information and Counseling Service for Older Persons,*
*Duke University School of Medicine, Durham, N.C.*

JUANITA M. KREPS, Ph.D.
*Professor of Economics, Department of Economics,*
*Duke University, Durham, N.C.*

ERDMAN PALMORE, Ph.D.
*Associate Professor of Medical Sociology,*
*Department of Psychiatry, Duke University School of Medicine,*
*Durham, N.C.*

ERIC PFEIFFER, M.D.
*Associate Professor of Psychiatry,*
*Department of Psychiatry, Duke University School of Medicine,*
*Durham, N.C.*

GRACE H. POLANSKY, M.S.S.A.
*Associate in Psychiatric Social Work,*
*Department of Psychiatry, Duke University School of Medicine,*
*Durham, N.C.*

ETHEL SHANAS, Ph.D.
*Professor of Sociology,*
*University of Illinois at Chicago Circle,*
*Chicago, Ill.*

JOSEPH J. SPENGLER, Ph.D.
*James B. Duke Professor of Economics,*
*Department of Economics, Duke University,*
*Durham, N.C.*

VIRGINIA STONE, Ph.D.
*Professor of Nursing, and Director of Graduate Studies,*
*Duke University School of Nursing,*
*Durham, N.C.*

ADRIAAN VERWOERDT, M.D.
*Associate Professor of Psychiatry,*
*and Director of Geropsychiatry Training Program,*
*Department of Psychiatry, Duke University School of Medicine,*
*Durham, N.C.*

F. STEPHEN VOGEL, M.D.
*Professor of Pathology,*
*Department of Pathology, Duke University School of Medicine,*
*Durham, N.C.*

H.- SHAN WANG, M.D.
*Assistant Professor of Psychiatry,*
*Department of Psychiatry, Duke University School of Medicine,*
*Durham, N.C.*

# Preface

In this book we have tried to bring together basic information which has a bearing on how people adapt to growing old. We feel that no single discipline, whether it be psychiatry, sociology, biology, or economics, can claim to offer a comprehensive explanation of how aged people act, think, and feel, or what the multiple determinants of their behavior are. Moreover, we feel that a mere collection of unrelated essays by experts from differing fields is not satisfactory, but that instead an integration of the diverse contributions is needed. We have sought to accomplish this integration in several ways. First, we invited as contributors to this volume investigators and clinicians who, as members of a common faculty, or as members of the Duke Center for the Study of Aging and Human Development, or through shared committee and organization work over a period of years, had come to know each other's work and point of view. Second, at the start of the project we made available to all contributors an overall outline of the proposed volume, thus allowing each of them to see how his or her chapter fitted into the entire scheme of the book. Third, we continued to refine the goal and scope of the book in weekly discussion sessions in which drafts of chapters were read and discussed, criticized, rewritten, and discussed again. These sessions were attended by many of the authors; but other staff members of the Duke Center also participated and contributed immeasurably to the final product presented here.

The deluge of new information about the aging process and the rapid obsolescence of present skills and knowledge have, in our opinion, demanded that a determined effort be made to present under a single cover a broad range of material. We further felt that we had to do so succinctly and in understandable terms so that the book might be useful to a wide spectrum of people.

This book is written for those with an interest in any of a number of aspects of aging, with the anticipation that their understanding of their own area of interest will be enhanced by an awareness of other forces also impinging on aged persons. It is our hope that the book will prove useful to psychiatrists who see aged persons in their practice, and to internists and general practitioners who do likewise. We feel the book contains information relevant to health planners, social welfare workers, and state and local health and welfare administrators. We hope this book will also be read by gerontologists from a variety of disciplines—sociologists, anthropologists, economists, psychologists, biologists—in short, all professionals whose topic of investigation is the aging process. College undergraduates or graduate students studying human development or normal or abnormal psychology, as well as their teachers, may find this a useful summary of present knowledge in this field. Furthermore, the book is relatively nontechnical so that it can be read by the general reader who wants to know more about aging, especially if he has aged parents whom he may need to care for or whom he at least wishes to understand. Finally, we feel that the aged themselves may obtain from this book a broader perspective of what they are experiencing.

We are indebted to many persons for their help with this project. In particular, we would like to acknowledge the help of Dr. Carl Eisdorfer, Dr. Walter Obrist, and Dr. Erdman Palmore, who in many ways assisted us in determining editorial policy. We are also extremely grateful to all those who participated in our discussion sessions, including Dr. Kurt Back, Dr. Daniel Gianturco, Mrs. Dorothy Heyman, Miss Frances Jeffers, Dr. Jesse McNiel, Dr. John Nowlin, Dr. Larry Thompson, Dr. Adriaan Verwoerdt, Dr. H.- Shan Wang, Dr. A. D. Whanger, and Mrs. Frances Wilkie.

We are especially appreciative of the two authors not on the Duke faculty who joined our Duke colleagues in this venture and added their highly specialized knowledge. We also wish to express regret that several distinguished members of the Center research staff were unable to collaborate with us on this volume because of previous commitments on their time, and we are sorry that we did not have the total benefit of their combined experience and wisdom. Readers familiar with the structure of the Center will notice, however, the frequency with which reference is made to their work throughout the book.

Special recognition is due Mrs. Rosa Absalom and Mrs. Ann Rimmer for their coordination of the entire editorial and production effort as well as for efficient handling of editorial correspondence. Finally, our gratitude must be expressed to all our contributors who worked diligently to maintain the original writing and production schedule.

EWALD W. BUSSE
ERIC PFEIFFER

*Durham, N.C.*
*June 1969*

# Contents

CONTRIBUTING AUTHORS                                             *v*

PREFACE                                                        *vii*

1. INTRODUCTION                                                   *1*
   *Ewald W. Busse and Eric Pfeiffer*

2. THEORIES OF AGING                                            *11*
   *Ewald W. Busse*

3. SOCIOLOGICAL ASPECTS OF AGING                               *33*
   *Erdman Palmore*

4. ECONOMICS OF RETIREMENT                                     *71*
   *Juanita M. Kreps*

5. THE AMBIGUITY OF RETIREMENT                                 *93*
   *Kurt W. Back*

6. HEALTH EXPERIENCE IN THE ELDERLY                           *115*
   *E. Harvey Estes, Jr.*

7. LIVING ARRANGEMENTS AND HOUSING
   OF OLD PEOPLE                                               *129*
   *Ethel Shanas*

8. SEXUAL BEHAVIOR IN OLD AGE                                 *151*
   *Eric Pfeiffer*

9. HOW THE OLD FACE DEATH                                     *163*
   *Frances C. Jeffers and Adriaan Verwoerdt*

10. FUNCTIONAL PSYCHIATRIC DISORDERS IN OLD AGE               *183*
    *Ewald W. Busse and Eric Pfeiffer*

11. INTELLECTUAL AND COGNITIVE CHANGES
    IN THE AGED                                                *237*
    *Carl Eisdorfer*

# Contents

12. THE BRAIN AND TIME      *251*
*F. Stephen Vogel*

13. ORGANIC BRAIN SYNDROMES      *263*
*H.- Shan Wang*

14. INSTITUTIONAL CARE OF THE AGED      *289*
*Alvin I. Goldfarb*

15. NURSING OF OLDER PEOPLE      *313*
*Virginia Stone*

16. SOCIAL CASEWORK AND COMMUNITY SERVICES
FOR THE AGED      *323*
*Dorothy K. Heyman and Grace H. Polansky*

17. TRAINING IN GEROPSYCHIATRY      *345*
*Adriaan Verwoerdt*

18. THE AGED AND PUBLIC POLICY      *367*
*Joseph J. Spengler*

INDEX      *385*

# Behavior and Adaptation in Late Life

# 1
# Introduction

EWALD W. BUSSE AND ERIC PFEIFFER

This book is the result of both multidisciplinary and interdisciplinary labor. The terms *multidisciplinary* and *interdisciplinary* are often used interchangeably and—we believe—erroneously [3]. For instance, multidisciplinary research is a type of *group* research involving investigators from several distinct scientific disciplines working in parallel with one another. The investigators are identified as a group because they work in proximity to one another and because their research deals with a common topic. The group usually plans to maximize communication among the various investigators, hoping to increase the breadth and potential of their work.

Interdisciplinary research, on the other hand, is a team effort by two or more individuals representing different scientific disciplines. Because of their particular skills and interests, these individuals have accepted responsibility for certain segments of a jointly defined research goal. The meaning of the prefix *inter-* is "mutual," not merely "among" or "between."

A glance at the great variety of scientific disciplines represented by the contributors makes it clear that the entire volume must be viewed as a multidisciplinary product, although many of its sections are of an interdisciplinary nature. All the authors share a common concern with the processes of aging and the problems of the aged. This does not mean, however, that each necessarily agrees with the approach used or the conclusions reached by the other authors. And while the editors hold themselves principally responsible for the selection of topics included in this book, the particular points of view expressed in each chapter are those of the individual contributors.

## ESTIMATES OF THE OLDER POPULATION

There has not been a census in the United States since 1960. For this reason the number of older persons (usually defined as persons above age 65) now living in the United States can only be estimated. Such estimates have been made by several governmental and private agencies, but they do not necessarily agree with one another. In May of 1968, Brotman, Chief of Research and Statistics of the Administration on Aging in the Department of Health, Education, and Welfare, estimated that in 1967 there were 8,069,000 men and 10,619,000 women or a total of 18,688,000 persons over age 65 in the United States [1]. This figure has of course increased since then, but by exactly how much is not certain. The reader should not be surprised, therefore, that several of the contributors to this volume have adduced slightly disparate figures, ranging from 19 to 20 million persons, for the estimated number of aged persons in the United States in 1969, or in 1970. There is general agreement, however, that old people make up about 9.4 percent of the entire population, and that this figure is less subject to change over a short number of years than the absolute number of older persons.

## ARE THE ELDERLY A MINORITY GROUP?

Since the elderly constitute such a sizable fraction of the entire population, it may at first be somewhat surprising that the question of the elderly as a minority group should be raised at all. But numbers alone do not determine minority status, as can be seen by comparing the elderly with a more clearly defined minority group, namely, Negroes in this country. In 1967 the elderly accounted for 9.4 percent of the population while Negroes accounted for 10.9 percent of the population [6]. Yet the latter clearly constitute a minority group in our society. In any case the question whether the elderly are a minority group has been raised, at times only subtly. Sometimes it has been answered in the affirmative; occasionally it has been answered negatively. The editors believe that the status of the aged as a deprived minority group is substantiated by the observations of several of the contributions to this volume. They believe that retired persons in particular rarely share in the advantages enjoyed by the majority of our society, and they believe that prejudices exist which restrict opportunities for the elderly to achieve personal satisfaction and participation in the entire range of activities open to other members of the society.

## THE NATURE OF MINORITY GROUPS

Minority groups will always exist in any sizable group of human beings. How minority groups are defined and recognized is rather complicated. Minority groups can be distinguished by such factors as their expressed beliefs and behavior, their physical appearance, their characteristic clothes, eating habits, religious expression, social behavior, or fixed and recognizable patterns of handling such experiences as insecurity, fear, grief, and aggression. At certain points in the history of a nation minority groups are more easily recognized and are seen as more deviant than at other points in time. Minority groups often become less visible as they gradually alter their own patterns or effect changes in the majority so that distinctions between the majority and the minority become increasingly blurred. There is still considerable fluctuation in the degree to which the aged are regarded as a minority group in this country. This is reflected in the rapidly changing and often contradictory public policies with regard to many aspects of the lives of the elderly.

Taking the point of view for the moment that any definable

group of people who share specific characteristics is in effect a minority group, then the question arises if it is possible for any minority group to have opportunities equal to those of the majority. Equal opportunity is highly unlikely so long as the minority group voluntarily or involuntarily maintains social expectations and behavior which are different from those of the majority. Paradoxically, this may even be true of what might be called affluent minority groups. It is obviously true of retired persons. It is also true that there are some minority groups which elect to bypass the opportunities offered by the majority in order to maintain their own value systems. Minority groups can exist in relatively contented fashion when the advantages offered them by their own group satisfactorily meet their needs or when, if they so elect, the opportunities of the majority are also open to them.

If one accepts the view that elderly Americans constitute a deprived minority, then it is important to understand how and why they have acquired this status. The elderly differ from many other minority groups in the way in which they have come by their status. They were neither born into it, nor did they achieve it through any action on their part; rather they had their minority status thrust upon them as a result of the accumulation of a certain number of birthdays. Whether lifelong discrimination or recently acquired discrimination is harder to bear is a question the editors are hardly prepared to answer; but they do feel that this difference is worthy of note.

## THE NATURE OF PREJUDICE

In primitive societies social and health problems are often complicated by the existence of folklore, myths, and superstitions. In so-called affluent societies unexpressed and unrecognized individual prejudices and group biases can be equally troublesome. The complications arising from them are often difficult to recognize since they are not sufficiently distinct to be classed as myths or superstitions. Nevertheless they can affect thought and behavior and be manifested by a lack of interest, a misinterpretation of facts, or inappropriate reactions, such as overconcern.

The abode of prejudice is largely in the unconscious mind. The conscious recognition that a prejudice exists is usually transient. Prejudices can be acquired throughout life, but the mechanisms that facilitate their development are primarily rooted in childhood fears and in childhood modes of thinking. Consequently prejudices carry the intense emotionality of childhood, although the "reasons" for them are couched in adultlike terms. Therefore prejudiced adults hold to their convictions with intense feelings which resist reality and logic. Prejudiced adults must first recognize that the excessive feelings which accompany their attitude are indeed unreasonable, and they must then be willing to unlearn by actual personal experience the faulty learning, replacing it by a rational approach.

The professional or volunteer worker who is involved with elderly persons brings into his relationships with them predetermined attitudes and patterns of reacting. Many members of the health and welfare professions have difficulty relating effectively to elderly persons. There are several factors contributing to this. We all instinctively fear physical and mental decline. When we observe a patient deteriorating despite our best efforts to the contrary, we are reminded that we, too, are vulnerable and will inevitably experience the changes of the aging process, including death. Also, members of the health disciplines are frequently frustrated because elderly patients often have multiple and chronic physical as well as psychological complaints which, moreover, are often exacerbated by the patients' life circumstances. The physician is made to feel he is of little value since he cannot relieve the symptoms, and he has neither the knowledge nor the prerogative of altering the socioeconomic conditions [2]. Comfort, considering these same problems, has coined the term *gerontophobia* to refer to the reluctance on the part of some health professionals as well as others to become involved in the problems of the aged [4].

## THE YOUNGER AGED AND THE OLDER AGED

Many of the chapters in this volume make it clear that, although all elderly people share certain problems, the elderly cannot be considered a homogeneous group. Important differences exist among the younger aged (those between ages 65 and 75) and the older aged (those over age 75). For instance, the prevalence of disabling physical conditions is far greater among those over age 75 than in the younger age group, although those between ages 65 and 75 who are disabled may have many more things in common with those age 75 and over than with their nondisabled age mates [1]. That the needs of the extremely old are substantially different from those of the younger group of elderly persons will emerge throughout this volume. This differentiation is particularly clearly drawn in Chapters 7 and 18. Elsewhere in the book age differences are sometimes explicitly stated; at other times they are merely implied. The editors believe that in the years ahead gerontologists will become increasingly cognizant of the subgroups which make up our aged population.

## THE DUKE LONGITUDINAL STUDIES

The reader will quickly notice that several of the authors of the various chapters make reference to results obtained from a longitudinal study carried out at Duke University. Many of them are coinvestigators either in that continuing study or in a more recently begun study which also deals with changes observed in individuals over time.* It was thought that a brief summary of the samples and the methods used in these studies might be useful.

The first longitudinal project was initiated in 1954. Its title is "The Effect of Aging Upon the Central Nervous System." The aim of this long-term study is to identify social, psychological, and physiological factors influencing the behavior of elderly people and

* This research is currently supported by U.S. P.H.S. Grant H.D.–00668, the J. P. Gibbons Fund, and Duke University.

to relate these changes to intellectual function, personality, and social competence.

The original sample was composed of volunteers who were 60 years of age or over at the beginning of the study. When initially screened and accepted, they were believed to be relatively free of disease, and they were functioning at an acceptable level in the community. The age range for the group at the onset of the study was 60 to 94 years, with a median age of 70. The sample contained both white and Negro, male and female, subjects, in proportions that approximated but did not coincide with the race and sex distribution of the community from which the sample was drawn [5]. Subjects were examined and studied over a two-day period. These studies were then repeated at two- to three-year intervals, and to date five series of studies have been completed. During this time the original sample of 260 individuals has been reduced to 127 subjects (as of June 30, 1969) because of attrition due to death and other causes.

It is recognized that individuals volunteering to participate in a study such as this one may possess characteristics that distinguish them from elderly persons who are unwilling to participate. Another limiting factor of the study is the unknown extent of the influence of this long-term research project upon the lives of the participating subjects. Only 6 percent of the original sample have been lost over the years because of refusal to continue to participate. In order to minimize losses the project has recently acquired a mobile laboratory to permit continuing detailed examination of any subjects who are confined to their homes, to hospitals, or to other institutions.

Masses of data have been acquired. At each full longitudinal examination over 1,000 variables per subject are coded, recorded, and transferred to magnetic tape for computer uses. The items include 336 medical observations, 109 psychiatric-neurological, 109 routine psychological, 234 social items, and a varying number of so-called special items. The investigators have utilized the accumulated resulting data cross-sectionally and longitudinally. Additional data come from so-called satellite projects and are available to the investigators. These projects are conducted independently on the same subjects by an individual investigator with the permission of the interdisciplinary team.

A second longitudinal investigation has recently been initiated and is entitled "Adaptation to Change." Many of the hypotheses and questions, observations, and methodology of this new study have been influenced by the first study. The new study is primarily concerned with the aging process and adaptation to stressful events during middle age and the retirement years.

A sample of slightly more than 500 subjects, ranging in age from 45 through 69, has been drawn. A random selection was employed, and the sample was designed so that there will be approximately 40 persons in each of ten age-sex cohorts in 1973. This design will make possible basic comparison between age groups, controlling for sex. It is intended to permit the partialing out of the effects of aging from differences between age cohorts by comparing differences over time with differences between adjacent age cohorts at one point in time. Individual differences will be studied after stressful events such as death of spouse or close relative, serious illness, menopause, departure of children, retirement, or economic changes by comparing differences between age cohorts and time intervals for the same cohort and by time-lag analysis which examines the adaptations that are likely to follow an identified change. Extensive planning for this study extending over several years resulted in careful definition of terms, the setting up of hypotheses and questions, clear elucidation of the variables to be studied, and the standardization of techniques.

---

It is one of the ironies of scientific work that many of the contributors to this volume are presently engaged in the gathering of new observations which in all likelihood will make at least portions of this volume obsolete.

## REFERENCES

1. Brotman, H. B.   Who are the aged: A demographic view. *Useful Facts*, 42. Washington, D.C.: U.S. Administration on Aging, August 9, 1968. Table 8.
2. Busse, E. W.   Problems affecting psychiatric care of the aging. *Geriatrics* 15:673–680, 1960.
3. Busse, E. W.   Administration of the interdisciplinary research team. *J. Med. Educ.* 40:832–839, 1965.
4. Comfort, A.   On gerontophobia. *Med. Opinion Rev.* September 1967. Pp. 30–37.
5. Maddox, G. L.   A longitudinal multidisciplinary study of human aging; Selected methodological issues. *Proc. Soc. Statistics Sect. Amer. Statistical Assoc.* 122:280–285, 1962.
6. U.S. Bureau of the Census.   *Statistical Abstracts of the United States, 1968*. Washington, D.C.: U.S. Government Printing Office, 1968.

# 2
# Theories of Aging

E W A L D   W .   B U S S E

The study of aging in all of its aspects, including biological, psychological, and sociological, is known as the science of gerontology. Consequently, gerontologists view attempts to prolong life which fail to also improve the lot of the aged as having limited value. In fact, the mere prolongation of life may be more of a detriment than an asset for all concerned. Although the desire to prevent or retard the progress of aging has obsessed humans for thousands of years, it has been appreciated that to extend life without maintaining vigor has enormous dangers. For example, Swift in *Gulliver's Travels* reports how his hero encountered pathetic creatures called "Struldbrugs." These unfortunate persons could not die but had all of the gradually increasing incapacities of aging, both physical and mental. Greek mythology teaches a similar lesson. The goddess Aurora with great effort persuaded Zeus to grant her husband Tithonus immortality. Unfortunately she did not ask and Zeus did not give Tithonus eternal youth, and he became more and more disabled, praying fervently for death.

Alex Comfort, a British scientist who has made significant contributions to gerontology, particularly to the biology of aging, has skillfully reviewed past efforts to extend the life-span [5, 6]. He points out that over the centuries the hope of delaying aging has been focused on the continuation of sexual vigor and reproductive capacity. In fact, in Darwin's concept of survival of the fittest, reproductive capability plays a central role. This point will be elaborated shortly.

Perhaps the best known of the attempts to find prolonged youth is the medieval European search for the Fountain of Youth. It seems incredible that this story was taken seriously. It was based upon a second-century account by a writer, Pausanias, whose works were revived and popularized by Jean de Mandeville. It is highly likely that this intensive search is particularly remembered because of Ponce de Leon's discovery of the state of Florida. For it is a fact that his 1512 expedition was actually organized and financed to specifically search for the Fountain of Youth.

Comfort also reviews a number of Near and Far Eastern rejuvenation efforts. These efforts to maintain youth were primarily rooted in what is called *gerocomy*. Gerocomy is the belief and practice that a man absorbs virtue and youth from women, particularly young women. This idea permeated many societies. King David in the Old Testament believed it and practiced accordingly. There is clear evidence also that the Romans held similar views. Further, as Comfort reports, this concept has some support from the modern experimental laboratory. Aged male rats will respond favorably when a young female rat is placed among them. Her presence and activities greatly improve their condition and promote their survival [7].

## AGING DEFINED

The biological processes of aging are usually associated with a decline of efficiency and functioning which eventually results in death. Some biologists define aging as a progressive loss of functional capacity after an organism has reached maturity, while others insist that aging begins with the onset of differentiation. Still others contend that a definition of aging is not useful or possible [30]. Many investigators prefer to separate declines in functioning into primary and secondary aging [3].

The biological processes called *primary aging* are apparently rooted in heredity. They are inborn and inevitable detrimental changes which are time-related but independent of stress, trauma, or disease. However, the various aging processes are not recognizable in all people, and those that are present do not progress at the same rate. *Secondary aging* refers to those disabilities resulting from trauma and chronic disease.

The designation *aged* is often used arbitrarily to describe or define persons who have achieved a certain chronological age within a given population. The wide variation in who is considered old is evidenced by the fact that a person 40 years of age is old in so-called undeveloped nations, while in an industrialized or advanced society one must survive many more years before he is considered aged.

## LONGEVITY AND THE CONTRIBUTION OF BENJAMIN GOMPERTZ

Since 1900 the percentage of the United States population age 65 and over has more than doubled, from 4.1 percent in 1900 to 9.4 percent in 1965, while the actual number of aged persons has increased sixfold from 3,000,000 to nearly 19,000,000. There has also been a clear reversal in life expectancy trends for men and women. In 1900 in the United States there were 98 old women to every 100 old men. Women have had longer life expectancies from 1900 onward [21]. During the period 1900 to 1902 life expectancy for white females below age 20 was lower than for males of a like age but slightly higher for females through the adult years.

In 1964 the longevity of the young female had improved remarkably and had considerably surpassed that of the young male. Apparently this was not the result of selective immigration—that is, more men than women coming into the country—but a shift in health as related to sex.

Women are now outliving men. In fact, there are about 129 older women per 100 older men. Life expectancy for women is still increasing faster than for men. During the next 20 years, although it is unlikely that the percentage of the population of older people in the population will increase significantly, their actual number will go up to about 25,000,000. Assuming that the current life expectancy trends continue, by the year 2000 the ratio of women to men will be 148 women to 100 men. Differences between aging in men and women are clearly presented in a number of chapters in this volume.

Human longevity is influenced by a complex of interacting factors which include genetic makeup, environmental, and nutritional factors, and psychological, social, and economic influences. The increase in average life expectancy has been largely due to a decrease in deaths attributable to infectious diseases. However, it is highly likely that measures which succeed in improving health and reducing death risk in early life positively affect the health in the adult years also, thereby diminishing the death risk.

Life expectancy is a computed projection, not an observed or estimated phenomenon. The projection is based upon the assumption that the death rate experienced in a single year or the average experienced in a few years will remain completely unchanged in the future. Obviously any natural or man-made events that influence future death rates, such as changes in medical knowledge and care, sanitation, nutrition, reduced traffic deaths, and war, automatically affect the accuracy of the prediction.

Primary aging has been described as a time-related process which results in a decline in rate or efficiency of various functions in plants or animals. Obviously a deterioration in function adversely affects an individual's chances of staying alive; the probability of death per unit time increases. The mortality rate for man, when early life deaths and deaths from violence are disregarded, tends to increase exponentially with age (Fig. 1). Benjamin Gompertz, an English insurance actuary, in 1825 published a description of an empirically derived mathematical equation which is concerned with the probability of dying at any given age. Although this equation is relatively simple, its accuracy has been repeatedly demonstrated. It continues to closely approximate real systems.

Gompertz' equation is as follows: $R = R_0 e^{at}$, where $R$ is the chance of dying at any age; $R_0$ is a mathematical constant related to the predicted chance of dying at age $o$; and $a$ is a constant that describes the rate of increase of the mortality rate as a function of

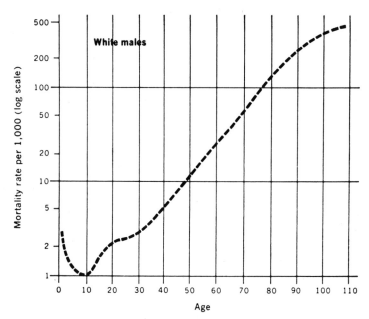

FIGURE 1.   *Gompertz plot. Mortality rate as a function of age, United States, 1939–41. Between age 30 and 90 the data obey the equation* $R = R_o e^{at}$. $R_o$ *(the initial mortality rate at time o) and* a *(the increase in the mortality rate over time) are constants which depend on the population;* e *is the base of natural logarithms and* t *is the age in years. (Reproduced from B. L. Strehler, Dynamic Theories of Aging. In N. W. Shock, Aging—Some Social and Biological Aspects. Publication No. 65. P. 286. Copyright © 1960 by the American Association for the Advancement of Science.)*

age; while *e* is the base of natural logarithms, and *t* is the age in years [12].

## SURVIVAL AND IMMORTALITY

Survival of the fittest is a common biological cliché. In the Darwinian sense fitness means the ability to contribute a maximum number of live and fertile offspring so that succeeding generations are assured. Thus evolution is concerned with the perpetuation and improvement of the species but not with the health or longevity of individuals after they have passed the period of reproduction. Further, it is possible that the biological traits that are basic to maximum reproductive capacity may be detrimental to the prolongation of life after cessation of the reproductive life.

An interesting question has been whether some animals are immortal, that is, whether they are capable of continuous and total cell replacement. This is far from a settled issue. What is clear is that in those animals that are incapable of cell replacement, either initially or for a limited period, a decline in vigor (aging) is seen. The sea anemone, a multicellular invertebrate, apparently is capable of replacing all cells continuously throughout life. The cells making up an individual are in a constant state of turnover and replacement. But even in this system the notion of immortality is open to some challenge since the sea anemone divides in two at some point in time. The half that retains the old nervous system ages and dies, while the half that has to grow a new system survives. Consequently, at least one part of the original animal continues indefinitely.

Based on the assumption that immortality exists in the lower, simple forms of life, it has been held that some animal cells that are capable of dividing are immortal if removed from the body's regulatory mechanisms. This belief in the capacity of animal cells to achieve immortality was given considerable support by the work of Alexis Carrel, a French surgeon who lived between 1873 and 1944. Carrel was the winner of the Nobel Prize for physiology and medicine in 1912. He reported that he had kept fibroblasts from chicks growing and multiplying in glass vessels for more than 30 years. Thus it seemed he had proved that these cells were capable of living far beyond the usual life expectancy of a chicken. Using similar techniques other experimenters claimed similar success with embryonic cells from laboratory mice. Unfortunately Carrel's success, and apparently that of the other investigators, was the result of errors in techniques. Carrel fed the cell culture with a crude extract taken from chick embryos. This embryo extract actually contained a very few but sufficient number of living chick cells. The introduction of these new fibroblasts permitted the culture to survive. If the extract used for feeding is carefully prepared and the fibroblasts eliminated, the cell colony will die.

Other experiments have suggested that human cells have the capacity to be immortal. But at the present time the only human cells which are apparently immortal are transformed or abnormal cells. So-called HeLa cells were originally taken from cancerous cervical tissue and grown in glass cultures by George O. Gey in 1952 at the Johns Hopkins University School of Medicine. Normal human cells have two sets of chromosomes and are therefore known as diploid cells. The normal number of chromosomes is 46. HeLa cells are mixoploid cells and may have anywhere from 50 to 350 chromosomes per cell, and the chromosomes differ considerably in size and shape from the chromosomes found in the normal human cell.

## COMPONENTS OF THE BODY AND AGING

The human organism consists of three biological components; two are cellular and one is noncellular. The first component is made up of cells capable of multiplying throughout the life span. Examples of such cells are epithelial cells (skin) and white blood cells. The second biological component is made up of cells that are incapable of division, as exemplified by the neurons of the brain.* The third biological component is the noncellular or interstitial material. The various theories of aging that will be presented often deal with only one of the three components. For example, one theory centers upon dividing cells by postulating that new cells in old animals are not as good as new cells in younger animals. A second group of theories focuses upon the possibility that irreplaceable cells, that is, nondividing cells, either are totally lost or decline in function. A third suggested theoretical basis for aging is that damage takes place in the noncellular material of the body,

* There are also some cells, e.g., endothelial cells, which rarely divide but which are at least capable of doing so.

interfering with nutrition, respiration, and excretion (the accumulation of waste products).

It is clear that biological aging can be studied at a number of levels, utilizing differing techniques. Consequently, numerous theories—often overlapping and frequently differing only in semantics, not in substance—can be found in the scientific literature. Only a few of these will be reviewed here.


## SELECTED BIOLOGICAL THEORIES OF AGING

One early biological explanation of aging rested upon the assumption that a living organism contained a fixed store of energy, not unlike that contained within a coiled watch spring. When the spring of the watch was unwound, life ended. This is a type of *exhaustion theory*. Although it may have some validity, scientific knowledge has become so extensive that such a simple explanation no longer suffices. Another simple theory relates to the *accumulation of deleterious material*. This particular theory is given some support by the observation that pigments, such as lipofucsin, accumulate in a number of living cells throughout the life-span. To date, however, there is no evidence that the accumulation of these pigments actually affects cellular efficiency.

Sinex believes that in attempting to understand the biochemistry of aging one must decide if the aging process constitutes *deliberate biological programming* or if the usual life-span of an individual is all that can be expected of an organism as chemically complex as that which comprises the total human being [25]. Aging in plants and in lower forms of animals often appears to be regulated by deliberate programming which in turn is tied to the seasons of the year. But where the memory for these programmed changes is stored is unclear. It is not necessarily in the nucleus of a cell; for example, the human erythrocyte has no nucleus but appears to be programmed to live 120 days. At present there is no known way to increase the survival of circulating erythrocytes. On the other hand, the life-span of the erythrocyte can be reduced, as in vitamin E deficiency.

The absence of a nucleus in an erythrocyte has focused attention upon the cytoplasmic content and possible evidence of deterioration there. It does appear that there are changes in the level of certain enzymes as well as a gradually increasing osmotic fragility with advancing cell age. The survival of circulating erythrocytes does not vary nearly as much from one species to another as does the animal's total life-span. Roughly speaking, however, there is a correlation between the survival of the erythrocyte and the total life-span. Not only does the erythrocyte provide a challenge for investigators interested in the program theory of aging, but it also challenges those interested in the possibility of exhaustion of critical intracellular constituents.

Similarly, there is considerable controversy over what part of a cell is the most important in cellular renewal. There is evidence that renewal of the nucleus or the cytoplasm may be beneficial. Conjugation (the union of one organism with another for the exchange of nuclear material) in many protozoa initiates a cycle of reproductive activity which gradually decreases [28, 29]. If subsequent conjugation is prevented, the clones die. In other species of protozoa, autogamy, that is, the replacement of the macronucleus by a new macronucleus derived from a micronucleus, restores vigor. If autogamy is prevented the clones die. If the deterioration of the clones is due to deterioration of genetic information in the macronucleus, how would conditions differ in the micronucleus so that this would not occur? On the other side of the coin, if deterioration is of cytoplasmic origin, how is it corrected by a new nucleus?

Other investigators working with amoebae have reported that they can significantly prolong the life of the amoeba by continuous renewal of cytoplasmic elements. Furthermore, the mating of paramecium shows that an old cytoplasm has profound adverse effects on an exchanged young nucleus.

The reader will recall that it has been demonstrated that it is highly unlikely that normal human cells are immortal. Only abnormal cells possess this ability. Furthermore, Leonard Hayflick has demonstrated that normal human fibroblasts will divide roughly 50 times and then die [14]. Hayflick utilized human fibroblasts from the lung. Cells derived from embryonic tissue achieve approximately 50 population doublings. Cells obtained at about age 20 will double 30 times plus or minus 10, and cells derived at still later ages show progressive declines in their doubling capacities.

The possibility exists that this phenomenon is the result of programmed aging. Although this idea is given some credence by Hayflick, he advances another view derived from the engineering concept called *mean time to failure*. Engineers contend that every machine has built-in obsolescence and that its lifetime is limited by the durability of its parts. Repair or replacement of parts of the machine extend its life-span, but barring total replacement of all of the elements, eventual failure of the machine is inevitable. The question is, What determines mean time to failure? And here it appears that one must turn to another theory, and that is *the accumulation of copying errors*. This theory holds that man's life is eventually terminated because his cells not only develop errors in copying but errors in copying in turn reduce metabolic efficiency and interfere with the capacity for repair.

Theories that focus on cell loss or on mutation, both random processes, are called *stochastic theories*. Stochastic implies "a process or a series of events for which the estimate of the probability of certain outcomes approaches the true probability as the number of events increases." Radiation seems to speed up aging by the random hitting of cells, either killing them or inducing mutations in them.

The atomic scientist, Leo Szilard, advanced a stochastic theory based upon what he termed a *hit*. It has been assumed that Szilard implied that such a hit was the result of radiation; but this apparently was not the case, since he considered any event that would alter a chromosome a hit. In addition, Szilard believed that every animal cell carries a load of what he termed *faults*. A fault is a congenital absence or impairment of one of the genes essential to cell function. A cell is capable of operating as long as one of a pair of genes continues to function; but when both of a pair of essential genes are incapable of functioning, the cell dies. Therefore, a cell will cease to function if one of the pair carries a fault and the other is the victim of a hit, or if both pairs are the victims of hits. The problem in Szilard's theory is that it is only applicable to irreplaceable cells. But perhaps the greatest objection to the fault-hit approach is that homozygous individuals that contain many pairs of genes that are alike should survive hits much more readily than heterozygous individuals having many dissimilar gene pairs. The fact is that hybrids, that is, heterozygous individuals with dissimilar genes, are consistently longer-lived than inbreds or homozygous individuals.

*Exposure of a living organism to repeated small doses of ionizing radiation* or to a larger sublethal dose appreciably reduces the life-span of the organism. Consequently, numerous attempts have been made to study the changes brought about by radiation for any possible similarity to the aging process. Radiated animals and aging animals both show an increase in the number of somatic cell mutations. Longevity in an aging animal is inversely proportional to the rate at which the animal develops mutations. Thus dogs live about six times longer than mice and develop mutations at about one-sixth the rate. It appears that the changes and mutations that are brought about by radiation are not the same as the chromosomal aberrations resulting from aging. When one compares the number of chromosomal aberrations produced by radiation to the life-shortening effect that would be expected proportional to the number of aberrations, there is not nearly the amount of expected life-shortening. Aging produces fewer chromosomal aberrations yet in proportion produces more life-shortening. No satisfactory explanation is as yet at hand for this discrepancy.

Howard J. Curtis, the radiation biologist, has advanced a theory which he elects to call the *composite theory* [10]. Curtis, in his earlier discussions of the somatic mutations viewpoint [9], stressed that somatic cell types differed from one another in frequency of cell division, some dividing frequently, some seldom, some not at all, as has already been discussed. Defects develop over time in all cells, but in those organs that can replace cells, the cell division process allows them to discard aberrant cells. Tissues having non-dividing cells do not have this mechanism of rejuvenation and thus are primarily responsible for the aging of the total organism. Consequently the fundamental aging process is the accumulation of defectively functioning cells in those organs whose cells are non-dividing. Aberrations occurring in dividing cells produce another serious problem, cancer. This, however, would not be considered an aging event. According to Curtis, the composite theory considers aging fundamentally "an increasing probability of developing a degenerative disease" [11]. As an individual ages, he becomes increasingly susceptible to degenerative diseases; furthermore, as each individual becomes older, he develops virtually all of the degenerative diseases—but at different rates. The disease which plays the major role in eventual death statistically appears to be a matter of chance.

The composite theory includes the postulate that aging changes take place in the somatic cells and that these changes cause them and their progeny to function to the detriment of the organisms. Although mutation is an important step in this detrimental change, the extent of the change cannot be explained as the result of a single mutation. Curtis believes that for the human an average of five steps is required to initiate one of the degenerative diseases. The nature of all of the steps has not been identified, but the occurrence of each step is a chance occurrence of a certain probability, for example, mutation rate. The probability of each step occurrence can be expressed in quantitative terms utilizing a mathematical formula devised by Armitage and Doll [1].

The *error theory* of cellular aging proposes that, with senescence, alterations (not necessarily mutations) occur in the structure of the DNA (deoxyribonucleic acid) molecule. These errors are transmitted to messenger RNA (ribonucleic acid) and ultimately to newly synthesized enzymes. Such defective enzymes could result in a number of problems. It is conceivable that the enzymes would be inactive and therefore accumulate substrates within the cell. Not only might the accumulation of substrates be detrimental to the cell, but the normal metabolic processes might be seriously disturbed. To compensate for this deficiency, it is possible that there would be an increase in RNA production and of protein turnover to compensate for the defective enzymes. If the number of defective or inactive enzymes proceeded to a point at which synthesis within the cell was no longer sufficient to compensate for the defective processes, then the death of the cell or its failure to contribute to the organism would result in the death of the organism.

The error theory is linked with the mutation theory in that it has been shown that chromosomal aberrations in the liver cells of normal mice increase linearly with age. Furthermore, these aberrations can be dramatically increased by a dose of x-ray. Following a single radiation dose, however, chromosomal aberrations gradually decrease toward normal. The defective chromosomes can be traced through a number of cell divisions, but then they disappear. The number of aberrations that occur are roughly proportional to the amount of radiation. Small doses of radiation are not as effective as a large dose. Since chromosome aberrations decline, it would appear that there is an inherent capacity to correct the damage inflicted by x-ray. The picture is further complicated by the fact that neutron exposure produces much more damage than x-ray. It has been shown that there is a relationship between the amount of chromosome damage and the shortening of life. But the effect of the mutation may take longer to manifest its detrimental influence than might be suspected. A possible explanation is that somatic cells may ordinarily contain a large reserve supply of RNA which permits them to function for a lengthy period without DNA. Actually several cell divisions may take place before the supply of RNA becomes so low that the cell no longer can function.

The *cross-linkage* or *eversion theory* is primarily applicable to the noncellular material of the body. The investigation substantiating this theory rests upon the study of collagen. Collagen is the most abundant protein in the body. It is one of the four major constituents of connective tissue and constitutes 30 to 40 percent of the body protein. A collagen molecule is composed of three polypeptide strands. Each polypeptide strand contains four subunits which are held together by pairs of ester bonds. With the passing of time there is a switching of the ester bonds from within to between the individual collagen molecules. Thus a cross-linking between the strands is accomplished, not only altering the structure of the collagen molecule but also changing its characteristics, particularly its elasticity. Although there is little doubt that the cross-linking phenomenon in collagen is an aging process, the change is found only in extracellular collagen and has not been demonstrated to occur in intracellular proteins.

The apparent stimulation of *autoimmune mechanisms* during senescence raises many questions [31, 32]. Is it possible that the gradually increasing amounts of antibody detected in the plasma and the increased incidence of autoimmune disease may be directly or indirectly linked to the lifelong accumulated exposure to immunochemical insults? Is it possible that the coding of self-recognition in either DNA or RNA alters with the passage of time so that cellular antigens are not properly recognized? Do the antibody-producing cells accidentally or in some programmed manner contribute to senescence through the release of antibodies to the body's own tissue, thus producing an autoimmune condition? Although autoimmunity increases with aging, resistance to infection decreases [24]. There is much knowledge to be gained regarding the various types of immune responses which begin to deviate with aging from that encountered in the young adult.

Many attempts have been made to relate life expectancy to physical characteristics of various species. The so-called *index of cephalization,* that is, the excess of brain weight over the expected amount in relationship to body weight, correlates the most closely with longevity. Since the neurons of the brain are irreplaceable and since they do die, it appears that the number of cells that serve as a reserve against continuing loss in some way favorably affects the coordination of the complex body and makes for its longer period of survival.

With regard to the *genetic determinants of aging,* it is frequently stated that there is no known gene responsible for the extension of the life-span, but there are genes responsible for defects that result in the shortening of life.

Not only genetic but environmental factors as well influence the life-span [2]. A small animal that has been utilized for research purposes by a number of investigators is the rotifer. This tiny aquatic animal, about one-half millimeter in length, is composed of a rigidly fixed number of cells. No new cells are formed after hatching, and the animal's size is dependent upon increasing the size of the individual cell. Rotifers are particularly useful for research because they multiply by parthenogenesis. Consequently the genetic characteristics of the offspring are theoretically the same as those of the parent.

The rotifer is poikilothermic, that is, its body temperature is always the same as its surroundings. Barrows and his colleagues discovered that a substantial increase in the rotifer's life-span could be effected by reducing the temperature of its environment or by cutting down on its food supply. That reduction of food intake positively affects the life-span had been noted by a number of investigators. In this instance, however, it is of particular interest. Barrows reports that the reduced diets result in a gain in life-span when applied to younger animals while the reduction in temperature was effective in animals who had reached full maturity and had ceased to lay eggs.

Man is not poikilothermic as is the rotifer. If one wanted to lengthen the human life-span by changing the effect of temperature, one would have to consider utilizating temperature-reducing drugs. This is very unlikely.

That traumatic life experiences alter the life-span is an established fact. However, that such experiences may differentially influence the life-span of men as opposed to women has not been given a great deal of attention. One can obtain some evidence for this idea by comparing age of death in twins, utilizing male, female, identical, and fraternal twins. When each of the pair has died of natural causes, there is a much greater variation in the age of death in identical male twins than in identical female twins. It can be assumed, therefore, that at least one of the identical twin males has been exposed to a more hostile environment or to a greater accumulation of traumatic events. Further, although the life-span of identical twins is more similar than that of fraternal twins, discrepancy in age of death is again greater between male than between female fraternal twins [15].

Shock points out that although physiological characteristics differ widely from individual to individual at any specific age, the averages of these values show a gradual but definite decline between the ages of 30 and 90 [22]. Although this decline does occur with age, Shock emphasizes the fact that certain functions in a specific individual at age 80 can be as good as those of the average 50-year-old man. One of the obvious manifestations of aging is the decline in the ability to exercise and do work. The ability to do work depends upon several variables, including the strength of the muscles, coordination involving the nervous system, and a number of other factors such as the adequacy of the heart and vascular system, respiration, and the like. Shock has made a series of estimates of the remaining function and tissues in an average 75-year-old person when compared to an average 30-year-old person. Shock reports that the average 75-year-old man has 90 percent of his original brain weight and 56 percent of his vital capacity. His maximum work rate is 70 percent of his former ability. He retains 63 percent of the original number of nerve trunk fibers and 90 percent of his original nerve conduction velocity.

An intriguing question is often asked. Is it true that space travelers will age at a different rate than earthbound humans? Einstein's theory of relativity includes two suppositions. They are: (1) Time actually runs slower for an object as its speed increases. This is called the "time dilation effect." (2) Time speeds up for an object as it moves away from a body exerting a gravitational force. Thus astronauts engaged in missions strictly of an earth orbital nature are primarily influenced by the time dilation effect. Hence they age more slowly since they are moving much faster than they were on earth. If an astronaut is engaged in an earth orbital mission for two weeks, he will be approximately 400 microseconds younger than he would be if he had remained on earth. Moon missions produce a somewhat different problem because here the space travelers virtually escape earth's gravity; therefore time and aging speed up. At this time it does not seem to be entirely worthwhile to worry whether space travelers will age more rapidly or less rapidly.

## SOCIOLOGICAL THEORIES OF AGING

Social scientists have developed a number of theories relevant to the aging and elderly and to the structure of society and social change. One of these theories holds that the status of the aged is high in static societies and tends to decline with the acceleration of social change [18]. Another theory is that the status of the aged is inversely related to the proportion of aged in the population— that the aged are most highly valued in societies in which they are scarce, and that their value and status decrease as they become more numerous. A third theory is that the status and prestige of the aged are high in those societies in which older people, in spite of physical infirmity, are able to continue to perform useful and socially valued functions [23]. It is apparent that we are living in a rapidly changing society and world. In fact, it is viewed by a very prominent sociologist as "the chaotic society" [13]. If the first theory has any validity, then it is apparent that elderly persons in the United States will decline even further in their already doubtful status position. As to value being tied to scarcity in an age group, it does not appear that by the year 2000 the actual percentage of elderly will change, although the number obviously will increase. The third theory has a pessimistic quality. It holds that early retirement is a rapidly accelerating pattern that will make it increasingly difficult for the elderly person to be involved in socially valued functions.

A few years ago a group of investigators advanced the so-called *disengagement theory*. This theory maintains that high satisfaction in old age is usually present in those individuals who accept the inevitability of reduction in social and personal interactions [8]. The *activity theory* of aging, on the other hand, holds that the maintenance of activities is important to most individuals as a basis for obtaining and maintaining satisfaction, self-esteem, and health. In one study the changes in activities and attitudes of 127 aged subjects were studied over a span of 10 years [16]. It was found that there was no significant overall decrease in activities or alteration in attitudes among men, while there was some decrease among women. The supporters of the disengagement theory base their belief predominantly on cross-sectional surveys; hence it is possible that this study is presenting important contrary evidence. Further, it was found that in these aging persons reduction in some activities or attitudes resulted in compensating increases in others. In addition, data correlating such measures as mental and physical status and socioeconomic and activity levels all support the activity theory as the basis for the promotion of vigor and satisfactory adjustment in the elderly.

One cannot ignore the fact that there are differences in lifelong patterns of living and that there are some people who tend to maintain relatively high or relatively low levels of activity. It does appear that those who reduce their activities as they age tend to suffer a reduction in overall satisfaction [19].

The pathological consequences of social deprivation and hostile social influences upon the infant have been reported by a number of investigators including Goldfarb, Provence, Bowlby, Kagan, and others. There is reason to think that similar deprivation in old age can have similar pathological effects. For elderly people deprivation can take many forms and guises. Economic deprivation is a common problem among the elderly, especially for those in voluntary or involuntary retirement. Devastating effects can sometimes be seen. The economically deprived older person must constrict his opportunities for living experience. He cannot buy all the things he immediately needs much less those for which he supposedly has saved all his life. He does not have the security that comes with a stable financial situation. In addition he now belongs to a subgroup of society whose values are no longer the same as those of the dominant middle-age adult society. Furthermore, society has failed to provide learning and recreational opportunities for the elderly to the same degree that it has for the young and middle-aged. Many aged thus lack methods of maintaining self-esteem. An individual must feel that he is valued or appreciated by others in order to have a reasonable esteem of his own self [4]. There is little doubt that the elderly American can be identified as belonging to a deprived minority.


## PSYCHOLOGICAL AND COMBINED THEORIES OF AGING

Psychological theories of aging are often the extension of personality and developmental theories into middle and late life. Personality theories usually consider the innate human needs and forces that motivate thought and behavior and the modification of these biologically based energies by the experiences of living in a physical and social environment. Just as the developmental theories of personality in early childhood take into account the physiological changes of the growing child and such factors as interaction with the mother, the study of personality in old age must consider possible alterations in the physiological processes of the elderly person and the interacting relationship that exists between the individual and his environment. To further complicate the problem of understanding personality changes with aging is the fact that as humans pass through their life experiences they become increasingly different rather than similar. Infants at six months of age are more similar than children at age 12. This divergence continues as a response to the large array of possible learning and living experiences. It is possible that in extreme old age people tend to return to greater similarity in certain characteristics as they share similar declines in biological functioning and as society constricts their opportunities.

A number of investigators have attempted to explore patterns of personality in middle and late life. Neugarten and associates have concluded that 60-year-olds, when compared to 40-year-olds, seem to see the environment as more complex and dangerous. They are less ready to attribute activity and affect to persons in the environment, and they move from an outer- to an inner-world orientation. In addition, older men seem to be more receptive than younger men of their own "affiliative, nurturant, and sensual promptings." Older women become more self-accepting of their own "aggressive and egocentric impulses" [17].

Else Frenkel-Brunswick, Reichard, and colleagues have also studied the personalities of older men. They were able to classify the men they studied into five major categories according to their patterns of adjustment to aging: the mature, the rocking-chair men, the armored, the angry, and the self-haters. These investigators found that the majority adjusting poorly to aging had had a life-long history of personality problems [20].

Throughout this book a number of combined approaches to the problems of the aged will be utilized. A theoretical approach of the combined type is the *cybernetic theory.* Cybernetics is the study comparing control systems within the central nervous system with computing machines [27]. This theory essentially could be called an *activity theory* or an *atrophy-of-disuse theory.* The authors state: "To become functional early in life . . . neurons must be activated. To retain their position of control, they must be reactivated repeatedly. We believe that aging involves deterioration of neuronic control which proceeds more rapidly if the cybernetic control systems are not used" [26]. It therefore implies that previously established patterns of learning and social activity are the determinants of patterns in late life. As such it is contrary to the disengagement theory previously discussed.

## REFERENCES

1. Armitage, P., and Doll, R. The age distribution of cancer and a multi-stage theory of carcinogenesis. *Brit. J. Cancer* 8:1–12, 1954.
2. Barrows, C. H., and Strehler, B. L. Program biological obsolescence. *Johns Hopkins Med. J.* 19:18–19, 1968.
3. Busse, E. W. Psychopathology. In J. Birren (Ed.), *Handbook of Aging and the Individual.* Chicago: University of Chicago Press, 1959, pp. 364–399.

4. Busse, E. W.   Social Forces Influencing the Care and Health of the Elderly. In J. C. McKinney and F. T. deVyver (Eds.), *Aging and Social Policy*. New York: Appleton-Century-Crofts, 1966. Pp. 268–280.

5. Comfort, A.   *Ageing, The Biology of Senescence*. London: Routledge & Kegan Paul, 1964.

6. Comfort, A.   *The Process of Ageing*. London: Weidenfeld and Nicolson, 1965.

7. *Ibid.*, p. 5.

8. Cummings, E., and Henry, W. E.   *Growing Old*. New York: Basic Books, 1961.

9. Curtis, H. J.   Biological mechanisms underlying the aging process. *Science* 141:686–694, 1963.

10. Curtis, H. J.   A composite theory of aging. *Gerontologist* 6:143–149, 1966.

11. Curtis, H. J.   Radiation and Ageing. In *Aspects of the Biology of Ageing*. Great Britain: Cambridge University Press, 1967. Pp. 51–64. (21st Symposium of the Society for Experimental Biology.)

12. Gompertz, B.   On the nature of the function expressive of the law of human mortality and on a new model of determining life contingencies. *Philos. Translations Royal Society* (London) 115:513–585, 1825.

13. Hauser, P. M.   The chaotic society: Product of the social morphological revolution. Presidential address at the annual meeting, American Sociological Association, Boston, Aug., 1968.

14. Hayflick, L.   Human cells and aging. *Sci. Amer.* 218:32–37, 1968.

15. Kallmann, F. J., and Jarvik, L. F.   In J. Birren (Ed.), *Handbook of Aging and the Individual*. Chicago: University of Chicago Press, 1959. Pp. 216–263.

16. Maddox, G. L.   Activity and morale: A longitudinal study of selected elderly subjects. *Social Forces* 42:195, 1963.

17. Neugarten, B. L., and associates.   *Personality in Middle and Late Life*. New York: Atherton, 1964. Pp. 189–190.

18. Ogburn, W. F., and Nimkoff, M. F.   *Sociology*. Boston: Houghton Mifflin, 1940.

19. Palmore, E.   The effects of aging on activities and attitudes. *Gerontologist* 8:259–263, 1968.

20. Reichard, S., Livson, F., and Peterson, P. G.   *Aging and Personality*. New York: Wiley, 1962. Pp. 170–171.

21. Riley, M. W., and Foner, A.  *Aging and Society*. New York: Russell Sage Foundation, 1968. P. 28.
22. Shock, N. W.  The physiology of aging. *Sci. Amer.* 206:100–110, 1962.
23. Simmons, L. W.  *The Role of the Aged in Primitive Society*. New Haven: Yale University Press, 1945.
24. Sinex, F. M.  Biochemistry of aging. *Perspect. Biol. Med.* 9:216, 1966.
25. *Ibid.*, p. 208.
26. Smith, K. U., and Smith, F. G.  *Cybernetic Principles of Learning and Educational Design*. New York: Holt, Rinehart, and Winston, 1965. P. 29.
27. *Ibid.*, p. 529.
28. Sonneborn, T. M.  The relation of autogamy to senescence and rejuvenescence in Paramecium aurelia. *J. Protozool.* 1:38–53, 1954.
29. Sonneborn, T. M.  Breeding Systems, Reproductive Methods, and Species Problems in Protozoa. In E. Mayr (Ed.), *The Species Problem*. Washington, D.C.: American Association for the Advancement of Science, 1957. Pp. 155–324.
30. Strehler, B. L.  *The Biology of Aging*. Washington, D.C.: American Institute of Biological Sciences, 1960.
31. Wolford, R. L.  Auto-immunity and aging. *J. Geront.* 17:281–285, 1962.
32. Wolford, R. L.  The immunologic theory of aging. *Gerontologist* 4:195–197, 1964.

# 3

# Sociological Aspects of Aging

In this chapter aging as a social process will be considered. Students of aging are often so impressed by the obvious physical deterioration and intellectual slowing which may accompany chronological aging that they overlook the central role of culture and society in determining individual and group variations in the aging process. Even when some group differences in the behavior of the aged are noted, it may mistakenly be assumed that these differences are caused by biological differences. For example, the fact that almost three times as high a proportion of U.S. men compared to women continue to work past age 65 is less related to any biological differences between men and women than it is to our cultural expectations that man's primary role should be work outside the home, while woman's primary role should be inside the home [55]. Similarly, the fact that professionals, managers, and farmers continue to work much more frequently than do other men is less a reflection of their better health than it is a result of the greater work opportunities for aged men in these more highly skilled or self-employed occupations.

In our youth-oriented culture, many people believe that the aged inevitably suffer a steady deterioration in physical and mental abilities and therefore should withdraw from the central arenas of our society. We often forget that in other cultures the aged are the most powerful, the most engaged, and the most respected members of the society. When some aged persons show depression, hopelessness, inferiority, and paranoia, we may forget that these symptoms may have been caused by deprivation of basic satisfactions, reduction to an inferior status, and discrimination against those with 65 or more birthdays, rather than by any biological process.

At the turn of the century Charles Horton Cooley developed the concept of the *looking-glass self*. By this he meant that the attitudes and behaviors of others toward a person serve as a mirror in which the individual sees himself. To a large extent this mirror determines the image a person forms of himself which, in turn, strongly influences his behavior. This concept can help us understand why two aged persons with similar health and physical abilities can respond in quite diverse ways to the same situation. For instance, compulsory retirement may make one man withdraw and become depressed, while it may give a second man an opportunity to develop activities and satisfactions he had been wishing for all his life. The first man may have been encouraged to "take it easy" in his retirement and to reminisce about the "good old days" from his rocking chair. In contrast, the second man may have been convinced by his associates to see retirement as a golden opportunity for adventure with freedom from responsibilities.

In order to clarify the nature of aging as a social process this discussion will consider, first, the differences between cultures in the functions and status of the aged; second, the differences between various aged groups within our society; third, the extent to which our aged are treated as a minority group and their reactions to this treatment; fourth, the basic controversy and evidence in regard to activity versus disengagement; and finally, some predictions about the aged in our future society.

## CROSS-CULTURAL DIFFERENCES IN AGING

A review of aging in preindustrial societies concluded that "every possible plan for a successful old age has been tried out sometime and somewhere in the world in mankind's attempts to enrich and round off the last years of life" [69]. While this may be an exaggeration, it is clear that an extremely wide variety of plans for successful aging have been tried. But despite these differences in plans for aging, most of the aged in all societies, primitive or contemporary, seem to share certain basic needs and interests. These basic interests have been summarized in five categories:

1. To live as long as possible, or at least until life's satisfactions no longer compensate for its privations.
2. To get some release from the necessity of wearisome exertion at humdrum tasks and to have protection from too great exposure to physical hazards.
3. To safeguard or even strengthen any prerogatives acquired in mid-life such as skills, possessions, rights, authority, and prestige.
4. To remain active participants in the affairs of life in either operational or supervisory roles, any sharing in group interests being preferred to idleness and indifference.
5. Finally, to withdraw from life when necessity requires it, as timely, honorably, and comfortably as possible [69].

Since these are apparently universal needs of the aged, any plan for successful aging should try to meet them as far as possible.

This section outlines the broad trends in the degree to which these needs have been met throughout human history. A summary on a graph of the rise and fall in the security, satisfactions and status of the aged throughout different societies would take the following general form. The baseline or zero point would be represented by animal groups in which there seem to be no instincts or inborn propensities to sustain aged parent or grandparent. The usual pattern among animals is to abandon the aged of the species as soon as abilities to function have seriously declined [69]. It is only through the development of human culture that the aged have been able to achieve any security. With the beginning of primitive hunting, fishing, and collecting societies, the status and security of the aged rises until it reaches its peak in the highly developed agricultural societies. It has usually been assumed that the graph would show substantial decline as it moves to our modern industrial societies [70]. Actually, the evidence is not clear as to how much, if any, decline has occurred in industrial societies. This point will be returned to after the next section.

*Peak in Agricultural Societies*

A few examples from the anthropological literature will illustrate the high status and great satisfactions achieved by the aged in most agricultural societies.

The aged among the Palaung in North Burma were given great prestige and privilege. Long life was considered a great privilege due to virtuous behavior in a previous existence. Milne states that most aged Palaung had "happy lives." Everyone was careful to avoid even stepping upon the shadow of an older person. The children periodically anointed the stool of the father after his death. A typical prayer of the son was, "Thou art gone, my father, but I still respect these things that belonged to thee. Give me long life and health, Oh, my father." As soon as a girl married she was usually eager to appear older than her age because the older woman had more privilege and honor [47].

The Balinese believe that a child is born close to heaven but moves away from heaven until maturity when he is at his lowest status. After maturity he rises in status until old age, and the very old person is regarded as being almost in heaven [71].

The aged Kafir man has both high prestige and access to more creature comforts than any other group in the society. He is allowed to sing and dance at pleasure, spear bucks, plot mischief, or make bargains for his daughters. He no longer has responsibilities for hard work. He may take another young wife for a concubine because it is believed that as long as he can obtain a youthful bride he will not grow old [37].

As a final example, the American patriarchal family of the nineteenth century often gathered four generations around the old parents. The power of the father was justified by his long experience and he was able to hold children and grandchildren in submission to the Bible and to customs. Responsibility between generations was the key to the family solidarity. This family system assured a great sense of security to aging persons [21].

The reasons for the rise in status of the aged from the primitive to the stable rural societies involve six factors which may be summarized as follows:

1. Stable agricultural societies were able to develop greater surpluses of food and shelter to share with the aged. As long as the next day's or the next week's meals were uncertain, as long as food storage was inadequate, as long as families had to migrate from one area to another when the local supply of food was exhausted, the aged and infirm were likely to suffer and to be left behind. It is true that, in order to counter this tendency, the aged in many primitive societies developed food taboos or food preferences which gave them some advantage over the younger tribe members in the competition for scarce food. But when food became more plentiful and more assured with the development of grain storage and animal husbandry, the security of the aged increased markedly.

2. Stable agricultural societies developed more capital and more personal property which increasingly came under the control of the aged. Through their ability to dictate who had access to the property, who would inherit it, and so on, the aged were able to exert a strong influence on the society as a whole, and thereby maintained their position of power.

3. The growing importance of the extended family relations could also be manipulated by the aged to support their status and power. The aged members of the extended family usually were able to influence marriage and birth rates and the economic and social roles that various members of the family assumed, thus assuring the well-being of the clan and of their own position in it.

4. In agricultural societies there are generally more opportunities for auxiliary but useful tasks for the aged than in the more primitive ones. As societies shifted to cultivation of the soil and

animal husbandry, the aged could move more easily to lighter tasks so that they seldom suffered from abrupt retirement and usually found useful functions until near the end of life. Simmons states, "Self employment or ancillary services in agrarian systems probably have provided the most secure and continuous occupational status that society at large has yet afforded for the majority of its aged" [69].

5. Stable agrarian societies accumulated more and more knowledge and technical skills for adapting to the environment and meeting the needs of its members. The aged tended to be the best authorities on this accumulated knowledge and often the most skilled practitioners of the growing arts and crafts. When most of what was known had to be retained by memory, the aged were the best source of information and were usually in the best position to make the best judgments. This semimonopoly on knowledge, wisdom, and skills reinforced the high status of the aged.

6. Similarly, because of their greater experience and knowledge, the aged were usually able to become the main leaders in the growing political, civil, judicial, and religious institutions in the agrarian society. These roles were even more rewarding than the auxiliary tasks described above. Simmons found that most of the tribes he surveyed had old men as chiefs, councilmen, and advisors. He pointed out that the term *elder* had commonly implied leader, head man, or councilman. Also, as magic and religion developed complex ceremonies and institutions among the sedentary societies, the aged were usually able to control the most important roles in these structures.

Two qualifications to this general picture of the high status of aged in agricultural societies should be borne in mind. First, there are both kinds of exceptions: The aged in some foraging, hunting and fishing societies had relatively high status, and the aged in some agricultural societies had relatively low status [28]. Secondly, among all societies the extremely old and helpless person is viewed as a living liability [69]. Our discussion does not refer primarily to this final pathetic stage.

*Decline in Industrial Societies?*

It has been assumed by most writers that the status and satisfactions of the aged have declined in industrial societies. But Friedmann has questioned the basis for this assumption [28]. In order to evaluate this question further, it will be useful to examine the same factors that contributed to the aged's rise in rural societies to see whether they may have contributed to a decline for the aged in industrial societies.

1. The surplus food and shelter have remained or increased, and this has remained a major source of security for the aged. Very few aged these days actually starve to death or die from exposure. However, *relative to younger persons* (see Chapter 4), the smaller amounts and poorer quality of food, shelter, and other comforts available to the average aged person often produce feelings of "relative deprivation." Research has shown that it is usually the relative advantages, rather than absolute amounts, that influence satisfaction and status. Relative to incomes of persons between the ages of 25 and 65, the income of the average aged person is less than one-half as high [79]. Also there are about twice the proportion of aged with poverty incomes compared to those under 65 [53].

2. Real and personal property have, of course, continued to grow, and this too has been a source of continued high status for those few aged fortunate enough to accumulate substantial amounts of property. The difficulty is that most aged actually have not been able to accumulate much property, apart from the house in which they live. Not counting home equity, the average couple over age 65 in the United States had a net worth of $2,740, and the average nonmarried person had less than one-third that amount [24]. Only one in five persons over 65 had a net worth (again excluding home equity) of as much as $10,000. Compared to families with a head aged 55 to 64, the median net worth of families with a head over age 65 is about one-third lower [26]. Furthermore, the actual day-to-day control of productive property (e.g., farms, businesses) has tended to pass from the hands of the aged to the younger and

middle-aged members of our society with the growing trend toward earlier retirement. Thus, the respect and power derived from control of productive property has declined for the aged.

3. In industrial societies the power of the extended family, and the power of elders within the family, have declined sharply. The growth of specialization, division of labor, production in factories, and the general movement of such functions as education and protection from the family to specialized institutions outside the family, all have contributed to a decline in the importance of the family structure in industrial society. The extended family is generally replaced by the small conjugal family typically composed of the father, mother, and two or three children under age 18. This type of family seems better adapted to the demand for rapid spatial and social mobility imposed by a rapidly changing industrial technology. In such a family, the aged can no longer effectively influence the number of children their children will have and thus ensure themselves room in their children's home, nor can they any longer effectively assign economic and social roles.

4. Because fewer of the productive functions are carried out within the family home, there are fewer opportunities for auxiliary but useful tasks for the aged. The aged, if they wish to perform an economically useful role, must compete in the open marketplace with younger men for jobs. This competition is made more difficult by the rapidly changing technology which makes obsolete the skills and knowledge of many of the aged. The result has been an increase in early retirement and in technological unemployment among the aged [55].

5. The control of essential knowledge and skills by the aged declined as knowledge was stored in writing and became more generally diffused. Libraries, rather than the aged, became the repository of the culture's knowledge. Information and entertainment are transmitted by books and the mass media rather than by word of mouth from the elders. Also, the knowledge and experience stored by the aged in modern society often becomes out of date and irrelevant to changed conditions.

6. In our increasingly secularized industrial society some aged

still maintain positions of power in religious institutions, but their power has declined as the power and relevance of religious institutions have tended to decline in recent years. In the political and civil arena control probably is shifting more and more to the younger and middle-aged majority as democracy spreads in modern societies. Notable exceptions to this trend are such institutions as the U.S. Senate and the judiciary whose power remains great and whose positions are filled primarily by the elderly.

Thus, most of the changes in these six factors indicate that the status and satisfactions of most aged relative to those of younger people have probably declined in industrial societies. Of course the status and satisfactions of some fortunate aged in our society are still quite high. It should be remembered that the United States is a composite of industrial and agricultural sections, and in the more rural sections of our country the aged's status may have remained fairly high. Perhaps in summary, rather than attempt to generalize to all sections of all industrial societies, it would be more useful to summarize the variables that appear to contribute to lower status and satisfactions for the aged, viz.: decreased importance of land and capital as a source of income and status; decreased importance of the extended family; high rates of geographical mobility; rapidly changing technology; and rapidly changing social structure and cultural values.

## SOCIAL AND ECONOMIC DIFFERENCES AMONG U.S. AGED

### Age and Sex Differences

Age and sex grading is probably the most pervasive basis of differentiation in all societies. These differences continue among the aged.

A basic difference between the sexes is that women live longer than men. In our society women live seven years longer than men (see Chapter 6). One consequence of this is that, while two-thirds of the aged men are still married, only one-third of the women are still married [24].

When women become widowed, they are more likely to live with their children or other relatives, while widowed men are more likely to live alone or end up in an institution. In general, men have fewer contacts with their families. They live further away from their families; they see their children less often, and they exchange services less with their families [68]. (These points are discussed in greater detail in Chapter 7.) The differences described may be related to the general cultural expectation that women should remain closer to their families while men should be more independent and more interested in things outside their families.

Aged men also claim to be healthier than aged women; they less often say they are house-bound; they report fewer incapacities; they report fewer illnesses within the past year; and they go to the doctor less often [68]. It is difficult to tell whether this is due to actual better health among men or whether it is due to the cultural expectation that men should be "tough" and should not admit illness as readily as women. Since women actually outlive men, it seems likely that the cultural expectation is the major explanation of these differences in reported health.

A clear and fundamental difference between the sexes is that aged men are more often employed than aged women, just as they were in their younger years. Thirty-eight percent of the men over age 65 continue some employment compared to 14 percent of the women [55]. Among those who are retired, more of the men were forced to retire because of compulsive retirement policies, poor health, and the like, while women more often report voluntary reasons for retiring. These differences are explained by the cultural expectation that man's primary role should be gainful employment, while the married woman's primary role is usually thought to be "in the home." Men also are able to earn about twice as much as women, even when the number of hours and weeks is controlled [56]. Partly as a result of this difference in earning power, there are about two times as many aged women in poverty as there are aged men [53].

Age differences also continue among persons over 65. In general, the older aged (those over 75) are in poorer health, are hospitalized more often, are more often widowed, live alone, are isolated and lonely, are rarely employed, and have less income than those between ages 65 and 75 [68].

## Class Differences

Socioeconomic differences also persist among the aged, although there is some evidence that these differences become somewhat attenuated in comparison with younger groups. For example, income differences become smaller because the income of the upper groups is reduced with retirement and the income of the lower groups is supported with Social Security and welfare payments [24]. But the general stratification patterns remain among the aged: Those with less income had less education and came from the blue collar or manual occupations; they have less adequate diets and poorer housing; they see doctors less often; as a result, their health is poorer, they are more incapacitated, and they have a higher death rate; they are more likely to double up and live with their children; and they have more serious unmet needs [24, 58, 68]. Lower strata groups in general have such characteristics as belonging to organizations less, being church members less often, traveling less, reading newspapers less, believing such fundamentalist ideas as the existence of the devil, and being more often anomic, depressed, and unhappy [14a]. The same characteristics probably apply to the aged poor also.

## Race

An extensive review of research on aged Negroes concluded:

A significantly higher proportion of Negroes than white aged persons occupy the lowest socioeconomic positions, a fact already apparent from existing data on comparative socioeconomic positions of Negroes and whites. Hence, when judged by the usual objective (demographic) indices of social adjustment to aging, the corresponding rank position of aged Negroes as compared with aged whites was also lower. Further, the studies definitely demonstrated that aged Negroes, as other aged groups, do not constitute a homogeneous entity. Health status and socioenvironmental conditions, including their previous and present life-styles, also affected and were affected by their adjustment to aging [38].

Beyond these generalizations, there is some scattered evidence that aged Negroes have some relative advantage compared to aged whites, e.g., aged Negroes do not usually suffer as great a reduction in income as do aged whites [52, 58]. There is also some evidence that Negro aged, compared with white aged, feel generally more accepted by their children and receive more assistance from their children [64]. It may well be that relative to their previous status and insecurity during youth and middle age, many of the Negro aged now enjoy somewhat higher status and security because of a more stable income, because surviving to old age is an achievement in itself, because intergenerational family ties are fairly strong, and because some progress toward racial equality has been made.

*Religious Differences*

In general, the Judeo-Christian tradition in our culture regards aging and long life positively. The Old Testament often describes long life as good and a reward for righteous living. Old age is so often associated with wisdom and good judgment as to give the impression that most old men were wise men. Respect for parents and especially aged parents was one of the primary duties and virtues. This view is in contrast to that of ancient Greek and Roman writers who usually depreciated old age unless the aged person had achieved unusual power [46].

In comparing our three major religious traditions, Jews appear to show the most respect and responsibility for their aged. They seem to have developed especially intense family feelings, perhaps as a result of discrimination and segregation. Certainly, Jews have developed extensive community services and homes for aged Jews.

Catholics also have a tradition of respect for the aged. They, too, have developed extensive welfare services and institutions for their own aged, partly because Catholics view most of the public institutions as being quasi-Protestant. However, it must be remembered that Christianity developed in a Greco-Roman setting and was also influenced by the Germanic culture, neither of which highly regarded its aged. Thus Christians, in general, seem not to have quite as high respect and feelings of responsibility for their aged as do the Jews [46].

The greatest diversity of attitudes toward the aged exists among Protestants. They tend more often to consider misfortune and failure as due to moral turpitude or to lack of responsibility and planning. Thus Protestants are often less sympathetic toward the misfortunes of their aged. They also tend to regard the state and the local community as more responsible for the care of the unfortunate aged. There is, in contrast to this general attitude, the pietistic Protestant tradition which founded and maintains many institutions for the aged.

## The Importance of Religion for the Aged

The theories and evidence regarding the importance of religion for the aged are somewhat contradictory. On the one hand there are assertions in the literature such as "Many older persons buffeted on many sides, exhibit in their attitudes and interests the growing importance of religion in their lives" [85]; and that religion is "the key to a happy life in old age. . . . A sense of the all-encompassing love of God is the basic emotional security and firm spiritual foundation for people who face the end of life" [45]. And to support these assertions, there is some evidence that there is a small increase in interest in religion among the aged as measured by responses to questionnaires [48, 57]. A national survey found that somewhat more of those over 65 said religion is "very important" in their lives [17]. Also, substantially larger proportions of older people in all denominations believe in the orthodox dogmas of their denomination [30].

Despite this subjective evidence of greater importance of religion for the aged, this interest does not seem to be carried out in greater religious activity such as church attendance and Bible reading. Nearly all the studies of religious activities and leadership roles in the church agree that there is no general increase in religious activities among the aged; rather, there is usually a decline [3, 6, 17, 35, 51, 57]. The general tendency is for religious habits of the midyears to persist into the later years as long as physical health permits. When there is a decline in church activities, the reason usually given is a decline in physical health and mobility. Poor health is undoubtedly a major factor, but there is some suspicion that it may often be used as an excuse for other reasons. A related piece of evidence is that only 17 percent of a sample of aged urban males claimed to read the Bible and the Bible was read less than any other kind of literature [6].

As for the assumption that religious interest and activities help in adjusting to old age and increasing satisfaction in aging, the evidence is again conflicting. On the negative side, two different studies using the Chicago Inventory of Activities and Attitudes show little or no association between religious attitudes and other aspects of satisfaction [32, 57]. Also, Barron found no relationship between religious attitudes and worry about getting older [6]. On the positive side, at least eleven separate studies have found a direct relationship between church attendance and good adjustment among the aged [48]. At least one of these studies had a large sample (5,000) and used extensive controls in its analysis. The main weakness of this study is that three of the 24 items making up the adjustment score were religious satisfaction items, thus contaminating the dependent variable with items that belong in the independent variable. This illustrates the general problem of getting reliable and valid measures of religiosity and of personal adjustment. Also, longitudinal study would solve some of the problems of cross-sectional associations. In summary, it is probably true that the aged are more orthodox religiously and believe more in the importance of religion, but this is not carried through to greater religious activity, perhaps because of increasing physical infirmities. However, despite some counterevidence, most of the studies agree that church attendance and other religious activities are associated with good personal adjustment in old age. Certainly, religious belief and activities usually continue to be important for the adjustment of those aged for whom religion was important earlier in life.


## THE AGED AS A MINORITY GROUP

A recurrent and controversial issue in social gerontology is whether or not it is useful to view the aged as an emerging minority group. Several gerontologists have argued that minority group concepts and theory help to explain the facts that many of the aged suffer from negative stereotyping, segregation, discrimination, and, as a result, often develop feelings of inferiority and group consciousness [7, 12, 65]. Others argue that the aged are different from racial and ethnic minority groups in several respects [73]. In considering this question, the various negative stereotypes about the aged will first be summarized, and then the evidence for or against the stereotypes (such as illness, sexual activity, mental abilities, morale, activities, productivity, and isolation) will be examined; second, the extent of voluntary and involuntary segregation of the aged and employment discrimination against the aged will be examined; and finally, the reaction of the aged to these forms of prejudice and discrimination will be discussed.


### Negative Stereotypes

ILLNESS. Perhaps the most common stereotypes about the aged have to do with their health status. From one-fifth to two-thirds of various groups, depending on type of group and on the statement, agree with the following statements. Older people "spend much time in bed because of illness," "have many accidents in the home," "have poor coordination," "feel tired most of the time," and "develop infection easily" [76, 77]. Other common stereotypes are that large proportions of the aged are living in hospitals, nursing homes, homes for the aged, or other such institutions, and that the health and abilities of the aged show a fairly steady decline with each passing year.

The fact is that most of these stereotypes are not true of the vast majority of aged persons. For instance, it comes as a great surprise to those unfamiliar with study findings that less than 4 percent of persons age 65 and over live in homes for the aged, nursing homes, hospitals, or other institutions [24]. In an ordinary group of uninformed persons the estimates of what proportion of the aged live in institutions usually range from 10 to over 50 percent.

As for the idea that the aged spend much time in bed, due to illness, it is true that they spend almost two times as many days per year in bed as younger persons, but this is still only 3 percent of the total days in the year (10 days per year in bed for men, 13 days for women) [49]. Also, most aged are able to carry on their major activity most of the time. Only 16 percent of the aged say they are unable to carry on their major activity, and the average number of restricted activity days is only 38 per year [49].

In relation to the stereotype that the aged get infection easily and have many accidents, there are actually fewer acute conditions among the aged than among the younger (1.3 per person per year for the aged compared to 2.1 for all ages [see Chapter 6]) [49]. It is true that the aged have more chronic conditions (81 percent), but this is only one-half more than those aged 17 to 64 (54 percent), and includes such minor conditions as needing glasses, mild hearing loss, and allergies [49].

Regarding the belief that the health and physical ability of most aged decline steadily, the Duke longitudinal study found that from 44 to 58 percent of survivors who returned for examinations had *no* decline in physical functioning or actually had some improvement over time, depending on the time interval (3 to 13 years) [59]. The aged actually show great variability in patterns of change. A few decline precipitously and quickly become totally disabled. For a majority of aged, health and abilities seem to remain fairly level or go up and down slightly when illnesses are contracted, accidents occur, and recoveries are made. Fifty-one percent of the aged rate their health as "good," 33 percent as "fair," and only 16 percent as "poor" [24]. Some aged pride themselves on remaining extremely healthy and capable. There are frequent reports of aged persons who run marathons, climb mountains, swim great distances, and carry out other feats demonstrating their high level of physical functioning. A recent study reports that a one-year program of exercise for men 70 and over so improved their health and fitness that their body reactions became similar to those of men 30 years younger [23]. Such evidence suggests that much of the decline in abilities that does occur among the aged may be due more to declining exercise and activity than to any inevitable aging process itself.

SEXUAL ACTIVITY AND INTEREST. Another generally held belief about the aged is that most no longer have any sexual activity or even sexual desires. Evidence from both the Kinsey survey and the Duke longitudinal study indicates that substantial proportions of the aged continue to engage in sexual activity and even larger proportions report continuing interest in sexual activity (see Chapter 8). This stereotype often causes resistance to remarriage and other normal sexual interest among the aged.

MENTAL ABILITIES. An additional common belief is that mental facilities tend to decline from the twenties onward, especially ability to learn and remember. Many believe that the aged "cannot learn new things," "are slow," "are forgetful," and "become less intelligent" [76, 77]. The evidence related to this belief is reviewed in Chapter 11, but it will suffice here to summarize some of the evidence countering or qualifying the idea of a general and steady decline in intellectual functioning among the aged. Longitudinal studies have found little overall decline in intelligence scores. Tests of vocabulary and information show less decline than other parts of intelligence tests. Several studies have found that there is more decline in speed of response than in the accuracy of response. Seven different studies have concluded that subjects with advanced education and superior ability, working without time pressure, show little or no deterioration with age [29, 30]. There is considerable evidence that many aged continue to be creative in later life [15]. Murphy and Cabrini, quoted in Soddy, concluded that the potential peak performance for abstraction and philosophy occurs between the ages of 45 and 83 [71]. Dennis found that creativity remained high among inventors and scholars in the humanities, mathematics, and botany through their seventies while dropping sharply among biologists, chemists, geologists, and artists [22].

MORALE. Another set of stereotypes about the aged is that they are "grouchy," "feel sorry for themselves," "touchy," and "cranky" [76, 77]. The evidence on this stereotype is somewhat mixed. Most studies have found somewhat more depression, neuroticism, and unhappiness among aged persons, although these studies do not show large differences by age [1, 10, 14, 31]. On the other hand a recent detailed item analysis of the Minnesota Multiphasic Personality Inventory found greater amounts of satisfaction and happiness indicated in the young *and in older ages* compared to the middle ages [61]. Also, older persons are no more likely to express worry than others [31]. A recent review concluded that "the typical older person is not only as likely as a younger person to have a sense of adequacy and self-worth but also as likely to seem content with his occupational and familial roles" [63]. The Duke longitudinal study found little or no significant decline in happiness or life satisfaction over a 10-year period [57]. The discrepancies in the conclusions of these various studies are probably due to the different groups studied, the different aspects of happiness or depression measured, and the different methods used. However, none of the studies would support the stereotype that the majority of aged are extremely depressed or unhappy.

ACTIVITIES. As for stereotypes about the aged's activities, about half of various groups believe the aged are "unproductive" and "spend most of their time reading or listening to the radio" [76, 77]. Actually, surveys show that people over 60 spend less time on mass media activities than people in their 20's [62]. Studies also show that interest in hobbies increases after the age of 50 [13, 18]. Two studies have found no marked decrease in role performance with age in the years 40 to 70 [33, 74]. Finally, the Duke longitudinal study also found little or no significant decline in activities among those aged 60 to 90 over a 10-year period [57]. One study even found that the degree of participation in community activities increased with age after the middle years among those with higher incomes and education [27].

PRODUCTIVITY. Concerning productivity of the aged, 36 percent of men age 65 or over engage in some employment, and earnings from employment are the largest single source of income for persons age 65 or over [56]. A review of most of the extensive studies of productivity has shown that there is either a slight *positive* relationship between productivity and age, or none at all [71]. A 1956 survey by the U.S. Labor Department showed that older workers had an attendance record 20 percent better than that of younger workers and that they had fewer disabling and fewer nondisabling injuries [7]. Other studies of absenteeism show that older workers generally have better attendance records than those under age 35. Frequency of accidents and illnesses tends to decrease with age, though the time off needed for recovery tends to increase [71]. The 1961 White House Conference on Aging concluded that extensive studies reveal no sound basis for the widespread belief that older workers, as an age group, are less productive, less reliable, and more prone to accidents and absenteeism than younger workers.

ISOLATION. The idea that most aged are lonely and isolated from their families and normal social relations is clearly false. About four-fifths of the aged in the United States live with someone else, three-fourths say they are not often alone, and 86 percent say they had seen one or more relatives during the previous week [68] (see Chapter 7). Two studies have also found that there is even more social interaction and less isolation among aged who live in neighborhoods with a high proportion of aged like themselves [66, 67].

WHO BELIEVES STEREOTYPES?   In terms of how similar the aged are to other minority groups, it is significant that persons with more unfavorable attitudes toward the aged are those persons who tend to have more negative attitudes toward ethnic minorities, especially Negroes, and toward the physically and mentally disabled [40]. To put it another way, those who are prejudiced against other minority groups tend also to be prejudiced against the aged. Two studies also found that those who had physical or mental symptoms themselves tended to project more symptoms onto the aged [5, 78].

*Segregation*

It is known that a sizable and growing proportion of the aged are concentrated in certain states and counties, in certain sections of cities, and in special residences for the aged. The latest surveys show that only about one-quarter of the aged live with their adult children [24, 68]. This is a decline from 1952 when one-third of the aged lived in a two or more generation household [72]. The concentration of the aged in certain counties is dramatically shown in the special Census Bureau map of the United States which color codes each county in terms of the proportion of aged [80]. The urban aged are more and more concentrated in the central sections of the city, and the rural aged are more and more concentrated in villages [28]. Breen describes the growing segregation of the aged:

Homes for the aged, public housing projects, medical institutions, recreation centers, and communities which are devoted to the exclusive use of the retired have been increasing in number and size in recent years. Retirement "villages" have been sponsored by philanthropic organizations, unions, church groups, and others. Even established communities which are now known as "retirement centers" have become inundated by older migrants seeking identification and spatial contiguity with "the clan" [12].

The question that cannot be answered at present is how much of this segregation is voluntary or "self-segregation" and how much of it is subtly or overtly forced on the aged by the younger majority. Probably more of the segregation is voluntary among the aged than among other minority groups. However, regardless of the causes of the segregation, the consequences to the aged and to the rest of society may well be similar to those familiar consequences of segregation of other minority groups. For example, Friedmann warns that the duplication of community facilities and services for segregated aged communities may prove to be as economically unfeasible as attempts to provide "separate but equal" facilities for other groups in our society. He also points out other costs such as loss of needed skills in the industrial system and loss of the potential contributions of this new leisure class in performing nonpaid functions essential in the conduct of political and civil affairs [28].

## Discrimination in Employment

There are many forms of discrimination based on age. Employment discrimination, such as compulsory retirement and failure to hire or promote, is probably the most widespread and the most serious in its consequences for the aged. Not only in our nation, but apparently throughout the world, most employers are generally not eager to retain or hire older workers. As Abrams commented, "Nowhere in the world do employers generally equate the plus factors of age, such as experience, judgment, know-how, with the energy, adaptability, and growth prospects of younger job seekers" [2].

This reluctance to hire older workers is especially intense when the labor supply is high in relation to demand, when the technology is rapidly changing and making older skills obsolete, and when the social status and political power of the aged are low.

It is, of course, difficult to determine how much of the forced retirement and failure to hire and promote is due to discrimination based on age alone and how much of it is due to a realistic and fair appraisal of the aged employees' abilities and efficiency. Un-doubtedly many of the aged who are forced to retire or are not hired are actually no longer capable of doing as good a job as a younger worker. But an arbitrary compulsory retirement age is, by definition, discrimination against an age group. Also, there is widespread agreement that many employers do discriminate against older workers in general simply because of negative stereotypes that they hold and other mistaken or irrational beliefs about older workers. Surveys of employment agencies and employers show that many accept the negative stereotypes discussed in the previous section, such as the beliefs that the older worker is hard to please, set in his ways, less productive, frequently absent, and involved in more accidents [7].

In addition to these negative stereotypes, employers have several other reasons or rationalizations, it is hard to say which, for discriminating against the aged. For example, they may believe older workers do not stay on the payroll long enough to justify hiring expenses. Yet, studies show that separation rates for older workers are much lower than for younger employees [7]. Employers may believe it is too costly to provide older workers with adequate pensions or employee group insurance. This generalization may or may not be true depending on the type of plan, the number of employees, and the average age. In addition, even if there are somewhat higher costs, there may be balancing advantages to offset these costs. Employers may believe that older workers do not have needed job skills. On the contrary, surveys show that older workers are *more* likely to possess skills, training, and know-how than younger job hunters.

In attempting to combat such discrimination, several states and the Federal government in 1967 passed laws "to prohibit age discrim-ination in employment" [82]. These laws appear to have been a useful step in the direction of reducing discrimination, but they have several serious limitations. Perhaps the most serious is that most of them do not apply to anyone age 65 or older, which is precisely the age range in which discrimination is most intense. Other limitations of these laws have been summarized as follows:

1. They do not wipe out stereotypes and prejudices against older workers.
2. They do not strike at employer concern with increased costs of pensions, insurance, or with personnel policies of promotion-from-within.
3. Evasion is simple and widespread [7].

*Subculture of the Aged*

The usual reaction to discrimination and segregation is for a minority group to form a distinctive subculture. Such subcultures usually are characterized by a sense of group identity, distinctive beliefs and behaviors, protection of members from the dominant majority, and social action to win benefits and reduce discrimination against its members. There is growing evidence that such a subculture is forming among our aged.

Rose and Peterson [65] present a number of reasons for the growth of a subculture of the aged:

1. The growing number of persons who live beyond the age of 65.
2. The growing proportion of the aged in physical vigor and health because of advances in medicine and sanitation.
3. The growing segregation of older people.
4. The increase in compulsory and voluntary retirement and the corresponding decline in employment of older people.
5. The long-run improvement in the standard of living and in educational level which increases the proportion of aged with the means (in terms of funds, knowledge, and leisure) to do something they consider constructive.
6. The development of special social welfare services for the elderly, particularly group work activities that bring older people together, for identifying with each other.
7. The decline in the pattern of adult children living in the homes of their aged parents.

Mixed group self-hatred and group pride, a characteristic of other subcultures, is documented by the finding that aged persons more often accept both the negative and the positive stereotypes about the aged than do younger persons [41, 76, 77]. There is also evidence that the aged do, in fact, tend to associate more with other older persons than with younger persons [65, 67]. Other behaviors of the aged which contrast with those of younger persons are less employment and more leisure activities, decreased sexual activity, lower crime rates (one-eighth that of those aged 25 to 29), life review, and preparations for death.

Attitudes characteristic of the aged subculture include a diminished emphasis on income and wealth as a basis for status because variation in income has been reduced; a reduction in the importance of occupation and former positions of power and influence; and an increase in the importance of present health and social activity as a basis for status and prestige [65]. In terms of political attitudes, the aged are likely to be more conservative except on issues that would benefit the aged directly, such as Medicare [63].

Finally, there are signs that the aged are developing more social and political power in order to reduce discrimination against them and to win benefits to compensate for discrimination. Many groups start out as "golden age clubs" or "senior citizens clubs," but through sharing common problems, they may develop an awareness that some of these problems occur to them as a group. They begin to talk in terms of taking concerted action, not merely individual action, to correct the situation. They may then join or cooperate with larger organizations such as the Townsend Movement for pensions for the aged, the McLain Movement to eliminate the means test in Old Age Assistance (California Institute of Social Welfare), the American Association of Retired Persons, the National Retired Teachers Association, the National Council on the Aging, and the National Council of Senior Citizens to gain benefits for aged persons. Or they may form local pressure groups to achieve local benefits such as reduced bus fares for those past age 65 as in San Francisco and Los Angeles.

Thus, among a growing proportion of the aged there are all the signs of group identification characteristics of ethic minority groups:

There is a desire to associate with fellow-agers, especially in formal associations and to exclude younger adults from these associations. There are expressions of group pride and corollary expressions of dismay concerning the evidence of "moral deterioration" in the out-group, the younger generations. With this group pride has come self acceptance as a member of an esteemed group, and the showing off of prowess as an elderly person (for example, in "life begins at 80" types of activities). There are manifestations of a feeling of resentment at the "way elderly people are being mistreated," and indications of their taking social action to remove the sources of their resentment [65].

Barron [7], on the other hand, argues that the aged are not a genuine minority group but only a "quasiminority group" because they are not socially organized as independently functioning subgroups in American society. However, this is obviously a matter of degree. The evidence seems to indicate that the degree to which the aged are socially organized and functioning independently is growing, along with the growing segregation, growing group consciousness, and growing local and national organizations for the aged. Others argue that the aged are no more like minority groups than are women, children, and other such groups. While these other groups may have some minority group characteristics, we believe that there is more prejudice, segregation, and discrimination directed toward the aged than toward women and children.

In summary, it appears that the aged already possess many minority group characteristics and that they are becoming increasingly like other disadvantaged minority groups.

## DISENGAGEMENT VS. ACTIVITY

A second controversial theoretical issue in social gerontology is the conflict between disengagement and activity theories. In 1961 the theory of disengagement was first systematically introduced along with some supporting evidence from a cross-sectional study in Kansas City. The basic ideas of disengagement theory are: (1) that the process of mutual withdrawal of aging individuals and society from each other is modal or typical of most aging persons; (2) that this process is biologically and psychologically intrinsic and inevitable; and (3) that this disengagement process is not only correlated with successful aging but is usually necessary for aging [20]. In contrast, activity theory would say: (1) that the majority of normal aging persons maintain fairly level amounts of activity and engagements; (2) that the amount of engagement or disengagement is more influenced by past life styles and by socioeconomic forces than by any intrinsic and inevitable process; and (3) that maintaining or developing substantial levels of physical, mental, and social activity is usually necessary for successful aging [34, 35, 43, 57]. This summary of the two theories is deliberately stated in an extreme form in order to contrast the positions. It should be clear that the issue contains far-reaching theoretical and practical implications.

A major reason why this controversy has not yet been finally settled is that usually cross-sectional data are used to support one or another position, even though the theories deal primarily with change over time. This presents various methodological problems which can confuse the issue. For example, some cross-sectional surveys show that older aged groups have somewhat lower average activities and morale scores than the younger aged. However, rather than reflecting change within the same individuals, such cross-sectional differences may be due to: (1) differences between generations (the older generation may always have been somewhat less active); (2) biased sampling (the older aged who were interviewed happened to be those who stayed at home and thus tended to be less active than those who were away from home); or (3) strongly influenced by a few individuals whose activities dropped sharply just prior to death.

Recent evidence from the Duke longitudinal study shows that the men had almost no overall reduction during a ten-year period in activities or life satisfaction and that women had small (less than

7 percent) but statistically significant reductions in both activities and life satisfaction [57]. Two-fifths of those who returned for examinations after 10 years showed less than 8 percent change in activities and one-fifth actually showed increases of 8 percent or more in activities. It was concluded that while many of the aged may disengage or reduce activities in some areas, the majority tend to compensate by increasing activities in other areas. Often a temporary decrease in activities due to illness may be compensated for by subsequent increase. Those who do reduce permanently are balanced by those who increase permanently. Therefore, the net effect is that there is little or no change in the average activities score.

It should be understood that this study was based on relatively healthy aged who were community residents and who survived for more than 10 years. It may be that disengagement is more typical of the less healthy aged who die earlier. But this study indicates at least that disengagement is *not* inevitable, even over long periods of time. With regard to whether the disengagement that does occur is an intrinsic process or more due to past life-style and to external events, even some of the original proponents have subsequently questioned this aspect of the theory [34, 36]. There is substantial evidence that when age is held constant there is still substantial variation in the indicators of social and psychological disengagement which are related to such factors as sex, health, ability, skill, and intelligence [10, 43, 44, 65]. The Duke study found high levels of consistency within individuals over time in amounts of activity [44, 57].

On the question of whether activity is related to high or to lowered morale and life satisfaction, the evidence is overwhelmingly on the side of the activity theory. The Duke longitudinal study found correlations of .42 for the men and .40 for the women between changes in activities and changes in life satisfaction. This means that when activities remained high or increased, life satisfaction tended to remain high or increase, and that when a person reduced activities his life satisfaction tended to decrease. Most other investigators have also found a positive relationship between activity or social interaction and morale or life satisfaction [16, 19, 34, 42, 65, 75].

Most of the evidence, then, supports the activity theory: continued engagement appears to be typical of the majority of normal aging persons; disengagement is not inevitable, except perhaps just before death; the amount of activity is strongly related to past life-styles and to external factors; and, most important from a practical standpoint, maintaining activity is usually associated with more successful aging and life satisfaction. It may be that activity theory is especially applicable to American culture with its emphasis on a "work ethic," on active mastery versus passive acceptance of nature and the world, on extroversion, and the like.

If the activity theory is generally valid, the practical implications are widespread and profound. If the maintenance of high levels of social interaction and other activities contributes to successful aging, then perhaps legislation should be enacted, agencies should be created, programs developed by government and private organizations, physicians and anyone interested in helping the aged adjust and have satisfying lives should encourage the maintenance of high levels of employment, membership in organizations, frequent contacts with friends and relatives, the development of skills, crafts, and hobbies, and the general development of more useful and meaningful roles for the aged.

## THE AGED AND FUTURE SOCIETY

Predicting the future has always been a hazardous occupation. Nevertheless, just as some planning for the future is usually better than no planning, tentative predictions are usually more useful than no predictions at all. In the concluding section of this chapter four tentative predictions will be ventured about the aged and our society in this century.

The first prediction is that the percentage of persons in our society over 65, estimated at 9.4 percent in 1970, will remain fairly level for the remainder of this century. The Census Bureau has estimated that the proportion aged 65 and over will still be 9.4

percent in 1990 [81]. This projection is based on two somewhat uncertain assumptions: that the birthrate will remain relatively high and that death rates among the middle-aged and older will not decline much. The assumption that birthrates will continue at a fairly high level is somewhat questionable in view of the fact that between 1960 and 1967 the birthrate dropped sharply by about one-quarter [83]. However, since 1967 the birthrate appears to have begun leveling off again. We are assuming that despite widespread use of contraceptives in the future, the average family will still want and will produce three or four children, a situation which would continue to make the population grow. The assumption that death rates among older persons will not decline much is based on a projection of the trend over the past 30 years which shows only small declines for persons age 55 and over compared to the marked decline in death rates for younger persons.

The dramatic increase in life expectancy at birth since 1900 has been due primarily to conquering infectious diseases which affect the death rate of infants, children, and young adults much more than those of older persons. Medical science has made relatively little progress in controlling the killers of the aged, the degenerative diseases. It is true that recent developments in transplants and in the control of cancer offer the hope of significant breakthroughs in reducing degenerative diseases. However, the practical application of such developments is not likely within the next 10 or 20 years—thus, our prediction that there will be no significant increase in the proportion of persons over age 65 in our society.

The second prediction is that euthanasia, defined as permitting terminally ill and suffering patients to die, will become more accepted and widely practiced. This prediction is based on the present growing interest and acceptance of euthanasia by laymen and professionals as reflected in the increasing number of articles and newspaper accounts sympathetic to the practice of euthanasia [25, 84, 86, 87]. Most of these articles agree that when a person has a hopeless and terminal illness, is suffering from intense and increasing pain, or is completely unconscious and his life is being prolonged only by complex and costly machines and personnel, it may often be most humane and ethical to stop protracting the death. Representative of this growing acceptance by physicians is the concluding statement on the aged in the American Medical Association's 1962 National Congress on Mental Illness and Health:

It was suggested, indeed, that the science and art for the preservation of life needs, as a counterpart, a science and art for the closure of life, and especially for very long and completed lives [4].

The following trends, it is believed, will tend to increase the acceptance of euthanasia:

1. The increasing number of persons who reach very old age when prolonged but terminal illness becomes the typical cause of death.
2. The trend toward more rational allocation of scarce and expensive medical equipment (e.g., kidney machines) and personnel to those persons who can benefit most.
3. The growing belief in the right of all persons to do what they want with their own bodies, so long as it does not harm others, as reflected in the growing acceptance of contraceptives, abortion, masturbation, premarital intercourse, and cremation. The right to die under certain circumstances may become another generally accepted civil right.

The third prediction, that a minority group subculture will increase among the aged, has already been discussed earlier under Disengagement vs. Activity. Hopefully, the negative stereotypes and discrimination against the aged will decline with increased knowledge and protective legislation and public programs. However, as we have seen with other minority groups, decreases in negative stereotypes and discrimination are not necessarily followed by less group consciousness and subculture formation. On the contrary, the reduction of prejudice and discrimination against Negroes has been accompanied by increasing group awareness and militant pressures for greater change. If this is the pattern followed by the aged, we can expect a growth in the subculture of the aged, and a

growth in pressures to increase benefits for the aged and opportunities for employment and other useful roles.

This brings us to our final prediction, that American society
will develop new roles for the aged and expand their present useful
roles. It is realized that this is contrary to the present trend toward
more and earlier retirement, toward segregation of the aged, and
the like. Perhaps this last prediction is based more on hope for the
future than on a projection of present trends. However, there are
scattered signs that give some basis for this hope. Several recent
nationwide projects have demonstrated many ways in which retired
persons can be usefully reengaged in the service of society. For
example, the Foster Grandparent Project supplied 4,000 men and
women in their 60's with work caring for 8,000 deprived children
in 1968. Project FIND employed 372 older persons in 12 communities throughout the country to interview and help over 44,000
elderly Americans in their homes. Project Green Thumb employed
many older persons to beautify the highways, parks, and cities
through the planting and cultivation of flowers, shrubs, and trees.
Many gerontologists have pointed out that because of the aged's
extensive experience and practice, many have developed high levels
of skill, emotional stability, wise judgment, and altruism. They
agree that these abilities can and should be channeled into constructive roles. Talcott Parsons sums up this point of view:

My suggestion, then, is that the roles in which our oldest people
have most to contribute, if they have survived the strains and the
previous phases of their life cycle successfully, are roles that stand
toward the top of this scale of social development. They are the
roles in which the broadest problems of adjustment, orientation,
and assumption of responsibility should operate. They are the roles
where judgment and what is often called wisdom should be at a
premium, but where the more confining operative responsibilities
are less pressing than in, for example, executive roles. The whole
range of fiduciary roles is important in this connection, and there
are a good many social precedents for permitting retaining such
roles to rather advanced ages as in the clergy, judiciary, and
teaching . . . . Another positive aspect of the aging persons in such
roles is his being in a favorable position to take a broad view and
to minimize parochial and personal self-interest. He is likely not to

be ambitious in a personal sense, simply because by his age he is excluded from the kind of opportunity that may be open to a younger person [60].

The idea that society can provide only a limited number of jobs, and that therefore it cannot possibly provide enough jobs for aged workers, is no longer accepted by most modern economists. Society could create a useful role for *every* adult *if* it were willing to devote the necessary attention and resources to this end. Certainly there would be major economic and political problems involved. But there is an unlimited number of goods and services needed and desired in American society. There are thousands of hospitals, libraries, schools, colleges, highways, and recreation areas that could and should be built and staffed. There is an unlimited amount of counseling, social service, community organization, group thereapy, tutoring, and training that could usefully be done if enough people were willing to organize the resources for these purposes. And one of the greatest resources that could be channeled toward these ends is the experience, skill, and devotion of millions of aged persons. The fact that much of this resource is currently being wasted is a shame for the present and a hope for the future.

## REFERENCES

1. Aaronson, B. F. Aging, personality change and psychiatric diagnosis. *J. Geront.* 19:144–148, 1964.
2. Abrams, A. J. Discrimination in Employment of Older Workers in Various Countries of the World. In M. L. Barron (Ed.), *The Aging American.* New York: Crowell, 1961.
3. Albrecht, R. The Meaning of Religion to Older People— The Social Aspects. In D. Scudder (Ed.), *Organized Religion and the Older Person.* Gainesville: University of Florida Press, 1958.
4. American Medical Association. Proceedings of National Congress on Mental Illness and Health, 1962. In F. C. Jeffers (Ed.), *Proceedings of Seminars, 1961–65.* Durham: Regional Center for the Study of Aging, Duke University, 1965. P. 167.

5. Arnhoff, F. V., et al. Projected symptoms of old age and present personal assessment. *J. Genet. Psychol.* 6:37–41, 1960.
6. Barron, M. L. The Role of Religion and Religious Institutions in Creating the Milieu of Older People. In D. Scudder (Ed.), *Organized Religion and the Older Person*. Gainesville: University of Florida Press, 1958.
7. Barron, M. L. (Ed.). *The Aging American*. New York: Crowell, 1961.
8. Birren, J. E. (Ed.). *Handbook of Aging and the Individual*. Chicago: University of Chicago Press, 1959.
9. Birren, J. E., and Morrison, D. F. Analysis of the WAIS subtests in relation to age and education. *J. Geront.* 16:363–369, 1961.
10. Birren, J. E., et al. (Eds.). *Human Aging: A Biological and Behavioral Study*. Washington, D.C.: U.S. Government Printing Office, 1963.
11. Botwinick, J. *Cognitive Processes in Maturity and Old Age*. New York: Springer, 1967.
12. Breen, L. Z. The Aging Individual. In C. Tibbits (Ed.), *Handbook of Social Gerontology*. Chicago: University of Chicago Press, 1960.
13. Briggs, E. S. How adults in Missouri use their leisure time. *School and Society* 47:805–808, 1938.
14. Britton, P. G. The MMPI and the aged: Some normative data from a community sample. *Brit. J. Psychiat.* 112:941–943, 1966.
14a. Broom, L., and Selznick, P. *Sociology*. New York: Harper & Row, 1968.
15. Butler, R. N. The Destiny of Creativity in Later Life. In S. Levin and R. Kahana (Eds.), *Psychodynamic Studies on Aging*. New York: International Universities Press, 1967.
16. Cameron, P. Ego strength and happiness of the aged. *J. Geront.* 22:199–202, 1967.
17. *Catholic Digest.* How important religion is to Americans. 17:7–12, 1953.
18. Cavin, R. S., et al. *Personal Adjustments in Old Age*. Chicago: Science Research Associates, 1949.
19. Clark, M., and Anderson, B. *Culture and Aging*. Springfield, Ill.: Thomas, 1967.
20. Cumming, E. and Henry, W. *Growing Old: The Process of Disengagement*. New York: Basic Books, 1961.
21. Dell, F. *Love in the Machine Age*. New York: Farrar and Rinehart, 1930.

22. Dennis, W. Creative productivity between twenty and eighty years. *J. Geront.* 21:1–8, 1966.

23. deVries, H. A. *Report on Jogging and Exercise for Older Adults.* Washington, D.C.: U.S. Administration on Aging, HEW, 1968.

24. Epstein, L. A. *The Aged Population of the United States: The 1963 Social Security Survey of the Aged.* Washington, D.C.: U.S. Government Printing Office, 1967.

25. Euthanasia Society. *A Plan for Voluntary Euthanasia.* London: Euthanasia Society, 1962.

26. Federal Reserve System. Survey of financial characteristics of consumers. *Federal Reserve Bull.* 50:285–293, 1964.

27. Foskett, J. M. Social structure and social participation. *Amer. Sociol. Rev.* 20:431–438, 1955.

28. Friedmann, D. A. The Impact of Aging on the Social Structure. In C. Tibbitts (Ed.), *Handbook of Social Gerontology.* Chicago: University of Chicago Press, 1960.

29. Ghiselli, E. E. Relationship between intelligence and age among superior adults. *J. Genet. Psychol.* 90:13, 1957.

30. Glock, C. Y. *American Piety.* Berkeley: University of California Press, 1968.

31. Gurin, G., et al. *Americans View Their Mental Health.* New York: Basic Books, 1960.

32. Havighurst, R. J. Validity of the Chicago attitude inventory as a measure of personal adjustment in old age. *J. Abnorm. Psychol.* 46:24–29, 1951.

33. Havighurst, R. J. The social competence of middle-aged people. *Genet. Psychol. Monogr.* 37:297–375, 1957.

34. Havighurst, R. J. Disengagement, Personality and Life Satisfaction in the Later Years. In P. F. Hansen (Ed.), *Age with a Future.* Philadelphia: Davis, 1964.

35. Havighurst, R. J., and Albrecht, R. *Older People.* New York: Longmans, Green, 1953.

36. Henry, W. The Theory of Intrinsic Disengagement. In P. F. Hansen (Ed.), *Age with a Future.* Philadelphia: Davis, 1964.

37. Holden, W. C. *The Past and Future of the Kaffir Races.* London: The Author, 1871.

38. Jackson, J. J. Social gerontology and the Negro: A review. *Gerontologist* 7:168–178, 1967.

39. Jones, H. E., and Conrad, H. S. The growth and decline of intelligence. *Genet. Psychol. Monogr.* 13:233–298, 1933.

40. Kogan, N. Attitudes toward old people: The development of

a scale and an examination of correlates. *J. Abnorm. Soc. Psychol.* 62:44–54, 1961.

41. Kogan, N. Attitudes toward old people in an older sample. *J. Abnorm. Soc. Psychol.* 62:616–622, 1961.

42. Lipman, A., and Smith, K. J. Functionality of disengagement in old age. *J. Geront.* 23:517–521, 1968.

43. Maddox, G. L. Disengagement theory: A critical evaluation. *Gerontologist* 4:80–83, 1964.

44. Maddox, G. L. Fact and artifact: Evidence bearing on disengagement theory from the Duke Geriatrics Project. *Hum. Develop.* 8:117–130, 1965.

45. Mathiasen, G. The Role of Religion in the Lives of Older People. In *New York State Governor's Conference on Problems of the Aging.* Albany: The Conference, 1955.

46. Maves, P. B. Aging, Religion, and the Church. In C. Tibbitts (Ed.), *Handbook of Social Gerontology.* Chicago: University of Chicago Press, 1960.

47. Milne, L. *The Home of an Eastern Clan.* Oxford: Clarendon Press, 1924.

48. Moberg, D. O. Church Participation and Adjustment in Old Age. In M. P. Rose (Ed.), *Older People and Their Social World.* Philadelphia: Davis, 1965.

49. National Center for Health Statistics. Data from the *National Health Survey.* Series 10, Nos. 13, 17, 24, and 26. Washington, D.C.: U.S. Government Printing Office, 1964–1965.

50. Nisbet, J. D. Intelligence and age. *Brit. J. Educ. Psychol.* 27:190–198, 1957.

51. Orbach, H. L. Age and religion. A study of church attendance in the Detroit metropolitan area. *Geriatrics* 16:530–540, 1961.

52. Orshansky, M. The aged Negro and his income. *Social Security Bull.* 27:3–13, 1964.

53. Orshansky, M. The shape of poverty in 1966. *Social Security Bull.* 31:3–32, 1968.

54. Orshansky, M. Living in retirement: A moderate standard for a couple. *Social Security Bull.* 31:3–12, 1968.

55. Palmore, E. Differences in the retirement patterns of men and women. *Gerontologist* 5:4–8, 1965.

56. Palmore, E. Employment and Retirement. In L. A. Epstein (Ed.), *The Aged Population of the United States.* Washington, D.C.: U.S. Government Printing Office, 1967.

57. Palmore, E. The effects of aging on activities and attitudes. *Gerontologist* 8:259–263, 1968.

58. Palmore, E. *The Aged Poor.* New York: National Council on the Aging, 1969.

59. Palmore, E. *Normal Aging.* Durham, N.C.: Duke University Press. In press.

60. Parsons, T. Sociocultural Pressures and Expectations. In A. Simon (Ed.), *Aging in Modern Society.* Washington, D.C.: American Psychiatric Association, 1968.

61. Pearson, J. S. Age and sex differences related to MMPI response frequency in 25,000 medical patients. *Amer. J. Psychiat.* 121:988–995, 1965.

62. Pressey, S. L., and Kuhlen, R. G. *Psychological Development Through the Life Span.* New York: Harper, 1957.

63. Riley, M. W. *An Inventory of Research Findings.* Aging and Society, vol. I. New York: Russell Sage Foundation, 1968.

64. Roberts, R. E. *Ethnic and Racial Differences in the Characteristics and Attitudes of the Aged in Selected Areas of Rural Louisiana.* M. A. Thesis, Baton Rouge: Louisiana State University, 1964.

65. Rose, M. P. and Peterson, W. A. (Eds.). *Older People and Their Social World.* Philadelphia: Davis, 1965.

66. Rosenberg, G. S. Age, poverty, and isolation from friends in the urban working class. *J. Geront.* 23:533–538, 1968.

67. Rosow, I. *Social Integration of the Aged.* New York: Free Press, 1967.

68. Shanas, E., et al. *Old People in Three Industrial Societies.* New York: Atherton, 1968.

69. Simmons, L. W. Aging in Preindustrial Societies. In C. Tibbitts (Ed.), *Handbook of Social Gerontology.* Chicago: University of Chicago Press, 1960.

70. Smith, T. L. The Aged in Rural Society. In M. Derber (Ed.), *The Aged and Society.* Champaign, Ill.: Industrial Relations Research Association, 1950.

71. Soddy, K. *Men in Middle Life.* Philadelphia: Lippincott, 1967.

72. Steiner, P. O., and Dorfman, R. *The Economic Status of the Aged.* Berkeley: University of California Press, 1957.

73. Streib, G. F. Are the Aged a Minority Group? In A. W. Gouldner and S. M. Miller (Eds.), *Applied Sociology.* New York: Free Press, 1965.

74. Sussman, M. B. Intergenerational family relationships and social role changes in middle age. *J. Geront.* 15:1, 1960.

75. Tobin, S. C., and Neugarten, B. L. Life satisfaction and social interaction in the aging. *J. Geront.* 16:344–346, 1961.
76. Tuckman, J., and Lorge, I. The effect of institutionalization on attitudes toward old people. *J. Abnorm. Psychol.* 47:337–344, 1952.
77. Tuckman, J., and Lorge, I. Attitude toward aging of individuals with experiences with the aged. *J. Genet. Psychol.* 92:199–204, 1958.
78. Tuckman, J., and Lorge, I. The projection of personal symptoms into stereotypes about aging. *J. Geront.* 13:70–73, 1958.
79. U.S. Bureau of the Census. *1960 Census of Population,* Vol. 1. Washington, D.C.: U.S. Government Printing Office, 1963.
80. U.S. Bureau of the Census. *Older Americans in U.S. by Counties, 1960.* Washington, D.C.: U.S. Government Printing Office, 1965.
81. U.S. Bureau of the Census. *Current Population Reports, Series B.* Washington, D.C.: U.S. Government Printing Office, 1966.
82. U.S. Congress. *Age Discrimination in Employment Act of 1967* (Public Law 90–202). Washington, D.C.: U.S. Government Printing Office, 1967.
83. U.S. Public Health Service, Division of Vital Statistics. *Vital Statistics of the United States.* Washington, D.C.: U.S. Government Printing Office, 1960–1968.
84. Verwoerdt, A. Euthanasia: A growing concern for physicians. *Geriatrics* 22:44–60, 1967.
85. Welfare Council of Metropolitan Chicago. *Community Services for Older People: The Chicago Plan.* Chicago: Wilcox and Follett, 1952.
86. Whitlow, B., and Rosner, F. Extreme measures to prolong life. *J.A.M.A.* 202:374–376, 1967.
87. Williamson, W. P., and Reid, F. W. Prolongation of life or prolonging the act of dying? *J.A.M.A.* 202:162–163, 1967.

# 4

# Economics of Retirement

JUANITA M. KREPS

Every American—whether poor or rich, black or white, uneducated or college-trained—faces a common aging problem: How can he provide and plan for a retirement period of indeterminate length and uncertain needs? How can he allocate earnings during his working lifetime so that he not only meets current obligations for raising children and contributing to the support of the aged parents but has something left over for his own old age?

The economic situation of the aged today speaks ill of the solutions to this problem in the past. But people now old were hampered in their efforts to prepare for their future by two world wars, a major depression, and lifetime earnings which were generally low. The important question persists: What are the prospects for the future aged?

As a Nation, what do we intend for ourselves when aged and what for those who are already old? How are older people, now and in the future, to share in our economic abundance?*

The Task Force members, from whose report the above quote was taken and whose purpose it was to call attention to the economic problems of the future aged, began by describing the plight of today's old people. To live in retirement in the 1960's, they pointed out, is to suffer an income gap that separates the old from the young—a gap that has widened since the beginning of the decade. In brief:

1. Median incomes of families with an aged head were 51 per-

* *Economics of Aging: Toward a Full Share in Abundance.* Prepared by a Task Force (Dorothy McCamman, Juanita M. Kreps, James H. Schulz, Agnes W. Brewster, and Harold L. Sheppard) for the Special Committee on Aging, U.S. Senate, 91st Congress, 1st Session, March 1969, p. 1.

71

cent of that for younger families in 1961, but only 47 percent in 1967.

2. Three out of ten old people (as compared with one in nine of the young) lived in poverty in 1967.

3. About half the families with an aged head had incomes below $4,000; one-fifth had less than $2,000.

4. About half the older unattached individuals had incomes below $1,500; one-fourth had $1,000 or less.

Low incomes, now the number one problem of the aged, are likely to persist. Particular attention is currently being drawn to the income problems of aged widows; to health needs and rising medical costs; to problems associated with home ownership and taxation; and to the implications of early retirement from the labor force. Unless positive action is taken, the future elderly will suffer the depriviation characteristic of today's old people.

Some of the social forces that shape the condition of retirees are peculiar to the United States. These institutional arrangements mirror our attitudes toward work and leisure, and the priorities we give to private consumption versus social transfers of income to nonworkers. In the final analysis, these institutions reflect our appraisal of the needs of young families in comparison with those of the elderly. Some of the issues involved in the support of retirees are common to all industrialized nations, however, for all advanced economies have reached a stage at which leisure in old age need not invite starvation. It is important to cover the common ground first and then to identify the particular set of problems now confronting our own economy.

## INCOME AND LEISURE ISSUES IN ADVANCED ECONOMIES*

The distribution of lifetime between working years and leisure years apparently depends primarily on the nation's stage of eco-

* The discussion in this section is drawn from the author's earlier work, *Lifetime Allocation of Work and Leisure* (Washington, D.C.: U.S. Department of Health, Education, and Welfare, Social Security Administration Research Report No. 22, 1968). Chap. 4.

nomic development or, more precisely, on the productivity of labor and hence the extent to which nonworking time can be supported. Labor force activity rates for men are highest in agricultural and lowest in industrialized countries; the downward trend among the industrially advanced nations continues, moreover, with the major declines appearing at the beginning and at the end of the worklife span. Since mid-century, the rates of decline in the activity of young men have differed in the advanced nations, as have the rates for men aged 65 and over; yet the overall effect has been to increase the number of nonworking years for men in all of these countries.

The scientific and technological progress that increases productivity per manhour also increases life expectancy, with the result that both working and nonworking years have increased during the twentieth century. Male worklife expectancy in the United States saw its first downturn in the 1950's, but the number of years spent outside the labor force has grown throughout the century, and it seems likely that additional years of life will henceforth be allocated to education, training, and retirement rather than to work.

There is clear evidence of an inverse relation between income level and amount of work performed in terms of both workyear and worklife. The important consideration for retirement studies relates to the level of income provided during nonworking years, an issue that becomes increasingly important as the proportion of the population living to retirement age grows and the retirement span lengthens with longer life and possibly earlier retirement. For while average earnings in a particular society may be high, the apportionment of these earnings may be bunched in such a way as to permit the incomes of nonworking persons to be low. Differences, then, between earnings and retirement income may be sufficiently large to argue for temporal redistribution of earnings through whatever mechanisms, public or private, the society elects.

## The Inverse Relation Between Income and Work

Inactive years for men are few in the underdeveloped countries, as John D. Durand noted a decade and a half ago. Rurality and low incomes, he suggested, were the major reasons for high activity rates in those countries; hence, the appearance of nonagricultural industries, the growth of cities, and increases in output per worker should lead to a decline in the labor force activity of men at both ends of working life [4].

This tendency for growth in productivity and real income to be accompanied by increasing amounts of time free of work has been noted often, but rarely has attention been given to international comparisons of income and work. Winston's 1966 study, however, addressing itself to the question of whether as incomes rise people systematically change their distribution of time between work and leisure, employs aggregate international cross-sectional data. The author concludes that there is a significant negative correlation between income and the aggregate allocation of effort to income acquisition, and that the values of the estimated relationship are strikingly similar to those from earlier studies using intercity and industrial cross-sectional data and cross-sectional data on occupational subgroups within societies [10].

Winston uses hours worked per capita, which is the product of average hours worked and the rate of labor force participation, as the indicator of the amount of effort devoted to income acquisition. For the labor force participation rate, two measures are employed: (1) the participation rate for persons aged 14 and over, standardized for population composition, and (2) the participation rate for men of prime working age, 20 to 64. For hours of work, again, alternatives are used: average hours per week, using aggregate-hours data, and average hours in manufacturing. Regardless of the combination of hours and participation rates, the negative relationship between income and social effort was maintained. For example, the fully aggregated data (the standardized participation rate multiplied by general hours) regressed against per capita national income indicate a highly significant negative relationship (at the 0.5 percent level). The value of the regression coefficient would indicate a 1.074 percent reduction in per capita working time with a 10 percent increase in per capita real income. In the case of one underdeveloped country, the author points out that if such a relationship held for Peru, a doubling of its per capita income ($125 in 1957) would be accompanied by a per capita decline of 135 working hours per year.

Of the variables other than income that explain the allocation of effort, the most important, Winston concludes, is the state of aggregate demand as indicated by the level of unemployment. Positive deviations from the fitted regression occur in countries with low levels of unemployment, while negative deviations appear in cases of high unemployment levels. It is interesting to note the relation of the two variables, per capita national income and level of unemployment, to social effort in five advanced economies: the United States, the United Kingdom, West Germany, Switzerland, and Sweden. The United States has by far the highest income; she has also suffered the greatest unemployment. The United Kingdom, West Germany, Switzerland, and Sweden have much lower income and unemployment levels [11].

Although generalizations are perhaps not in order, it does appear that the United States high-income/high-unemployment position has lessened the amount of effort allocated to work. Questions may well be posed for those European countries whose productivity and income levels are rising rapidly: How successfully will a portion of their higher standards of living be translated into greater leisure, including retirement? Will they be able to make the transfer more smoothly, avoiding the unemployment problem that has constituted the primary pressure for the growth of leisure in the United States?

### Income Levels and Work in Old Age

International comparisons of income levels can be drawn either from per capita income data or from wage rates in the different countries. In the United Kingdom, West Germany, and Switzerland the general wage per hour is less than half that in the United States; even the Swedish general wage is only two-thirds the United States rate (Table 1). Rapid growth in output in West Germany, which in the earlier year had the lowest per capita income, nevertheless raised that nation's income per person to only 52 percent of the United States level for 1964 (Table 2). The United Kingdom had slower

TABLE 1.  *Average hourly earnings*[a] *for men in selected countries, 1957 and 1964*

|  | 1957 | | 1964 | |
|---|---|---|---|---|
| Country | General | Manufac-turing | General | Manufac-turing |
| West Germany | $0.562 | $0.551 | $1.045 | $1.025 |
| Sweden | [b]1.039 | 1.031 | [b]1.550 | 1.482 |
| Switzerland | 0.707 | 0.717 | 1.080 | 1.064 |
| United Kingdom | 0.730 | 0.761 | 1.062 | 1.110 |
| United States | [b]1.900 | [c]2.050 | [b]2.300 | [c]2.530 |

a Derived from rates reported in local currency by the International Labour Office and converted to U.S. currency at the exchange rates reported by ILO.

b General wage level not reported. Entry computed by weighting sectoral wage levels reported by ILO and Bureau of Labor Statistics by sectoral distribution of the labor force. However, data were not complete and may not be comparable to the other entries in these columns. In addition, computed rate is for both men and women.

c Rate for both men and women, which thus understates the male rate.

Sources: ILO *Yearbook of Labour Statistics, 1965,* tables 18, 19A, 20–22 (Geneva: International Labour Office); U.N. *Statistical Yearbook, 1962,* tables 39, 67, *1965,* tables 53, 82. 139 (New York: United Nations); U.S. Department of Labor, *Monthly Labor Review,* December 1958, tables A–2, C–1, November 1966, tables A–9, C–1.

TABLE 2.  *Per capita gross domestic produce and national income in selected countries, 1957 and 1964 (current dollars)*

|  | Per Capita Gross Domestic Product at Factor Cost | | Per Capita National Income | |
|---|---|---|---|---|
| Country | 1957 | 1964 | 1957 | 1964 |
| West Germany | $0,837 | $1,541 | $0,741 | $1,409 |
| Sweden | 1,273 | 2,013 | a | a |
| Switzerland | 1,308 | 2,003 | 1,220 | 1,815 |
| United Kingdom | 1,039 | 1,472 | 0,955 | 1,275 |
| United States | 2,345 | 3,002 | 2,110 | 2,696 |

a National income data not available in United Nations sources.

Sources: U.N. *Yearbook of National Accounts Statistics, 1958,* table 1, *1965,* tables 1, 9A; *Statistical Yearbook, 1958,* table 1, *1965,* table 19 (New York: United Nations).

economic growth during the period and consequently achieved a per capita income only 47 percent of that in the United States in 1964. Income in the United States thus continued to be one and one-half to two times as high as the income in the other countries, despite recent differences in rates of growth [9].

In contrast to the much higher per capita incomes and wage rates in the United States, the proportion of earned income maintained for persons in retirement in this country is relatively low (Table 3).

TABLE 3. *Average old-age benefits as a percentage of average wages in manufacturing, and pensionable age, in selected countries, most recent year available*

| Country | Year | | Average Benefits As a Percentage of Average Wages for All Workers | Normal Pensionable Age[a] | |
|---|---|---|---|---|---|
| | Benefits | Wages | | Men | Women |
| West Germany | [b]1963 | [c]1963 | 31.4 | 65 | 65 |
| Sweden | [d]1962 | 1961-62 | 22.4 | 67 | 67 |
| Switzerland | [e]1963 | [f]1963 | 18.0 | 65 | 62 |
| United Kingdom | [g]1965 | 1965 | 15.2 | 65 | 60 |
| United States | [h]1964 | 1964 | 18.2 | 65 | 65 |

[a] Earlier retirement, under varying conditions, is provided in most countries.
[b] June.
[c] May; includes family allowances paid directly by employer.
[d] January; old-age pensions.
[e] Old-age and survivor payments.
[f] Adult male (skilled and unskilled) and all women workers weighted by the number of persons in each category.
[g] Retirement pensions.
[h] Old-age, survivor, and disability awards.
Sources: Germany: Georg Tietz's summary of data in *Zalenwerk zur Sozialversicherung* (Berlin, 1963). Sweden: *Statistisk Årsbok för Sverige, 1964,* tables 253, 272. Switzerland: *Statistisches Jahrbuch der Schweiz, 1965,* pp. 296, 371. United Kingdom: *Report of the Ministry of Pensions and National Insurance for the Year 1965,* pp. 78, 132; *Ministry of Labour Gazette,* August 1965, p. 525. United States: U.S. Department of Health, Education, and Welfare, *Social Security Bulletin,* March 1966, table Q–6; U.S. Department of Commerce, *Survey of Current Business,* July 1966, pp. S–14, S–15. Pensionable age: U.S. Department of Health, Education, and Welfare, *Social Security Programs Throughout the World, 1967* (Washington, D.C.: U.S. Government Printing Office, 1967).

West Germany, which has next to the lowest per capita national income, assures the highest proportion of average wages to old-age recipients. These benefits are payable, moreover, without regard to whether the older person has retired. Sweden's average benefit is also a substantially higher proportion of average wages than is our own retirement benefit; pensionable age is also later.

The relation between average earnings and retirement benefits would seem to be more relevant to the retirement decision of an individual than earnings as such, at least when full employment prevails and retirement is optional within the age range of, say, 65 to 69. In the case of West Germany, the lower participation rate of men in this age group bears out this hypothesis (Table 4). Swedish figures are not comparable, since pensionable age is 67, and the proportion of older men at work in the United Kingdom is slightly

TABLE 4. *Labor force participation rates for men aged 65 to 69 in selected countries, recent years*

| Country | 1950 | 1960 | 1964 |
|---|---|---|---|
| West Germany | [a]26.8 | [b]33.2 | 36.6 |
| Sweden: | | | |
| Census (excluding unemployed) | 56.4 | 50.6 | [c]47.8 |
| Survey | [d] | 58.6 | 48.5 |
| Switzerland | 65.9 | 59.2 | [d] |
| United Kingdom | [e]48.7 | [f]39.5 | [g]39.6 |
| United States | 59.8 | 43.8 | 42.6 |

[a] Aged 65 and over. Excludes West Berlin.
[b] 1961 data. Excludes West Berlin.
[c] 1965 data.
[d] Not available.
[e] 1951 data.
[f] 1961 data.
[g] Forecast.

Sources: 1950 and 1960 columns: U.N. *Demographic Yearbook, 1955,* table 15; *1964,* table 8 (New York: United Nations). 1964 column: Germany: *Arbeits- und Sozialstatistische Mitteilungen,* July–August 1965, p. 172. Sweden: *Tilgången På Arbetskraft 1960–1980,* Statens Offentliga Utredningar, 1966, tables 6, 9. United Kingdom: *Ministry of Labour Gazette,* January 1965, p. 4; Central Statistical Office, *Monthly Digest of Statistics,* No. 220 (April 1964), table 13. United States: U.S. Department of Labor, *The Older American Worker,* June 1965, p. 145.

lower than in the United States, despite the somewhat larger proportion of earnings maintained in the latter country.

Examination of the pension/earnings ratios for other countries may reveal a direct relation between the ratio and the proportion of men who retire in the five-year span following pensionable age. But such comparisons are hazardous for several reasons: measures of part-time work in old age, which are crucial to such analysis, are poor; the data on other sources of income of the elderly are sparse except for older people in the United States [5]; and, finally, there is considerable variation in the practice of using a retirement test as a condition of drawing pensions [7].

Although the relevant group would seem to be men aged 65 to 69 for countries with pensionable age of 65, this age group typically has the highest incomes among the elderly because of continued work and higher benefits. The lower benefits accrue to men aged 70 and over, older women of all ages, and, in the United States, to retired men aged 62 to 64, whose characteristics often suggest that the pension is a form of unemployment compensation. Pension incentives probably have little to do with the act of retiring in such cases; retirement is not optional, but is a product of economywide circumstances that for the older group seem unlikely to change. For the early retirees in the United States the present high level of economic activity is somewhat more promising.

*Pensionable Age and the Age of Retirement*

An inverse relation between average earnings and time spent at work has been demonstrated, using international cross-sectional data. Similarly, an inverse relation between the proportion of earnings maintained as pension and the labor force participation of men in the early years of eligibility might well be shown if reliable data were available. However, the influence of normal pensionable age on actual retirement age is obviously of primary significance, despite variations in pension arrangements among various countries. It is important to note the extent to which actual retirement age has come to approach pensionable age and then to examine the factors that account for the establishment of, or change in, pensionable age.

In a recent survey, more than one-third of the responding nations stated that the average exact age of initial receipt of pension was either the same as or within one year of normal pensionable age, i.e., the earliest age at which the normal old-age pension becomes payable. When there were differences between pensionable and actual retirement age the latter was higher, but for schemes having 65 as the pensionable age the variation was generally small. The observance of a "normal" retirement age is noteworthy, particularly in view of the availability of advanced pensions in more than half the countries; many of these advanced pensions were not reduced [2].

Deferred retirement credits were also available in 24 of the 57 schemes covered in the report, but there is not sufficient evidence to demonstrate that a delayed retirement credit induces workers to postpone retirement, even when the amount of the increment is substantial. The role played by a retirement test is also unclear. Thirty-seven schemes imposed some sort of retirement condition, ranging from the stipulation that the worker give up all remunerative work to less stringent rules, such as limitations on earnings up to a specified age. With only one exception, the 20 schemes having no retirement test were content with their arrangements, whereas almost half the 37 having such tests reported some sentiment for changing the regulations. The estimated costs of eliminating the retirement condition ranged from "negligible" in Italy to a 40 percent increase on the island of Jersey in the Channel Islands. The estimated long-run rise in cost in the United States was 10 percent [3].

Higher costs resulting from removal of a retirement test would presumably be more than offset by an increase in the total output of the larger labor force. If the state of the economy called for additional manpower and retirees constituted a potential labor source, waiving the retirement test could be justified, since it would furnish the inducement to older workers to remain in the labor force. The three countries in the present study with the tightest labor markets impose no retirement provision. In Sweden, entitlement to benefits does not depend on financial participation of the worker or on any qualifying period; the scheme is tax-financed and allows concurrent receipt of wages and benefits. Switzerland and West Germany have social insurance schemes in which the pension is again not contingent on retirement or income. Moreover, the German worker may claim an advanced pension at age 60 or afterwards if he has been unemployed for a year and is unlikely to find work. The United Kingdom and the United States apply earnings tests up to age 70 and 72, respectively.

The tendency for actual retirement age to approach pensionable age is easy to understand in an economy of labor excess. The bidding for limited jobs must either force some of the workers out of jobs or push down the wage rate; the latter would require considerably more downward flexibility of wages and prices than has prevailed in the postwar economy in the United States. Thus, those workers who have pensions are expected to vacate their jobs in favor of younger men who have not only better education and more up-to-date skills but also greater financial needs. It is precisely the logic of this retirement-on-schedule pattern that compels attention to any movement toward a lowering of pensionable age or even any increase in the prevalence of early-retirement provisions in private-pension schemes. The question of whether the age at which one may retire is to become the age at which one is expected to retire must be kept clearly in mind.

## Retirement Policy and Manpower Needs

The imposition of a retirement condition and the selection of pensionable age itself are likely to reflect the policymaker's view of the manpower situation. One of the major considerations in the establishment of old-age benefits in the United States was the intent of drawing elderly persons off the labor market and thus helping to restore the balance between the supply of and demand for labor. It followed that the benefit would have to be contingent on actual retirement. The lowering of pensionable age for men further recognized the need to provide income for men aged 62 to 64 who for reasons other than disability could no longer find employment. But perhaps the clearest example of the relation between manpower problems and retirement policy is the pension scheme negotiated by the United Automobile Workers. Here the need to remove the excess of labor from a rapidly automating industry led to extremely generous private pensions, permitting workers to retire as early as 55.

In contrast, the nations of Western Europe have attempted to keep older persons at work, and the advantages of a flexible retirement age are frequently cited.* Although pensionable age clusters at 65 for both men and women in the member countries of the Organization for Economic Cooperation and Development, inducements to continue working, such as West Germany's scheme for increasing the size of the pension if retirement is postponed, are frequent. In Sweden the pensionable age is 67, with provisions for a .6 percent reduction for every month the pension is taken prior to that age, down to 63; a similar increment is added for each month beyond age 67 that the pension is postponed. In Great Britain the graduated pension, not being subject to a retirement test, may provide some incentive to work beyond age 65.

Although convincing arguments are being made for flexible retirement age in European countries suffering labor shortages, there has been no attempt to raise pensionable age. It is understandable that there is also no movement to lower the age of retirement, given the need for manpower. Curiously, while incentives are being offered to older workers to keep them at work, there is strong pressure for shortening the workweek and lengthening annual vacations. Moreover, there are many inducements to bring women into the labor force: child-care centers, special arrangements for rest periods on the job, and extensive maternity- and sick-leave provisions.

These attempts to serve manpower needs by increasing the number of workers, while still allowing each employee gradually to reduce his workyear, are in direct contrast to the situation in the United States, both as to manpower needs and the manner of

---

* See, for example, Sven O. Hyden, *Flexible Retirement Age* (Paris: Organization for Economic Cooperation and Development, 1966). Other OECD studies dealing with retirement and older-worker problems are: A. Heron, *Age and Employment* (1962); Stephen Griew, *Job Re-design* (1964); R. M. Belbin, *Training Methods* (1965); Bert Andersen, *Work or Support* (1966), and *The Employment of Older Workers* (1965).

meeting these needs. Demographic developments here have been markedly different. The population of working age has been growing rapidly and will continue to do so; comparable data on the percentage increase from 1966 to 1976 in the United States and in European nations, summarized in OECD studies, are shown in Table 5.

TABLE 5. *Percentage increase in working age population, 1966-67*

| 0–4 percent | 5–9 percent | 10–14 percent | 15–19 percent | 20–29 percent |
|---|---|---|---|---|
| Austria | France | Netherlands | United States | Turkey |
| Belgium | Norway | Portugal | | |
| Denmark | | | | |
| West Germany | | | | |
| Ireland | | | | |
| Italy | | | | |
| Sweden | | | | |
| Switzerland | | | | |
| United Kingdom | | | | |

In addition to the much greater increase in persons of labor-force age in the United States, the faster pace of technology in this country has reduced the demand for labor per unit of output, thereby creating a further labor market imbalance. The solution to this imbalance has resulted in growth of leisure in a form that differs from any added free time in the European nations. Here the labor force has been reduced at both ends of the worklife span. Despite the fact that our age of entry into the labor force has traditionally been much later than in European nations, the movement toward further postponement continues here, with Sweden the only close competitor in number of years of schooling provided youth.

The allocation of a substantial portion of the growth in leisure to the retirement period has the advantage of making the free time available to all workers who survive to retirement age. Conceivably, leisure in the form of extended vacations might be somewhat less evenly apportioned over the labor force, accruing, initially at least,

most generously to workers whose bargaining strength enables them
to gain contractual concessions providing for reduced working time.*
Moreover, there is the broader question of the extent of the practi-
cability of tradeoff between retirement leisure and vacation (or
other workyear) arrangements. The difficulties inherent in a reap-
portionment of the amount of nonworking time now available are
clearly evident in the discussions surrounding any proposal for
reductions in working hours. Finally, we know very little about
workers' actual preferences as to the distribution of free time. The
question of whether increased leisure in old age is in fact preferred
directs attention to a consideration of the broader issue of the allocation of future leisure, which promises to grow rapidly. Evidence that
other advanced countries are choosing patterns of leisure time that
are somewhat different from our own underscores the importance of
discerning actual preferences before policy is established.

## INCOME MAINTENANCE IN THE UNITED STATES

In summary, both real incomes and the number of hours free of
work have grown rapidly in the United States and most Western
European nations during the past decade. The amount of free time
currently available to a worker varies in the different countries, and
there are important differences in the forms the additional leisure is
taking. The European nations surveyed have distributed the year's
leisure more heavily in annual and public holidays and less in a
shortened workweek than has the United States; however, there are
now strong drives throughout Western Europe to reduce hours
worked per week. As to change in worklife, the pattern varies from
one country to another. Sweden has decreased significantly the labor
force participation of young persons while increasing the activity of
all women beyond adolescence. West Germany and the United
Kingdom have lowered somewhat their traditionally high work
activity in youth, with the participation of older persons changing

* The author is indebted to Robert L. Stein, formerly of the Office of Research
and Statistics, Social Security Administration, for raising this question and making
other valuable criticisms.

less significantly. Switzerland continues to have a long worklife for men and low participation rates for women, the rates for both changing more slowly than in other nations.

## Growth of Leisure in the United States

Growth of leisure in the United States promises to be even greater as technology continues to raise productivity per manhour. As a rough dimension of past growth in free time, the employed worker has about 1,200 hours per year more nonworking time than his 1890 counterpart. The additional time is apportioned over the year in the following forms: reduction in workweek (from 61.9 to 40.5 hours), approximately 1,100 hours; increase in paid holidays (4 days), 32 hours; increase in paid vacation (6 days), 48 hours; increase in sick leave (1 week), 40 hours. The shortened workweek has thus accounted for most of the century's rise in free time during worklife. In addition to a shortened workyear, nonworking years have grown by about 9 for a male at birth, with present life and worklife expectancies. This increased free time, therefore—bunched at the beginning and end of worklife—amounts to about one-third the amount added through workweek reductions, added vacations, and the like.*

The amount of time free of work in the United States not only has grown rapidly during this century but also is destined to expand to much greater dimensions in the coming decade. What forms this new leisure will take is of great significance—as important, perhaps, as the composition of the goods produced. A greater amount of free time at the end of worklife is but one of several forms in which leisure could be allocated. Its desirability over other forms of free time, moreover, is in part dependent on the financial arrangements made for the retirement period, or on the temporal distribution of income.

---

* Estimates prepared for Juanita M. Kreps and Joseph J. Spengler, "The Leisure Component of Economic Growth," in *Employment Impact of Technological Change*. Appendix Volume II of *Technology and the American Economy*. (Washington, D.C.: U.S. Government Printing Office, 1966.) P. 355.

## The Problem of Retirement Income

To the extent that the growth in nonworking time takes the form of a shortened workyear, the cost of the leisure, measured in terms of product foregone, is concealed in the wage/price relationship, and income-maintenance arrangements are not affected. Increased leisure in the European nations, being apportioned largely in shorter workweeks and longer vacations, has not magnified the problem of income maintenance in old age. Tight labor markets, moreover, have encouraged the utilization of older persons who cared to continue working. In the United States, by contrast, the level of unemployment during the past two decades has led industry and the Congress to make early retirement possible. Meanwhile, few incentives have been offered to induce continued labor force participation past the age of 65.

As F. Le Gros Clark has pointed out, the acceptance of 65 as the age of withdrawal from work occurred earlier in the United States than in the United Kingdom, and an inching down below age 65 has now begun in this country. Whether such a movement will continue here and develop in other nations as their income levels approach our own is difficult to predict. Nevertheless, it is clear that certain retirement-related problems are peculiar to the United States, if for no other reason than the fact that we reached a certain level of economic development somewhat earlier than other countries [1].

Perhaps the best indicator of this nation's economic advance is its faster pace of technology and the resulting acceleration of real incomes during the past two decades. Higher postwar rates of economic growth in Western Europe have narrowed but by no means eliminated the United States' lead in per capita income. Paradoxically, the higher per capita income rises, the more acute become the income problems of certain groups of people, i.e., those groups who are not current participants in the economic process. For the higher income reflects higher productivity per manhour, and such increases in our economy are expected to accrue to the workers who are actually at work rather than to those of the preceding or succeeding generation of workers.

Considerable disparity between income during working and retirement years may be more acceptable in an economy that places great stress on the output of the individual worker. Job performance is supposedly rewarded by a wage roughly commensurate with productivity; in fact, the promise of higher income provides the incentive for greater worker effort. Given a wage structure explained largely in terms of output per manhour, it is easy to develop a rationale for variations in wages for different jobs (or individual performances on a particular job), a gradual decline in income if productivity declines with age, and a still lower assured income during retirement.

The social security program justifies a transfer of income from workers to nonworkers on the basis of previous earnings and contributions. The essence of the retirement benefit—this transfer of income claims from workers to nonworkers—is not always recognized, however. That such a transfer is necessary may also be obscured, and the range of options as to methods of transfer may not be systematically explored. Intergenerational transfers of income, once made chiefly within families, have come increasingly to be made between workers and nonworkers, irrespective of family ties [8], and the remaining issue has to do with the amount of the transfer, i.e., the extent of the smoothing-out process.

In explaining the development of a scheme of retirement benefits, the role played by economic ideology cannot be overlooked, even though its quantitative importance is difficult to assess. For whatever reason, reluctance to apportion larger percentages of the nation's income to retired persons in this country—in contrast to the allocation made from much lower incomes in West Germany, for example—results in a marked difference between the income of the worker and that of the retiree, even when the savings and part-time earnings of the latter are included.

Along with the problem of the income drop at retirement is the equally pressing question: What happens to the retiree's relative income position during the years of his retirement?* The retirement

* The argument in this and the next three paragraphs follows the author's discussion in "Higher Incomes for Older Americans" published in *Foundations of Practical Gerontology*, edited by Rosamonde Ramsey Boyd and Charles G. Oakes,

span is now long enough to permit a significant worsening of his income relative to that of persons still at work. At age 65 a man's life expectancy is about 13 years, and that of his wife, who is probably slightly younger, is almost 20 years. If there is any lowering of retirement age or increase in life expectancy, the couple's non-working period may extend to two full decades.

During these 20 years dramatic changes are likely to occur in the income position of those persons in the labor force. If the economy's real rate of growth were as high as 4 percent annually, the total output of goods and services would roughly double in two decades. Working persons and their families would thus enjoy a 100 percent increase in real incomes, while the bulk of the retirees continued to live on incomes that were fixed. To the extent that prices rose, the aged's income position would be worsened even further.

Offsets to their relative decline in income would be available only insofar as older persons were able to continue working, at least on a part-time basis, or retirement benefits grew in some rough accord with the overall growth of the economy. Arrangement for tying the social security benefits to the cost of living, although an important safeguard in periods of inflation, would not meet the need to keep retirement incomes in line with the incomes of persons still at work. The central question comes to be, then, to what extent (and through what mechanisms) older people are to share in the growth in national output.

Growth in real income for persons of all ages comes from the same source: increased output. The rate of economic growth thus sets the limit to the pace at which we can raise incomes. The better our technology, the more efficiently we use our manpower and other resources, the faster incomes can rise. But whereas productivity will provide the goods and services with which to raise future levels of living for all age groups, persons share in this growth in accordance with their income claims—claims which accrue to retirees via the tax mechanism (and OASDHI benefits) or through private saving. If we would raise the income of the future retiree, we must therefore increase his capacity to save during worklife, or raise the social security benefit by transferring a larger income claim to him through the taxation-benefit scheme. In either case, consumption is foregone during worklife in return for consumption during retirement. For the present generation of retirees, further private savings are not possible; their incomes can be increased only by raising retirement benefits.

### The Temporal Distribution of Income and Leisure

To the extent that free time is chosen by the individual in lieu of income, the worker maximizes his satisfactions, given the overall time constraint [6]. There are, however, instances in which time is not convertible into income, although such a conversion would greatly increase total utility. Unemployment is the prime example, but involuntary retirement may result in much the same removal of the income alternative. Free time may in fact have no utility in periods when it is excessive, nor work any disutility when it is very scarce.

It is a balancing of goods (i.e., income) and leisure that maximizes satisfactions, and this balance may be disturbed by too much free time in one stage of life and too little in another. Similarly, a some-what more even distribution of income throughout the life-span might increase the total utility of any given amount of lifetime earnings. Such a smoothing of income can be and often is accomplished by individual savings arrangements; many people, on the other hand, have extremely high time-preferences for goods and relatively little willpower for saving. Reliance on some form of forced savings is therefore quite common.

Since it is not possible to save the goods one produces this year for consumption several decades hence, today's worker can only acquire deferred claims against the goods produced later in the form of an annuity or "rights" to retirement benefits. In the case of an annuity, he knows how many dollars of income he will receive (though he does not know what their purchasing power will be); rights to retirement benefits, however, are not guaranteed in amount.

He knows only that if payroll taxes go up now he will have fewer present dollars, retirees will have more dollars, and (since benefits have never been reduced) his own benefits will probably be at least as high as those that beneficiaries are currently receiving and presumably will reflect to some extent changes in earnings levels as well as in purchasing power.

The smoothing of lifetime earnings roughly in accordance with family needs throughout the life cycle is more easily accomplished the longer the worklife or the more heavily the leisure is apportioned during the worklife and the less it is bunched into retirement. The more concentrated the working time, obviously, the more concentrated will be total earnings. If retirement age is lowered, the volume of income transferred from workers to nonworkers must be increased just in order to hold benefits to their present level. Attempts to set percentage limits on the payroll tax—if this is to continue to be the sole source of revenue for benefits—are therefore tied to the question of the temporal distribution of leisure.

At present our most vexing income-maintenance questions pertain to the issue of early retirement—its financing and the extent to which the retirement years are to absorb the leisure component of the nation's economic growth. The positive value to retirees of leisure in this extended form has been given little thought, and there are no parallels in other advanced countries that one can study. It is clear, however, that any significant trend in the direction of early retirement calls for reexamination of the income-maintenance rules for at least two reasons: (1) the retirement benefits available to early retirees are particularly low, and private-pension coverage, though growing, is still limited to a small proportion of the total labor force; and (2) the added length of the retirement period thins the annual income from savings and other assets meant to be spread over the nonworking period.

Whether additional leisure in the form of early retirement is the most desired allocation of any new free time is also a question for consideration. Although the European nations, with lower incomes and less free time, do not face this question immediately, it is evident that reduction in retirement age has a very low priority in their range of leisure preferences, which are for shorter workweeks, additional holidays in some cases, and extended education and training periods. These might well be preferred by workers in this country if they were, in fact, alternative options. Preferences for a shorter workyear might be expressed even among those workers whose retirement incomes are adequate; certainly this would be true for persons retiring on reduced social security benefits alone.

## REFERENCES

1. Clark, F. L. G. *Work, Age, and Leisure.* London: Michael Joseph, 1966. P. 137.
2. David, A. M. Problems of retirement age and related conditions for the receipt of old-age benefits. Report IX of the Fifteenth General Assembly. *Bull. Int. Soc. Sec. Assoc.* 18:97–109, 1965.
3. *Ibid.,* pp. 105–106.
4. Durand, J. D. Population Structure as a Factor in Manpower and Dependency Problems of Under-developed Countries. *Population Bull. U.N.,* 3. New York: United Nations, 1953. P. 10.
5. Epstein, L. A., and Murray, J. H. *The Aged Population of the United States.* Washington, D.C.: U.S. Government Printing Office, 1967.
6. Gallaway, L. E. The aged and the extent of poverty in the United States. *South. Econ. J.* 33:212–222, 1966.
7. Higuchi, T. Old-age pensions and retirement. *Int. Labour Rev.* 90:1–19, 1964.
8. Kreps, J. M. Economics of Intergenerational Relationships. In E. Shanas and G. Strieb (Eds.), *Social Structure and the Family: Generational Relations.* Englewood Cliffs, N.J.: Prentice-Hall, 1965. Pp. 267–288.
9. United Nations. *Statistical Yearbook, 1965.* New York: United Nations, 1966. Table 179.
10. Winston, G. C. An international comparison of income and hours of work. *Rev. Econ. Stat.* 48:28–39, 1966.
11. *Ibid.,* p. 35.

# 5

# The Ambiguity of Retirement

KURT W. BACK

## THE CHANGING MEANING OF RETIREMENT

*Retirement and Type of Society*

Retirement has been considered an aging problem primarily in industrial societies. However, retirement itself is not a phenomenon peculiar to these societies. It has always been the case that with diminishing powers the aged person becomes unable to perform his normal economically gainful work. Since he can no longer maintain himself, society must find some way to maintain him, if he is to survive at all. In some societies, both the society and the aged person feel that he has contributed sufficiently to the physical welfare of the society and is now entitled to a different, perhaps a more contemplative, life. He must relinquish the role of provider and find another role.

In industrial as well as nonindustrial societies the working role may be linked to the possession of power and implicated in feelings of individual worth. Thus the aged person may be reluctant to retire and relinquish this power. For example, in peasant societies the act of turning over the property by the parent in exchange for a guarantee of support signifies the end of the parent's farming activities and the start of independent work—frequently the possibility of marriage—for the son (see Chapter 3). Since the timing of this change is within the discretion of the parent, this form of retirement is sometimes achieved by bitter negotiation. Similar power struggles occur frequently between occupants of positions and their prospective successors in the political world, these strug-

*93*

gles being the most visible manifestations of the continual small struggles that occur between generations.

Thus the phenomenon of retirement has existed in many non-industrial societies. However, both the status and meaning of retirement have been transformed by the exigencies of an industrial economy. We shall first indicate the importance to society of retirement as a condition of life today, and then discuss, from the point of view of the individual, the meaning of the status change, the retirement process, the importance of the previous occupation, and the use of free time.

*Prevalence of Retirement in the United States*

In 1900 more than two-thirds of all men age 65 and over were gainfully employed. This proportion had dropped to 32.2 percent by 1960 and is expected to fall to 23.4 percent by 1975. The one exception to this general decrease occurred during the period of World War II, indicating that many of the men in this age bracket are available to work if they are needed [20].

The impact of retirement falls unevenly on different population groups. In general, men with higher degrees of education, and those in professional and managerial positions, are more likely to keep on working. For instance, slightly more than half the men over 65 who had a college degree were working in 1960, as compared with less than a quarter of those with a fourth grade education or less [20]. Thus retirement is less prevalent among those who can be presumed to have had higher incomes during their working lives.

With women the picture is somewhat different. The extent of their participation in the labor force has increased during this century, especially for those women in the age bracket preceding usual retirement age. This trend has offset the general trend for leaving the labor force in those 65 and older, with the result that the rate of labor force participation of women aged 65 and older has stayed fairly constant at 10 percent or just below [20]. The question of retirement of women is complicated by the fact that they do not necessarily enter the labor force in their younger years, although more and more are doing so. Currently, half the women in the age group 45 to 54 are working, as compared with 90 percent of the males [10].

The proportion of workers who are covered by social security and private pension plans has been increasing steadily in recent years; today an overwhelming proportion of the aged obtain benefits from such coverage. In 1962 social security payments were made to 70 percent of the aged, while 16 percent of married couples and 5 percent of nonmarried persons reported income from private pensions. By 1975 it is expected that 90 percent will be receiving social security payments, and the number of private pension plans is increasing markedly. By way of contrast, as recently as 1948 only 13 percent of persons aged 65 and over obtained social security benefits, and the number receiving payment from private pension plans was only one-fourth of the number who received such payments in 1962 [20].

## Economic and Social Retirement

In this chapter retirement will be treated as an emerging status in present-day society; that is, it is becoming a recognized position during a man's life. Throughout his working life man is characterized in many ways by his occupation. When he retires his identification changes; he is now socially in a different status, which may have various consequences, especially economic ones. The discussion will attempt to distinguish the social definition of retirement from the economic one.

It has been observed that many persons who are classified as "retired" actually work either full-time or part-time. For instance, in 1962 40 percent of men between the ages of 65 and 72 who were beneficiaries of social security reported some work experience [19]. Persons who work after retirement may be driven to work through economic necessity because the retirement income is not sufficient to satisfy their needs. Alternatively, they may prefer the activity involved in gainful employment to the other possible ways of spending their time. Some organizations, such as the military and other governmental units, set the minimum period for reaching retirement so low that the retiree feels easily able to start a second career. In fact, we would hardly have called Dwight D. Eisenhower or Charles de Gaulle "retired officers" while they were serving as presidents of their respective countries. In many of these cases the possibility of early retirement is considered to be a purely economic advantage rather than true retirement, somewhat in the same manner in which short weekly hours specified in construction unions' contracts are often really a vehicle for higher weekly wages through overtime pay.

It seems fruitful, therefore, to make a distinction between economic and social retirement. When studying retirement plans, especially from the point of view of the company from which a person retires, the economist must define retirement as the point at which the worker severs relations with the employer and receives a pension of some kind. However, a person may or may not feel himself to be retired at this point. A social definition of retirement would specify it as that condition in which a person concedes that he is no longer active in the work role or work activity with which he identified his active career. This definition is clearly subjective and may be hard to apply to individual cases. However, it has the advantage of pointing out that the main problem in retirement (apart from the financial loss) is the loss of identification with the work role and separation from the network of relationships which the work role involved.

The situation is different for women, both socially and economically. At all ages only a minority of women are gainfully employed, and many of them interrupt their working careers during the child-bearing and family-rearing years. Thus, speaking in strictly economic terms, neither retirement nor employment is as widespread in women as in men. In addition, women do not have as much identification with the work role; many of them enter the labor force late, after children are grown, and their economic and social position is less dependent on their own than on their husbands' work. It may be that for many women the equivalent of retirement is the loss of the mother role, when the last child leaves home. Family theorists have spoken of this as the "empty nest" stage of life [7]. For all these reasons the impact of retirement on women in today's society is less predictable than it is on men. For some women—career women, for instance—retirement may have the same effect that it does on men. For many other women its importance will depend on individual circumstances.

The present chapter will concentrate on the personal and social implications of retirement as opposed to the economic and financial ones. It will concentrate primarily on men, since for them the work role (and hence separation from it) is universally applicable.

### Retirement in Industrial Society

Five kinds of factors have influenced the importance of retirement in industrial society and the conditions under which it takes place. They have all tended to make retirement more prominent and more visible in industrial societies than in others.

DEMOGRAPHIC FACTORS. Both the number and proportion of individuals in the older age groups have increased during this century. The proportion of people aged 65 and over has increased from 3 percent in 1850 to 4 percent in 1900 and to 9 percent in 1960 [20]. However, the proportion does not tell the whole story. With the increase in population the increased proportion means, of course, a vastly larger number of people over age 65. From 3.1 million in 1900, the number of people age 65 and over has risen to 16.7 million in 1960 [20]. The aged today, being more numerous, are more visible as a segment of society. Because of this, society's planning for the aged, as evidenced by senior citizen communities, special activities, and general concern with the status of retirees, has also increased.

ECONOMIC FACTORS. Technological advance has led to increased productivity per worker in all industrial countries. In the United States this increase occurred at the rate of 1.5 percent per year before World War I, 0.5 percent per year between World Wars I and II, and at a rate of almost 3 percent since World War II [25]. This increased productivity per worker makes it possible to decrease the total working time of the individual worker and still assure a considerable increase in total production and standard of living [15] (see also Chapter 4).

REQUIRED SKILLS.  The nature of the skills required in work in modern industry has acted in two ways to increase the pressure to retire the older worker. First, in many industrial jobs, skills, once learned, cannot be improved upon. Thus the aged worker does not have any advantage in wisdom such as the advantage he used to have when jobs were less dependent on specific skills. Thus, even if there is no actual decrement in performance, the older worker is at no particular advantage. Second, rapid changes in job require- ments, and even in the creation and obsolescence of whole occupa- tions, which occur in a rapidly expanding technological society, force the worker to keep learning new skills and ceasing to practice old ones. We may disregard here the question of whether an older worker has more trouble than a younger one in acquiring a new skill. Even the fact by itself that the older worker has to relearn, while the younger worker, especially one just entering the labor force, has to learn only the one skill, might be expected to put the older worker at a psychological disadvantage. For these reasons a rapidly changing industrial society will tend to put a premium on rapid turnover of the labor force.

SIZE OF ECONOMIC UNIT.  Industrial society has in general larger economic units than preindustrial society, even in the agricultural and bureaucratic sectors. In fact, the creation of modern industrial societies is in great part a function of the societies' organizational capacity. One of the by-products of this capacity is the establishment of definite policies which are applied generally, with little regard for individual differences. Thus retirement does not depend any more on the individual capacity of the older worker to hold his job and to fend off rivals, but on an imposed negotiated policy of retirement at a certain age. In certain positions outside the organi- zational pattern, e.g., in the top positions in management, labor, and government, retirement at a certain age is not enforced and the aged are able to hold their own. In these power positions the aged are probably overrepresented. Hunter in 1958 compiled a list of the one hundred most influential Americans [12]. Of these more than a third were age 65 or over. However, among the great mass of people in the labor force, where organizational policies prevail, retirement has been taken out of the realm of individual decision.

SEGREGATION OF WORK AND LEISURE. Because of the nature of industrial work, modern society makes a sharp distinction between work and leisure [31]. Special times and places are assigned to work, as opposed to the preindustrial situation in which work could be performed around the home and no definite times for work were established. In consequence, retirement has become abrupt in industrial society. The retired person does not go to work any more; he does not spend a definite time period at a working activity. His social contacts are interrupted, and he is suddenly faced with large blocks of free time.

## SOCIETY CREATES THE AMBIGUITY

### The Privilege and Obligation to Retire

The foregoing discussion has tried to show the extent and origins of the retirement status in contemporary society. The next consideration will be, from an historical point of view, how retirement has come to be an achievement and a problem at the same time.

Note must first be made of a basic ambiguity inherent in the way retirement plans have developed in modern society. Social legislation makes it possible for the aged to withdraw from the work force and still receive income. This has been regarded as a privilege, and political and economic groups have fought and still fight for an early age limit and adequate compensation in retirement. However, this right to retirement shifts subtly to an obligation to retire at the time retirement pay becomes effective. Retirement is more and more becoming regarded as a role for the aged. Transition to this role arouses concern in the aged person and creates problems regarding his adaptation to retirement, his morale, and his ways of spending time.

In a society that is able to support an increasing proportion of nonproductive members, we are faced with the fact that all of the values of the society are directed at the glorification of economic roles, at work within the society, and in general at the activities related to youth. Here we have the crux of the sociopsychological problem of retirement. Retirement is regarded as an achievement in principle but dreaded as a crisis when it actually occurs.

The prevalence of retirement and society's acceptance of it are still increasing; we cannot at this time tell with certainty how far retirement will become the norm for older people and how completely society will accept the idea of retirement. This transition period is made far more complex by the fact that the provision of reasonably adequate retirement pay, increasing number of years spent in retirement, and social acceptance of the retirement state proceed at an uneven pace. Until the prevalence of retirement becomes constant, we will be faced with these problems of transition.

### Development of Retirement Policy

Policy-makers may be motivated by any of several different lines of thought in preparing plans for retirement of the aged. They can start from humanitarian motives, using such rationales as:

Retirement is a right an individual possesses after devoting many years to productive labor.

or

Retirement is a necessity in order to protect the aged who cannot perform gainful work any more.

They may also be motivated by considerations which have little to do with the aged, but which are aimed at solving problems affecting society as a whole, such as:

Retirement is an economic necessity allowing the young to enter the labor force and advance in their occupational career.

or

If some people have to be eliminated from the labor force, it is best that these be the aged.

The first type of reason for retirement is usually given explicitly in discussions of social insurance schemes and other retirement legislation. The second type is more likely to be present implicitly. This type is important, however, in society's transition from permissive to normative attitudes toward retirement, and the eventual social expectation that retirement is a natural stage of life. Both the humanitarian and the economic motives are present in society's thinking, and may be simultaneously held by a single individual. The ambiguity inherent in this double approach underlies the problem retirement poses in dealing with the aged. How did it develop?

The values which originally influenced the acceptance of retirement policies as a social necessity were humanitarian. They were opposed to the extreme individualism of some preindustrial societies which assumed that people should be responsible to provide for their own old age and that only in extreme cases should society take steps to care for the poor, as expressed in the old English Poor Law. This policy was inadequate in that it led to many destitute aged persons being consigned to poorhouses. As society became industrialized, individualism became completely unrealistic. Workers were unable to put aside substantial savings, nor could the gainfully employed easily support the aged and infirm. Even more, the threat of an impoverished old age put pressure on the worker during his younger years, contributing to the precariousness of his existence and his feelings of disaffection. The diverse social insurance schemes which arose, such as those covering accidents, illnesses, disability, and aging, were probably as much a help to the people who would anticipate these calamities as a direct aid to those who had suffered them [5].

Europe preceded the United States in the passage of social insurance acts: Germany in 1889 and England in 1910 passed laws that showed genuine concern for the problems of the worker. Bismarck in Germany and Lloyd George and Churchill in Britain in their speeches proposing these plans expressed concern for the dignity and security of the working man, and dismay at the cruelty of punishing him for not accomplishing what was clearly beyond his means [4, 5]. In the United States, the acceptance of this responsibility on the part of society came in the 1930's. Here, two factors stood in the way of acceptance of a comprehensive insurance scheme: a strong tradition of individualism and an equally strong devotion to the idea of autonomy of communities and states. The depression of the 1930's made the problem of the aged overwhelming, since they were most likely to be unemployed, and the states could not provide for them unassisted. The work of the commissions and committees which eventually led to the Social Security Act showed awareness of this rapid shift in values, and eventually the principle of social insurance was also accepted in the United States [6].

Other, less obvious motives also played a part in this process. Especially in Germany and probably to a lesser extent in the other industrialized nations, one motive of the policy-makers was to mitigate industrial unrest and prevent the workers from seeking radical solutions. Bismarck openly campaigned for social legislation on the grounds that it would counteract socialism, and, in fact, the socialist delegates voted against the bill. Soon afterward, however, the socialists became enthusiastic supporters of the system, and even of its contributory features (rather than entirely state-supported, which Bismarck had wanted) which gave the worker dignity and conferred the sense that old age payment was a right the worker had earned. In England, the motives of the Liberal Government were similar, in that they were trying to hold their own against the Labor Party. In the United States, the New Deal measures were partially influenced by similar fears, as well as by a new factor: Because of the high unemployment rate, a regulated way to get the older worker out of the labor force was very appealing. The possibility of obtaining work for the young and middle-aged by encouraging retirement is still instrumental in the efforts of many unions to lower the retirement age.

These historical observations show how much the problem of retirement is linked to the total functioning of the industrial system. It became clear that, as Churchill put it, "It is a great mistake to suppose that thrift is caused only by fear" [3]. For a variety of reasons, the solution was found of giving the worker a stake in the system by guaranteeing him a pension to which he has usually contributed himself. Even when the premiums are only contributed by the employer, both the employer and the worker can rightly feel that this is a substitute for a payment which the employer would have given otherwise in the form of direct wages. There may be other, incidental effects of retirement on modern society, among them a possible braking effect on the birth rate, since individuals do not need to have grown children to support them in their old age.

The principal effect of systematic retirement plans on society which concerns us here, however, is the regularizing of passage through the labor force which an old-age insurance system brings about, i.e., the removing of choice from the individual. Retirement benefits are given to the worker for his use when he is no longer able to work. For a long time it was assumed that every worker would keep working as long as he was able to do so. In line with this point of view, the argument was put forth that the amount of the premium should depend on the hazards of the industry, as is frequently the case in accident insurance. However, under the pressure of circumstance a subtle inversion of emphasis occurred. From being the provision of aid at a time when the worker was unable to work, the benefits have become a basis for the definition of this disability; i.e., whenever a worker can have the full benefits, he should then retire.

This shift in emphasis has become widespread, and has resulted in the age of 65 becoming an almost inviolable borderline between work and retirement. Even legislation against job discrimination because of age does not apply to individuals over this age. In population statistics the economically active population is defined as being between the ages of 14 and 65, and the ratio of this age group to the total population is defined as the "dependency ratio," assuming that individuals outside these age limits are not economically active. Thus retirement has become the social norm for the aged—defined usually as age 65 and older—and this norm is becoming more and more universally enforced. Provision of security for the worker has become a rule to follow which may not be altered to fit individual cases. We can now ask how the individual deals with the problems created by this system.

## THE INDIVIDUAL FACES THE AMBIGUITY

### Kinds of Status Change

Although more and more people expect to retire and although retirement is becoming a natural stage of life, the step itself represents an important status transition. In many ways contemporary American society identifies the individual by his occupation. Thus retirement is still, in great part, a giving up of a role and not an acquisition of a new status. There are a number of transitions of this kind in life, some pleasant and some less pleasant. They all share some common problems. The person has to give up patterns of behavior and expectations in which he has been trained and acquire new ones. This becomes a problem for the individual as well as for the group which he leaves. Society has developed mechanisms which make this transition easier.

We can distinguish different kinds of status change. One kind is an improvement in status, such as graduation or promotion. Another kind is one in which a person voluntarily relinquishes a role and takes on another which is neither better nor worse, e.g., starting a second career. A third kind of status change takes place when one is deprived involuntarily of a role [9]. The basic ambiguity of retirement consists in the fact that it is questionable whether it belongs in the second or third category. Retirement may be accepted as a new beginning, similar to the one a woman makes who gives up a career for marriage or motherhood. On the other hand, it can be seen as an involuntary loss of status which may or may not reflect on a person's worth.

## The Retirement Process

We can look at the retirement process as a status change which is only vaguely defined. The tendency of both the individual retiree and of the persons in charge of the process is to make the change look as good as possible, i.e., as a regular status change, or at worst as an involuntary change which does not reflect on individual worth. The process of preparation for retirement, the change itself, and the individual's adjustment to it all influence the success of these attempts to view it optimistically.

In current society, most persons accept the social prescriptions and expect or want to retire. They have some idea of their future financial arrangements and what immediate changes may occur in their way of life. They are less certain about other repercussions, the effect on their interpersonal relations with family, community, and former co-workers. In general, however, they seek little information except for the details of their future income.

Looking at the trend of the last two decades, we may presume that retirement will become more accepted by society in future years. In the recent past there is evidence of an increasing acceptance of retirement by people still in the working force. This change has been as rapid as the increase in development of retirement plans. Studies in the 1950's found that a substantial proportion of working people opposed retirement [28, 30]; later studies have shown a greater degree of acceptance and favorable expectation of retirement [14, 21]. In fact, many younger respondents would prefer a younger retirement age than they actually expect [11]. Workers in the age group immediately preceding retirement, on the other hand, were less likely to look forward to it. This may be due to either of two factors. One is that the necessity of facing imminent retirement devalues it in the eyes of the workers. The other is that the trend toward greater public approval of retirement is reflected in the younger workers' showing greater enthusiasm for it, whereas the older workers came from a previous generation which did not have such a positive attitude. In the present stage of transition in attitudes toward retirement the latter alternative seems plausible. However, there are some data to suggest that actual retirement is viewed by the older worker as a crisis, lending support to the first, more pessimistic, hypothesis. Further support is given by the finding that younger people tend to anticipate greater happiness in old age in general than older people actually experience.

In spite of people's increasing acceptance of retirement, there is usually little preparation for the change. Financial preparation seems to be the most necessary kind of planning, and Katona has found that individuals who are enrolled in pension plans are most likely to have additional savings [14]. This corresponds to the theory of levels of aspiration, which would predict that people raise their sights with success. Looking at this question another way one can say that people will plan for retirement if there is something to plan for. Social provisions will precede individual plans.

The relation between planning for retirement, exposure to information about it, and attitude toward it is complex. In a study involving individuals within five years of retirement, the majority had been exposed to some material about retirement. Those who had most exposure were also most likely to have some plans for retirement. However, both exposure and planning were related to the degree of favorableness of the subjects' anticipation of it [22].

Taking these findings into consideration, it might be hypothesized that the virtual certainty of being covered by social security and the increasing likelihood of a pension plan at one's place of employment make retirement a state to look forward to. Those increasingly numerous individuals who accept the retirement role also seek out more information about retirement and are thus able to plan for retirement [22]. The studies previously cited enable us to understand why, in general, formal preretirement programs have not been effective. Those who are interested will seek out information, while those who dread retirement will not appreciate a reminder of the future. People generally tend to seek information that is consonant with their attitude.

The worker who finds himself in the process of retiring may experience it either as a crisis which he has done his best to make unexpected or as a normal event, the achievement of a reward which is due him for his long service to society. It can be said that a minority of workers retire completely voluntarily. In a 1963 study of retirees who had started receiving social security benefits during the previous five years, almost half had retired for poor health, and only a quarter said they had retired voluntarily, because they preferred leisure or for similar reasons. The remaining quarter retired because of company policy, layoff, or similar constraints. However, the proportion of voluntary retirees, although small, had doubled over the past 12 years [19]. It is therefore becoming more acceptable to admit that one wants to retire just because one does not want to work.

Although retirement is such a ubiquitous event, little attention has been given to the actual process of retirement. Contemporary society places little ritual emphasis on status change. Thus retirement may pass unnoticed or be marked only in a minor way. One study indicates that the marking of retirement by some ritual act is a portent of favorable adjustment in retirement; somewhat surprisingly, even the kind of retirement gift given is an indication of the retiree's later adjustment. If the gift indicates a new retirement activity (such as golf clubs), this is a sign that the prognosis for gratification later on is better than if a merely formal gift (such as a gold watch) is given. The more retirement is looked on as a change to a new status, and the less it is perceived as the giving up of a prized status, the better the transition will be accomplished [26].

## Work Status and Retirement*

We have seen that social trends are leading to an increased general acceptance of retirement, but there are still large differences among individuals and among groups in this respect. One important determinant of the person's attitude toward and adjustment to retirement is the nature of the work he has been doing. Two different kinds of

* Unless otherwise stated, the material in this section is based on Section One (Chapters 2–7), "Work and Retirement," in I. H. Simpson *et. al.* (Eds.), *Social Aspects of Aging* [21, 22, 23].

work involvement may facilitate adjustment to retirement. One is the feeling of involvement in one's work and the possession of high prestige which work may confer; this gives support to the person and can carry him through the status change involved in retirement. The second kind is the attitude of separating one's work from one's real life, and considering only the extrinsic rewards in work to be important. In this case retirement is eased because not much had been invested in the work role to begin with. In accord with the preceding rationale, retirement should be easiest either for people in high-prestige positions—professionals and management men—or for those in low-prestige positions.

There is, in fact, some evidence for both alternatives. Both the high- and low-prestige groups show good adjustment to retirement if the conditions that are appropriate for each of them are met. Individuals in high-prestige occupations will be satisfied in retirement if they felt successful and satisfied with their former work and if they have some chance to continue the former work activities. Among middle-class workers (white collar and skilled) successful adjustment to retirement depends on factors less related to their occupation: If they are attracted to their work and miss it, they have less of a chance than the high-prestige workers to recapture in retirement those features of the work they liked. In distinction to the high-status occupations, the middle-class jobs depend in general on social contacts or intricate tools, neither of which are available in retirement. Thus the factors determining the happiness of the retired middle-class worker are not as easy to pinpoint as those influencing the high-status worker.

Perhaps because the middle-class worker may have more trouble than the upper- or lower-class worker in making the transition from work to retirement, he reports more of a need for information about retirement than the other two. The upper-class group apparently has gained through normal channels all the information it needs about the sort of retirement its members can look forward to, and the low-prestige group is mainly interested in the financial arrangements that are possible. Labor unions, the associations most closely affiliated with the middle group, are the organizations which, more than any other, claim the continued participation of their retired members [29].

Work status differences also play a part in determining attitude during the retirement process itself. Preretired individuals in high-prestige occupations are least enthusiastic about retirement, while those in low-prestige occupations are most enthusiastic. Later on, this is reversed: The professional men find retirement better than they expected, while the semiskilled workers do not find it as attractive as they had thought they would. This shift probably occurs during the first two years of retirement. Thus the immediate retirement experience represents more of a crisis for the professional, but he recovers over the next few years, whereas the opposite pattern is true for the blue-collar worker [27].

One other difference among occupational groups is that workers in high-prestige positions are less subject to fixed retirement ages than are other workers. It is difficult to find retired physicians and lawyers. This freedom, however, is bought by a corresponding detrimental effect on self-image when they do retire. Professionals, who work as long as they can—as all workers used to do—have to face the fact that in retiring they are giving up a status, which makes a smooth transition more difficult. Workers who are retired according to a criterion unrelated to their personal worth, such as chronological age, can more easily accept retirement as a transition to a new, equivalent status.

*Free Time*

One of the major consequences of retirement, in addition to economic and status considerations, is the sheer availability of time. Thus much of the practical concern society has shown for the retiree has been directed toward the problem of the use of leisure time. During the working years, leisure is a small segment of one's total available time, and therefore activities may be chosen merely to contrast with or to escape from the working activities. This sort of leisure activity may prove to be unsatisfactory when it occupies the major portion of one's life. Thus attempts to expand the working man's leisure-time activities to fill the new-found time of the retiree are frequently useless. The retiree has to work out a meaningful new pattern of life, and this is frequently difficult. Time, which is scarce for the working man, becomes suddenly excessive and can acquire a negative value. As Wilbert Moore has said succinctly, retirees may have "too much time for much too short a future" [18].

There is little consensus on how retirees spend their time, and little systematic research has been done. Most writers merely prescribe how the retired person ought to spend his time, or classify the various activities he might pursue. Case studies of patterns of successful and unsuccessful retirement show the variety of activities that might be enjoyed. But the picture which emerges indicates that it is not the activities themselves but the meaning which the individual is able to give to the activities which determines his adjustment [13, 16, 24]. Puttering around with toys may be the last resort of a desperate, bored man; it may also be a satisfying activity of a man whose life-style has consisted in general of devotion to others, especially if the toys are for his grandchildren [2].

Thus retirees spend their time in a variety of ways, just as people in the labor force do. There is no particular reason why people should change their whole style of life merely because they have retired. In effect, people adjust to retirement in a way analogous to that in which they adjusted to their previous life.

In particular we find the same occupational differences we noticed previously. For retirees from the professional and managerial coterie, continuity of activity from the preretirement period becomes important. This may consist, for instance, of reading in the case of a man whose job activities involved working with symbols. In middle-status jobs no such relation between previous activities and post-retirement activities is found; there may even be a negative relation [23]. Similar results are found when we consider working among the newly retired. The incidence of working has been reported to be positively related to occupational status and also positively related to morale in high-status groups. Here again, high involvement in his work makes the retiree desire continuity in his life [8].

From these pieces of evidence we can see that provision of mean-ingful activities for retirees is a difficult and frequently impossible task. The meaning of life in retirement is continuous with the meaning one gives to life over a range of years. Life cannot become suddenly meaningful because one has retired if it was not mean-ingful before. Many of the morale problems attributed to retirement may be in reality a function of the total life-style of the person.

## CONCLUSION

Hannah Arendt has in *The Human Condition* demonstrated how the meaning of work has changed in the last few centuries [1]. The central figure in today's society is no longer the contemplative, think-ing man, nor even the manufacturing man, but the laboring being (*animal laborans*). Life and values are oriented around activity, the act of working, and all other activities are made subordinate to this central concern. To the degree that high energy levels are prereq-uisite to this activity, our society can be called youth-centered. The aged person tries to retain his position by showing that he can be as active as the young person. We have seen that the aged can retain power if they are in positions in which they can remain within the competitive world of activity; but even the leisure-time activities of the retiree are defined by the value of leisure to the young [17]. "Eighty years young" is the highest compliment the aged person can be paid.

It may be that the social trend toward early retirement will help inaugurate a new conception of man's relation to work. Taking into consideration the trends toward increasing longevity and decreas-ing age at retirement, the proportion of the individual's life spent in the labor force will soon be less than half. It is difficult to predict from the present trends what form retirement will take under these conditions. Today's retirees have spent most of their working life during a time when retirement pay was not guaranteed and the status of retirement could not be clearly envisaged. In consequence, he is a victim of change, caught between two patterns of work and retirement. Members of today's labor force, the retirees of the future, can give new meaning to work and leisure, and plan for a new pattern of life which includes placing a positive value on retirement.

REFERENCES

1. Arendt, H. *The Human Condition.* New York: Doubleday, 1959.
2. Buhler, C. Meaningful Living in the Mature Years. In R. W. Kleemeier (Ed.), *Aging and Leisure.* New York: Oxford University Press, 1961.
3. Churchill, W. S. *Liberalism and the Social Problem.* London: Hodder and Stoughton, 1909.
4. Dawson, W. H. *Social Insurance in Germany 1883–1911.* London: T. Fisher Unwin, 1912.
5. Donahue, W., Orbach, H. L., and Pollak, O. Retirement: The Emerging Social Pattern. In C. Tibbitts (Ed.), *Handbook of Social Gerontology.* Chicago: University of Chicago Press, 1961.
6. Douglas, P. H. *Social Security in the United States.* New York: McGraw-Hill, 1936.
7. Duvall, E. M. *Family Development.* New York: Lippincott, 1957.
8. Fillenbaum, G. *The Working Retired.* Durham, N.C.: Center for the Study of Aging and Human Development, Duke University Medical Center, 1968. Unpublished manuscript.
9. Goffman, E. On cooling the mark out. *Psychiatry* 15:451–463, 1952.
10. Goldstein, S. Socio-economic and migration differentials between the aged in the labor force and in the labor reserve. Presented at annual meeting of the Gerontological Society, New York, 1966.
11. Harris, L. "Pleasant" Retirement Expected. *The Washington Post,* November 28, 1965 (reported in Riley and Foner).
12. Hunter, F. *Top Leadership, U.S.A.* Chapel Hill: University of North Carolina Press, 1959.
13. Kaplan, M. The Uses of Leisure. In C. Tibbitts (Ed.), *Handbook of Social Gerontology.* Chicago: University of Chicago Press, 1961.
14. Katona, G. *Private Pensions and Individual Saving.* Ann Arbor: University of Michigan Press, 1965.
15. Kreps, J. M. The Allocation of Leisure to Retirement. In F. M. Carp (Ed.), *The Retirement Process.* Bethesda, Md.: Public Health Service Publication No. 1778, 1966.

16. Linder, M. E. Preparation for the Leisure of Later Maturity. In W. Donahue, W. W. Hunter, D. H. Coons, and H. K. Maurice (Eds.), *Free Time: Challenge to Later Maturity*. Ann Arbor: University of Michigan Press, 1958.

17. Meyersohn, R. B. Americans Off Duty. In W. Donahue, W. W. Hunter, D. H. Coons, and H. K. Maurice (Eds.), *Free Time: Challenge to Later Maturity*. Ann Arbor: University of Michigan Press, 1958.

18. Moore, W. E. *Man, Time, and Society*. New York: Wiley, 1963.

19. Palmore, E. Employment and Retirement. In L. A. Epstein and J. H. Murray (Eds.), *The Aged Population of the United States*. Washington, D.C.: U.S. Government Printing Office, 1967.

20. Riley, M. W., and Foner, A. *An Inventory of Research Findings*. Aging and Society, vol. I. New York: Russell Sage Foundation, 1968.

21. Simpson, I. H., Back, K. W., and McKinney, J. C. Attributes of Work, Involvement in Society, and Self-evaluation in Retirement. In I. H. Simpson *et al.* (Eds.), *Social Aspects of Aging*. Durham, N.C.: Duke University Press, 1966.

22. Simpson, I. H., Back, K. W., and McKinney, J. C. Exposure to Information on, Preparation for, and Self-evaluation in Retirement. In I. H. Simpson *et al.* (Eds.), *Social Aspects of Aging*. Durham, N.C.: Duke University Press, 1966.

23. Simpson, I. H., Back, K. W., and McKinney, J. C. Continuity of Work and Retirement Activities, and Self-evaluation. In I. H. Simpson *et al.* (Eds.), *Social Aspects of Aging*. Durham, N.C.: Duke University Press, 1966.

24. Soule, G. H. Free Time—Man's New Resource. In W. Donahue, W. W. Hunter, D. H. Coons, and H. K. Maurice (Eds.), *Free Time: Challenge to Later Maturity*. Ann Arbor: University of Michigan Press, 1958.

25. Spengler, J. J. Some Economic and Related Determinants Affecting the Older Worker's Occupational Role. In I. H. Simpson *et al.* (Eds.), *Social Aspects in Aging*. Durham, N.C.: Duke University Press, 1966.

26. Stokes, R. G. *Transition: Factors in the Adaptation to Major Status Transitions*. Durham, N.C.: Duke University, 1967. Unpublished M.A. thesis.

27. Stokes, R. G., and Maddox, G. L. Some social factors on retirement adaptation. *J. Geront.* 22:329–333, 1967.

28. Streib, G. F., and Thompson, W. E.   Adjustment in retirement. *J. Social Issues* 14:1–64, 1968.
29. Tibbitts, C., Convery, J. M., Livingston, D., Loomis, O. E., and Shanas, E.   Panel on: Social Attitudes Toward Retirement and Support of Older People. In H. L. Orbach and C. Tibbitts (Eds.), *Aging and the Economy.* Ann Arbor: University of Michigan Press, 1963.
30. Tuckman, J., and Lorge, I.   *Retirement and the Industrial Worker.* New York: Bureau of Publications, Columbia University Teachers College, 1953.
31. Wax, R. H.   Free Time in Other Cultures. In W. Donahue, W. W. Hunter, D. H. Coons, and H. K. Maurice (Eds.), *Free Time: Challenge to Later Maturity.* Ann Arbor: University of Michigan Press, 1958.

# 6

# Health Experience in the Elderly

E. HARVEY ESTES, JR.

When is a person healthy? When is he ill? These questions are difficult ones at all ages, but for the older individual the answers are especially obscure. Many an older person has low back pain, stiff joints, or diminished hearing, yet considers himself in the best of health. Experience has taught him that these are common symptoms, that there is little to be done for them in a curative sense, and that life can be pleasant in spite of them, once the anxiety about their potential significance has been put aside.

In this chapter no attempt has been made to cover all the illnesses of the elderly. But certain broad areas important to the health care of the elderly, as well as some of the diseases which have a higher incidence in this age group, are discussed.

## ILLNESS PATTERNS IN THE ELDERLY

*Acute Illnesses*

One characteristic of older persons is that they are apparently less often affected by acute illness than younger individuals (Table 1). When such illness occurs, however, it usually leads to more days of restricted activity than illness in younger individuals (Table 2). Older females spend about three more days per year in restricted activity due to acute illness than their male counterparts (9.5 and 6.2 days, respectively, at age 65 and older).

*115*

TABLE 1.  *Number of acute illnesses per 100 persons per year by age*

| Age | No. of Illnesses |
|:---:|:---:|
| Under 5 | 340 |
| 5–14 | 244 |
| 15–24 | 195 |
| 25–44 | 166 |
| 45–64 | 125 |
| 65+ | 103 |

Source: *Acute Conditions: Incidence and Associated Disability, United States—July 1966–June 1967.* National Center for Health Statistics, Series 10, No. 44, March 1968 (Table 11, p. 22).

TABLE 2.  *Days of restricted activity associated with acute illnesses per 100 persons per year by age*

| Age | Days of Restricted Activity |
|:---:|:---:|
| Under 5 | 829 |
| 5–14 | 797 |
| 15–24 | 661 |
| 25–44 | 663 |
| 45–64 | 640 |
| 65+ | 811 |

Source: *Acute Conditions: Incidence and Associated Disability, United States—July 1966–June 1967.* National Center for Health Statistics, Series 10, No. 44, March 1968 (Table 12, p. 23).

These data were obtained by household interviews conducted by the National Center for Health Statistics on a probability sample of the civilian population of the United States. Restricted activity was defined in this study as a substantial reduction in activity normal for that day, and covered restrictions up to and including complete inactivity.

Why there should be a decreased incidence of acute illness in the elderly is not clear. A greater degree of immunity to common respiratory pathogens, a diminished level of awareness of symptoms, and a diminished concern leading to less acknowledged illness are all possibilities.

As in all other age groups, the group consisting of upper respiratory infections, influenzal illnesses, and other respiratory ailments accounts for the majority of the episodes of acute illness, and for most of the days of disability. Injuries are the second most common cause of illness and days of disability. Contusions are the most frequent type of injury, followed by fractures, sprains, and dislocations. Digestive system conditions are the third most frequent type of acute illness in the elderly. These three categories alone account for four-fifths of the acute illness problems of the elderly (58, 14, and 7 percent, respectively) [11].

Thus the majority of acute illness seen in the elderly are relatively simple in terms of devices and professional skills required for diagnosis and treatment. They do not differ substantially from acute illness in other age groups in this respect. The superimposition of these illnesses in a group of patients with underlying senility and chronic disease leads to greater disability as measured by days of restricted activity.

## Chronic Illnesses

The exact prevalence of chronic diseases in the elderly is not known due to the inadequacy of methods of obtaining information. The two general types of survey techniques used are (1) a clinical examination of a sample population and (2) a questionnaire given to a sample population. Those diseases requiring medical tests or observations (such as hypertension and diabetes mellitus) appear more frequent when a clinical examination is used, whereas those diseases that are largely self-diagnosed (such as chronic sinusitis) appear more frequent when a questionnaire technique is used [10].

Using data from an examination type survey [1], the chronic illness seen most frequently in the elderly is heart disease. Over half of individuals over age 65 (575/1,000) suffer from this disorder, with hypertensive heart disease and coronary artery disease leading the list of specific types. Arthritis is only slightly less frequently seen, and again over half the individuals examined were affected (515/1,000). Osteoarthritis was the specific type seen in over 90 percent of these cases. Other frequently diagnosed chronic disorders, with the rate per 1,000 persons, are as follows: obesity, (380), abdominal cavity hernias (212), cataracts (148), varicose veins (148), hemorrhoids (142), hypertension without heart disease (142), and prostate disease (135, per 1,000 males).

The incidence of all chronic disease, including relatively mild and non-disabling chronic diseases, rises steadily with advancing years. Under age 15 there are 400 chronic diseases per 1,000 population, and at age 65, there are 4,000 per 1,000 population, a ten-fold rise in prevalence [2]. Thus there are multiple chronic illnesses in many older members of the population. With respect to the disability caused by these chronic diseases, this is, as expected, more severe in the elderly. About 30 percent of those over age 65 considered themselves to be limited in one or more daily activities (moving about, feeding self, climbing stairs) as a result of chronic disease [3]. The limitation was usually at the level of inconvenience or discomfort, with a much smaller number requiring assistance from others. Less than 1 percent of persons surveyed were limited in their ability to feed, dress, and bathe themselves, or perform toilet functions, but when limitation was present help was usually required. Locomotion could usually be carried out with help, though with difficulty. Two-thirds of those reporting limitation of ability to move about were still able to function without aid. Three-fifths of those reporting limitation of ability to climb stairs were able to function alone. Of particular importance is the fact that travel on public conveyances was an exception to this trend. Three-fourths of those who reported limitations in this function required help to travel or were unable to travel at all. This fact has obvious implications in planning for delivery of proper medical care to an elderly population.

## MORTALITY AND ITS CAUSES IN THE ELDERLY

The average length of life in the United States in 1966 was 70 years [12], a figure which has remained essentially the same for

10 years. On the average, the female outlives the male by 7 years (74 vs. 67 years). This average expectation of life at birth is strongly influenced by infant and childhood mortality, and therefore gives little information about the expectation of life at a given age.

At age 60, the average remaining years of life are 17.9; at age 65, 14.6 years; and at age 70, 11.6 years. The same trends exist with respect to sex and color as in the preceding paragraph. For example, at age 60 the average remaining lifetime for white males is 15.9 years, for white females 20.0 years, for nonwhite males 14.9 years, and for nonwhite females 18.1 years.

The 20 most important causes of death in the elderly are listed in Table 3. Arteriosclerotic heart disease is the most important cause of death in all age ranges, with cerebral and subarachnoid hemorrhage as the second in rank order. Hypertensive heart disease is the third most common cause of death in the age ranges from 65 to 84, and though it remains an important cause of death beyond 85 years, it is outranked by generalized arteriosclerosis and cerebral thrombosis and embolism.

While most of the 20 listed causes of death show an increasing death rate with progressively older age ranges, neoplasm of the lung is a notable exception. The death rate from this cause declines with older age ranges. The death rate from emphysema is also noteworthy in that it is relatively constant with progressively older age ranges.

## SOME DISEASES AFFECTING THE ELDERLY

### Arteriosclerotic Heart Disease

There is some evidence that mortality from arteriosclerotic heart disease has increased in recent years. This is true for both sexes, and at all age groups. This fact raises many questions regarding the influence of external factors on both the incidence of, and the response to, coronary atherosclerosis. There is also a notable varia-

TABLE 3.  *Age-specific death rates per 100,000 population per year by cause, 1959–61*

| Cause | All Ages | 65–74 | 75–84 | 85+ |
|---|---|---|---|---|
| Neoplasm, stomach | 12 | 67 | 123 | 156 |
| Neoplasm, colon | 16 | 87 | 167 | 220 |
| Neoplasm, lung | 22 | 123 | 105 | 74 |
| Neoplasm, breast[a] | 14 | 55 | 82 | 135 |
| Neoplasm, prostate[a] | 7 | 45 | 116 | 171 |
| Diabetes mellitus | 16 | 96 | 167 | 174 |
| Subarachnoid and cerebral hemorrhage | 60 | 261 | 749 | 1686 |
| Cerebral embolism and thrombosis | 32 | 152 | 517 | 1341 |
| Other CNS vascular diseases | 8 | 34 | 137 | 449 |
| Arteriosclerotic heart disease | 278 | 1433 | 1306 | 6878 |
| Endocarditis and myocardial degeneration | 29 | 118 | 438 | 1465 |
| Other heart disease | 11 | 47 | 116 | 277 |
| Hypertensive heart disease | 35 | 179 | 446 | 933 |
| Other hypertensive diseases | 7 | 26 | 81 | 221 |
| General arteriosclerosis | 18 | 56 | 300 | 1394 |
| Chronic and unspecific nephritis | 6 | 21 | 45 | 101 |
| Influenza and pneumonia | 32 | 102 | 316 | 999 |
| Emphysema | 5 | 33 | 43 | 46 |
| Senility, ill defined | 7 | 22 | 49 | 183 |
| Accidental falls | 11 | 33 | 137 | 513 |

a Incidence per 100,000 males *and* females. Incidence per 100,000 of the particular sex at rise would be approximately double the reported rate.

Modified from: Duffy, E. A., and Carroll, R. E. *United States Metropolitan Mortality 1959–61.* P.H.S. Publication No. 999-AP-39, National Center for Air Pollution Control, Cincinnati, Ohio, 1967.

tion in mortality in various areas of the United States. The states in the Northeast have one and one-half times the incidence seen in the central plains states. These facts serve only to remind us that this disease, though a well defined entity, still has many unknown facets.

The underlying pathological lesion is coronary artery obstruction. This process begins as an intimal lipid deposition early in life, and is progressive in nature. The process is spotty in location, and affects certain areas preferentially (first portion of the anterior descending branch of the left coronary artery, first part of the right coronary artery, the right coronary artery as it bends at the acute margin). Superimposed on this chronic, progressive process are other related processes which may cause a sudden increase in the degree of obstruction. Subintimal hemorrhage into the hyper-vascular base of a lipid deposit may cause a thrombosis within the narrowed lumen. Thrombosis may also occur without subintimal hemorrhage.

Potential collateral channels exist at all ages, but channels interconnecting coronary arteries become more frequent and of larger size with advancing years. The interplay between advancing obstructive disease and increasing collateral channels, and the anatomical location of the obstructive disease, are important determinants of acute myocardial infarction, as evidenced by the fact that many such events develop in the absence of coronary thrombosis, subintimal hemorrhage, or other acute obstructive events.

The most important clinical event in arteriosclerotic cardiovascular disease is myocardial infarction. About one-third of cases of acute infarction terminate fatally before medical attention is obtained. Of those who reach the hospital, another 20 to 30 percent die within the period of hospitalization, the highest risk being within the first 24 hours. These deaths are of several types. Most are due to acute arrhythmia, the rest due to congestive failure or cardiogenic shock. The development of coronary care areas within community hospitals is a significant recent development. These areas feature continuous monitoring of the cardiac rhythm of patients, and a staff specially trained for emergency treatment of arrhythmic and other events. Drastic reduction in the mortality from arrhythmia has been achieved in such units, but the mortality from cardiogenic shock and congestive failure remains essentially the same.

## Presbycardia

The presence of a specific disease of the heart, related to aging and involutional changes in the heart muscle, and independent of the presence of coronary artery disease, has been proposed by William Dock [4]. The high incidence of coronary artery lesions in the elderly makes it difficult to judge the independent effect of involutional changes in heart muscle, but rare cases are seen in which no other apparent cause of congestive heart failure can be found.

## Complete Heart Block

At one time, the occurrence of complete heart block, particularly in an older individual, was considered another manifestation of coronary artery disease. More recent observations have shown that the appearance of stable atrioventricular block in older individuals is usually a result of an idiopathic fibrotic change in the upper interventricular septum, extending downward and interrupting the common bundle. Heart block due to coronary artery disease is seen, but is usually accompanied by a clear clinical event, such as a myocardial infarction. Thus stable atrioventricular block may represent a form of heart disease related to aging, in that it is caused by an extension of a process normally present, but slowly increasing with time.

## Cerebral Thrombosis and Hemorrhage

A previous section of this chapter cites the rising incidence of both cerebral thrombosis and hemorrhage in older age groups. Ischemic infarction of the brain and intracerebral hemorrhage are listed as separate entities, in spite of the frequent difficulty in antemortem clinical differentiation between the two entities. It is also noteworthy that both entities are strongly related to the presence of arterial hypertension.

Ischemic infarction is usually ascribed to progressive vascular narrowing, leading to slowed vascular flow and thrombosis. Intracerebral hemorrhage is a result of arterial rupture, but the events leading to the rupture remain obscure. R. W. R. Russell has suggested that hemorrhage may be caused by a rupture of small microaneurysms which he has found to be present in certain sites in the brain in close correlation with advancing age and arterial hypertension [9]. Such lesions are seen in greatest numbers in older patients with hypertension, and the site of occurrence is similar to the site of cerebral hemorrhage. Russell suggests that such lesions are a direct result of damage associated with age and hypertension.

Thrombosis is often seen in the sac of such aneurysms. Hoobler has suggested that certain stages of the evolution of these aneurysms could lead to small nonhemorrhagic strokes related to thrombosis [7]. He thus explains the reduced incidence of both ischemic infarction and intracerebral hemorrhage seen with antihypertensive therapy.

## Osteoporosis

This condition, characterized by a thinning of the cortex of long bones and thinning of the vertebral bodies due to decreased formation of bone matrix, is not usually listed among the most common ailments of the elderly, yet underlies some of the increased morbidity of the elderly in response to trauma.

Osteoporosis has many causes, including immobilization, decrease of estrogen production (postmenopausal osteoporosis), and steroid administration. A specific form, related to senility, is recognized. Its etiology remains obscure, but diminished androgen production probably plays an important role.

Except for back pain, the condition is usually asymptomatic, and is usually an incidental finding or is discovered as a result of a fracture. It is more severe in the spine and pelvis, and may lead to vertebral collapse. Normal levels of serum calcium, phosphorus, and alkaline phosphatase usually distinguish it from other bone disorders, but differentiation from multiple myeloma presents special problems, since alkaline phosphatase levels may not be elevated, and the radiological picture may be indistinguishable. For this reason, bone marrow aspiration should be performed in cases of unusual osteoporosis, especially when accompanied by anemia or proteinurea.

## CONSTRAINTS TO PROPER HEALTH CARE
## IN THE ELDERLY

As discussed in previous sections of this chapter, the elderly patient suffers from relatively few illnesses that are unique to his age group. The special problem in the elderly is the fact that a given illness is usually superimposed on an assortment of pre-existing chronic illnesses and on organ systems which have lost their wide margin of reserve capacity. The elderly patient thus represents a delicately balanced mechanism in which even a "minor" illness can lead to major consequences.

This fragile state of affairs poses problems for both the elderly patient and his physician. The patient has multiple problems, and treatment for one may produce adverse effects with respect to the other. Aspirin prescribed for arthritic pains may cause a flare of a peptic ulcer, or a diuretic prescribed for mild congestive failure may cause a painful exacerbation of gout. "Usual" doses of medications may also cause unusual effects. A sedative dose of a barbiturate may cause mental confusion, for example. The physician (and his patient) may be unprepared to accept the chronic nature of the medical problems, resulting in discouragement, frustration, and even anger.

In treating elderly patients, many physicians wisely follow a general policy of extreme caution in prescribing drugs, changing activity routines, or removing the patient from familiar surroundings. Patience and understanding on the part of physician, family, and patient is highly rewarding.

*Manpower and Facilities*

The elderly patient faces many problems in seeking assistance for health and illness problems. First, a physician may not be available. Second, the patient usually has several medical problems (e.g., hypertension, prostatic hypertrophy, and glaucoma), and each of these problems may require services of a separate physician-specialist. Third, he has difficulty in obtaining guidance in matters of general hygiene, the application of techniques to prevent illness (e.g., dietary measures, exercise), and in advice for minor day-to-day illnesses, due to crowding of the physician's schedule.

Many recent publications have noted a growing shortage of physicians [6, 13]. In addition, most (approximately two-thirds) of today's physicians are specialists, and they are therefore less available to the patient as a personal physician than the generalists whom they have replaced.

Maldistribution of physician manpower is also a growing problem, and is particularly likely to affect the elderly. The younger physician usually settles in a practice location which is most likely to provide good hospitals, capable colleagues, and good living conditions for his family. These conditions are most often found in areas of economic growth and higher per capita income [5]. The older, declining areas of large cities, and the smaller towns and rural areas are those areas which have failed to attract new physicians. These are the same areas in which older persons are found in greater proportion.

Such areas are often dependent on elderly physicians. For example, in North Carolina's rural counties, 40 percent of the physicians are over age 60 and 20 percent over age 70 [8]. It should be recognized that an ill-defined but very important service of a personal physician is that of providing an interface with, and an input pathway into, the increasingly complex system of medical care. Even though an elderly physician may be unable to provide the special skills required for certain illnesses, he can nevertheless provide the access to these skills. The loss of a long time physician because of illness, retirement, or death often forces the older patient to seek entry into the health care system with no guidance, and to consult a new, much younger physician who may not transmit the same sense of security as the older man.

Medical facilities are also becoming more complex as they arrange and equip themselves to deliver more complex medical treatment. While this is a laudable development, it also creates problems. The physician is much more dependent on the services of these facilities—in clinics, hospitals, and the like—than in the past, and has largely abandoned the practice of seeing the patient in the home. The advantage of the available laboratory and radiographic facilities in hospitals and clinics for proper diagnosis and treatment is obvious. However, as noted earlier, the older patient is often limited in his ability to drive and to utilize public transportation. A high percentage requires assistance with these functions. Even when transportation is arranged, the complexity of the hospital or clinic may deter the older patient from utilizing its services unless compelled to do so.

*Economic Factors*

Most older persons face the unknowns of the future (an unknown span of life, an unknown degree of economic inflation, unknown expenses) with a fixed amount of savings or income. Medical care is costly, and is becoming more so month by month. It is therefore not difficult to understand why many older persons, with a fixed reserve to cover an unknown period of years, delay or avoid altogether seeking medical care for economic reasons. Medicare has provided a partial answer to the problem, but by uncovering personnel shortages and inadequate facilities, it has undoubtedly forced all medical care costs even higher.

A wider scattering of family members in modern society has heightened the economic threat of illness. Family members who were once available to care for an ill mother or father may now live in distant cities. For many, hospitalization or professional nursing care is now the only alternative, one which requires considerable financial outlay.

## *Attitudinal Factors*

Most older persons, perhaps to a greater extent than younger generations, have grown up with a conception of themselves as strong, productive, independent individuals, relying on no one. Hard work and "something for a rainy day" are important components of their value system. Many wish to retain enough of their material goods to pass along an inheritance to their heirs. The acceptance of illness, with its dependency on others, is extremely difficult, and denial of illness is common, particularly in men.

Fear of discovery of a fatal or progressive illness is another common factor leading to delay or avoidance of medical care. A questionable symptom or sign is ignored until pain or other symptoms force a medical consultation, or until concern by other family members leads to the same result. While the consequences of such denial are difficult to quantitate in terms of greater mortality, greater disability, and greater overall cost, these are presumed to result.

## SUMMARY

The acute illnesses of the elderly are not unique in type, but result in more prolonged disability and probably constitute an increased threat to life because of restricted organ system reserve. Chronic disease is relatively common, but usually results in mild limitation in function. Some few illnesses seem directly attributable to aging and its effects. The problems which have led to poor delivery of health care to the population at large have a more profound effect on the elderly.

128

REFERENCES

1. Commission on Chronic Illness. *Chronic Illness in a Large City,* Vol. IV. Cambridge: Harvard University Press, 1957. P. 539.
2. *Ibid.,* p. 51.
3. *Ibid.,* p. 64.
4. Dock, W. Presbycardia or aging of the myocardium. *New York J. Med.* 45:983, 1945.
5. Estes, E. H., Jr. The critical shortage—physicians and supporting personnel. *Ann. Intern. Med.* 69:957, 1968.
6. Fein, R. *The Doctor Shortage: An Economic Diagnosis.* Washington, D.C.: The Brookings Institution, 1967.
7. Hoobler, S. W. Cooperative Study on Stroke and Hypertension. In J. W. Toole (Ed.), *Cerebral Vascular Diseases, Sixth Conference.* New York: Grune & Stratton, 1968.
8. Research and Evaluation Division. *General Information for Regional Study Committees.* North Carolina Regional Medical Program, 1968.
9. Russell, R. W. R. Pathogenesis of Primary Intracerebral Hemorrhage. In J. F. Toole (Ed.), *Cerebral Vascular Diseases, Sixth Conference.* New York: Grune & Stratton, 1968.
10. Sanders, B. S. Have Morbidity Surveys Been Oversold? In A. M. Lilienfeld and A. J. Gifford (Eds.), *Chronic Disease and Public Health.* Baltimore: The Johns Hopkins Press, 1966.
11. U.S. Bureau of the Census. *Statistical Abstract of the United States, 1967* (88th ed.). Washington, D.C.: U.S. Government Printing Office, 1967. Table 111, p. 84.
12. U.S. Department of Health, Education, and Welfare. *Vital Statistics of the United States, 1966,* vol. II, sec. 5. National Center for Health Services. Washington, D.C.: U.S. Government Printing Office, 1968.
13. Warren, J. V. The problem of providing health services. *Ann. Intern. Med.* 69:951, 1968.

# 7

# Living Arrangements and Housing of Old People

ETHEL SHANAS

There are now some 19 million people aged 65 and over in the United States. Who these people live with, that is, their household arrangements, and where they live, that is, their housing or physical environment, have become matters of increasing concern. Are most old people isolated, living apart from family and friends? Or, alternatively, are they part of family networks? Are most old people living in poor housing? Or is the housing of most persons adequate for their needs? It is questions such as these that concern those responsible for social policy and programs of social betterment.

The kind of living arrangements in which old people are found reflects many factors. Most important among these is the sex of the old person; how old he is; whether he is married or unmarried; whether or not he has children; the state of his health; and his income level. Just as household composition varies, the actual housing of the old person also varies. He may live in his own home or apartment, the home of children, a home for the aged, a nursing home, or a hospital. The living arrangements of old people, that is, the composition of the household of the old person, are not the same as his housing, that is, the physical aspects of the old person's environment. It is important to distinguish between the two, since physically adequate housing alone cannot compensate for inadequate or unsatisfactory social relationships.

This chapter deals with both the living arrangements of older people and housing for the aged. It is thus divided into two parts, the first of which is concerned with whom the old person lives with, the second, where he lives. The first section begins with a general discussion of the living arrangements of older people. It points up some of the differences between the institutional and noninstitutional populations and stresses the fact that only a small proportion of the aged are institutionalized. It then treats with the household composition of the noninstitutional aged, and with the role of children, relatives, neighbors, and friends in maintaining the social integration of the aged. Special attention is then given to the characteristics of old people living in institutions. The second part of the chapter focuses on housing for the aged. Here there is a discussion of the characteristics of housing occupied by the elderly and of the various types of housing now available to them. The chapter concludes by integrating the two parts in a consideration of the multigeneration family, its increasing importance in the United States, and its effect on future trends in living arrangements and housing for the elderly.

## LIVING ARRANGEMENTS OF OLD PEOPLE

Old people, like younger persons, live in a wide variety of households. Some old people live alone, while others live with family members or with other persons. An individual's living arrangements usually reflect his position in the life cycle. As young people become self-sufficient, even before marriage, they may leave the family home and set up households of their own or share households with friends. As they marry they start their own households. Thus in the United States we find most young and middle-aged adults living in a household with a spouse and children. The households of the elderly, however, differ from the households of middle-aged adults. When the elderly are compared with the middle-aged there is a substantially lower proportion of elderly households with both husband and wife present.

Not all households of the elderly are the households of widows or widowers, however. Just as those over age 65 differ in their living arrangements from the middle-aged, persons in their 60's are apt to be found in different kinds of households than persons in their 90's. The composition of one's household in old age is a reflection of whether one is a man or a woman, under 75 or over 75, married or unmarried, sick or well, a parent of children or childless, and, finally, whether one's income is large enough to permit a housing choice. All of these factors are interrelated. To illustrate, a man age 65 is apt to be married, he may have unmarried children still living at home, he is likely to be in either good or fair health, and his income, while reduced from that of his working years, is likely to still be above the poverty level. The chances are about eight out of ten that he is still the head of a household. A woman of 80, on the contrary, is probably widowed. If she has children they are all married. She is likely to be in frail health, and her income is probably below the poverty level. The chances are better than seven out of ten that she no longer is either the head of a household or the wife of the head.

Table 1 gives the living arrangements of older men and women in the United States. Because age and sex are the major deter-

TABLE 1. *The older population: percentage distribution of living arrangements by sex and age (1967)*

| Living Arrangement | Aged 65+ | | Aged 65–74 | | Aged 75+ | |
|---|---|---|---|---|---|---|
| | Men | Women | Men | Women | Men | Women |
| Total | 100 | 100 | 100 | 100 | 100 | 100 |
| Living in families | 81 | 62 | 84 | 66 | 74 | 56 |
| Family head, spouse present | 68 | — | 76 | — | 54 | — |
| Wife of head | — | 33 | — | 44 | — | 18 |
| Family head, no spouse | 4 | 11 | 3 | 10 | 6 | 12 |
| Relative of head | 9 | 18 | 5 | 12 | 14 | 26 |
| Living alone or with nonrelatives | 16 | 34 | 13 | 32 | 20 | 36 |
| Alone | 13 | 30 | 10 | 29 | 16 | 32 |
| With nonrelatives | 3 | 4 | 3 | 3 | 4 | 4 |
| Living in an institution | 4 | 4 | 2 | 2 | 6 | 8 |

Source: Adapted from Brotman, H. B. [2: Table 8].

minants of living arrangements, the table divides the elderly into men and women and those under 75 and those over 75.

There is a widespread belief in this country that most old people live alone. The facts are contrary to this belief. The majority of both men and women live not alone but in families, either maintaining their own households with a spouse, or living with relatives either in their own or the relative's home. Although the census uses the categoric term *relative,* those relatives with whom the elderly share housing are usually adult children. Among households with a head aged 65 or more, one-fifth have adult children in the home. In the same way, roughly three-fifths of all old people who are not household heads and who live in the home of relatives are the parents or parents-in-law of the household head [5].

Women outlive men, and men tend to marry women younger than themselves. As a result, widowhood is more usual among older women than among older men. Even at the very advanced ages, 85 and over, when less than one of every ten women are married, four of every ten men are married [20]. With advancing age and increasing widowhood, the proportion of old people living in the homes of relatives increases. Among those over 75, compared to those aged 65 to 74, almost three times as great a proportion of men and twice as great a proportion of women live with relatives. Again as a result of widowhood, the older the person the more likely he is to live alone. Reflecting the higher incidence of the widowed among aged women, the proportion of old women who live alone is two and one-half times as great as the proportion of old men.

Institutional living is not common among the elderly in the United States or in European countries. Only about four of every hundred older men and women in the United States live in institutions. Old people who live in institutions differ markedly from other old people. A much higher proportion among the institutionalized have never married or are widowed. The proportion of old people in institutions who are single (25 percent), is about three times as great as the proportion of single persons in the older population (8 percent). Similarly, widowed and divorced persons are almost 60 percent of the institutional population but only about 40 percent of the older population [26]. These findings suggest that those older persons who have a spouse or children to care for them are far less likely to be found in institutions. This will be discussed later in this chapter.

To summarize the discussion to this point, most old people live in families; living alone is associated with widowhood and advanced age; more old women than old men live alone; and the elderly in institutions are only a small proportion of the total aged population.

## The Role of Children, Relatives, Neighbors

Living with adult children is not a preferred living arrangement in the United States, nor for that matter in any of the countries of Western Europe in which the situation of the old has been extensively studied [4, 6, 7, 8, 15, 22]. In contemporary societies older parents and adult married or widowed children share a home only under certain well-recognized circumstances.

Housing shortages sometimes make sharing a necessity. In many of the countries of Europe, particularly where housing was severely damaged in World War II, limited housing supply makes the sharing of quarters inevitable. Historically, economic dependence has been one of the main reasons for parents and adult children to continue to live together. In some rural areas of Europe this type of dependence may still be found with older parents and adult children working together on the same farm [23].

This type of economic dependence is far less common in the United States. In this country, however, economic support from children to older parents often takes the form of providing housing and maintenance for an aged parent in the child's household. The roles of giver and receiver of help may also be reversed. It is sometimes the aged parent who is helping to maintain a dependent adult child—a widowed daughter and her children, for example, may share the parent's household. At times, the old parent or the adult child requires services one from the other which cannot be supplied in separate households. Old people may require nursing care; working mothers for their part may need a grandparent in the home to take care of grandchildren. As many old people (2 percent) are totally bedfast at home as live in all nursing homes and hospitals. An additional 5 percent of the elderly are housebound. Many of these bedfast and housebound persons live with their children who provide nursing care and other services [16]. Similarly, a working woman may only be able to work because another adult is in the household to look after a child. This adult usually is an aged parent. As an example of the exchange of services and help between the generations, a young couple were both able to complete their work for advanced academic degrees because the husband's 82-year-old grandfather lived with them and looked after their small son when they both had to be away.

Although aged parents and adult children do not commonly share households in this country, this does not mean that older parents and children live at great distances from one another, or that they do not see one another often. Despite the vast physical distances of the United States, most older persons who have children live in close proximity to at least one child. Less than three old persons in ten live in the same household with a child, but an additional five in ten live within a half-hour's distance of a child (see Table 2). Eight of every ten old people then either live with a child or within a half hour of him. Among the aged with living children only about one in twenty are more than a day's journey from their nearest child.

Men are less likely to live in the same household with an adult child than are women. As has been pointed out, this results from the fact that a greater proportion of men are married and that a separate independent household is the preferred housing pattern for married couples in the United States irrespective of their age. However, men are equally as likely as women to live close to their children. Proximity to children and the opportunity to see them easily may compensate the widow or widower for the loss of a spouse. Widowed persons with children are more likely to live with children than are married persons. Indeed, 43 percent of all

TABLE 2. *The proximity of the nearest child to persons aged 65 and over*[a]

| Proximity of Nearest Child | Percentage Distribution |
| --- | --- |
| Total | 100 |
| Same household | 28 |
| 10 minutes or less | 33 |
| 11–30 minutes journey | 16 |
| 31 minutes–1 hour | 7 |
| Over 1 hour but less than 1 day | 11 |
| 1 day or more | 5 |
| N = | 2012 |

[a] Non-institutional population only.
Source: Adapted from Shanas, E. [14: Table 3].

widowed persons who have children live in the same household with their children, and an additional 40 percent live within a half-hour's distance of them.

Old people who have children not only live near their children, they also see their children often. In a national sample study, almost two-thirds of all persons with children saw at least one of their children within a 24-hour period [19].

Just as the proximity of children operates to compensate for the loss of a spouse, the extended family compensates old persons who have no children. Among widowed and single persons who have no children, four of every 10 live with brothers, sisters, and other relatives [14]. In many instances persons without children are especially attached to some young relative. About one-half of all persons without children (about 10 percent of the total elderly) say that they see a young relative every day or several times a week [11]. To all intents and purposes these relatives assume the responsibilities of children. The extended family, through children and grandchildren, brothers and sisters, nieces and nephews operates to maintain the old person in society. In general, the data indicate that the old people are integrated within a family network whether or not they live with children. The extended kin family system operating along kin lines, and vertically over several generations, serves to expand the immediate living arrangements of the elderly and to integrate them into the community and the larger society [24].

In addition to the supportive roles played by children, siblings, and other relatives, neighbors also play a part in integrating the aged into the larger community. Most old people in the United States are long-time residents of the area in which they live. Twenty-five or more years of residence in a given area is not uncommon. Neighborhood friendships, however, are important for less than half of the aged. Only about two persons in every five interviewed in a national study said that they visited neighbors daily, several times a week, or even once a week. About the same proportion of old people said that they never visited their neighbors or visited them only under special circumstances, when the neighbor needed help or when there was an illness in the neighbor's family. There was no difference in the proportion of older men and women who visited neighbors. Reviewing these data, the writer said: "Apparently, whether an older person visits his neighbors or not is a function of the particular neighborhood pattern rather than of the sex of the older person" [12].

In a study of 1,200 older people in Cleveland, Ohio, Irving Rosow has isolated the factors that determine whether or not neighbors will play a major part in the social relationships of the aged. Rosow shows clearly that the greater the density of other old people in the immediate neighborhood of the old person the greater will be his number of neighborhood friends. Indeed, in areas where there are many old people, when family care in illness may be lacking or insufficient, neighbors will substitute for the family [9].

In keeping with the earlier discussion of the importance of children in the social integration of the aged, Rosow also points out that while neighbors and friends are important in the integration of old people they cannot take the place of children and family: "Involvement with children and relationships with friends constitute two completely *independent systems* . . . friends are not functional equivalents of the family . . . whatever intergenerational supports may be built into a system for older people, this particular relationship cannot be duplicated nor can another effectively stand in its place" [10].

## The Function of the Institution

In contrast to the usual living arrangements of the elderly the institution as a form of living arrangement stands outside the general pattern of social life. Its residents are physically located in a community but are not part of it. Four percent of all old people in the United States live in institutions. Who are these old people? How do they happen to have this type of living arrangement?

It has already been pointed out that single and widowed persons are more likely than married persons to be residents of institutions. For persons in any marital status the proportion of persons institutionalized is likely to rise with age. Seven percent of those aged 75 and over are resident in institutions compared to only 2 percent of those aged 65 to 74.

About half of all people living in institutions are residents of nursing homes and hospitals. These findings suggest that the institution meets the needs of the older frail person and the sick. Not all frail old people are in institutions, however. Seven percent of all old people are either totally bedfast or totally housebound at home. Peter Townsend, the British sociologist, has hypothesized that "the likelihood of admission to an institution in old age is partly contingent on family composition, structure and organization, and not only on incapacity, homelessness and lack of socioeconomic resources" [25]. The institution then meets the needs of the frail and sick with certain family characteristics. This means that those enfeebled persons who are unlikely to have supportive families are more likely than other feeble old persons to be residents of institutions. This hypothesis is confirmed by British data which show that institutions in that country have disproportionate numbers of single persons, widowed persons with no surviving children or only one child, and persons with no surviving brothers or sisters [17].

Old people in the United States are generally opposed to institutional living. The institution continues to be associated in their thinking with the poor house, senility, and physical decline. Among every ten old people queried about possible living arrangements six said that they would least like to live in a home for the aged, even if they needed physical care. The American public, however, is less opposed than the elderly to the idea of institutional living. Among every ten of a cross-section of adults, four say a home for the aged is the least desirable living arrangement for old people, while one in eight says it is the best [13].

Institutional living for the old, whether in a nursing home or a home for the well aged, is disliked by the elderly, and only tolerated by their children. As a result, it is suggested that old people with children reach a more advanced stage of illness or dependency than do the single or childless before seeking admission to the institution. The institution serves first those frail persons without resources and without family, and then those with families who are enfeebled.

To this point only the living arrangements of the aged in terms of household arrangements has been discussed. It has been shown that most old people do not live alone but in families. The role of children, relatives, and neighbors in the social environment of the old person have been considered, and the major role played by the extended family has been stressed. Finally, consideration has been given to the institution for the aged and to how differential use is made of the institution by old persons with different kinds of family structure.

The physical housing of the aged will now be discussed. Housing by itself cannot solve the social or physical problems of the elderly. However, housing may indeed compound or ease these problems.

## HOUSING OF OLD PEOPLE

Where old people live, the physical environment of older people, may be described in different ways. It is possible to concentrate one's description solely on the physical characteristics of housing occupied by old people, or, alternatively, one may stress the sociological implications of such physical characteristics. In this discussion first where old people live in terms of the population distribution of the elderly will be considered; second, the characteristics of the housing of the elderly; and third, the opportunities for independence within different housing environments. Throughout the discussion the emphasis will be on the sociological implications of the physical aspects of housing.

## *Where Do Older People Live?*

POPULATION DISTRIBUTION. Old people in the United States, like other people, are primarily residents of cities and towns. While children may still sing of going "over the river and through the woods to grandmother's house," some 70 percent of the elderly live in urbanized areas, that is, in places of 2,500 or more persons, and in central cities and their suburbs. Fifty-one percent of all old people live either in cities of 50,000 or more persons or in the suburban fringe of such cities [2]. Old people, then, are concentrated in the central city, particularly in its older sections, and in its older suburbs. Few old people can be found in new suburbs unless these have been built as communities for the elderly. The new suburb attracts younger persons with young families.

Some parts of the United States have higher proportions of elderly residents than do others. In the states of Maine, New Hampshire, Vermont, and Massachusetts, among the New England States, in Iowa, Missouri, Nebraska, and Kansas, among the North Central States, and in Florida, old people make up more than 11 percent of the population. Old people in the New England and West North Central states, however, are largely persons born in these areas who have chosen to stay while others have chosen to migrate, while old people in Florida have usually moved to that state after retirement. In the New England and West North Central states, then, most old people continue to live in the same communities and often in the same houses in which they have spent their lives, while in Florida one finds many new types of housing for the elderly. Retirement communities, retirement hotels, mobile homes, and other modes of housing are available to Florida residents.

HOUSING CHARACTERISTICS. Old people in the United States are primarily home owners, not renters. About three of every four old people who are still household heads own their own homes [1]. This is understandable since in this country "a home owner is regarded as a stable, responsible and successful member of his community. Moreover, particularly in the period prior to the establishment of the social security system, the outright ownership of a home provided a kind of insurance against the financial insecurities of old age" [21].

Most of the homes owned by older people were purchased when these people were younger. As a consequence the elderly usually own houses that are older than the houses owned by younger persons. Because the older person lives in an older house, it is more likely to be substandard than are houses occupied by younger persons. Rental housing occupied by the elderly is especially likely to be substandard since old people who rent housing are usually unable to compete economically for standard housing with younger persons (see Table 3). Since older homeowners bought their homes some time in the past, their houses are apt to be in older neighborhoods. Such neighborhoods, particularly in central cities, are often the focus for redevelopment activities. The housing unit occupied by the old person may be relatively easy to replace. The ties of the old person to his familiar surroundings and to his total environment, however, are extremely difficult to replace. Some studies of relocated old persons suggest that for many old persons the familiarity of objects in an older home, the accessibility of neighborhood facilities, the long-time patterns of shopping, churchgoing, visiting, and the like are not compensated for by better physical surroundings [3].

Since old people usually purchased their homes when their families were larger, the old person, in comparison with other home owners, lives in a house that is "underoccupied," that is, his house

TABLE 3. *Characteristics of housing units by age of head, 1960*

| Characteristic | Head Aged 65–75 | | | Head Aged 75 & Over | | |
|---|---|---|---|---|---|---|
| | All | Owner-occu-pied | Renter-occu-pied | All | Owner-occu-pied | Renter-occu-pied |
| Percent substandard | 20.1 | 16.2 | 29.1 | 25.7 | 22.0 | 33.5 |
| Percent built 1939 or earlier | 75.4 | 72.9 | 81.2 | 81.7 | 81.4 | 82.3 |
| Percent moved in since 1950 | 44.4 | 34.1 | 67.6 | 36.9 | 24.4 | 63.5 |

Source: Adapted from Sheldon, H. D. [20: Table 9].

is too big for him. While older people often cling to familiar surroundings, the situation of the old person in the overlarge house
may be equally as difficult as that of the old person in an over-
crowded single room. The larger the house, the more it entails in
terms of upkeep, maintenance, and care.

The houses of the elderly, then, are distinguished by their age,
their poor condition in comparison to other housing, and their
larger than usual ratio of number of rooms to number of residents.

OPPORTUNITIES FOR INDEPENDENCE. Housing for the elderly may
also be evaluated in terms of the degree of independence called for
within a given housing setting. From this point of view housing
for the elderly may be arranged along a continuum ranging at one
extreme from that which requires the most independence, the
house or apartment in an age-integrated neighborhood, to that
which requires the least independence at the other extreme, the
nursing home or the hospital.

Most older people live in housing which requires them to be
independent. The forms of this housing vary. An old person may
live independently in a house or an apartment in a neighborhood
in which his neighbors are persons of various ages. He may also

live independently in a community in which most of his neighbors
are older people or in an apartment project for the elderly which
provides him no special services.

As physical strength wanes, old people must relinquish some of
their independence. Retirement hotels and other living facilities in
which meals may be taken in a central dining room serve the needs
of many old people who no longer can do their own shopping or
who prefer to have fewer housekeeping responsibilities. While some
of these facilities are labeled as hotels for the aged, others retain
their facade of serving all age groups while they become in effect
halfway houses for old people between independent and congregate
living.

In congregate living arrangements the old person exchanges his
independence for dependence. Congregate living arrangements for
the elderly vary from homes for the well aged who require a
sheltered environment to nursing homes and hospitals. Most homes
for the well but feeble aged encourage their residents to do things
for themselves, but exactly what the old person can do and when
he can do it is prescribed for him by the institution. The old lady
who, before entering a home slept all day and then viewed television all night, finds her waking and sleeping hours regulated in
the institution so that she will not interfere with the living patterns of the other residents or the work patterns of the staff. In the
same way, meals can no longer be catch-as-catch-can affairs but
must be eaten at regular hours. Erstwhile favorite foods may never
appear on the menu. These changes in the scheduling of time and
in matters of taste are sacrifices of independent choice which old
people must make in the congregate setting.

Finally, in the nursing home or hospital, the physically decrepit
old person becomes totally dependent on other people. These others are not only the providers of physical care but they also com-
prise the meaningful environment with which the old person inter-
acts insofar as he is able. It should be stressed that only a small
proportion of old people (about 2 percent at any one time) come
the full circle from active independent living to completely dependent living in a nursing home or hospital.

To this point, the housing of old people has been considered in terms of the sociological correlates of population density, housing characteristics, and degree of independence required of the old person. It has been shown that the elderly are primarily urban dwellers, that when they live in their own homes these houses likely are older and more dilapidated than the homes of younger persons, and that as people become enfeebled the degree of independent housing they can manage steadily diminishes. The discussion will now consider new types of housing for the aged which have emerged in the United States within the last score of years and which are designed to meet the housing needs of this heterogeneous population.

*New Forms of Housing*

A variety of types of housing for the aged are now being developed in this country in response to the special requirements of this age group. The motivating force behind this new housing varies. Some developments are sponsored by voluntary organizations such as church and fraternal groups; others are instigated by private investors who find a profitable market among the "younger" elderly in particular; and still others are instigated by the Federal government which through the Department of Housing and Urban Development (and earlier through the Housing and Home Finance Agency) has taken an active role in stimulating construction for the elderly [27].

These new types of housing include both whole planned communities and individual projects. Among the new styles of housing are so-called retirement villages, communities in which the sale of housing is age-restricted, high-rise apartment projects, retirement hotels, mobile homes, and combinations of independent housing units and congregate living facilities.

Housing in retirement villages usually appeals to the "younger" segment of the aged population. In general, these planned communities offer standard housing at somewhat lesser costs than comparable housing in other communities. Some concession in physical planning is made to the age of the residents. Electric outlets, for example, may be placed higher on the wall so that they can be reached more easily, bathtubs may be equipped with "grab bars," and so on. The residents in the retirement community are expected to be independent. It is anticipated that they can meet their physical needs. Sometimes care of lawns and gardens is provided by the developers, but often it is expected that the resident will maintain his property. The planned community often offers its residents special community services such as medical centers or recreation centers, but these features are not its primary appeal. Its primary appeal is that in planned communities one finds standard housing which appears to be good value for the money.

In general, planned communities for the elderly are most successful when they are located in metropolitan areas, least successful when they are located at some distance from existing metropolitan centers. Planned communities in metropolitan areas are usually occupied by former residents of these areas. The older person, then, while he has changed his housing, is still close to his family and friends. Planned communities in nonmetropolitan locations are often difficult to reach by nonresidents. Living in such communities tends to have an isolating effect on the residents. Since retirement communities are usually occupied all at once by persons in their mid-fifties and sixties these communities face the problem of what will happen as their residents pass from what is essentially late middle age into the older ages of 75 or more. Experience with these communities is still too limited to speculate on their future as the bulk of the settlers who are couples become widowed and more frail.

High-rise apartments for the elderly have been sponsored by local housing authorities, private investors, and voluntary associations. Such apartments may offer amenities to their residents, such as a common dining room, a medical clinic, or an organized recreation program. These high-rise units may be located in central cities or in outlying areas. In urban redevelopment sites they often isolate their residents from the surrounding community and become islands within the total project. On the other hand, the high-rise development, like the retirement community, provides its residents with easy access to their age peers. Such age peers are at once the source of friendships and of various minor services.

Retirement hotels have some of the characteristics of high-rise projects and retirement communities. Like both these environments they bring together a large number of people of the same ages and usually of the same income level. They differ from high-rise projects in that their residents are likely to require more in the way of services. Retirement hotels offer more than meals and maintenance of living quarters to their residents. Often the hotel management serves as a monitoring service which keeps in touch with the residents and ensures them of medical care if it is needed.

Mobile homes parks for the elderly are found especially in those states with mild climates—California, Arizona, and Florida. The mobile home is less costly than a fixed home. Rents for sites are apt to be less than taxes for houses, although where spaces are purchased rather than rented the cost of the site often approximates residential land costs. The mobile home park, like the retirement community and the high-rise project, provides its residents with access to their age peers. Unlike the retirement community the usual mobile home park makes no effort to provide special amenities for its elderly residents. The responsibilities of the developer are assumed to have terminated with the physical maintenance of the site.

The combination of independent housing units and congregate living units is also becoming increasingly visible among housing for the aged. These developments, unlike the retirement community, appeal to the "older" segments of the elderly population. In these projects the resident has the privilege of living independently in his own home as long as he is able and then moving to congregate quarters if he needs them. The residents of independent living units associated with congregate quarters have access to the medical facilities of the institution as needed. Their yard work and often their house work is taken care of by the institution, and they may have their meals in the institution if they wish. This type of development has a special appeal for elderly couples, who may desire the independence of their own home in combination with the services of the institution.

While the variety of new housing alternatives now being developed for the aged would seem to provide for all segments of this heterogeneous population, participation in new housing is economically determined. Only old people with low incomes can live in certain housing projects and only old people with better than average income would appear to be eligible for most retirement communities, privately sponsored high-rise developments, mobile home parks, and many of the new facilities for congregate living. Many imaginative new developments in housing for the aged may be expected in the future. Whether these developments will meet the needs of this population is uncertain. At the present time, those who need given kinds of housing most would appear least able to afford it.

## FUTURE TRENDS

Future trends in living arrangements and housing for the aged will reflect two factors: changes in the income level of the elderly and changes in their family structure. It may be expected that the Federal government and voluntary bodies will continue to provide leadership in demonstrations of new sorts of housing. On the basis of past experience, however, the efforts of neither the government nor of voluntary organizations can be expected to meet the needs of old people for adequate housing. In the future, as now, this need will probably be met by private developers. Developers will be interested in this market only to the extent that the income level of old people rises so that they compete economically with other segments of the population. Up to now developers have found a limited but economically viable market among the elderly. With anticipated rises in real income among this population group, such a market should continue and probably expand in size.

The revolution in family structure now under way will affect the living arrangements of the elderly and their housing needs. The four-generation family is now emerging as the typical family pattern in old age. As of now, four of every ten people over age 65 who have adult children are great-grandparents. Among the total population aged 80 and over six of every ten men and seven of every ten women are great-grandparents [18]. What is happening in this country is that both grandparents and great-grandparents are becoming younger. The grandparent generation is likely to be composed of people in their fifties, sixties and early seventies. Most of the elderly now over 75 are in the great-grandparent generation.

The present grandparent generation is composed mainly of married couples. In the United States the accepted living pattern for couples is to continue to live in their own home as long as possible. With anticipated rises in income level and with earlier retirement it is the grandparent generation that will increasingly provide a market for single family retirement homes and for age-segregated apartment dwellings. In many instances the housing of the grandparent generation is not labeled as age-segregated housing, but is in effect housing for only the middle-aged or elderly because the housing design discourages the presence of children.

The grandparent generation see themselves as having fulfilled their adult responsibilities. They have raised their children and seen them established. Are they, who are themselves aging, to undertake the responsibility for the elderly? In general, while they assume financial responsibility if necessary, they do not want the responsibility of physical care for the aged parent. This attitude will increasingly affect the housing pattern of the great-grandparent generation. There will be an increased demand for congregate facilities to meet the needs of the great-grandparent generation. The increasing popularity of those institutional facilities which offer some combination of small house or apartments and single rooms reflects the pressures and the needs of the great-grandparent generation, a generation composed primarily of widowed persons.

Future trends in living arrangements for the elderly will continue to respect the autonomy of married couples and their desire for independent living. At the same time, the desire of older parents and adult children for housing which ensures physical proximity will continue to play a part in housing location. We can anticipate more physically independent housing for the elderly, a lesser proportion of old people living with adult children, and an increase in congregate facilities to meet the needs of the very old.

REFERENCES

1. Brotman, H. B. Home ownership by older households, by state, 1960. *Useful Facts*, 24. Washington, D.C.: U.S. Administration on Aging, June 7, 1967. P. 9.
2. Brotman, H. B. Who are the aged: A demographic view. *Useful Facts*, 42. Washington, D.C.: U.S. Administration on Aging, August 9, 1968. Tables 2 and 8.
3. Niebanck, P. L. Knowledge Gained in Studies of Relocation, a Challenge to Housing Policy. In F. M. Carp (Ed.), *Patterns of Living and Housing of Middle Aged and Older People*. Washington, D.C.: U.S. Government Printing Office, 1966. Pp. 107–116.
4. Paillat, P. Le degré d'isolement des francais agés. In Seventh International Congress of Gerontology, *Proceedings*. Vienna, Austria, 1966.
5. Riley, M. W., and Foner, A. *An Inventory of Research Findings*. Aging and Society, vol. I. New York: Russell Sage Foundation, 1968. Pp. 174–175.
6. Rosenmayr, L. Family relations of the elderly. *J. Marriage and the Family* 30:672–679, 1968.
7. Rosenmayr, L., and Köckeis, E. *Unwelt and Familie Alter Menschen*. Berlin: Luchterland-Verlag, 1965.
8. Rosenmayr, L., and Köckeis, E. Housing Conditions and Family Relations of the Elderly. In F. M. Carp (Ed.), *Patterns of Living and Housing of Middle Aged and Older People*. Washington, D.C.: U.S. Government Printing Office, 1966. Pp. 29–46.
9. Rosow, I. Housing, and Local Ties of the Aged. In F. M. Carp (Ed.), *Patterns of Living and Housing of Middle Aged and Older People*. Washington, D.C.: U.S. Government Printing Office, 1966. Pp. 47–64.
10. Rosow, I. *The Social Integration of the Aged*. New York: Free Press, 1968. P. 317.

11. Shanas, E. *The Health of Older People: A Social Survey.* Cambridge: Harvard University Press, 1962. Pp. 99–100.
12. *Ibid.,* p. 100.
13. *Ibid.,* pp. 103, 172.
14. Shanas, E. Family and Household Characteristics of Older People in the United States. In P. From Hansen (Ed.), *Age with a Future.* Copenhagen: Munksgaard, 1964. P. 452.
15. Shanas, E., Townsend, P., Wedderburn, D., Friis, H., Milhøj, P., and Stehouwer, J. *Old People in Three Industrial Societies.* New York and London: Atherton and Routledge Kegan Paul, 1968.
16. *Ibid.,* chap. 2.
17. *Ibid.,* p. 112.
18. *Ibid.,* p. 151.
19. *Ibid.,* p. 196.
20. Sheldon, H. D. *Changes in Family Composition and the Housing of the Older Population of the United States.* A paper prepared for the International Social Science Research Seminar in Gerontology. Markaryd, Sweden. August 5–9, 1963. Table 4.
21. *Ibid.,* p. 9.
22. Stehouwer, J. Relations Between Generations and the Three-generation Household in Denmark. In E. Shanas and G. F. Streib (Eds.), *Social Structure and the Family: Generational Relations.* Englewood Cliffs, N.J.: Prentice-Hall, 1965.
23. *Ibid.,* pp. 148–149.
24. Sussman, M. Relationship of Adult Children with Their Parents in the United States. In E. Shanas and G. F. Streib (Eds.), *Social Structure and the Family: Generational Relations.* Englewood Cliffs, N.J.: Prentice-Hall, 1965.
25. Townsend, P. On the Likelihood of Admission to an Institution. In E. Shanas and G. F. Streib (Eds.), *Social Structure and the Family: Generational Relations.* Englewood Cliffs, N.J.: Prentice-Hall, 1965.
26. U.S. Bureau of the Census. *U.S. Census of Populations: 1960 Subject Reports.* Inmates of Institutions, Final Report PC (2)–8A. Washington, D.C.: U.S. Government Printing Office, 1963. Table II.
27. Wilner, D. L., and Wakeley, R. P. Special Problems in Alternates in Housing Older Persons. In J. C. McKinney and F. T. de Vyver (Eds.), *Aging and Social Policy.* New York: Appleton-Century-Crofts, 1966. Pp. 235–236.

# 8

# Sexual Behavior in Old Age*

ERIC PFEIFFER

As survival into old age has become increasingly more common-place, the aged themselves and the larger society have become interested in not only the fact of survival but the quality of survival as well. This has led to activity on two fronts. Governmental and private agencies have increasingly concerned themselves with the provision of services to the elderly, particularly in the areas of income continuance, job availability, medical care, and housing. These same institutions have also increasingly encouraged research into basic and applied aspects of aging, and a number of comprehensive reviews of the physiology, psychology, and sociology of old age have appeared [1, 3, 13, 14].

One aspect of old age which has hitherto received insufficient consideration by researchers and by clinicians alike has been the sexual life of elderly persons. In fact, until recently relatively little scientific information with regard to the range and scope of sexual behavior in the elderly has been available, either to the elderly themselves or to those who must care for and counsel them. But the picture has begun to change. With the publication of Kinsey's pioneering works [4, 5], with the investigations of Masters and Johnson [8], and, still more recently, with the Duke University publications on the natural history of sexual behavior in old age [10, 11, 15, 16] a small but significant body of knowledge has now been identified. Nevertheless, information about sexual behavior in the aged still

---

* The discussion in this chapter is drawn in part from the author's earlier work, "Geriatric Sex Behavior," published in *Med. Aspects Hum. Sex.*, volume 3, July 1969.

lags far behind similar information on adults or adolescents. Our society has to a considerable extent moved toward greater frankness in the study and discussion of many aspects of human sexuality. That is to say, the taboos concerning sex in adolescence and adulthood have largely been laid aside. Not so the taboo against sex in old age.

## THE TABOO AGAINST SEX IN OLD AGE

There is no doubt that a taboo against sex in old age exists and that it constitutes a serious impediment to systematic, in-depth investigations into patterns of sexual behavior in old age. The taboo operates at several different, if clearly related, levels. First, it is evident among potential subjects and their relatives. A number of investigators have commented on the difficulty of recruiting aged subjects for studies which are clearly labeled sexual in nature [4, 5, 8]. Even when cooperation has been gained, the data which can be collected are generally of a very limited variety. At times the aged themselves may be glad to participate in such studies, but relatives who learn of their participation may become upset and insist that they withdraw from the study. A recent fictional account of a survey type of sex study also depicts the experience as clearly disturbing to some participants [18].

Second, the taboo also operates among some physicians and behavorial scientists. Thus, referring physicians may express concern that such studies may prove upsetting to their patients, or they may contend that such matters are essentially private and should not be studied scientifically. As has been pointed out by Lief in several publications, physicians themselves may not be entirely comfortable with sexual matters since their training in general has but inadequately prepared them in this regard [6, 7].

Finally, investigators themselves must learn to overcome a degree of initial hesitancy and embarrassment before they can comfortably inquire into the sexual lives of their elders. For instance, in the Duke longitudinal study some of the young physician investigators found it difficult to inquire into the sexual lives, past or present, of aged women who had been single all of their lives. There were fourteen such women in the study panel; on only four of these were any sexual data obtained.

### The Nature of the Taboo

What is the explanation of this taboo? One frequently stated opinion is that it is merely a hangover from a Victorian age [12]. But the tenacity with which it persists makes it seem likely that present day processes are also active in maintaining it. Our society still holds that sexual activity should be engaged in primarily for procreative, only secondarily for recreative, purposes.* In adolescence and adulthood, when the production of offspring is a possibility, sexual activity can be tolerated. But in old age the fiction that coital activity is being carried on for reproductive purposes can no longer be maintained.

It also seems likely that the taboo against sex in old age is, in part, an extension of the incest taboo. In our society children of all ages often experience a great deal of anxiety from observing or imagining their parents engaged in sexual activity. Since the elderly represent the parent generation, some of the discomfort may be accounted for on this basis.

Finally, the taboo against sex in old age may serve the interests of the regnant generation. By creating and fostering a stereotype of the elderly as an asexual group, the younger group perhaps seeks to eliminate the aged as competitors for sexual objects.

Actually, a series of fictions or cultural stereotypes exist with regard to sexual behavior in old age [2, 12]. The most important ones can be summarized briefly. Many people believe that sexual desire and sexual activity cease to exist with the onset of old age; or that sexual desire and sexual activity should cease to exist with the onset of old age; or that aged persons who say they are still sexually active

---

* The Catholic Church still teaches that sex should have only one purpose, the production of children.

are either morally perverse or engaged in wish-fulfilling deceptions and self-deceptions.

These stereotypes have only minimal relationship to the actual data and, as is true of stereotypes generally, make little allowance for individual variation. Only the phrase "onset of old age" is variably defined, from the menopause to retirement to extreme old age. Having considered the taboo against sex in old age and the several stereotypes which exist about the topic, the actual data can now be considered. Three series of studies will be reviewed and evaluated: the findings of Kinsey and his associates; those of Masters and Johnson; and the Duke longitudinal data.

From the start it is possible to make one statement which runs as a theme through all the studies to be considered. There are substantial differences in sexual behavior between men and women at any given age, including old age. There are at least two implications of this observation: one, an implication for research, the other for clinical practice. Data concerning any given aspect of sexual behavior should be examined separately for men and women. Second, the sometimes unequal or unmatched sexuality of men and women can at different ages lead to sexual conflicts and frustrations, at least for some individuals.

## KINSEY'S FINDINGS

Kinsey studied the sexual histories of 14,084 men [4]. Included in this huge group were 106 men over age 60, only 18 of whom were over 70. It is therefore not an exaggeration to say that the aged were underrepresented in Kinsey's sample. For this reason some of the statements which Kinsey makes must be viewed somewhat cautiously since they were, in a number of instances, based on extrapolations from data on younger age groups. In addition, many of the analyses in his book do not include the aged at all [4: Tables 60–66, Figs. 53–88]. Kinsey nevertheless reached a number of interesting conclusions which he felt were justified on the basis of his data. One of these was that men were sexually most active in late adolescence (ages 16 through 20) and that their activity then gradually declined and that the "rate at which males slow up in these last decades does not exceed the rate at which they have been slowing up and dropping out in the previous age group" [4: p. 235]. This should be contrasted, however, with the fact that he then goes on to present on the succeeding page data on the rapid increase in the proportion of subjects who are impotent. His figures indicate that this rises from 20 percent at age 60 to 75 percent at age 80. Kinsey also noted that married men, when compared with either single men or with men who had been previously married, had frequencies of sexual activity which were only slightly higher than those of their nonmarried counterparts.

Kinsey also studied some 56 women over age 60 [5]. His conclusions regarding age-related changes in sexual behavior for the most part represent extrapolations from changes observed at younger ages. He noted a gradual decline in frequency of sexual intercourse between ages 20 and 60 but felt that this "must be the product of aging processes in the male" and that there is "little evidence of any aging in the sexual capacities of the female until late in her life" [5: p. 353]. Kinsey further observed that in contrast to the men, single and postmarital females had rates of sexual activity which ranked far below those of their married counterparts.

## MASTERS AND JOHNSON REPORT

Masters and Johnson [8] devote a considerably greater portion of their book to geriatric sexual responses than did Kinsey. Their data are divided into two categories: (1) findings with respect to sexual anatomy and physiology in old age, based on actual laboratory participation of a small group of aged subjects; and (2) findings with respect to sexual behavior in old age, based on interviews with a somewhat larger group of self-selected aged subjects. Masters and Johnson report that in their sample men past age 60 were slower to be aroused sexually, slower to develop erection, slower to effect intromission, and slower to achieve ejaculation. Accompanying physiological signs of sexual excitement, such as sexual flush and increased muscle tone, were also less pronounced than in younger subjects. The findings were similar for women. Degree of physiological response to sexual stimulation, as indicated by breast engorgement, nipple erection, sexual flush over the breasts, increased muscle tone, clitoral and labial engorgement, were diminished in women over age 60. However, capacity to reach orgasm was not diminished, especially among those women who had had regular sexual stimulation.

Masters and Johnson interviewed 133 men above age 60, 52 of whom were above age 70. They present their conclusions somewhat dogmatically and often without sharing with the reader the actual data upon which these conclusions are based. They state that "there is no question of the fact that the human male's sexual responsiveness wanes as he ages." Great emphasis is placed by them on the role of monotony in sexual activity in determining declining sexual activity. Why monotony should be more important in advanced age than earlier in life is not explained. Vincent has recently pointed out that monotony of sexual expression can be a significant problem in young marriages as well [17]. Masters and Johnson also conclude that men who have had a high sexual "output" during their younger years are likely to continue to be sexually active in old age. This is in congruence with the findings of Newman and Nichols who earlier reported a positive correlation between strong sexual feelings in youth and continued sexual interest in old age [9].

Masters and Johnson also interviewed 54 women above age 60, 17 of whom were above 70. They conclude on the basis of their sample that capacity for sexual intercourse with orgasmic response is not lacking in older women. Unfortunately, they do not address themselves to the actual incidence of continuing sexual interest or activity in these women. They agree with Kinsey that a sizable portion of the postmenopausal sex drive in women is related to the sexual habits established in earlier years.

Masters and Johnson also asked about masturbation in their sample of women. They conclude, again rather cavalierly, that "masturbation represents no significant problem for the older-age-group of women." They further state that "there is no reason why the milestone of the menopause should be expected to blunt the human female's sexual capacity, performance, or drive" and finally, that "there is no time limit drawn by the advancing years to female sexuality." While these statements may be true from a physiological standpoint, they ignore the social and psychological realities involved. Regular or even occasional satisfaction of sexual needs through coital activity is no longer available for many aged women, and considerable conflict may attach to the practice of masturbation; for it is a fact that the majority of aged women will spend a considerable portion of their old age in widowhood, without a sexual partner. Thus time indirectly does set limits upon female as well as upon male sexuality.

Despite these criticisms there can be no doubt that Masters and Johnson have ventured into an area of study that has long been closed to scientific investigation and that they have thus made an important contribution to the understanding of human sexual behavior.

## THE DUKE LONGITUDINAL DATA

At the Duke University Center for the Study of Aging and Human Development, a longitudinal, interdisciplinary study of older individuals has been carried out since 1954 and is still in progress. As part of the study which seeks to elicit somatic, psychological, and social changes associated with old age, data on past and present sexual behavior were also obtained. Subjects of the study were seen repeatedly at approximately three-year intervals. This technique made possible the observation of changes occurring within individual subjects over time, not merely changes in groups of subjects, as is the case in cross-sectional studies. Information was obtained on the degree of enjoyment of sexual intercourse and intensity of sexual feelings, both at the present time and in younger years. Also sought was information on the present frequency of intercourse in those subjects who were still sexually active and on the reasons for and age of cessation of coital activity in those subjects who were no longer sexually active.

Initially 254 subjects, ranging in age from 60 to 94 years, and roughly equally divided between men and women, were studied. At subsequent examinations this number gradually dwindled as subjects died, became seriously disabled, and a few failed to continue in the study for a number of personal and situational reasons. Included in the study panel were 31 intact couples who provided the investigators with a unique opportunity to cross-validate the information provided by each of the two marriage partners. This was important methodologically because the reliability and validity of data on sexual behavior obtained by interview techniques has at times been questioned.

The results of these studies have been presented in a number of related articles and papers [10, 11, 15, 16]. Only a brief summary of them can be presented here. From the longitudinal data the following major statements can be made. First, sexual interest and coital activity are by no means rare in persons beyond age 60. Second, patterns of sexual interest and coital activity differ substantially for men and for women of the same age.

About 80 percent of the men whose health, intellectual status, and social functioning were not significantly impaired reported continuing sexual interest at the start of the study. Ten years later the proportion of those still sexually interested had not declined significantly. In contrast, in this same group of men 70 percent were still regularly sexually active at the start of the study but ten years later this proportion had dropped to 25 percent. Thus there was a growing discrepancy with advancing age between the number still sexually interested and those still sexually active.

In the sample of women whose health, intellectual status, and social functioning were good at the start of the study only about a third reported continuing sexual interest. This proportion did not change significantly over the next ten years. Only about a fifth of these same healthy women reported at the start of the study they were still having sexual intercourse regularly. Again this proportion did not decline over the next ten years. Obviously and somewhat surprisingly, then, far fewer women than men were still sexually interested or coitally active. How can this phenomenon be explained?

The present author has suggested three tentative explanations. First, women may always have had lower levels of sexual interest than men. Kinsey reports a lower frequency of total sexual outlets for women than for men, at all ages [5]. Our own data also lend some support to this notion; most men but only a third of the women in our sample reported strong sexual feelings in their younger years [11]. Whether these differences between the sexes exist as a result of a cultural or of a biological double standard, however, cannot be said at this time. Second, there is reason to believe that the clearly demarcated menopause in women, signaling the end of reproductive capacity, may indeed have a negative influence on sexual interest and activity in at least some women. A new longitudinal study at Duke University of persons between ages 45 and 70 may shed some light on this supposition. Third, decline of sexual interest and activity in women may have occurred before their entry into the study (that is, before age 60). Our data indicate that the median age of cessation of intercourse occurred nearly a decade earlier in women than in men (ages 60 and 68, respectively) [10]. Interestingly enough, the overwhelming majority of women attributed responsibility for the cessation of sexual intercourse in the marriage to their husbands; the men in general agreed, holding themselves responsible.

A number of other important findings also emerged from the study. Among these were the following:

1. As Kinsey had found for the younger ages, we found that in old age, too, married men did not differ markedly from nonmarried men in degree of reported sexual interest and activity. On the other hand, married women differed substantially from nonmarried women; only a very few of the latter reported any sexual activity, and only 20 percent reported any sexual interest.

2. While our cross-sectional data indicated a gradual *decline* in sexual interest and activity with increasing age, our longitudinal data revealed that some 20 to 25 percent of the men, but only a few

percent of the women, actually showed patterns of *rising* sexual interest and activity with advancing age. Furthermore, rising patterns were more frequent among nonmarried than among married men.

3. Among the group of intact couples included in the study panel there was a very high level of agreement between husbands and wives with regard to reported frequency of sexual intercourse and reasons for stopping coital activity.

It must be admitted that the Duke longitudinal data on sexual behavior in old age are far from complete. Additional information is obviously needed to answer some of the following questions: What sexual conflicts and problems do the married and the nonmarried aged experience? What are their sexual fantasies, dreams, and concerns? How important is masturbation as a sexual outlet for those aged who no longer have a capable sexual partner available to them, and what conflicts does it arouse? To whom do the aged turn for help with their sexual or marital problems? Full and satisfying answers to these and other questions are not currently available, and more comprehensive studies are needed.

## PRACTICAL IMPLICATIONS

In the meantime, what are the implications for clinical practice of the above mentioned areas of ignorance and of knowledge? The practitioner—whether he be a psychiatrist, internist, general or family physician, social worker, or welfare agent—must be aware and accepting of the fact that many aged continue to have or desire an active sex life. Further, he must be able to convey this acceptance to his patient or client. But he must also be aware that not all in the larger society share this view of the legitimacy of the aged person's sexual strivings. He must therefore seek to educate and to temper prejudices where he can. Chapter 3 of this book addresses itself to the problem of the aged as an underprivileged minority. It is no exaggeration to say that the aged are sexually underprivileged.

Their sexual overtures, aspirations, and performances are often ridiculed. Elderly widows and widowers interested in dating or in remarrying are often placed under severe pressure to give up their aims by their "friends" or relatives; they are told "not to make fools of themselves." Aged couples living with their children or other relatives often are afforded no real privacy, even though their other needs may be well provided for. Many state hospitals, nursing homes, and homes for the aged practice segregation of the sexes or else permit men and women, even husbands and wives, to spend time with each other only in public dayrooms or under "supervision." An openness about sexual matters, availability of counsel for sexual problems, and living arrangements which permit sexual expression to the extent that the aged individual is still interested in and capable of would not appear to be too outrageous a list of demands on behalf of the aged.

That is not to say that the practitioner should exhort all of his aged patients or clients to vigorous sexual activity. Sexual needs vary tremendously from individual to individual, and past intensity of sexual desire and activity is probably the best predictor of sexual interest and activity in old age. Then, too, the gift of longevity has been distributed unequally between the sexes. As a result a very sizable portion of women will spend a major portion of their old age in widowhood, without a sexual partner. To exhort them to an active sexual life when none is available would be cruel advice indeed. In short, what is needed is for the practitioner to give concerned, equanimous attention to the aged person's individual sexual needs, past preferences, and current limitations and opportunities. In so doing he will significantly enhance the quality of survival for many persons in old age.

## REFERENCES

1. Birren, J. E. (Ed.). *Handbook of Aging and the Individual.* Chicago: University of Chicago Press, 1959.
2. Golde, P. and Kogan, N. A sentence completion procedure for assessing attitudes toward old people. *J. Geront.* 14:355–363, 1959.

3. Group for the Advancement of Psychiatry. *Psychiatry and the Aged: An Introductory Approach*. GAP Report No. 59. New York: Group for the Advancement of Psychiatry, 1965.
4. Kinsey, A. C., Pomeroy, W. B., and Martin, C. R. *Sexual Behavior in the Human Male*. Philadelphia: Saunders, 1948.
5. Kinsey, A. C., Pomeroy, W. B., Martin, C. R., and Gebhard, P. H. *Sexual Behavior in the Human Female*. Philadelphia: Saunders, 1953.
6. Lief, H. I. Sex education of medical students and doctors. *Pacif. Med. Surg.* 73:52–58, 1965.
7. Lief, H. I. Sex and the medical educator. *J. Amer. Med. Wom. Ass.* 23:195–196, 1968.
8. Masters, W. H., and Johnson, V. E. *Human Sexual Response*. Boston: Little, Brown, 1966.
9. Newman, G., and Nichols, C. R. Sexual activities and attitudes in older persons. *J.A.M.A.* 173:33–35, 1960.
10. Pfeiffer, E., Verwoerdt, A., and Wang, H.- S. Sexual behavior in aged men and women. I. Observations on 254 community volunteers. *Arch. Gen. Psychiat.* (Chicago) 19:753–758, 1968.
11. Pfeiffer, E., Verwoerdt, A., and Wang, H.- S. The natural history of sexual behavior in a biologically advantaged group of aged individuals. *J. Geront.* 24:193–198, 1969.
12. Rubin, I. *Sexual Life After Sixty*. New York: Basic Books, 1965.
13. Simon, A., and Epstein, L. J. (Eds.). *Aging in Modern Society*. Psychiatric Research Report 23. Washington, D.C.: American Psychiatric Association, 1968.
14. Tibbitts, C. *Handbook of Social Gerontology*. Chicago: University of Chicago Press, 1960.
15. Verwoerdt, A., Pfeiffer, E., and Wang, H.- S. Sexual behavior in senescence. I. Changes in sexual activity and interest of aging men and women. *J. Geriat. Psychiat.* In press.
16. Verwoerdt, A., Pfeiffer, E., and Wang, H.- S. Sexual behavior in senescence. II. Patterns of sexual activity and interest. *Geriatrics* 24:137–154, 1969.
17. Vincent, C. E. Sex and the young married. *Med. Aspects Hum. Sex.* 3:13–23, 1969.
18. Wallace, I. *The Chapman Report*. New York: Simon and Schuster, 1960.

# 9

# How the Old Face Death

FRANCES C. JEFFERS AND
ADRIAAN VERWOERDT

Professional persons working with older individuals are concerned that adjustment to the later years of life be as healthy and satisfying as possible, whatever the future may hold for such individuals or however long that future may be. Whatever the circumstances, at this phase of the life-span there can be no avoidance of the fact of death. To its approach the older person must either make some type of adjustment or he must build up defenses which shield him to some extent from facing the necessity that he, too, must die. According to Feifel "the adaptation of the older person to dying and to death may well be a crucial aspect of the aging process" [6]. To the extent that one agrees with this statement, the aging person's awareness of death, its personal meaning to him, and the effects of these on behavior, all become important factors in understanding and managing the problems of late life.

The realization of the inevitability of death, and thus of the extinction of the individual personality, is seen by many therapists as the ultimate threat to a human being. Koestenbaum, speaking from an existential point of view, interprets death anxiety as a dread of seeing the world itself disappear [18]. Our modern culture has attempted to alleviate such anxiety by taboos on the topic of death, by increasing the impersonality of memorial services, and by disguising cemeteries as ordinary parks [25, 39]. But from those persons on "the shady side of the hill" of life, death can scarcely be hidden. A realistic acceptance of death as the "appropriate" end of life may well be the hallmark of emotional maturity [40]. If

awareness and acceptance of death are characteristics of the emotional maturity of elderly persons, one may also ask to what extent
they occur in younger persons and what the effects may be of such
factors as age, physical illness, and personality adjustment. At the
present time, some research evidence is beginning to accumulate,
but much work remains to be done. Kastenbaum, in chairing a
Gerontological Society symposium in 1965, outlined some of the
difficulties and challenges of "death research" [15].

Several problems of research methodology exist in the area of
personal attitudes toward death and dying, awareness of death,
and means of coping with death anxiety. First, in reading the
literature it becomes clear that there are difficulties with regard to
the conceptualization of death and in arriving at operational definitions suitable for research purposes. Second, authors tend to utilize
diverse subject groups, methods, questionnaires, and/or interview
schedules, so that it is difficult to compare findings from different
studies. Third, some of the research methods utilized to date
(direct questioning, death attitude scales, sentence completions,
projective techniques, and so on) may be inadequate to measure
accurately and fully the degrees of death awareness and the meanings death has for different individuals. In addition, such data are
generally obtained at only one point in time. Data obtained from
serial interviews over a prolonged period of time might shed additional light on the "deeper" significance of death to the personality.
Thus far, reports on this type of material are not available except
tangentially (e.g., Lindemann's reports on the effects of grief and
bereavement [22]).

## AWARENESS OF DEATH

Awareness of external events, inner physiological processes, or subjective experiences is not an "all-or-none" phenomenon, but rather
it can be manifested in varying degrees of consciousness. It follows
that awareness of death may be revealed indirectly through the

existence of ideas that are related to death. Thus it may be that frequently awareness of one's own death occurs on a preconscious level.

A special instance of preconscious awareness of impending death was described by Verwoerdt and Elmore, who studied 30 hospitalized patients (age range 24 to 74) with fatal illness [37]. The data suggested a relationship between actual temporal distance to death, hopelessness, and decreased expectation of futurity. None of the patients could know, or alleged to know, exactly how long they still had to live. Nor was this interval before death known to the investigators at the time of the study; it was obtained instead from a follow-up study one year later. Patients who were closer to death expressed more hopelessness and evidenced a greater reduction of expectation of futurity. This same finding was reported by Lieberman in his study of 22 older persons a year or less distant from death [21]. In illness, especially in fatal illness, the patient may well be aware of the rate of decline in his physical status. By "monitoring" these internal physiological changes, he may be able to "estimate" the rate of his decline from the present to a terminal point [8]. It is possible that to some extent similar mechanisms may also be activated by the much slower biological changes which occur as a result of the aging process.

Studies of comparison on death awareness between younger and older persons in the general population are few and far between. Investigators appear to be primarily concerned with one group or with the other, in descriptive rather than in comparative studies. J. Riley reported, in a study of 1,500 adults, that most persons 61 years and older said they think at least occasionally, and 45 percent said they think often, about the uncertainty of their own life or of the death of someone close to them. Such thoughts were somewhat more widespread among people over age 60 than among the younger persons in his sample [30].

In a Duke study (1966) of frequency of death thoughts among 140 elderly noninstitutionalized persons (60 to 94 years old), it was found that 49 percent of them reported being reminded of death at least once a day, if only by reading the obituaries; 20 percent admitted to death thoughts about once a week, 25 percent less than once a week, while 5 percent denied they ever thought about it; and 1 percent were undecided [13]. It was reported by 7 percent of the subjects that they had thoughts related to death constantly on their minds. Several factors differentiated these subjects from the "deniers." The latter tended to believe that such awareness would affect enjoyment of life; they were more active, less "disengaged," and had higher "morale"; their subjective health assessment was higher, although there was no difference with regard to objective health ratings; they had higher IQ scores, and their occupations were primarily in the nonmanual categories. Finally, these subjects were younger than those who always had death thoughts on their mind.

Hence, those who shut out thoughts of death presumably felt more distant from it by reason of being chronologically younger and by considering themselves to be in better health. But it is interesting to note that when the two groups were given a sentence completion test in which they were asked to speak directly about personal meanings of death, they differed very little in type of emotional reaction: The incidence of positive (nonthreatened, accepting) reactions in each group was about 50 percent, with neutral or negative reactions making up the other 50 percent.

Richardson and Freeman found that thoughts of death were more common among those in poor than in good health [29]. This is in keeping with the above-mentioned finding at Duke of an inverse relationship between favorable self-health evaluations and frequency of death thoughts, and with the findings reported by Shrut [33] and by Rhudick and Dibner [28]. The latter two investigators, using death references from TAT stories, found additionally that neurotic patients showed much more death concern than did psychotic patients. This phenomenon is also mentioned by May, who states that whenever *concern* about death arises, it is to be assumed that a neurotic element may be present [23].

Summarizing these findings, current research evidence suggests that *frequency of death thoughts* may be higher in older age groups and also in conditions of physical illness. *Concerns about death* tend to occur in individuals with neurotic conflicts rather than in either normal or psychotic individuals.

## PERSONAL MEANINGS OF DEATH

Closely linked with awareness of death is the meaning of death to the individual. Doubtless the significance of death for the person has a great number of determinants, both personal and socio-cultural. "The meaning of death" is not to be equated with the actual experience of the event of dying, but is taken to signify the subjective anticipations, interpretations, inferences, or projections of personal feelings onto the fact of death. It is likely that there are as many meanings of death as there are human beings capable of reflection. In spite of such an infinite variety of meanings—with their subtle differences and nuances—a certain degree of classification would seem desirable even on an arbitrary basis. Several possible categories emerge from a scrutiny of the data obtained from sentence completion tests in the Duke study referred to above [13]. The elderly subjects were asked to complete the following phrases:

1. When a man dies, ——
2. Death is ——
3. I feel that when I die, I ——

It appeared that for the most part the responses could be categorized under one or another of the following headings:

1. *Continuation or cessation of life.* The greater part of the subjects expressed firm religious convictions (it must be remembered that North Carolina lies within the "Bible belt"), as for example: "When a man dies, he lives again," "Death is passing from this life into another world," or, "I feel that when I die, I think my spirit or soul will carry on." The end of life on this earth is seen by these persons as a stepping-stone to another life. Another thought expressed was that, "When a man dies, he will keep living

on in the minds and hearts of those still here." There were some persons, on the other hand, who thought of death primarily as extinction of the personality and loss of identity. One "ceases to exist," "he's buried," "he's dead all over," "he's soon forgotten." Or, "It's very final." Thus, death was seen as "inevitable" or—more positively—as rest and release: "I will be out of all my troubles," "I'll leave behind me the troubles and worries of life."

2. *Death as the enemy.* Only infrequently was death viewed as an enemy disrupting life patterns and relationships, e.g., "Death is a cruel master." However, more subjects expressed fear of the dependency, disability, or pain which they associated with the act of dying.

3. *Reunion or isolation.* Many persons expressed reunion beliefs, as, for example, "I am going to meet the ones who have gone ahead of me." For some, death involved departure from a known existence and separation from loved ones here with sadness but without the element of decreased self-esteem: "I wouldn't be afraid to die but I dread to leave my children and loved ones."

4. *Reward or punishment.* Most of the subjects viewed death as a transition to a better state of being, a reward for a life well lived: "I will go to heaven, and into the joys of the Lord." This was in keeping with the firm religious beliefs of the study panel members as a whole. Only seldom were there direct expressions that death meant punishment: "He's at rest if he lived right and he's gone if he didn't."

5. *The anticipated or the unknown.* Several subjects expressed uncertainty or curiosity, as follows: "I can't say," or, "I don't know what death is—tell me—what is it?" Or, "I wonder what it is going to be like—who knows?—sort of like going to Egypt." The anticipation of death as an event made familiar through religious rituals was observed in such responses as, "Death is going to my long home," and, "My spirit will go back to God."

In a similar manner Feifel categorized the two dominant outlooks of 40 disabled World War I veterans. One group visualized death as the dissolution of bodily life and the doorway to a new life; the other group, with a "philosophic resignation," looked on death as "the end" [6].

## EMOTIONAL REACTIONS TO DEATH AWARENESS

Typically, the older subjects studied at Duke seemed to experience feelings which were appropriate to the particular ideas about death which they had expressed; for example, it was commonly observed that beliefs in reunion after death were associated with feelings of happy expectation [13]. Those few subjects who felt threatened by the sentence completion test tended to view death as being cruel or as punishment: "Those questions are very tough, I tell you, they shook me up." There was also some evidence of ambivalent feelings. Several persons stated, for example, "Heaven may be my home, but I'm not homesick yet."

Notably absent were any expressions of angry protest or rage in response to the disruptive or cruel aspects of death. The death-defying mood portrayed by poet Dylan Thomas ("Rage, rage, against the dying of the light") is perhaps more characteristic of the attitude of younger persons.

A number of investigators are in agreement that only a relatively small proportion of older persons—only 10 percent or less in several studies—express fear of death [6, 12, 35]. In the National Institute of Mental Health sample of healthy older persons, overt fear of death was present in 30 percent of the subjects [1]. In a sentence completion test conducted by Kogan and Shelton, 200 individuals, aged 49 to 92, thought that death was more frightening to "people in general" than to old people. They also felt that old people were comparatively less likely to regard death as one of their greatest fears but rather thought of it as an escape or as inevitable [19]. Kogan and Wallach found, in comparing older persons with college students, that the responses to the concept of death, utilizing the semantic differential, were less negative among the older subjects than they were among the younger subjects [20].

In another study at Duke University, only 10 percent of the elderly community subjects answered the question "Are you afraid to die?" in the affirmative [12]. Thirty-five percent of the subjects denied being afraid, while 55 percent were hesitant or ambivalent in their answers. The responses admitting fear of death tended to be devoid of religious references; the finding that these particular subjects showed less belief in life after death confirms that in Swenson's study [35]. In addition, it was found at Duke that those persons who admitted fear of death gave fewer responses on the Rorschach test, had fewer leisure activities, and lower IQ scores. J. Riley reported a similar relationship between negative views of death and lower educational level in his sample of 1,500 adults [30]. Finally, the Duke subjects who expressed fear of death had a higher incidence of feelings of rejection and depression. Rhudick and Dibner suggest that death concern may not necessarily manifest itself as overt anxiety but may be accompanied by somatizing and withdrawal tendencies [28].

Butler points out that even though many older persons may not show any obvious fear of death, one cannot conclude that the problem of death does not exist for them. Rather, one may need to study the person at a particular stage of his adaptation to the reality of death [4]. As one of the elderly volunteers at Duke put it, "No, I'm not afraid to die—it seems to me to be a perfectly normal process. But you never know how you will feel when it comes to a showdown. I might get panicky."

In summary, it appears from the expressions of older persons that death is feared much less than prolonged illness, dependency, or pain, which may bring the several threats of rejection and isolation, as well as loss of social role, self-determination, and dignity as an individual. To some of the elderly ill who are cared for in their own homes, life may still seem worth living, but even here regret is often expressed for "the bother I am to those I love." Glaser and Strauss point out that terminal geriatric patients often decide to stay in the hospital in order not to be a burden to their families [9]. Experience in nursing homes suggests that, except for an occasional geriatric patient who clings tenaciously to life, death is seen by most of them as preferable to continued illness or chronic disability. These patients may have already become "socially dead"—according to Kalish's concept—in their own eyes as well as to others, and thus they view their impending death as timely and welcome [9, 14]. Kastenbaum quotes staff reports in a geriatric hospital to the effect that, among older persons who were dying, most of their references to death were positively valued, such as calm waiting for death or a desire for the end of all suffering [16].

There has been such a wide disparity between findings on the one hand of lack of fear of death in older persons and, on the other hand, the assumption of some clinicians of the universality of this fear that Kastenbaum, in taking note of the difference in opinion, has challenged the use of this concept altogether in the study of aging [15, 17].

## COPING WITH THE PROSPECT OF DEATH

It has become a truism that individual variations in adaptive behavior may exist to a greater degree among the elderly than in other age groups because their relative longevity may provide a greater quantity and variety of life experiences. Thus their coping behavior vis-à-vis death may be varied as well. Muriel Spark has written an absorbing piece of fiction, *Memento Mori,* in which she deals in some detail with the varied behaviors of several older persons in response to anonymous phone calls of four words only, "Remember you must die" [34].

Certain coping techniques or defense mechanisms may be adaptive for one person but maladaptive for another. Whether or not a particular defense is adaptive or not depends further on quantitative factors. Some of the determinants for the type of mechanism utilized may be: (1) the temporal factor: chronological age and distance from death; both of these were found to be of importance in the Duke geriatric studies [13]; (2) physical and mental health; (3) the influence of varying frames of reference such as religious orientation and socioeconomic and occupational status; (4) community attitudes; (5) family and personal experiences with death; (6) attitudes of persons currently in the immediate environment; and (7) the individual's own psychological integrity and maturity. A major determinant of the adjustment is probably how the individual has adjusted to changes and crises in his past life. Payne cites—as an additional determinant to a person's acceptance of his death—the nature of his emotional commitments during his lifetime to people and to productive endeavors [26]. Wahl hypothesizes that the well-loved child is more likely to retain an unconscious proclivity toward infantile omnipotence which he is able to put into use in handling the death anxiety, as he has had confidence to face new situations in the past [38].

In most instances of successful adaptation, an interlocking of several coexisting adaptive approaches may be utilized. By functioning simultaneously, one adaptational technique fosters, or even potentiates, another one.

To many persons is given the ability to cross into old age and to face death with a conscious, though perhaps unverbalized, feeling of satisfaction with past achievements and a sense of contentment with life as they have lived it. A decreased energy level may reconcile them to rest from struggle and facilitate a philosophical attitude toward closure. Wahl quotes Spinoza as having said that the adult who sees death as completion of a pattern and who has spent his time, unfettered by fear, in living richly and productively, can accept the thought that his self will one day cease to be [38].

Mastery and adaptation to the prospect of death may—in addition to the predominantly intrapyschic processes of synthesis and integrity—be achieved in other ways, as through the anchorage point of mature religious beliefs or the securities and sastifactions derived from social relationships.

Feifel's reports and others have confirmed that for many older persons a belief in life after death or a trust in religious support serves as a bolster against the threat of death [6]. The study of the geriatrics panel in North Carolina revealed that there was almost universal belief in a life after death, with only 2 percent of the number of 254 denying such a belief outright [12]. Twenty-one percent compromised by saying they were "not sure" of such after-life, but 77 percent wished to be counted among those who were sure, with almost as many variations as individuals in imagining what it might be like. On the other hand, for a few in the Duke panel and also for some persons in Feifel's studies strong belief in religion and in an after-life can be threatening if the person fears retribution at death for his sins. As Choron notes, belief in "immortality" may generate its own kind of death-fear [5].

One of the most satisfying adaptations to the ending of life is a close but nonambivalent relationship with children and grandchildren. This satisfies not only the mutual affectional needs but bestows on the older person the reminder of continuity of life and tangible evidence of his own ongoing contribution to mankind. The grandparents can participate, often without overstrained responsibility, in the pleasures of learning, wonder, and companionship of a new generation.

Planning by a person around whatever inheritance he may have to leave to his family and friends is often a tangible mark of his acceptance of the ultimate closure of his life, however near or distant that closure may be. Judging sheerly by the more probable proximity to the end, it would seem logical that, the older a person is, the more time he would have had for preparation and getting his affairs in proper shape for his death. For some persons, however, intervening variables—denial, hostility, fear, or disturbed reactions of family members—may operate to arouse resistance to such planning. Occasionally one can observe the superstitious fear that being prepared for death might actually hasten its coming. In a study at Duke (1965) on the extent of concern and planning for chronic illness, for example, the elderly persons studied expressed relatively little concern and little actual planning for such an eventuality. Many gave the impression that they did not wish to consider such a possibility [11].

In a current study at Duke, based on the Rosow Death-Awareness Scale, the older panel members appeared to be more practical with regard to such financial matters as keeping up their life insurance for funeral costs, making wills, and signing their homes over to their children. One 90-year-old woman had purchased her cemetery lot and her tombstone, and had even paid in advance for engraving the date of death after her name. More involvement in planning might well be expected by those who also indicated more awareness of death; Rosow found this correlation among the 100 community respondents in his study [31]. However, resistance to giving away a few of the most valued keepsakes before death is a hopeful sign, indicating a wish to live as fully as possible until the last; often such treasures are assigned to the appropriate recipients, who will get them "later." These preparations signify a realistic acceptance of personal death and the desire to "set one's house in order" well in advance. But such planning for separation from life is too often upsetting to the older person's family and friends and is viewed as morbid preoccupation with death.

The taboo in Western culture on open discussion of death presents peculiar difficulties both for those who work or live with older persons and for the older persons themselves [7]. Yet the one who is threatened by the prospect of his death has great need to communicate with someone about the problem. Often his own family members are unable to speak with him about this; the prospect of his death and his awareness of it disturbs them too greatly because of their own emotional involvement with him. The finding of J. Riley indicates that older persons may be more comfortable discussing the problems associated with death with clergymen or with doctors [30]. But even some of those associated with the medical profession—doctors, nurses, social workers—admit to uneasiness when faced with the care of dying patients or with older persons who seek to discuss their death. As Verwoerdt has pointed out, the physician "sides with health against illness and with life against death" [36]. Thus he and others concerned must come to terms with their own anxieties in order to communicate with empathy and to provide supportive therapy for the older person who is threatened by the prospect of dying [10, 27, 32].

In general, in those instances when the outcome of facing the threat of death has been unsuccessful or maladaptive for the aged person, it may be expected that he has automatically repeated old defenses, that his repertoire of coping techniques is only a limited one, that a few defenses are used rigidly and excessively, and/or that innovative techniques tend to be absent. The essence of maladaptive behavior is that it aggravates the very problem against which it is directed or creates new problems which require additional problem-solving techniques. Keeping in mind the importance of qualitative and quantitative factors, as well as the existence of the individual uniqueness of personality and interindividual variability, it may be well to review various types of coping with the prospect of personal death which have been observed by the present authors as well as by others.

Denial, which is aimed at avoiding clear awareness of a painful threat, has been considered by many psychiatrists to be a major mechanism for palliating fear of death. Attitudes of denial may manifest themselves in a great variety of ways. For example, an older person may acknowledge that "Death is inevitable," but in the privacy of his mind may add, "For me, however, it's only probable," or, "Only in the distant future," or even, "Inevitable— except for me." However, persistent denial is difficult to maintain, for the aged are surrounded by death's signposts: the sickness and death of contemporaries, as well as their own decreasing capacities. "Blinders" need to be powerful indeed to block out such ever-present and increasing stimuli. Other defenses which also serve the purpose of exclusion from awareness include suppression, rationalization, and externalization. Frequently these mechanisms occur in clusters rather than singly.

In another group of defenses, the goal of the coping behavior is not so much to exclude the threat from conscious awareness, but rather retreat from the source of anxiety. These defenses include such mechanisms as regression, withdrawal, "disengagement," or even surrender, as in certain cases of suicide. It is well known that direct death-seeking behavior occurs in old age. In fact, the rate of actual suicide increases sharply with advancing age, especially among men, and unsuccessful suicide attempts are of greater significance in old age than in younger years. These points are discussed more fully in Chapter 10 of this volume. Furthermore, attention should be given to what might be called occult or slow suicide in old age, due to depression, loss of appetite, or lowered vitality. No statistics are available on this point, but the impression of physicians and attendants in hospitals and homes for the aged is that death occurs much more rapidly when there is no will to live.

In cases of withdrawal and disengagement there is a move away from people. This defensive pattern may be aimed at protecting the individual against the painful loss, through death, of significant others. In the void of social isolation, the stage is set for hypochondriacal preoccupation with the bodily self. At the same time, hypochondriasis may imply a call for closeness, inasmuch as the physical complaints represent a wish for attention or support.

Among the less socially acceptable mechanisms employed against death fears is that of withdrawal and/or escape by way of alcohol and drugs. Because of social disapproval and the need to hide such behavior, it cannot be ascertained to what extent this mechanism is utilized by older persons, but clinical experience and occasional newspaper stories suggest that it is not uncommon.

A third category of coping behavior is characterized by its emphasis on attempts at mastery and resolution. Included here are defenses such as intellectualization, counterphobic mechanisms, hyperactivity, sublimation, and acceptance.

Butler cites counterphobic behavior as a defensive maneuver when old persons adopt greatly inappropriate dress and behavior in their effort to appear young: "One sees older people who cannot bear to look at themselves in a mirror and whose drawings show signs of dissolution despite intact cognitive and psychologic functions" [4].

Hyperactivity may be observed in certain vigorous older persons and may be vented on hobbies, restless travels, or civic enterprises; it is often accompanied by loquaciousness. This could be interpreted as an almost frenetic hold onto some phase of life which promises an opportunity for continued usefulness and a sense of past achievement, or it may be an anodyne to despair. On the other hand, losing oneself in activity adaptively can be observed in artists, musicians, or professional persons who continue to be absorbed in creative activity, thus keeping death at arm's length, often physically as well as psychologically.

Another important mechanism utilized—for better or worse—by the aged as they face the end of their existence is that of the life review. Butler postulates this as "a universal normal experience, intensifying in the aged, and occurring irrespective of environmental conditions" [2]. He views such life review as a primary factor in reminiscence and discusses its contribution to certain disturbances in later life, as well as its probable role in the evolution of more positive characteristics of old people, such as candor, serenity, and wisdom. When an individual cannot dodge the fact that time on this earth is running out for him, the nearness of death brings with it almost inevitably, if not a total life review, at least a recall of some of the major events and relationships in his past life. Perhaps this is related to the old belief that a drowning man's life flashes before his eyes before he goes down for the last time.

Thus it is not abnormal that the later years become for many persons a time for introspection and looking back, for creativity in the writing of an autobiography (or for compilation of material toward an autobiography which may actually never be written), for endless recitals of reminiscences often enjoyed only by the central figure himself, or—more unhappily still—for lapses into melancholia and depression triggered by unhappy memories of losses or of regret over misspent years or wrongs done for which it is now too late to atone [24]. Depression, for example, tends to predispose the older person toward a sensitization for previous unhappy experience, so that eventually a bleak perspective emerges. Finally, there are those tragic instances when the review and stock-taking lead to the discovery that one "missed the boat" and that it is now too late to repair previous mistakes. Particularly painful may be the awareness that large or significant areas of human experience had been avoided, that life had not been fully lived.

For those who cannot face the mirror of themselves, and the burden of their memories, the life review may be difficult if not shattering. The reminiscences of such persons appear repetitious, shot through with conscious or unconscious misrepresentations, without apparent purpose except to escape the present by filling time. Or they appear to be mere monologues with disturbing themes of old guilt or bitterness, obviating communication with others. Or should they be listened to carefully in an attempt to understand them as the older individual's efforts to establish a final identity in his own eyes as well as in that of the listener?

At the time of crisis when an individual comes to full realization of the foreshortening of his life-span and the approach of death, the self seeks to renew and establish itself before it may be lost. Robert Fulton puts it succinctly: "Death asks us for our identity" [7]. It is as if Charon, the boatman from Greek mythology, or St. Peter at the gate of heaven, were asking the mortal to present his passport.

From an existential point of view ("The essence of life is its mortality"), Koestenbaum argues that only through awareness of death can a man achieve integrity [18]. Under such pressure man will attempt to find the meaning and fulfillment of his life. "The vitality of death lies in the fact that it makes almost impossible the repression of unpleasant but important realities . . . and one is able to see all events in life from the perspective of his total existence."

Viewed in this way, the constructive and therapeutic aspects of the self-review—whether it be by spoken or silent reminiscing— are apparent when the individual can develop a satisfying pattern and meaning out of the conglomerate of events in his past life. Coming to terms with himself—his failures and achievements, his griefs and satisfactions—he seeks to integrate a new identity with a new acceptance of his own humanness, not judging himself too harshly for his limitations. This new crystallization of his self-awareness may affect his relationships with others and may bring increased tolerance, mellowness, and affection as he sees others in a different light as well. The factors that favor constructive reorganization of the personality through life review may include flexibility, resilience, and self-awareness; the reevaluation of the past may facilitate the person's "serene and dignified acceptance of death" [2]. This in turn may facilitate a better acceptance also of whatever life may bring before the final curtain.

## REFERENCES

1. Birren, J. E., Butler, R. N., Greenhouse, S. W., Sokoloff, L., and Yarrow, M. (Eds.). *Human Aging: A Biological and Behavioral Study*. Public Health Service Publication No. 986. Washington, D.C.: U.S. Government Printing Office, 1963.
2. Butler, R. N. The Life Review: An Interpretation of Reminiscence in the Aged. In R. Kastenbaum (Ed.), *New Thoughts on Old Age*. New York: Springer, 1964.
3. Butler, R. N. The Destiny of Creativity in Later Life: Studies of Creative People and the Creative Process. In S. Levin and R. J. Kahana (Eds.), *Psychodynamic Studies on Aging: Creativity, Reminiscing, and Dying*. New York: International Universities Press, 1967.
4. Butler, R. N. Toward a Psychiatry of the Life-Cycle. In A. Simon and L. J. Epstein (Eds.), *Aging in Modern Society*. Psychiatric Research Report No. 23. Washington, D.C.: American Psychiatric Association, 1968.
5. Choron, J. *Death and Western Thought*. New York: Collier-Macmillan, 1963.
6. Feifel, H. Attitudes Toward Death. In H. Feifel (Ed.), *The Meaning of Death*. New York: McGraw-Hill, 1965.
7. Fulton, R. *Death and Identity*. New York: Wiley, 1965.
8. Glaser, B. G., and Strauss, A. L. *Awareness of Dying*. Chicago: Aldine, 1965.
9. Glaser, B. G., and Strauss, A. L. *Time for Dying*. Chicago: Aldine, 1968.
10. Group for the Advancement of Psychiatry. *Death and Dying: Attitudes of Patient and Doctor*. New York: Mental Health Materials Center, 1967.
11. Heyman, D. K., and Jeffers, F. C. Observations on the extent of concern and planning by the aged for possible chronic illness. *J. Amer. Geriat. Soc.* 13:152–159, 1965.
12. Jeffers, F. C., Nichols, C. R., and Eisdorfer, C. Attitudes

of older persons toward death: A preliminary study. *J. Geront.* 16:53–56, 1961.

13. Jeffers, F. C., and Verwoerdt, A.   Factors associated with frequency of death thoughts in elderly community volunteers. *Proc. 7th Int. Cong. Geront.,* Vienna 6:149–152, 1966.

14. Kalish, R. A.   A continuum of subjectively perceived death. *Gerontologist* 6:73–76, 1966.

15. Kastenbaum, R.   Death as a research problem in social gerontology: An overview. *Gerontologist* 6:67–69, 125, 1966.

16. Kastenbaum, R.   The mental life of dying geriatric patients. *Proc. 7th Int. Cong. Geront.,* Vienna 6:153–159, 1966.

17. Kastenbaum, R., and Aisenberg, R. B.   *The Psychology of Death.* New York: Springer. In press.

18. Koestenbaum, P.   The vitality of death. *J. Existentialism* 5: 139–166, 1964.

19. Kogan, N., and Shelton, F. C.   Images of "old people" and "people in general" in an older sample. *J. Genet. Psychol.* 100:3–21, 1962.

20. Kogan, N., and Wallach, M. A.   Age changes in values and attitudes. *J. Geront.* 16:272–280, 1961.

21. Lieberman, M. A.   Psychological correlates of impending death: Some preliminary observations. *J. Geront.* 20:182–190, 1965.

22. Lindemann, E.   Symptomatology and management of acute grief. *Amer. J. Psychiat.* 101:141–148, 1944.

23. May, R.   *The Meaning of Anxiety.* New York: Ronald, 1950.

24. McMahon, A. W., Jr., and Rhudick, P. J.   Reminiscing in the Aged: An Adaptational Response. In S. Levin and R. J. Kahana (Eds.), *Psychodynamic Studies on Aging: Creativity, Reminiscing, and Dying.* New York: International Universities Press, 1967.

25. Mitford, J.   *The American Way of Death.* London: Hutchinson, 1963.

26. Payne, E. C., Jr.   The Physician and His Patient Who is Dying. In S. Levin and R. J. Kahana (Eds.), *Psychodynamic Studies on Aging: Creativity, Reminiscing, and Dying.* New York: International Universities Press, 1967.

27. Quint, J. C.   *The Nurse and the Dying Patient.* New York: Macmillan, 1967.

28. Rhudick, P. J. and Dibner, A. S.   Age, personality and health correlates of death concerns in normal aged individuals. *J. Geront.* 16:44–49, 1961.

29. Richardson, A. H., and Freeman, H. E.  Behavior, Attitudes and Disengagement Among the Very Old. Unpublished manuscript quoted in M. W. Riley and A. Foner (Eds.), *An Inventory of Research Findings*. Aging and Society, vol. I. New York: Russell Sage Foundation, 1968.

30. Riley, J.  Attitudes Toward Death. Unpublished manuscript quoted in M. W. Riley and A. Foner (Eds.), *An Inventory of Research Findings*. Aging and Society, vol. I. New York: Russell Sage Foundation, 1968.

31. Rosow, I., and Chellam, G.  An awareness-of-death scale. In *Proc. 7th Int. Cong. Geront.*, Vienna 6:163–165, 1966.

32. Saunders, C.  *Care of the Dying*. London: Macmillan, 1960.

33. Shrut, S. D.  Attitudes toward old age and death. *Ment. Hyg.* 42:259–266, 1958.

34. Spark, M.  *Memento Mori*. (Time Reading Program No. 17.) Chicago: Time-Life Books, 1964.

35. Swenson, W. M.  Attitudes toward death in an aged population. *J. Geront.* 16:49–52, 1961.

36. Verwoerdt, A.  *Communication with the Fatally Ill*. Springfield, Ill.: Thomas, 1966.

37. Verwoerdt, A., and Elmore, J. L.  Psychological reactions in fatal illness: I. The prospect of impending death. *J. Amer. Geriat. Soc.* 15:9–19, 1967.

38. Wahl, C. W.  The fear of death. *Bull. Menninger Clin.* 22:214–223, 1958.

39. Waugh, E.  *The Loved One*. London: Chapman and Hall, 1948.

40. Weisman, A. D., and Hackett, T. P.  Predilection to death: Death and dying as psychiatric problem. *Psychosom. Med.* 23:232–256, 1961.

41. Weisman, A. D., and Hackett, T. P.  Denial as a Social Act. In S. Levin and R. J. Kahana (Eds.), *Psychodynamic Studies on Aging: Creativity, Reminiscing, and Dying*. New York: International Universities Press, 1967.

# 10

# Functional Psychiatric Disorders in Old Age

EWALD W. BUSSE AND ERIC PFEIFFER

## DETERMINANTS OF ADAPTATION

It has been customary to say that an individual's adaptation at any given point in time is determined by an interplay of the biological, social, and psychological factors impinging on him at that moment and in his recent and distant past. This chapter will treat adaptation in old age as only one special instance of adaptation throughout the life cycle. Erikson, who has done pioneer work toward the development of a psychiatry of the life cycle, has rightly pointed out both the uniqueness of each phase of the life cycle and its essential continuity with all other phases [25, 26].

The unique aspects of old age are easily enumerated. This is the last phase of life, the phase in which the individual must come to grips with his own relatively imminent extinction. It is also the phase in which the individual's capacities for adaptation are for the first time clearly diminishing as contrasted with other phases of life, such as adolescence or early adulthood, in which adaptative capacities are either improving or remaining more or less on the same plane. In particular, the brain, the "organ of adaptation," is undergoing involutional changes (see Chapter 12). However, the magnitude of the task of adaptation is not diminished in old age.

Old age is also a phase of continued development. The self-image undergoes its final revision as the individual makes a summary assessment of the worth of his life [14, 25, 60]. The sphere of the individual's concern which has been expanding throughout the life cycle—including first the mother-child dyad, then the larger family, then the peer group, the community, the nation, and so on—may expand still further to fasten on basic concerns common to all men. Wisdom and judgment (however difficult these may be to define) come to full flower in old age, at least in some men. Certain qualities, such as statesmanship, seem to be found more often in those of advanced years.

But what, in more concrete terms, determines the balance between the successes and failures of adaptation in old age? On theoretical grounds we might say that the history of adaptation in younger years is probably one of the best predictors of adaptation in old age. Individuals who have been able to develop a basically trusting relationship with others; who have developed a sense of autonomy and a clearly defined, positively valued identity; who have developed satisfying relationships with others in marriage or in a work situation; who have previously confronted adversity without succumbing to it, will probably also make satisfactory adaptations to the stresses of old age. There is also some research evidence to support the notion that those who develop emotional disturbances in old age have had more emotional disturbances in younger years, while those who adapt well in old age have made good adjustments throughout their lifetime [55, 59, 76, 97]. In short, we can say that the past is prologue.

Of course many factors, biological and experiential, contribute to whether an individual in younger years has been well or ill adapted, has been happy or unhappy, productive or unproductive. Good health, intelligence, membership in intact families and in integrated communities, adequate food, shelter, and clothing, good education, and orderly careers can easily be counted on the positive side of the ledger. Extreme poverty, broken families, poorly integrated communities, membership in deprived minority groups, poor education, poor jobs, unavailability of medical care—amounting to what Berkman has called "cumulative deprivations" [4]—all would tend to prejudice adequacy of adaptation [40, 51, 68, 72, 97].

We also want to call attention to the importance of chance or adventitious factors, often ignored in psychological writings, in determining adaptation. Accidents of geography, history, politics, or economics may profoundly alter the lives of individuals or groups of individuals. For instance, let the reader consider the impact on individual adjustment of such monumental events as the Great Depression of the 1930's, World War II, the passage of social security legislation or of Medicare legislation, or the as yet unpredictable impact of a developing computer technology.

There is some evidence to suggest that those factors which contribute to good adaptation in younger years also continue to exercise determining influences in old age [68, 72]. This is not to deny individual variation in coping either particularly well or particularly poorly with the unique problem of old age.

## THE TASK OF ADAPTATION IN OLD AGE

What are the unique problems of old age? What are the specific tasks which biology and the culture have set up for the aged individual? These tasks are predictable only in a society that is reasonably stable. To the degree that ours is such a society and to the degree that it will remain so in the future, we can say that the tasks facing most aged persons in the United States are somewhat as follows. First, there is the problem of one's self-image or identity. The aged person must come face to face with the fact that he is now no longer young, no longer even middle-aged, but that instead he has entered the last phase of his life, the phase which precedes death. It is difficult to maintain a positive identity when one's usual props for such an identity, such as one's social and occupational role, have been taken away. Under these circumstances it may be difficult for the aged person to find a thread of continuity with his past identity. The degree to which this is a problem depends to a large extent on the nature of one's prior occupational status. For persons in some occupations retirement not only means an abrupt termination of income-producing activity but also the loss of a variety of job-connected social associations. For others, such as professional persons, the transition into retirement may be much more gradual, and even when retirement from work is complete, social contacts with one's professional associates frequently continue.

There is also an adaption to be made vis-à-vis one's relatives and friends. Age is a period of loss when, as one aged woman once put it, "All my friends have either gone to heaven or to Miami." It is a time when losses occur more frequently than the establishment of new relationships. But it is also a time of quietness and reflection when the individual can look back on his life, now more or less completed, gaining some distance from his own personal involvement with it, making some judgments about it, working toward the construction of a new and final identity.

## NORMATIVE REACTIONS TO OLD AGE

The actual transition from one phase of life to another is never automatic, simple, or quick. But the amount of upheaval or distress which results from a transition depends on whether the new phase is welcomed and whether adequate preparation has been made for it. Throughout earlier periods of life considerable preparation is made for each succeeding phase of the life cycle, and, as a result, the transitions are for the most part reasonably well accomplished by most people. For example, careful planning goes into readying the preschool child for his student career. As he advances through the years of formal education, he is constantly anticipating, or others are anticipating for him, his ultimate economic career. But during the working years very little preparation, formal or informal, is made for the last phase of the life cycle. Consequently, many of the changes which take place in old age come to be viewed as losses, pure and simple, in part because substitute ways of utilizing the person's energies have not been planned and alternative ways of maintaining security and self-esteem have not been developed.

But at other phases of life losses occur, too, and hitherto cherished rights and privileges (e.g., dependency, parental support, parental guidance) must be relinquished. Such losses in childhood, adolescence, and young adulthood are far outweighed by the gains realized (increased independence, prestige, power, sexual gratification). In contrast, the losses experienced in old age are more numerous and more visible, the gains fewer and less apparent.

But losses are already beginning to occur in middle age. In fact, middle age is ushered in by the end of the reproductive period. Sometime during middle age child-rearing activities cease. Toward the end of middle age or early in old age, cessation of work productivity occurs for the great majority of people in our culture. Unless retirement has been adequately anticipated, the loss of a job may lead to awareness of uselessness, and freedom becomes boredom.

Certain declines and losses are inevitable. It is an inescapable fact that all aged persons experience a decline in physical vigor and stamina [85]. There is a gradual decline in mental agility in all aged persons [5] (also see Chapter 11). Concomitant with retirement, many aged individuals experience significant declines in income, amounting for many to a drop of more than 50 percent from previous income levels (Chapter 4). The loss of loved ones through death becomes a frequent experience of old people and contributes to a growing social isolation and sometimes to intensively felt loneliness. Lastly, the death of others may bring forcefully to mind one's own impending and inevitable death.

But loss is only one side of the ledger. With planful anticipation, old age and retirement may bring with it many distinct achievements or gains. Taking events somewhat in the same order as we have before, let us look at this other side of the picture. The loss of reproductive capacity may bring for many a newly won sexual freedom, without fear of pregnancy or unwanted late-life offspring. The fact that the children are grown, that they have been educated and are able to make a life of their own, is for many a source of personal satisfaction. The retirement years, for individuals who have prepared for them, in terms of financial security and through lifelong participation in leisure activity, can indeed be "golden years." While the loss of physical abilities has no compensation as such, the expectations of society in this regard are lowered accordingly, and most older persons can still perform at levels which are in congruence with society's expectations. Much the same is true of the gradual decline in mental capacity. Here, too, the expectations of society are lowered as the age of a person advances. In regard to declines in income upon retirement, this is offset in part for many by a decline in work-related expenditures.

It is hardest of all to compensate for the loss of loved ones. This is especially true of the loss of the spouse. This loss is for many aged persons the most grievous assault of all. But even here new relationships can be established or old ones strengthened, either with other aged persons or with one or another of one's grown children. Finally, even one's own impending death can be dealt with by a philosophical attitude and by a "mannerly" acceptance of its inevitability [6] (also see Chapter 9).

## LONELINESS

In view of the ubiquity of loss in old age, it is often thought that the old are also frequently lonely. This is a natural expectation. But loneliness is not merely a matter of being alone. Solitude need not be experienced as loneliness, while loneliness can be felt in the presence of other people. For instance, persons residing in nursing homes often complain of loneliness, even though they are surrounded by people and, at a superficial level, are interacting with them. Loneliness is the awareness of an absence of meaningful integration with other individuals or groups of individuals, a consciousness of being excluded from the system of opportunities and rewards in which other people participate.

Loneliness is not confined to the old. It is a frequent, though often temporary, experience in adolescence; it is also experienced by many schizophrenic patients who have described feeling utterly and vastly alone while in the presence of others. The late Frieda Fromm-Reichmann devoted her last paper, published posthumously, to a discussion of loneliness, particularly as it is experienced by schizophrenic patients [31].

Only a few research studies of loneliness have been carried out. Shanas and her associates in their cross-national survey tried to study the problem by examining the relationship between subjectively experienced loneliness and social isolation in old age [84]. About half of those living alone reported they felt lonely only rarely or not at all. About three-fourths of those living with other people reported they were rarely or never lonely. Particularly vulnerable to feelings of loneliness were persons who had recently lost their spouses. Fairly frequent contacts with their children was a factor which seemed to mitigate somewhat feelings of loneliness among those living alone. Interestingly, persons who had been single all their lives complained of loneliness much less frequently than persons who were either still married or who had been widowed, separated, or divorced. Shanas concludes that it is loss (desolation), not isolation, which has the closer relationship to loneliness. It is also known that persons who have been separated, divorced, or widowed also have higher rates of suicide in old age than those with intact marriages. However, there have been no reported studies of the frequency of subjectively experienced loneliness among persons who have attempted or committed suicide.

It is obvious from what has been said that, as elsewhere in human affairs, given events in old age may have different meanings for different individuals. For some the transition into old age will be smooth and gratifying. For others there may be temporary upheavals in response to specific life circumstances, but psychic equilibrium will be reestablished eventually. For still others whose range of adaptive techniques has been narrow, or whose preparation for old age, both psychological and material, has been inadequate, or who have come to experience particularly grave misfortunes in old age, this period of life may lead to the development of overt psychiatric symptomatology requiring professional intervention.

In what follows a few epidemiological data in regard to psychiatric illness and psychiatric treatment in old age will be considered. Recent legislation which makes psychiatric treatment more readily available to increased numbers of aged persons than heretofore will also be discussed. The discussion will then turn to the minor and major psychiatric disorders occurring commonly in old age.

Psychiatric disorders in which organic disease of the brain underlies the behavorial disturbance will be dealt with in detail in Chapter 13. This chapter will deal principally with psychiatric disorders of functional (psychogenic) origin. It will conclude with a discussion of psychotherapeutic approaches which are especially adapted to the aged.

## EPIDEMIOLOGY

It is difficult to obtain precise data in regard to the incidence and prevalence of psychiatric disorders in old age. Different diagnostic criteria are used in different studies, and the cutoff between what is seen as still within normal limits and what is seen as pathological is by no means uniform. An additional methodological problem exists in that we do not know how the findings from a particular study population in a particular geographic area apply to the aged generally; i.e., we do not know how representative the findings are. Nevertheless, the data which are available deserve examination. They tend to fall into three broad categories: (1) data in respect to aged individuals residing in or newly admitted to public and private mental hospitals and psychiatric wards of general hospitals; (2) data in respect to aged persons receiving psychiatric care on an outpatient basis; and (3) data in respect to the proportion of individuals living in the community who manifest varying degrees of psychiatric disturbance, as measured most commonly by some type of psychiatric interview schedule. As might be expected, the findings from these three categories of studies are quite divergent, although the data from different studies in any one category show some consistency.

Slightly fewer than 1 percent of persons over age 65 are hospitalized in private or public mental institutions [49, 94]. Of these, roughly half were admitted for psychiatric disorders arising in old age (principally organic brain disease—see Chapter 13), while the other half are individuals admitted for functional psychosis, principally schizophrenia, who have grown old in the hospital. An additional 3 percent of old people are residing in nursing homes, homes for the aged, and geriatric or chronic disease hospitals [7]; probably about half of these suffer from significant psychiatric disturbances. Combining these data we can say that between 2 and 3 percent of old people live in institutions as a result of psychiatric illness. Additional information on institutional care of the aged is presented in Chapter 14.

While persons over age 65 make up nearly 30 percent of patients in public mental hospitals and 11 percent of those in private psychiatric hospitals, they account for only 2 percent of the patients seen in psychiatric outpatient clinics [35]. In terms of rates of utilization of outpatient facilities this amounts to only about one-tenth of 1 percent of old people receiving outpatient treatment. These figures do not include persons receiving ambulatory care from psychiatrists in private practice, but the number so involved is extremely small. We can conclude from these data that the aged are markedly underrepresented in outpatient or intermediate care facilities. This point will be discussed later. The observation assumes added significance, however, when we look at the findings on prevalence of psychiatric symptoms in community samples.

A number of surveys have also been conducted in this country and abroad to determine what proportion of old people living in the community, in addition to those already in institutions, have psychiatric disorders. Table 1 illustrates the range of findings in different studies.

The composite picture that emerges from the several studies is that some 5 percent of old people living in the community are either psychotic or else have severe psychopathology; when persons with neurotic and personality disorders are added this figure increases to some 15 percent; and when all degrees of psychiatric impairment are included, ranging from the mild to the severe, then from 25 to nearly 60 percent of the aged may be affected [57, 78].

It is important to note that the community surveys reported thus far have all been cross-sectional studies, assessing psychiatric disability of a population at only one point in time. Sizable longi-

TABLE 1.   *Prevalence of psychopathology in old age*

|                            |        | Degree of Pathology        |                               |
|----------------------------|--------|----------------------------|-------------------------------|
| Author, Location           | Severe | Moderate and Severe | Mild, Moderate, and Severe |
| Pasamanick, Baltimore      | 5%     | 12%                        | —                             |
| Lowenthal, San Francisco   | 5%     | 15%                        | —                             |
| Kay, Newcastle             | 8%     | 26%                        | —                             |
| Nielsen, Samsø             | 7%     | 22%                        | —                             |
| Leighton, "Stirling County"| —      | —                          | 50–60%                        |

Sources: [46, 51, 57, 64, 70].

tudinal studies of the problems of psychiatric disorders in sizable populations of old people are obviously desirable although the methodological problems are enormous. Further, such survey studies as have been reported do not differentiate psychopathology arising for the first time in old age from disorders continuing into old age from younger years. Nor do most of the studies make a distinction between organically based psychiatric disorders and those of functional origin.

Survey studies, such as the Leighton and Leighton studies and the Midtown study, indicate that the proportion of persons who have any degree of psychopathology does not increase significantly with age [51, 89]. However, the proportion of individuals suffering from psychiatric disorders requiring hospitalization increases dramatically with advancing age. The major cause for this increase is the increasing proportion of individuals suffering from organic psychoses in old age rather than an increase in functional psychoses. Organically based psychiatric disorders account for an increasingly larger proportion of the total amount of pathology. In the age group 65 to 74 more than half of the persons residing in mental hospitals have a functional diagnosis, while in the age group 75 and over this ratio is reversed, and organic psychosis now accounts for more than half of those in psychiatric hospitals [78].

It is one of the most interesting aspects of the epidemiological data mentioned thus far that the aged either seek or receive very little psychiatric treatment on an ambulatory basis. They either receive no psychiatric attention at all, or they are hospitalized for lengthy periods of time, often for life. This lack of intermediate care of aged persons is a puzzling phenomenon. It is not explained by a mere lack of intermediate care facilities, i.e., a lack of out-patient clinics, although this may be a contributing factor in some locations. Several other factors may also be important. Perhaps a certain amount of psychopathology is more easily tolerated by the aged themselves or by those who live with the aged because it is seen as part of "normal aging" [87]. Also, as Estes has pointed out in Chapter 6, there is a general reluctance on the part of the aged to seek medical examination or care; he has emphasized the attitudinal as well as economic and logistical impediments. There may also be generational differences; the acceptance of psychiatry as a legitimate medical speciality may be much less in the current generation of aged than among younger people. Finally, there may be a reluctance on the part of some therapists to take old people into treatment, because they themselves hold gerontophobic at-titudes (see Chapter 1), or because they have the mistaken notion that the aged do not respond to therapy or, more simply, because few psychiatrists or therapists have had adequate training in the techniques of treatment which are especially applicable to aged persons (also see Chapter 17).

## PREVENTIVE PSYCHIATRY IN OLD AGE

From what has been said it is obvious that many aged persons with psychiatric difficulties receive no psychiatric care until their disorders are far advanced. This raises the question of what preven-tive steps can be taken to reduce the prevalence of severe psychi-atric illness in old age. It is still an unsettled question whether psychiatric disorders can indeed be prevented at any age. In the last decade, however, public health concepts of primary, secondary, and tertiary prevention (also defined as prevention, early treatment, and rehabilitation, respectively) have been introduced into psychiatric thinking [16]. According to Caplan "primary prevention is a community concept. It involves lowering the rate of new cases of mental disorders in a population over a certain period by counteracting harmful circumstances before they have had a chance to produce illness. It does not seek to prevent any specific person from becoming sick. Instead, it seeks to reduce the risk of a whole population so that, although some may become ill, their number will be reduced." Caplan goes on to say that preventive psychiatry deals with general influences prevailing in a "population at risk" (such as the aged).

The existence of even severe pathology is generally not sufficient to lead to psychiatric hospitalization; a constellation of psychopathology plus a series of adverse environmental circumstances —e.g., death of a family member, physical illness, social isolation— is necessary before hospitalization is effected [56]. Thus while efforts to provide early psychiatric care for many more old people would no doubt be valuable, early help along a variety of other lines (the provision of good medical care, good housing, adequate retirement income, continued contact with remaining family members) may be equally significant in reducing at least some forms of psychiatric illness in old age. It has been the experience of medicine over the past 100 years that health measures focused on entire communities have been far more successful in reducing illness and mortality than have measures aimed only at individual patients.

## PAYING FOR PSYCHIATRIC CARE IN OLD AGE

Kreps in Chapter 4 has pointed out that a large proportion of old people have incomes which place them below the "poverty line," while Estes in Chapter 6 has discussed financial constraints on good medical care for the aged. In recognition of the aged's vulnerable position in this regard, Congress has recently passed legislation to lighten the financial burdens imposed by illness on the aged. While many readers are probably familiar with the basic legislation, it may be useful to review it briefly with an emphasis on provisions that apply to psychiatric care specifically.

The Social Security Amendments of 1965 (Public Law 89–97) created Medicare, a program of health insurance for the aged which became effective July 1, 1966. It consists of two parts. Part A—hospital insurance—provides for payment of the cost of almost all the services ordinarily furnished by hospitals, by extended care facilities, and by home health services. Definite time limits on the various coverages are fixed by law; thus hospital benefits are limited to 90 days during any one "spell of illness." This insurance plan is financed by social security contributions by persons still in the work force and by their employers. Part B—medical insurance—is a voluntary program in which individuals pay monthly premiums currently at $4.00 which are matched by funds from the Federal government. This insurance helps pay for physician services in the hospital, for certain other services not included in the hospital insurance, and for outpatient services. After an annual deductible of $50.00 has been paid by the patient, the insurance pays 80 percent of "reasonable charges" for the covered services [88].

In regard to psychiatric care, the limits of coverage are drawn much more narrowly than for general medical care [35, 39]. The hospital insurance part of Medicare covers inpatient services in psychiatric hospitals and psychiatric services in general hospitals. However, a lifetime limit of 190 days has been placed on coverage of inpatient service in mental hospitals, a provision designed to limit costs as well as to encourage active treatment rather than custodial care of mentally ill persons. No such lifetime limitation exists for other illnesses. This lifetime limit, however, does not apply to psychiatric care given in a general hospital. The reason for this distinction is that such care can generally be assumed to be active treatment, while that furnished in many mental hospitals, after the initial period of hospitalization, is more likely to be custodial. Custodial care is specifically excluded from coverage under the provisions of the statute. In fact, the present administration has recommended in its recent budget message to Congress a further reduction in the lifetime limits on psychiatric hospital care, from 190 to 120 days. To date, however, no definite action has been taken on this recommendation. Part B of Medicare also covers psychiatric outpatient treatment, but again the limits of coverage have been extremely narrowly drawn. The insurance coverage for such care, after the $50 deductible has been paid by the patient, is limited to 50 percent of actual expenses, or $250 per year, which-ever is less. This limitation is unfortunate since relatively inexpen-sive outpatient treatment can probably prevent relatively expensive psychiatric hospitalization in some cases. What impact Medicare will eventually have on patterns of utilization of treatment facili-ties and hence, on costs of the program, is a matter of great in-terest. Special studies by governmental agencies are currently under way to seek answers to these important questions. Once they are available, perhaps some modification of the present benefit struc-ture will be possible.

It should be realized that the legislation passed in 1965 addressed itself only to improving the ability of old people to pay for needed psychiatric services. It did not deal with the manpower problem at all. Increased ability to pay for services can only increase the total demand for such services, and, unless increased manpower needs are also attended to, deficiencies in services to other segments of the population are likely to occur.


## THE EXPERIENCE OF ANXIETY IN THE AGED

Anxiety plays a central role in most theoretical systems in psy-chiatry [23, 29, 92]. It is generally viewed as the result of intra-personal and/or interpersonal conflict, or as the result of threaten-ing external circumstances. Anxiety is a complicated psychophys-iological response. As used in this context, it may be defined as a subjectively experienced state of dread anticipation in which the object of one's dread is only vaguely defined; the term also includes the bodily manifestation of this uneasy mental state: muscular tenseness, restlessness, rapid heart rate, excessive sweating—all signs of preparedness for fight or flight. The psychophysiological manifestations of anxiety undoubtedly change with advancing age, possibly paralleling those of alteration in the nervous and endocrine systems. It appears that response to an anxiety-producing stimulus in the elderly is often delayed and may be increased or decreased, depending on which manifestation of anxiety is being measured. Furthermore, the same stimuli which produce anxiety in younger persons may not produce the same reaction in the elderly, and vice-versa [22, 74, 86].

From a practical point, anxiety is a common symptom in old age. In may be present intermittently in response to a specific stress situation; it may be present chronically in some individuals; or it may be a concomitant of other psychiatric disorders, to be discussed below. Anxiety may be experienced overtly or it may give rise, with or without being experienced overtly, to a variety of other symptoms or defenses.

When a precipitating circumstance for the anxiety can be determined, an exploration of the possible alternative ways of dealing with the situation need to be explored with the patient. Actually, a certain amount of anxiety in a given situation can improve alertness and efficiency for coping. Even a certain amount of anger can promote readiness for action. However, when fear and anger become extreme or persistent, they tend to have a disorganizing effect on the adaptive efforts of the individual.

Often clarification of the nature of the problem, or the discovery that the problem the person is facing is one which is common among old people, is enough to reduce the level of anxiety to manageable levels or to a point at which the individual's own coping devices can take over and resolve the difficulty. At other times concrete help may be needed. Additional family members may need to be involved, or the patient may need to be referred to other social agencies for help in arranging financial support, rearranging living conditions, initiating medical care, or other concrete help giving (see Chapter 16).

But anxiety in old age may also be related not to a specific circumstance but to the more general problem of growing old. Old people are apt to be experiencing increasingly frequent feelings of helplessness vis-à-vis life's circumstances. They can no longer manage on their own. They are dependent on others, a situation which evokes in many feelings of impotence, worthlessness, abandonment, and rage. The therapist can guide the patient toward a gradual acceptance of this dependency as age-appropriate, while at the same time identifying persons in the older person's environment upon whom he can indeed depend—adult children, a still capable spouse, a trusted paid companion or servant, or, if hospitalized, a familiar, rather than a constantly changing nursing staff, or even a trusted therapist. Dependency can be tolerated more easily if the individual can be sure that the support upon which he is relying will not be withdrawn at any moment. The provision of a stable physical and psychological environment can reduce anxiety. By a stable environment, however, we do not mean one which is devoid of stimulation.

It is important that, whenever possible, anxiety be relieved relatively promptly, since persistent anxiety can have a marked alienating effect on other persons in the old person's environment. Marked anxiety, and the irritability which often goes with anxiety, tend to evoke negative rejecting reactions from those persons around the aged individual, thus further increasing his interpersonal estrangement. In addition, such alienation robs him of further sympathetic interest and dependent supplies.

When simple psychotherapeutic intervention or environmental manipulation is insufficient, tranquilizing drugs may be used. However, several cautions about drug-giving to the aged should be expressed. First, drugs should not be given which impair cortical functioning since many aged already have minimal organic brain disease or since their reserve capacity has been reduced. For instance, drugs in the barbiturate category or other central nervous system depressants are generally contraindicated. Second, the aged are generally far more sensitive to the usual dosages of psychoactive drugs, and the lowest possible dosage which still produces the desired effects must be used. For nonpsychotic anxiety in old age chlordiazepoxide (Librium) in dosages of 5 mg. twice daily has been proved clinically useful. This dosage will often result in decreased anxiety as well as in mild elevation of mood. Higher dosages may be tried, but only under close supervision. Side effects of this drug include drowsiness, ataxia, and, occasionally, syncope. Since the rate of accidents is already high among aged persons, great care should be taken to avoid falls or other accidents. When the aged do fall the likelihood of their sustaining a serious fracture is markedly increased due to the age-related demineralization (osteoporosis) of their bones.

Anxiety is essentially an unstable affective state, designed for emergency situations. If the problems creating the anxiety cannot be resolved, psychological homeostatic mechanisms go into effect which seek to reduce the level of anxiety, usually by the elaboration of alternate defenses of symptoms. The prompt treatment of clinically significant anxiety is therefore important preventively since it can forestall the development of more troublesome or more fixed symptomatology.

In what follows it will be seen that the defenses used preferentially or most commonly by the aged are relatively primitive ones. Primitive defenses are "security operations," as Sullivan called them [92], which became available in early infancy and which are relatively simple but also poorly focused and nonspecific. This preferential use of primitive defense mechanisms is another way of saying that the overall capacity for adaptation of the older individual has been reduced, in part because of at least minimal cerebral deterioration, partly because of psychosocial losses which have already been mentioned and which lead to loss of self-esteem.

## SLEEP DISTURBANCES

Elderly persons frequently complain of sleep disturbances. Some complain of difficulty going to sleep, some of insufficient sleep, and others of restless sleep, with frequent awakenings. The complaint of sleeping too much is more often the concern of relatives and friends rather than of patients. Many older patients who complain of sleep problems are worried that poor sleep will lead to serious illness. These sleep disturbances may be related to anxiety in some instances, but in others they may reflect age-related changes in the physiology of sleep.

Although variations and disorders of sleep and activities during sleep have always been of considerable importance to physicians, until recently there was very little information of clinical relevance [18, 48]. Most physicians are aware that there are at least four major stages of sleep and that stage one, rapid eye movement (REM) sleep, is the stage of sleep in which dreams are most likely to occur. Further, it is appreciated that there are four to five REM episodes during a night's sleep and that these REM periods become progressively longer during nocturnal sleep. Sleep patterns and sleep requirements change throughout the life-span. A newborn infant sleeps between 16 and 17 hours a day. Within the first 6 months in most infants there is a gradual decline, but at least 12 hours is the usual pattern. By age three, 10 hours a night is the common rule, and the necessity for daytime naps is decreasing. During adolescence it is not unusual to encounter trouble waking up. This difficulty is probably the result of physiological changes. In young adulthood, and, in particular, in middle life and the later years, there are some individuals who claim an increased need for sleep, and some a decreased need. However, it is doubtful that any elderly person in reasonably good health requires more than 8 to 9 hours of sleep per night. It has been reported recently that men between the ages of 50 and 60 who sleep more than 9 hours a day have twice the death rate from stroke as those who sleep only 7 hours. If the men sleep more than 10 hours, they are four times as likely to have a stroke [37].

In elderly subjects there are some important changes in patterns of sleeping. Stage four sleep, that is, deep sleep, virtually disappears, and older people require a longer period to fall asleep [43, 44]. Their sleep is lighter, and more frequent awakenings occur. Feinberg has recently reported that these changes are still more pronounced in persons with significant organic brain disease [28]. It is important that people, as they pass into the latter part of their life-span, recognize that the process of going to sleep lengthens and that they, as part of the normal process, will be aware of more frequent awakenings. However, both of these phenomena are exacerbated if there is pain or other discomfort. In such cases an analgesic alone or in combination with a hypnotic can help an elderly person have a restful sleep.

Many of the so-called psychotropic drugs, including stimulants, hypnotics, and antidepressants, seem to alter the frequency and duration of REM periods, either during the time that medication is given or after it is withdrawn [66, 67]. These matters require additional elucidation. Barbiturates produce a sleep much like normal sleep, but unfortunately the elderly person often has a barbiturate hangover the next morning; task performances may be impaired for several hours after awakening. Paraldehyde continues to be a very reliable medication for assuring a reasonable length of sleep. It also appears that methyprylon (Noludar) may be particularly useful for elderly patients.

Sleep not only serves a normal physiological function but provides a period of escape from many stresses of life for some persons. Chronic insomnia, on the other hand, can most commonly be attributed to unsolved emotional conflict involving feelings of guilt and hostility with fear of retaliation. There is wide variation in the amount of sleep required by various individuals. A few persons can get along on as little as 5 or 6 hours a night, while the majority require a minimum of approximately 8 hours. Busse *et al.* found that, in a group of subjects over the age of 60, 7 to 10 percent used sleeping pills habitually [12]. In various groups of apparently well-adjusted community subjects over the age of 60, 20 to 40 percent of each series occasionally used sleeping pills. In elderly subjects who were free of physical pain, those who used sleeping pills excessively were found to have many other neurotic complaints and to be poorly adjusted socially. Kutner and his co-workers reported that 50 percent complained of chronic insomnia [50]. Nearly one-fourth of his subjects usually awoke tired and exhausted. This is somewhat in contrast to the study by Ginsberg who found that 18.6 percent of elderly nonpsychotic residents of a county home complained of insomnia [34]. In fact, sleep problems were the lowest on the list of ten complaints of these elderly county home residents.


## HYPOCHONDRIASIS

Hypochondriasis is an anxious preoccupation with one's own body or a portion of one's own body which the patient believes to be either diseased or functioning improperly. For many years hypochondriasis has been considered a syndrome rather than a distinct disease entity. But recently the second edition of the *Diagnostic and Statistical Manual of Mental Disorders* of the American Psychiatric Association (DSM-II) has established hypochondriacal neurosis as a separate neurotic condition [1]. The symptom constellation of hypochondriasis also continues to be described as a feature of other psychiatric disorders, such as some of the psychoses, psychophysiological reactions, or personality disturbances.

Hypochondriasis is frequent among elderly patients, particularly women [20]. Much of the early work on hypochondriacal patients was carried out by one of the present authors (E. W. B.) in a special clinic for such patients in a large university medical center. A survey of the patients in this clinic found that more than half of these patients were over age 60 and the majority were women [8]. Efforts in this clinic were devoted to the elucidation of the dynamics of hypochondriasis and to the development of a therapeutic approach. After considerable experimentation certain techniques were found to be quite effective, and these will be discussed below [9].


### The Dynamics of Hypochondriasis

In order to understand why some persons develop physical complaints as a way of solving psychological problems, an understanding of the "sick role" in our society is needed. In most Western cultures great emphasis is placed upon personal independence, financial success, and social prestige. There is little tolerance for the nonachiever or the person who is a failure. When a person falls ill, however, a different set of rules applies. Talcott Parsons has outlined the sick role in our society as follows: First, the sick person is exempted from his normal social responsibilities if his illness is severe enough; second, it is assumed that the sick person became sick through no fault of his own and that he therefore has a right to be taken care of; third, it is assumed that he will desire to get well, in fact that he is under actual obligation to want to get well; and fourth, it is assumed that he will seek competent medical help and cooperate fully in the process of getting well [69].

It is fair to say that society regards the person who becomes emotionally ill with much greater ambivalence. While gross psychosis may be acceptable as an excuse for nonperformance, more minor, so-called neurotic complaints are often seen by the society and by many patients themselves as an unacceptable admission of personal failure.

Escape from personal failure into the sick role is available at all ages but seems to be particularly frequently used by elderly individuals. This can be successful for varying periods of time. But if no organic illness exists, family members and associates usually recognize this and at such a point their attitudes toward the "sick" person begin to change. Recognition that the excuse of illness is physically unjustified makes people feel they are being exploited. No doubt most people have at times during their lives "played sick" to avoid trouble. Since they have used this defense only to a limited degree, they resent a chronic complainer who does not respect the same limits. As a result, the hypochondriac's problems become greater when friends and relatives become suspicious of the justification for his complaints.

Three psychological mechanisms play a major role in the dynamics of hypochondriasis: (1) a withdrawal of psychic interest from other persons or objects and a centering of this interest upon oneself, one's own body, and its functioning; (2) a shift of anxiety from a specific psychic area to a less threatening concern with bodily disease; and (3) use of physical symptoms as a means of self-punishment and atonement for unacceptable hostile or vengeful feelings toward persons close to the individual. An awareness of these mechanisms makes the patient's complaints more understandable and contributes to the development of a meaningfully designed treatment program. For instance, it is easy to see why an older worker who has had no other interest except his work, is a likely subject for the development of hypochondriasis upon retirement. Normal bodily functions, for instance, breathing and elimination, which he ignored in the past, may now merit as much attention as did his work before retirement. Or, elderly people who experience anxiety over loss of social prestige or financial security may find it more tolerable to shift their anxiety to concern over bodily functioning. More than one of these mechanisms may be active in a given patient.

*Treatment of Hypochondriasis*

Because treatment approaches to hypochondriasis are rarely presented in textbooks or papers, they will be discussed here in considerable detail. The treatment of hypochondriasis can be frustrating and time-consuming. It can be less so if a few techniques of proved value are used and if they are used as soon as the physician suspects that he is dealing with hypochondriasis. Delay in recognition can seriously impede effective treatment.

Before going on to a discussion of techniques which have proved useful, a few remarks will be made about techniques which are at best of doubtful value in dealing with this particular group of patients. Ordinarily, giving the patient a full explanation of his medical condition serves as a reassurance. This is not true in hypochondriasis. To explain the patient's physical complaints in psychiatric language is to rob him with one stroke of a carefully designed defense system, thereby undermining his self-esteem. The usual reaction to such explanations is a further increase in the patient's complaints. In addition, the relationship between the patient and the physician is seriously jeopardized. The patient may become extremely hostile or may seek medical help elsewhere.

Even less specific explanations of how emotional upsets can sometimes cause physical symptoms are likely to be unsuccessful. The patient may agree that this can happen to some people, but he is sure that such an explanation does not apply to him.

Another technique which has been tried without striking success has been to give the patient a specific organic diagnosis, then treat him for that disorder and suggest that he will get well within a certain period of time. Usually, improvement does occur, to varying degrees and for a varying period of time. But inevitably a reaction sets in, for the patient still requires his illness as a defense. New complaints develop, and old ones return in an exaggerated form. The patient will return to his physician who in desperation may start the process all over, only to fail again.

A particular caution should be expressed about surgical procedures for the relief of symptoms in hypochondriacal patients. It never helps the patient to have a scar which testifies to the fact that a competent physician believed that he had something wrong with his body. In addition, the operative scar can become the focus of new symptoms which are then attributed to "complications" or "adhesions" following the surgical procedure.

### Effective Techniques

Some techniques of positive value will next be discussed. In order for the hypochondriacal person to continue to live with his family and in society, his psychological defenses must be maintained and the physician must respect this need. He will need to listen attentively to the patient's veritable "organ recital," but until a positive relationship between physician and patient has been established, little can be gained from seeking to direct the patient into a discussion of areas of emotional conflict. A more important point to be made by the physician is that the patient is indeed sick and that the physician is taking care of him.

PLACEBOS.   In order to make this point more clearly medication or a placebo may be prescribed. In doing so the physician must be careful to avoid utilizing any medication which is likely to produce side effects, since this would only complicate an already confused clinical picture. Particular attention must be given to avoidance of drugs which have been used by the patient without success previously. The drug or placebo must be given with an assured manner, since these patients are alert to any expression of doubt on the part of the physician. This technique may be criticized in that it implies to the hypochondriacal patient that he does have an organic illness, however slight. This criticism must be accepted, but in turn it should be pointed out that many hypochondriacs actually do have changes in their physiological functioning which can respond to medication. The technique is extremely worthwhile in establishing a good doctor-patient relationship. It is useful principally because of its symbolic value. A hypochondriacal complaint is a distress signal, and the patient's anxiety may be reduced and his self-esteem increased by knowing that a highly regarded professional person is "taking care of me." Thus the placebo (Latin for "I will please") can symbolically represent to the patient security and satisfaction. The question may also be raised about the difference between the use of medication and surgical procedures. Very simply, operations leave scars which not only can permanently alter a patient's self image but also can lead to new complaints of "postoperative" complications. It must be admitted, however, that on very rare occasions placebos, too, may lead to complaints of "side effects" on the part of the patient.

HANDLING OF RELATIVES. Relatives, particularly those who have begun to suspect that the patient's symptoms are emotional, not physical, in origin may request an interview with the doctor in order to confirm their suspicions. Under these circumstances it is probably best to avoid saying that the patient's symptoms are of psychological origin. A comment to the effect that the patient is ill, that he is worried, and needs help, and that the doctor will do what he can for him, is far more helpful. The doctor may also seek to involve the relative in the patient's treatment by asking him to be more accepting, if not more sympathetic toward the patient's complaints. This will tend to reduce the negative feedback the patient receives from his surroundings and lessen his need to rely on physical complaints. One of the surest ways for the patient to lose confidence in the doctor is to be told by a relative that the doctor really thinks the patient's complaints are imaginary.

HANDLING OF INTERVIEWS.   Generally speaking it is wise to see a hypochondriacal patient at least once a week for the first several times. Later the time between appointments can be lengthened. When an appointment is given to hypochondriacal patients it is interesting how many will respond by saying that the time suggested is inconvenient for them and ask that another time be arranged. This is usually a way of testing the physician to determine the extent of his interest in the patient. Generally, the physician should insist that the patient adhere to the selected time for his appointment and also adhere to the therapeutic regimen. The patient will depart with new confidence, buoyed up by the fact that he has both medicine and another appointment. His anxiety concerning the possibility that his illness would be challenged has been reduced.

The length of the interview is necessarily limited. Although the first contact may require considerable time, return visits can be reduced to 15 to 20 minutes. The patient should be told how long his next appointment will last. This will discourage hypochondriacal patients from making bids for additional time. Not infrequently, when the duration of the interview has not been specified, the patient, sensing that the interview is about to be terminated, may "suddenly" remember something very important, thereby seeking to extend the period of contact with the doctor. If the diagnosis has been properly made, the important information can usually be taken up at the next visit.

When the patient returns for his second appointment, he finds that the physician's attitude has not changed. The doctor continues to be an interested and understanding listener. When the patient expresses hostility against his previous physicians, the present doctor must restrain himself from defending his colleagues and must confine his remarks to recognition of the patient's previous experiences as being both upsetting and disappointing to him. No diagnosis or prognosis is ventured by the physician. This restraint is difficult for the average doctor because this is foreign to his usual way of handling patients.

As progress from treatment is seen, the physician will become aware of a shift away from the patient's physical complaints to a greater emphasis on psychic conflicts related to family, work, and friends. When this change becomes apparent, treatment can follow two paths.

1. The patient may gradually lose the intensity of his preoccupation with his imaginary illness as a result of the confidence gained in the doctor-patient relationship. He may have exacerbations of his symptoms when his life problems increase, but in the meantime he can return to more active and more efficient participation in his social environment.

2. A still brighter outlook can be anticipated if the patient begins to develop some insight into his situation. When he begins to notice that his symptoms become worse after an argument, for instance, he may then be ready to face his problems more directly in counseling interviews or in psychotherapy. As a result, he may be able to abandon his physical complaints altogether.

Especially with older hypochondriacal patients, however, physicians must remain alert to the possibility that true organic illness can develop. Included in the high cost of being neurotic is the distinct possibility that physical illness may be overlooked because all the multiple symptoms previously complained of had been on a functional basis.

*Somatic Complaints in Nonmedical Settings*

What has been said thus far about chronic complainers applies principally to patients who have sought medical care repeatedly. Studies of community elderly, however, revealed that some 30 percent of them also had high levels of bodily concern [13, 58]. This term, high bodily concern, as used in the study did not imply anything about the basis of this concern; it might be reality-based, consistent with the presence of organic disease; or it might be of neurotic origin. Of the 30 percent with high bodily concern, one-half had neurotically based concerns, and at least another fourth had a physical basis for their concern but with some neurotic overlay. Interestingly, most of these patients did not seek medical care but used their concern instead as a *social crutch* in an attempt to defend against anxiety, and to solicit the sympathy, forgiveness, and help of others.

## DEPRESSION

Recurrent periods of depression, lasting from a few minutes to a few days, are common in old age. Busse and his colleagues have reported findings in a study of "normal community volunteers" over the age of 60. The study revealed that elderly persons were aware of the fact that they were experiencing more frequent and more annoying depressive periods than earlier in life. The subjects reported that during such episodes they felt discouraged, worried, or disgusted with their own uselessness, often to such a degree that they felt there was no reason to continue to live. Only a small number of subjects in the study admitted entertaining thoughts of suicide; but a larger percentage stated that during such depressive periods they would welcome death if it were a painless one [2, 11].

The dynamics of depression of course are well known and will be mentioned here only briefly. The most widely held of these is that depression is a pathological response to the loss of person or object which had been held ambivalently by the individual [61]. It postulates introjection of the lost object into the self and the directing of hostile impulses toward that object in the form of self-accusations, self-blame, and guilt. However, depressions may also occur in response to the "loss of narcissistic supplies." Here self-directed hostility and guilt are less of a problem. It would appear that in general in the depressions of old age guilt is a relatively unimportant dynamic force [10]. Their depressions instead seem to be more commonly linked with the loss of narcissistic supplies. The individual feels that he has lost everything, that nothing remains. Guilt mechanisms seem to play a more prominent role in the depressions of young people and in the more severe agitated psychotic depressions in old age to the degree that these are not related to biological factors.

First to be discussed is a treatment program applicable to the relatively mild depressive reactions occurring in older persons who are still able to live in their communities, and whose depressions are not of sufficient severity to require hospitalization. Precipitating circumstances for the depressive episodes can often be identified. Some of the losses likely to occur in old age have already been detailed.

A treatment approach to the milder depressions of old age is based on the assumptions that they have occurred in response to the loss of dependent or narcissistic supplies. An effort is therefore made to reestablish new or alternate sources of such supplies. In this the doctor can be one source. His interest and attention to the patient's problem can instill a renewed feeling of self-worth in the patient. In addition efforts should be made to see that the patient maintains or regains contacts with other persons in his own environment, that he participates in activities which are useful and productive. He may also be encouraged to have contact with other persons of his own age. This may initially have a further depressing effect on the elderly person, but with time he may discover common interests and problems in other old people and therefore see himself as less deprived.

As an illustration of the impact of continued activity it may be pointed out that in the above mentioned study from 44 to 48 percent of persons who were unemployed or retired experienced depressive episodes; among persons who continued to work, however, this percentage was only 25 percent. One should be cautious in concluding that work alone plays some vital role in preventing or decreasing the number of depressive episodes. It is possible that there are fundamental differences which permit some persons to continue work and to be relatively immune to depressive episodes. Other important defenses against depression would seem to be planned creative and recreational activity if these are a continuation of previous participation in such activities. Clinical experience has shown that the taking up of so-called hobbies upon retirement is of little value to elderly persons unless it results in the production of something which is appreciated by others. A hobby which contributes nothing to others but merely occupies the time of an elderly person is in the long run unsatisfactory.

*Depressive Psychoses*

While minor depressive reactions are extremely frequent in old age, major depressive reactions, often of psychotic proportions, also occur. Depressive psychoses may arise for the first time in old age, or they may represent recurring episodes of depression in persons who have previously experienced affective disturbances.

In private psychiatric hospitals patients with affective psychoses, particularly depressions, make up roughly one-half of newly admitted patients over age 60 or 65 [62, 82, 90]. In public mental hospitals they constitute a much smaller fraction, somewhere around 10 percent [57]. While attention to diagnosis of mental disorder is frequently deemphasized in current psychiatric thinking, correct diagnosis of the type of mental disorder, particularly a differentiation between organically and functionally caused disturbances, is of extreme importance in old age. The outcome of treatment in the affective psychoses is good, while the prognosis of the organically caused psychiatric syndromes is much less favorable (see Chapter 13).

Again, the major signs and symptoms of affective psychosis of the depressed type are well known [36, 71]. There is a pervasively melancholy mood, drastic reduction in self-esteem, a pessimistic outlook about the future; there may be frequent crying spells or, more rarely, an inability to cry. These symptoms may be coupled with certain of the biological signs characteristic of depression:

loss of appetite, weight loss, constipation, marked sleep disturbances, and sometimes either marked psychomotor agitation or
retardation. Sometimes severe depression in old age can mimic
an organic brain disease state. Patients who are depressed may be
unable to answer questions. They may be so slow in their thinking
that they cannot perform simple mathematical problems or they
cannot correctly produce information about their orientation in
time and place. Standardized psychological tests, however, if
administered slowly, will demonstrate that no organic impairment
exists and that the seeming dementia is a result of an inability to
produce answers rather than an inability to formulate answers.

### Treatment of Severe Depression in Old Age

The treatment of the major depressive psychoses in old age is
not markedly different from the treatment of these disorders in
younger years [27, 71]. When it is determined that the patient is
indeed profoundly depressed, he should be hospitalized, for two
reasons. First, the risk of suicide is great in elderly depressed
persons (see below); second, the depth of depression can be evaluated and treatment can be administered most effectively in a
hospital setting.

PSYCHOTHERAPY. Psychotherapy may be used as an adjunct to
other forms of therapy or, more rarely, it alone may be sufficient.
It has several serious limitations, however. (1) Profoundly depressed patients have great difficulty in engaging in ongoing psychotherapy, particularly therapy which depends on a continued
dialogue between patient and therapist. (2) Results can be
achieved only slowly, if at all, thus leaving the patient exposed to
suffering and to suicidal risks for needlessly long periods. (3) Since
the psychotherapeutic process is a slow one, and since spontaneous
remissions of depressions occur, it is difficult to tell whether improvement has occurred spontaneously or as a result of treatment.
Occasionally profoundly depressed aged persons do improve dramatically merely upon being hospitalized, responding perhaps to

the overall care-giving milieu. In such cases a real danger exists that the improvement is only temporary. If the patient is discharged to the same environment, without making provision for someone to continue to give interested care, relapse may be prompt. For example:

An 80-year-old widow living alone in an apartment was admitted to a psychiatric hospital following a suicide attempt. She said she had become deeply discouraged after the death of her pet parakeet. It was clear from psychiatric interviews that the parakeet had symbolized her remaining involvement with her environment. In the hospital she improved quickly, without specific therapy. She was discharged home in good spirits. Two weeks later she committed suicide by putting a plastic bag over her head.

DRUG THERAPY. Since 1957 a number of drugs with antidepressant properties have been introduced [45]. These drugs, while somewhat less effective than electroconvulsive therapy (ECT) in terminating depressive episodes, do have certain distinct advantages over ECT. Drug therapy is a more flexible and more convenient form of treatment, and one which is more readily accepted by patients and by their families. The compounds currently in greatest use are the nonmonamine oxidase inhibitors, such as imipramine (Tofranil), desipramine (Norpramine, Pertofrane), amitriptyline (Elavil), and nortriptyline (Aventyl). For younger patients the usual starting dose of these drugs is 25 mg. three to four times daily, to be increased if no side effects develop. For older persons the starting dosage should be somewhat lower. The central nervous system of aged individuals seems to be far more sensitive to psychoactive drugs in general, and its response to the antidepressant drugs is no exception. If the drugs are well tolerated, the dosages may be increased slightly, but they should not reach the high daily levels which may be administered safely to younger patients. The antidepressant compounds mentioned have multiple pharmacological actions, the antidepressant action being only one of many. Put another way, these drugs may have multiple side effects, and the doctor must be thoroughly familiar with them before prescribing.

ELECTROCONVULSIVE THERAPY. When hospitalization alone, supportive psychotherapy, or antidepressant drugs have been ineffective, electroconvulsive therapy should be considered. Research findings are that this mode of treatment is as effective in terminating depressive episodes in old age as it is in younger persons [45]. A thorough evaluation of the patient's overall health status is required with particular attention to the cardiovascular system. Apart from acute myocardial disease, however, few absolute contraindications to its use exist. That is, age alone is not a contraindication to its use. Details of the procedure and the precautions involved in administering ECT in old age are presented in Kalinowsky and Hoch's standard text on the somatic therapies used in psychiatry [45].

## MANIA

Depressive psychoses predominate among the affective disorders in late life as they do in younger years. However, manic psychoses do occur in old age. For instance, in Roth's study of 220 patients hospitalized for affective disorders, 13 percent had predominately manic symptomatology [80].

Clinically, mania is in many ways a direct mirror image of depression [71]. The patient feels elated ("like a million bucks"), optimistic, and all-powerful; speech is rapid; hyperactivity may be present; joviality is sometimes interrupted by short bursts of anger or paranoid thinking, but the euphoric mood usually returns quickly; there may be short periods of sadness or weeping which suddenly give way to flights into grandiosity. Occasionally a quiet, transfigured euphoria is observed. Until the introduction of lithium carbonate for the treatment of mania, the prognosis for mania in old age was generally regarded as poor. While the rate of survival is as good among aged manics as among aged depressed patients, continued institutionalization was necessary in over half of Roth's cases [80]. In the last decade, considerable experience has been gained with lithium carbonate in the treatment of manic states, at least at younger ages [33, 81]. Lithium carbonate is still labeled an experimental drug by the U.S. Food and Drug Administration, although at least one drug company is currently in the process of bringing the drug to market under FDA regulations. Special precautions must be taken to follow the electrolyte picture in aged patients extremely closely since fluid balance may be more easily upset in patients with marginal cardiac or renal status [82, 83]. In view of the poor prognosis in mania otherwise, trials of lithium therapy would seem to be warranted. If cardiac, renal, or electrolyte status contraindicates the use of lithium carbonate, phenothiazine may be of some help in controlling the overt symptomatology. They are less effective in bringing about a termination of the manic episode.

## PARANOID REACTIONS

Paranoid reactions are also frequent in old age. It is important to distinguish between the mild paranoid reactions which are at times only short-lived, poorly focused, and not at all disabling, and those severe and all-encompassing paranoid reactions which are intensely experienced, disruptive of social interaction, and which usually lead to hospitalization of the affected individual. Intermediate states between these two extremes also exist. Moreover, paranoid phenomena are not entirely outside the range of normal experience. Most people at one time or another have been unjustly suspicious of neighbors, friends, and associates, and have at times interpreted essentially neutral stimuli in a personal manner.

Paranoid symptoms occur throughout the life cycle. However, paranoid reactions are more frequent in old age [30]. One may well ask why this should be so. On reason may be that these factors which are thought to contribute to the development of paranoid reactions at any age tend to be more frequent in old age. Social isolation, general insecurity, solitary living, and sensory defects, particularly hearing loss, tend to increase in the population of older people. One might also be able to say that older persons use projective mechanisms which underlie paranoid symptom formation *faute de mieux.* Projective mechanisms are a relatively primitive defense that becomes available to the infant of one or two years. It is a mechanism which can be applied instantaneously to any given situation. More complicated and more highly focused defense operations may no longer be readily available to the aged individual. In addition, the use of projection may serve a reconstructive function. Due to declines in vision and hearing, the aged may perceive the external world only imperfectly. Large segments of their surroundings may therefore appear vague to them, and a kind of "filling in the blank spaces" may be necessary to be able to exist in this incompletely perceived world. Experiments with sensory deprivation or those "natural experiments" of being isolated in Antarctica or on a lonely sea voyage have pointed out clearly that the human mind does not well tolerate a lack of sensory patterning. In sensory deprivation a new world, to be sure a hallucinated one, is created in order to fill the void. This mechanism may well be operative in the aged as well. The unknown is often interpreted as hostile and at least threatening. It should not be surprising therefore that paranoid projections often are of hostile intent. While younger paranoid patients often blame powerful but somewhat remote and esoteric forces for their misfortunes, old people often blame persons either geographically or emotionally close to themselves. Thus paranoid ideas in old age often center on neighbors, on passers-by, on the mailman or milkman, or on members of the aged person's own household. For instance, neighbors are accused of laughing or talking about the old persons, of maligning his or her character; neighborhood children are accused of teasing them, or of peering through the windows at them or spying on them; relatives are accused of trying to push them into a nursing home or other institutions, or of trying to poison them. Occasionally some grandiose idea may be expressed.

A certain amount of suspiciousness may actually be adaptive in the face of a treacherous environment. There is no doubt that the aged encounter more hostility and fewer opportunities in their environment than do young people. Paranoia, like hypochondriasis, can provide an excuse for failure. The individual can say that the fault lies not with himself but with "them." "They" are trying to harm him, are taking away his powers, and "they" are trying to make him look ridiculous. Frequent as paranoid symptoms are in old age, it should be made clear that they do not have the same ominous significance that such ideas have in younger persons. In fact, paranoid ideas in old age, while usually indicating hostile intent toward the older person, may sometimes have rather child-like or whimsical qualities attached to them. The following brief case examples may be illustrative:

Mrs. W. was an 80-year-old widow, in good physical health, alert, and well informed about events around her. She was not disoriented, and there was no other evidence of organic brain disease. However, from time to time she became very concerned and upset over the "fact" that her neighbors were putting lint into her washer and dryer. On several occasions she went to the police station to lodge a complaint. She had no good explanation why the neighbors were doing this. Reasoning with her was to no avail. For instance, her daughter tried to prove that this could not be happening because there was nowhere the neighbors could obtain lint to dump into her machine. Apart from this she got along well, but on washdays her complaints and accusations returned.

Mrs. B., age 74, had a happy marriage of 53 years until her husband died. After spending the winter alone in her big house, her son suggested that perhaps she would enjoy going to the spring meeting of the Golden Age Society. This would give her an opportunity to meet new people, see old friends, and have an outing with people her own age. She thought this was an excellent idea, and she looked forward to going.

In the afternoon paper a few days later she saw an article about the meeting to be held the next morning. She noticed that the topic for the meeting was "Correct Way to Prepare Your Will." The article went on to state that questions could be asked, and anyone wishing to make a will could do so that morning. On reading this she "realized" why her son had told her about the meeting and insisted that she go. She became angry, refused to go, and was sure that her son was "in cahoots" with the man making out the wills, and this was his way of seeing to it that she left all her worldly possessions and savings to him.

## The Relationship Between Deafness and Paranoid Reactions

A number of authors have tried to relate sensory defects, particularly deafness, to the development of paranoid ideas [15, 42, 77].

Since some hearing loss is common in old age [96], this may in part account for the frequency of paranoid ideas among old people. Thus Houston and Royse, writing in 1954, commented as follows: "Often not knowing what his fellow men are saying the deaf person becomes doubtful about them: losing auditory contact with them he has to rely on an inner-world of auditory memories and images; he misinterprets auditory sense impressions . . . he projects his inner feelings of inferiority caused by his deafness onto his environment and develops ideas of reference. Systematization soon follows, with active delusions of persecution. If the personality is sufficiently unstable a psychotic illness results" [42]. In their study the above authors were able to demonstrate a higher proportion of paranoid symptoms among deaf psychotics than among nondeaf psychotics. Eisdorfer, in a Rorschach study of aged persons with sensory impairment, found that deaf aged were more likely to use primitive thought on the Rorschach cards than were aged who had no hearing impairment or who had some visual loss [21].

*Paranoid Psychoses*

In addition to the relatively minor paranoid reactions, paranoid psychoses also occur. Post has recently published a monograph on persistent persecutory states of the elderly in which he has reviewed a number of studies in the literature [73]. In addition, he reports his own experience with hospitalized paranoid patients. He concludes that in England paranoid psychoses account for nearly 10 percent of all patients admitted to psychiatric hospitals in old age. He is speaking here of paranoid psychosis in which there is no gross organic brain disease. Paranoid symptoms are not at all infrequent in the organic brain syndrome. In these paranoid psychoses of old age, females predominate markedly in all of the studies reviewed, with men accounting for only from 5 to 25 percent of the patients with this diagnosis.

The relationship of the paranoid psychoses of late life to the schizophrenias of younger years, particularly to paranoid schizophrenia, is not clear. In Post's study of some 93 patients with paranoid psychoses of late onset, approximately one-third had only paranoid auditory hallucinations without other classical symptoms of schizophrenia; another third had paranoid delusions which were fairly easily understandable on the basis of adverse living situations and on the basis of social and partial sensory isolation (about a third of his patients were deaf; many lived alone and had little or no social contact); only about a third had the more or less classical symptoms of schizophrenia, with autistic ideation, disorganized thought processes, and archaic symbolization and delusion formation. In Post's study, as well as in a number of other studies reviewed by him, the typical prehospitalization picture was that of a woman, unmarried (either never married or widowed or divorced or separated for a number of years), now living alone, with some hearing loss, who had been for much of her past life relatively socially isolated regardless of what the specific living arrangements were. About a third of the patients in Post's study were described as having been suspicious, unduly sensitive, quarrelsome, or hostile throughout most of their lives.

## Treatment of Paranoid Patients

The immediate treatment goal with paranoid patients is to reduce the anxiety which leads to the development of paranoid ideas. Basically, this can be accomplished by three differing but related techniques: by psychotherapeutic intervention, by reducing the threat from the external environment, and by anxiety-alleviating drugs. Any or all of these techniques may be used.

In psychotherapy the principal endeavor is aimed at restoring self-esteem through clear communication between the patient and persons in his environment. Empathic understanding of the frightened patient's life situation can be very calming. It is similarly helpful to consider with the patient alternative explanations of what is happening to him.

In terms of environmental manipulation, consideration has to be given to many different types of intervention. It is very important to have the patient in an essentially familiar and relatively uncomplicated environment. For other patients it may be essential to see to it that they have adequate glasses to correct visual defects, or hearing aids to correct auditory losses, or that they have adequate lighting in their home or apartment. Other patients may require financial assistance, medical care, companionship, housekeeping services, or other concrete help. Regardless of the nature of the intervention it is always important to state clearly what steps are to be taken and the purpose of each of these steps.

When the above techniques are insufficient or when insufficient personnel exists, tranquilizing drugs are indicated. The introduction of the phenothiazine drugs has wrought a major change in prognosis of the paranoid psychosis in old age. Until about the mid-1950's, the prognosis for most of these patients was seen as bleak. This in spite of the fact that they were generally physically well and did not follow the kind of declining course which is so frequently seen in patients with senile or arteriosclerotic brain disease. In fact, many of these patients survived for many years in institutions, without improvement. With the advent of phenothiazine therapy in the early 1950's, this picture has changed dramatically. Chlorpromazine (Thorazine) or thioridazine (Mellaril) in dosages from 25 to 100 mg. three or four times a day or haloperidol (Haldol) in dosages from 0.5 to 1.0 mg. two to three times daily have proven effective in abolishing paranoid symptomatology [41, 73, 91]. In general, patients have had to be maintained on these drugs for long periods of time for the improvement to be lasting.

*Paranoid Symptoms in Other Psychiatric Disorders*

In addition to those syndromes in which paranoid symptomatology is the principal feature, paranoid symptoms may also be present as part of an affective psychosis. In such cases the persecutory ideas are generally in congruence with the dominant affect. Paranoid symptoms may also be seen in the framework of an acute (reversible) or chronic (irreversible) brain syndrome. In such cases signs of organic brain disease are generally recognizable [17].

SUICIDE IN OLD AGE

In 1966, the latest year for which complete statistics are available, there were 21,281 persons who committed suicide in the United States [95]. Of these, 5,967 or 28 percent, were persons over age 60. Thus the aged account for an inordinately high proportion of the overall suicide problem. Especially among men there is an almost linear increase in suicide rates with advancing age, as can be seen in Table 2.

TABLE 2.  *Suicide rates in the U.S. for 1966 by age, sex, and color*

| Age Range | White Males | White Females | Nonwhite Males | Nonwhite Females |
|-----------|-------------|---------------|----------------|------------------|
| 15–19 | 6.7 | 2.1 | 4.8 | 2.4 |
| 20–24 | 14.2 | 4.5 | 14.1 | 3.6 |
| 25–29 | 16.1 | 6.8 | 17.3 | 6.4 |
| 30–34 | 18.4 | 8.8 | 18.6 | 6.0 |
| 35–39 | 21.0 | 10.2 | 12.6 | 3.6 |
| 40–44 | 24.4 | 12.3 | 10.2 | 2.6 |
| 45–49 | 27.5 | 13.1 | 15.1 | 4.4 |
| 50–54 | 32.8 | 12.8 | 12.9 | 2.6 |
| 55–59 | 37.6 | 12.1 | 14.6 | 4.4 |
| 60–64 | 39.3 | 10.7 | 14.1 | 2.2 |
| 65–69 | 37.8 | 10.1 | 16.4 | 3.4 |
| 70–74 | 40.0 | 9.3 | 13.5 | 4.1 |
| 75–79 | 48.7 | 7.9 | 15.6 | 2.0 |
| 80–84 | 55.4 | 6.7 | 15.1 | 3.4 |
| 85+ | 59.0 | 4.3 | 23.9 | 3.3 |

Source: *Vital Statistics of the United States,* vol. II. Mortality, part A. Washington, D.C.: U.S. Public Health Service, 1968.

For the entire population of the United States the suicide rate was 10.9 per 100,000, but among aged white males the rate was four to six times greater than this average. Several investigators have reported slightly different absolute suicide rates in different locations, but the finding of relatively high suicide rates among aged males is uniform in all these studies. Thus Gardner in a study of an upstate New York county reported suicide rates of 36 per 100,000 for males at age 70 [32], while Dublin has estimated the rate to be 70 per 100,000 for the same age and sex group [19], with findings of Hartelius, who studied a Swedish population, falling somewhere between these figures [38]. The significance of these findings is increased still further by the fact that the reported figures almost certainly represent falsely low figures. Suicide is not sanctioned by society; therefore it tends to be underreported. Thus death certificate diagnoses of "accidental death" or of "death by asphyxiation" are sometimes made to camouflage suicide by gunshot wounds or by carbon monoxide poisoning.

As has been mentioned, the most dramatic increase in suicide with advancing age occurs among white men. The suicide rate for white women also increases with age up to about age 50; thereafter it gradually declines. Negroes have lower suicide rates than white persons, but the pattern of increased suicide with advancing age is beginning to appear among Negro men, paralleling the pattern among white men.

From year to year there is little variation in the overall suicide rate. But over a long period there have been significant changes. Suicide rates were high during the Depression; they reached a low during the war years, and currently they are stable from year to year.

Marital status has a significant influence on suicide rates [38]. The highest suicide rates are seen among men who are divorced, followed by the widowed, who are in turn followed by those who have never married; suicide rates are lowest among persons with intact marriages. Other characteristics of persons who commit suicide in old age are lack of employment, solitary living arrangements, and residence in the deteriorating central sections of our cities [32].

*Psychiatric Diagnoses of Persons Committing Suicide*

Evidence from several studies indicates that more than half of the older persons committing suicide have been depressed [32, 79].

A smaller fraction is made up of persons who have used alcohol to excess where this is either the primary psychiatric problem or else a symptom of a depressive illness. A still smaller fraction is made up of persons who suffer from organic brain disease, while a few percent of those who commit suicide suffer from a terminal medical illness. Other psychiatric disorders, such as schizophrenia or personality disorders, account for only a few percent of those committing suicide. Hartelius has remarked that the suicide rate among the elderly in Sweden increased following legislation which changed a previously restrictive policy on liquor consumption to one of free availability [38]. In connection with this point, it is interesting that public drunkenness is the most common cause of arrest among older persons in this country (discussed later in this chapter).

To date there is no satisfactory explanation of why suicide is more common among men than women. Depression, the psychiatric disorder most frequently associated with successful suicide in old age, is at least as common among women as it is among men. One can speculate that the impact of retirement, of physical decline, or of physical illness is more devastating to the self-esteem of men than of women in modern society. But this does not amount to an explanation. Nor is a truly good explanation available for the increase in suicide with advancing age. Batchelor quotes Swinson (1951) as saying that "suicide in the last 50 years has increasingly become a disorder of elderly people," and he has suggested that "as the present century has advanced, the old may have found their environment more hostile than the young" [3].

### Attempted Suicide

While many more young persons attempt than commit suicide (the ratio has been estimated at about 7 : 1), the number of old people attempting suicide is roughly the same as the number actually committing suicide [3, 19, 65]. Among younger persons suicide attempts often represent an expression of hostility toward someone or an attempt to bring someone to terms. These are rarely the motivations for attempted suicide in old age. Rather, when an old person attempts suicide, he almost always fully intends to die. Rescue from a suicide attempt in old age is often accidental or due to poor planning of the attempt. Persons attempting suicide in old age should be hospitalized. The psychiatric diagnoses of those attempting suicide are similar to diagnoses of those actually committing suicide, a finding which is in contrast to young attempters who are diagnosed as having neurotic personalities or transient situational reactions.

*Prevention of Suicide*

Many suicides in old age can be prevented by early and effective treatment of psychiatric disorders, particularly depressions, which arise in old age. But general health and welfare measures aimed at keeping older persons active, useful, and socially involved can undoubtedly also contribute to a reduction of suicide in this age group. As is true in younger years, in old age, too, the suicidal intent is always only temporary. If a person can be helped through a stressful period toward a new and satisfying adjustment, a life will have been saved.

## CRIME AMONG THE AGED

Crime, though not to be equated with psychiatric illness, nevertheless represents a pattern of deviant behavior. It is therefore of interest to know what crimes aged persons do commit and whether the pattern of criminal behavior differs from that of younger age groups. Keller and Vedder [47] have recently analyzed the *Uniform Crime Reports* published by the U.S. Department of Justice and the Federal Bureau of Investigation. Beginning in 1964 these reports contained information on crimes committed by the age groups 60 to 64, and 65 and above. They are concerned with arrest rates rather than rates of conviction. Drunkenness and disorderly conduct are the most frequently preferred charges in the over-65 age group as they are for all age groups. There is some decline in crimes of violence in the aged perhaps related to declining physical strength.

It is frequently said that sexual offenses are common in old age. Their importance, however, seems to have been highly overrated both in the public press as well as among some criminologists. Sutherland, writing in 1934, seems to have established this idea firmly in the minds of many [93]. A close reading of his work, however, indicates that he used the term *aged* to refer to all persons over age 50. The *Uniform Crime Reports* do not support Sutherland. Sex crimes rank low among the list of crimes for which aged persons are arrested. Violent sexual offenses, such as rape, are rare in this age group; the majority of sexual offenses are of a more infantile nature. They include "indecent exposure," touching or fondling of children, or "impairing the morals of a minor."

Epstein et al. recently reported a study of arrests of individuals 60 years of age and over in San Francisco [24]. They report that the arrest rate for aged persons in San Francisco was only one-fourth the arrest rate for the city as a whole. Their most striking finding was that slightly more than 80 percent of all arrests of persons age 60 or older were for drunkenness. An additional 6 percent involved petty theft, 4 percent traffic offenses, and 5 percent a variety of miscellaneous, usually minor, offenses. Only 2 percent involved offenses against persons, including one for murder. Fewer than 1 percent were arrested for sexual offenses. The authors point out that these findings certainly do not fit the stereotype of the elderly offender as being frequently arrested for sexual or other serious offenses.


## PSYCHOTHERAPY WITH OLDER PATIENTS

In 1959 Rechtschaffen published a thoughtful and well-balanced review of the literature on psychotherapy with geriatric patients [75]. The review contains 72 references; it deals specifically with face-to-face psychotherapy, not with psychiatric treatment generally.

Now, a full decade later, the review still stands as an excellent summary of this aspect of the aging problem.

By beginning with a focus on the "Martin" method Rechtschaffen sets the tone of the entire discussion. Psychotherapy with old people must differ from psychotherapy with the young, both in aim and method. On the whole the goals are much more highly focused, more specific, though not necessarily more limited—only more limited in the sense that they are more circumscribed. The methods tend to be far more directive, involving the therapist in much greater "activity," where activity sometimes means only greater verbal input, but sometimes also refers to greater motor input on the part of the therapist.

Dr. Lillien J. Martin was a psychologist who, after her own retirement, founded the Old Age Counseling Center of San Francisco in 1929. Hers was an active, enthusiastic, inspirational approach to the problems of old age. In a series of short interviews Dr. Martin attempted to instill in her aged clients an attitude of purposeful activity and a "will-to-do" attitude. Clearly, she supported an activity theory of aging, not a disengagement theory. In her own hands this method was apparently quite successful but gained few adherents outside of her own immediate circle of influence. Rechtschaffen ventures the notion that her approach failed after her death because there was nothing scientific or objective in it which could be transmitted to other therapists.

Rechtschaffen quotes Freud on three points, all of which are of questionable validity in the light of present findings. "Near or above the fifties the elasticity of the mental processes, on which the treatment depends, is as a rule lacking—old people are no longer educable." He is also quoted as saying that "the mass of material to be dealt with would prolong the duration of the treatment indefinitely." Freud is also quoted as saying that when a younger person is cured of a neurosis he has 30 or 40 or 50 good years of life ahead of him, but that therapy with the aged is less valuable since they have only a few years remaining.

Abraham is quoted as introducing the first note of optimism regarding the analysis of the aged. He said, ". . . the age of the neurosis is more important than the patient." S. E. Jelliffee, of Boston, said that "chronological, physiological, and psychological age do not go hand in hand" and proceeded with the analysis of several aged patients. Jelliffee felt that it was important to modify classical psychoanalytic techniques, feeling that many of the aged had arrived at their defensive structure intuitively and that it could not be dismantled without doing a disservice to the patient. Grotjahn, writing in 1940, was the first to give strong emphasis to the real and immediate needs the analyst was called upon to fill in the life of the geriatric patient. He wrote: "Not only is the senile person's relationship to reality changed by his psychotic withdrawal, but the reality situation itself is fundamentally changed by the biological and social dependence and helplessness of an old man . . . the analyst is not a more or less unreal image, but a vivid active part of reality engaged in the management of the patient's hospital life." Rechtschaffen comments that with these remarks Grotjahn seems to have anticipated the development of modified analytic techniques in the treatment of the aged.

Alexander in 1944 delineated two forms of psychotherapy— insight-oriented therapy and supportive therapy. He said that the primary consideration in the treatment of the aged should be the degree of ego strength available. Through the writings of a number of authors also reviewed by Rechtschaffen rings the warning that the established defenses of the aged should not be tampered with unless some modification of the aged person's real life situation is also possible. A rekindling of old conflicts, even though they have not been handled in an entirely satisfactory manner in younger years, is often not indicated. Meerloo has also championed continued therapeutic efforts with the aged. He has called attention to the need for education, environmental modification (especially in conjunction with home visits by social workers), and he has reemphasized the role of the therapist as a real figure in the life of the patient. Meerloo even went so far as to say that the aged might have less resistance to therapy and that this might be more receptive to input from a therapist. Meerloo also called attention to the fact that the aged often see their therapist as their child, the reverse of what usually happens in the transference reaction. Rechtschaffen continues as a vague generality a statement by Lawton that psychotherapy with older persons "differs only in degree, not kind, from that employed with younger age groups. No new principles nor techniques of therapy need to be involved, though old ones need to be modified." However, he credits Lawton with being the first to propose specific training programs for therapy with the aged (also see Chapter 17) and with pointing out that the aged are often in the highest positions of leadership; therefore their mental health is important to the rest of society.

Rechtschaffen also reviews the contribution of Goldfarb who has developed techniques of brief psychotherapy with disturbed aged patients with some brain damage. Goldfarb's experience is extensive. He attributes great importance to the phenomenon of dependency in old age. He feels that acceptance of this dependency is an important goal in therapy, and to some degree he deliberately encourages a limited illusion in which the aged person can see the younger therapist as a child who will take care of the older person. There is obviously the danger that the illusion may go too far and that real disappointment may follow such an approach. Goldfarb's technique, too, runs somewhat counter to the goal of mastery over one's environment. It appears to the present authors that the difference between these two approaches, one seeking acceptance, the other independence and continued activity, may reflect a difference in the residual capacity by the types of patients the several therapists have dealt with. It is our impression that with Goldfarb's patients there was relatively little hope of their ever functioning independently again and that his approach was essentially intended for institutional populations.

## GROUP THERAPY WITH OLDER PATIENTS

Group therapy with aged patients has been attempted, primarily in institutional settings, by a number of authors, including Lichtenberg, Linden, and Wolff [52, 54, 98, 99]. Obviously there are several immediate advantages to group psychotherapy of aged patients. First, such therapy allows the usually scant treatment personnel in such institutions to reach a significantly large number of patients than with individual psychotherapy. Second, the interaction with other group members may be at least as therapeutic as the interaction with the group leader.

It should be apparent, however, that the aims of group psychotherapy in institutions, such as state hospitals or homes for the aged, are not the same as those ordinarily sought in group therapy. Thus there is much more focus on matters of simple resocialization, ward adjustment, and participation in ward activities, than there is on a restructuring of the personality or basic conflict resolution. Wolff has pointed out that groups containing both male and female elderly patients tend to do better in terms of socialization than those of one sex alone [98].

It has been the experience of one of the present writers that, when vigorous therapeutic efforts have resulted in improvement in ward behavior, there is generally a quick relapse to the preintervention status when these efforts are stopped. Thus, while group therapy and remotivation programs on geriatric wards are extremely gratifying to observe and obviously worthwhile, they must be continued in order for the improvements to be maintained.

A few isolated efforts have also been made to conduct group therapy with aged patients on an outpatient basis. Notably, Liederman has reported his experience at UCLA [53]. As has already been pointed out elsewhere in this chapter, more intermediate or ambulatory care is needed in an attempt to reduce the number of persons requiring total hospitalization.

REFERENCES

1. American Psychiatric Association. *Diagnostic and Statistical Manual of Mental Disorders* (2d ed.). Washington, D.C.: American Psychiatric Association, 1968.
2. Barnes, R. H., Busse, E. W., and Silverman, A. J. The interrelationships between psychic and physical factors in the pro-

duction of mental illness in the aged. *N.C. Med. J.* 16:25–28, 1955.

3. Batchelor, I. R., and Napier, M. B.   Attempted suicide in old age. *Brit. Med. J.* 2:1186–1190, 1953.

4. Berkman, P. L.   Cumulative Deprivation and Mental Illness. In M. F. Lowenthal, P. L. Berkman, and associates, *Aging and Mental Disorder in San Francisco*. San Francisco: Jossey-Bass, 1967. Pp. 52–80.

5. Botwinick, J.   *Cognitive Processes in Maturity and Old Age*. New York: Springer, 1967.

6. Brosin, H. W.   Discussion, *Death and Dying: Attitudes of Patient and Doctor*. New York: Group for the Advancement of Psychiatry, 1965. Pp. 642–643.

7. Brotman, H. B.   Who are the aged: A demographic view. *Useful Facts*, 42. Washington, D.C.: U.S. Administration on Aging, August 9, 1968. Table 8.

8. Busse, E. W.   The treatment of hypochondriasis. *Tri-State Med. J.* 2:7–12, 1954.

9. Busse, E. W.   Hypochondriasis and Its Treatment. In A. Verwoerdt (Ed.), *Introduction to Psychosomatic Medicine*. Mimeographed. Durham, N.C.: Duke University Dept. of Psychiatry, 1963. Chapter 12, pp. 121–130.

10. Busse, E. W.   Research on Aging: Some Methods and Findings. In M. A. Berezin and S. H. Cath (Eds.), *Geriatric Psychiatry: Grief, Loss, and Emotional Disorders in the Aging Process*. New York: International Universities Press, 1965. Pp. 73–95.

11. Busse, E. W., et al.   Studies of processes of aging: VI. Factors that influence the psyche of elderly persons. *Amer. J. Psychiat.* 110:897–903, 1954.

12. Busse, E. W., et al.   Studies of processes of aging: X. The strengths and weaknesses of psychic functioning in the aged. *Amer. J. Psychiat.* 111:896–901, 1955.

13. Busse, E. W., Barnes, R. H., and Dovenmuehle, R. H.   The incidence and origin of hypochondriacal patterns and psychophysiological reactions in elderly persons. First Pan-American Congress on Gerontology, Mexico City, September, 1956.

14. Butler, R. N.   The life review: An interpretation of reminiscence of the aged. *Psychiatry* 26:65–76, 1963.

15. Cameron, N.   Paranoid Conditions and Paranoia. In S. Arieti (Ed.), *American Handbook of Psychiatry*, vol. I. New York: Basic Books, 1959.

16. Caplan, G.   *Principles of Preventive Psychiatry*. New York: Basic Books, 1964.

17. Davidson, R. Paranoid symptoms in organic disease. *Geront. Clin.* 6:93–100, 1964.
18. Dement, W., and Kleitman, N. The relation of eye movements during sleep to dream activity; An objective method for the study of dreaming. *J. Exp. Psychol.* 53:539, 1957.
19. Dublin, L. I. *Suicide.* New York: Ronald, 1963.
20. Earley, L. W., and von Mering, O. Growing old the outpatient way. *Amer. J. Psychiat.* 125:963–967, 1969.
21. Eisdorfer, C. Developmental level and sensory impairment in the aged. *J. Projective Techniques* 24:129–132, 1960.
22. Eisdorfer, C., et al. The characteristics of lipid mobilization and peripheral disposition in aged individuals. *J. Geront.* 20: 511–514, 1965.
23. Engel, G. Anxiety and depression-withdrawal: The primary affects of unpleasure. *Int. J. Psycho-analysis* 43:89–97, 1962.
24. Epstein, L. J., Mills, C., and Simon, A. The elderly offender: I. The elderly alcoholic: The jail as a substitute for hospitalization. Paper read at the annual meeting of the Gerontological Society, Denver, Col., October 31–November 2, 1968.
25. Erikson, E. H. *Identity and the Life Cycle.* Psychological Issues, vol. I, no. 1. New York: International Universities Press, 1959.
26. Erikson, E. H. *Childhood and Society.* New York: Norton, 1963.
27. Ewalt, J. R., and Farnsworth, D. L. *Textbook of Psychiatry.* New York: McGraw-Hill, 1963.
28. Feinberg, I., Braun, M., and Shulman, E. EEG sleep patterns in mental retardation. *EEG and Clin. Neurophysiol.* In press.
29. Fenichel, O. *The Psychoanalytic Theory of the Neuroses.* New York: Norton, 1945.
30. Fish, F. J. Senile paranoid states. *Geront. Clin.* 1:127–131, 1959.
31. Fromm-Reichmann, F. Loneliness. *Psychiatry* 22:1–15, 1959.
32. Gardner, E., Bahn, A. K., and Mack, M. Suicide and psychiatric care in the aging. *Arch. Gen. Psychiat.* (Chicago) 10: 547–553, 1963.
33. Gershon, S. Use of lithium salts in psychiatric disorders. *Dis. Nerv. Syst.* 29:51–55, 1968.
34. Ginsberg, R. Sleep and sleep disturbances in geriatric psychiatry. *J. Amer. Geriat. Soc.* 3:493–511, 1955.
35. Goldstein, M. S. Medicare and care of mental illness. *Health Insurance Statistics* HI-4, March 7, 1968. Washington, D.C.:

U.S. Department of Health, Education, and Welfare, Social Security Administration, Office of Research and Statistics.

36. Grinker, R., Sr., et al. *Phenomena of Depression*. New York: Hoeber, 1961.

37. Hammond, E. High risk factors in death of heart disease. (Symposium, Albany Medical College). *Geriatric Focus* vol. 8, April 1969.

38. Hartelius, H. A study of suicides in Sweden 1951–63, including a comparison with 1925–1950. *Acta Psychiat. Scand.* 43:121–143, 1967.

39. Hess, A. E. Medicare and mental illness. *Amer. J. Psychiat.* 123:174–177, 1966.

40. Hollingshead, A. B., and Redlich, F. C. *Social Class and Mental Illness: A Community Study*. New York: Wiley, 1958.

41. Holstein, A., and Chen, C. Haloperidol—a preliminary clinical study. *Amer. J. Psychiat.* 122:462–463, 1965.

42. Houston, R., and Royse, A. B. Relationship between deafness and psychotic illness. *J. Ment. Sci.* 100:990–993, 1954.

43. Kahn, E. and Fisher, C. The sleep characteristics of the normal aged male. *J. Nerv. Ment. Dis.* 148:477–494, 1969.

44. Kales, A., et al. Sleep and dreams—recent research on clinical aspects. *Ann. Intern. Med.* 68:1078–1099, 1968.

45. Kalinowsky, L. B., and Hoch, P. A. *Somatic Treatments in Psychiatry*. New York: Grune & Stratton, 1961. P. 103.

46. Kay, D. W. K., Beamish, P., and Roth, M. Old age mental disorders in Newcastle-upon-Tyne: I. A study of prevalence. *Brit. J. Psychiat.* 465:146, 1964.

47. Keller, O. J., Jr., and Vedder, C. B. The crimes that old persons commit. *Gerontologist* 8:43–50, 1968.

48. Kleitman, N. *Sleep and Wakefulness* (rev. ed.). Chicago: University of Chicago Press, 1963.

49. Kramer, M., Taube, C., and Starr, S. Patterns of Use of Psychiatric Facilities by the Aged: Current Status, Trends, and Implications. In A. Simon and L. Epstein (Eds.), *Aging in Modern Society*. Washington, D.C.: American Psychiatric Association, 1968.

50. Kutner, B., et al. *Five Hundred Over Sixty: A Community Survey on Aging*. New York: Russell Sage Foundation, 1956.

51. Leighton, D., et al. *The Character of Danger: Psychiatric Symptoms in Selected Communities*. The Stirling County Study of Psychiatric Disorder and Sociocultural Environment, vol. III. New York: Basic Books, 1963.

52. Lichtenberg, J. D. A study of the changing role of the psychiatrist in the state hospital. *Psychiat. Quart.* 28:428–441, 1954.
53. Liederman, P. C., Green, R., and Liederman, V. R. Outpatient group therapy with geriatric patients. *Geriatrics* 22: 148–153, 1967.
54. Linden, M. E. Group psychotherapy with institutionalized senile women: Study in gerontologic human relations. *Int. J. Group Psychother.* 3:150–170, 1953.
55. Lowenthal, M. F. Antecedents of isolation and mental illness in old age. *Arch. Gen. Psychiat.* (Chicago) 12:245–254, 1965.
56. Lowenthal, M. Social and related factors leading to psychiatric hospitalization of the aged. *J. Amer. Geriat. Soc.* 13:110–112, 1965.
57. Lowenthal, M. F., Berkman, P. L., and associates. *Aging and Mental Disorder in San Francisco.* San Francisco: Jossey-Bass, 1967.
58. Maddox, G. L. Self-assessment of health status. A longitudinal study of selected elderly subjects. *J. Chronic Dis.* 17:449–460, 1964.
59. Maddox, G. L. Retirement as a Social Event in the United States. In J. C. McKinney and F. T. deVyver (Eds.), *Aging and Social Policy.* New York: Appleton-Century-Crofts, 1966.
60. Maugham, W. Somerset. *The Summing Up.* Garden City, N.Y.: Doubleday Doran and Co., 1938.
61. Mendelson, M. *Psychoanalytic Concepts of Depression.* Springfield, Ill.: Thomas, 1960.
62. Meyers, J. M., Sheldon, D., and Robinson, S. S. A study of 138 elderly first admissions. *Amer. J. Psychiat.* 120:244–249, 1963.
63. National Institute of Mental Health. *Patients in Mental Institutions, State and County Mental Hospitals, Part II, 1966.* Washington, D.C.: U.S. Government Printing Office, 1968.
64. Nielsen, J. Geronto-psychiatric period-prevalence investigation in a geographically delimited population. *Acta Psychiat. Neurol. Scand.* 38:307–330, 1962.
65. O'Neal, P., Robins, E., and Schmidt, E. H. A psychiatric study of attempted suicide in persons over sixty years of age. *A.M.A. Arch. Neurol. Psychiat.* 75:275–284, 1956.
66. Oswald, I., and Thacore, V. R. Amphetamine and phenmetrazine abnormalities in the abstinence syndrome. *Brit. Med. J.* 1:5382, 1963.

67. Oswald, I., and Preist, R. G.   Five weeks to escape the sleeping pill habit. *Brit. Med. J.* 2:1093, 1965.
68. Palmore, E.   Physical, mental and social factors in predicting longevity. *Gerontologist.* In press.
69. Parsons, T.   *The Social System.* Glencoe, Ill.: Free Press, 1951. Pp. 436–437.
70. Pasamanick, B.   A survey of mental disease in an urban population: VI. An approach to total prevalence by age. *Ment. Hyg.* 46:567–572, 1962.
71. Pfeiffer, E.   *Disordered Behavior: Basic Concepts in Clinical Psychiatry.* New York: Oxford University Press, 1968.
72. Pfeiffer, E.   Short-term vs. long-term survival in old age: Physical, psychological and social correlates in two polar groups. Paper read at the 8th International Congress of Gerontology, Washington, D.C., August 1969.
73. Post, F.   *Persistent Persecutory States of the Elderly.* London: Pergamon, 1966.
74. Powell, A. H., Eisdorfer, C., and Bogdonoff, B.   Physiologic response patterns observed in a learning task. *Arch. Gen. Psychiat.* (Chicago) 10:192–195, 1964.
75. Rechtschaffen, A.   Psychotherapy with geriatric patients: A review of the literature. *J. Geront.* 14:73–84, 1959.
76. Reichard, S., Livson, F., and Peterson, P. G.   *Aging and Personality.* New York: Wiley, 1962. Pp. 170–171.
77. Retterstol, N.   *Paranoid and Paranoiac Psychoses.* Oslo: Universitetsforlaget, 1966.
78. Riley, M. W., and Foner, A.   *An Inventory of Research Findings.* Aging and Society, vol. I. New York: Russell Sage Foundation, 1968. Pp. 361–406.
79. Robins, E., et al.   The communication of suicidal intent: A study of 134 consecutive cases of successful (completed) suicide. *Amer. J. Psychiat.* 115:724–733, 1959.
80. Roth, M.   The natural history of mental disorder in old age. *J. Ment. Sci.* 101:281, 1955.
81. Schlagenhauf, G., Tupin, J., and White, R. B.   The use of lithium carbonate in the treatment of manic psychoses. *Amer. J. Psychiat.* 123:201–207, 1966.
82. Schou, M.   Lithium studies: I. Toxicity. *Acta Pharm. Tox.* 15:70–84, 1958.
83. Schou, M.   Lithium studies: II. Renal elimination. *Acta Pharm. Tox.* 15:85–98, 1958.
84. Shanas, E., et al.   *Old People in Three Industrial Societies.* New York: Atherton, 1968. Pp. 258–287.

85. Shock, N. W. The physiology of aging. *Sci. Amer.* 206:100–110, 1962.
86. Shmavonian, B. M., and Busse, E. W. Psychophysiological Techniques in the Study of the Aged. In R. Williams, C. Tibbitts, and W. Donahue (Eds.), *Processes of Aging,* vol. I. New York: Atherton, 1963. Pp. 168–183.
87. Simon, A. The geriatric mentally ill. *Gerontologist* 8:7–15, 1968.
88. Social Security Administration. *Medicare: A reference guide for physicians.* Washington, D.C.: U.S. Government Printing Office, 1968.
89. Srole, L., et al. *Mental Health in the Metropolis: The Midtown Manhattan Study.* New York: McGraw-Hill, 1962.
90. Straker, M. Prognosis for psychiatric illness in the aged. *Amer. J. Psychiat.* 119:1069–1075, 1963.
91. Sugerman, A., Williams, B., and Adlerstein, A. Haloperidol in the psychiatric disorders of old age. *Amer. J. Psychiat.* 120:1190–1192, 1964.
92. Sullivan, H. S. *Conceptions of Modern Psychiatry.* Washington, D.C.: William A. White Foundation, 1947.
93. Sutherland, E. H. *Principles of Criminology.* Philadelphia: Lippincott, 1934.
94. U.S. National Center for Health Statistics. *Prevalence of Chronic Conditions and Impairments Among Residents of Nursing and Personal Care Homes.* United States, May–June, 1964 (P.H.S. Publication No. 1000, Series 12, No. 8). Washington, D.C.: U.S. Government Printing Office, 1967.
95. U.S. Public Health Service. *Vital Statistics of the United States, Volume II, Mortality, Part A.* Washington, D.C.: U.S. Public Health Service, 1968.
96. Weiss, A. D. Sensory Functions. In J. E. Birren (Ed.), *Handbook of Aging and the Individual.* Chicago: University of Chicago Press, 1959.
97. Wilensky, H. L. Orderly careers and social participation: The impact of work history on social integration in the middle mass. *Amer. Sociol. Rev.* 26:521–539, 1961.
98. Wolff, K. *The Biological, Sociological and Psychological Aspects of Aging.* Springfield, Ill.: Thomas, 1959.
99. Wolff, K. Group psychotherapy with geriatric patients in a psychiatric hospital: Results of a ten year study. *Psychiatric Studies and Projects,* vol. 3, no. 2, 1965.

# 11

# Intellectual and Cognitive Changes in the Aged

CARL EISDORFER

One of the most salient questions in the study of the human life-span concerns the nature and degree of changes in intelligence and in cognitive ability in late life. Among the most frequent subjective impressions of the aged is the view that the aged characteristically show a loss of recent memory and impaired learning ability. Indeed, difficulty with recent memory, leading to progressive deterioration of other intellective functions, may be the earliest indication of a variety of disorders classified as senile brain disease, presenile dementia, and the like. Consequently, it is particularly important to appreciate that the empirical data concerning intellectual changes in the aged are not often clearcut but instead are confusing and contradictory.

The findings from long-term longitudinal investigations of middle-aged and aged persons have raised doubts about the validity of the simple hypothesis that there is a progressive, generalized loss of intellectual and learning ability in all older persons. Such studies have also raised fundamental problems in the field of human aging. The relationship between initial levels of intellectual ability and age-related decline on the one hand, and the role of physical illness in affecting cognitive behavior on the other hand, are two of the more important sets of relationships which require reappraisal.

Intelligence has been a central focus of study not only for research psychologists but for practitioners of a wide variety of disciplines, including educators, personnel managers, clinical neurologists, and general physicians. For the practitioner intelligence is a descriptive concept with a variety of meanings. Educators in particular appear to define it as the capacity of the individual to acquire and utilize information for the purpose of reaching some "appropriate" goal. Not only is intelligence defined as the capacity to use the environment, but certain other aspects of behavior are also termed intelligence; e.g., "reasonable" or "smart" behavior is highly valued, in contrast to "stupid" or ineffectual behavior. It becomes clear that this latter approach, i.e., focusing upon particular activities, has a high social loading since adaptive behavior is often bound to a particular culture. Clinicians and attorneys are often called upon to make judgments concerning the appropriateness of particular actions. Accordingly, poor judgment in the handling of money may be seen as implying loss of intelligence and as an indication of inability to continue to be a responsible agent.

## THE CONCEPT OF INTELLIGENCE

For the psychologist, however, intelligence is an intervening variable. It is not directly measurable but must be inferred. Thus the criteria for intelligence or intelligent behavior are variable, and a variety of measuring devices have been employed in the search for the most acceptable ways in which to make meaningful statements concerning the intellectual capacity of an individual or group. There is no question that many factors, e.g., maturation, physical condition at the time of testing, and previous test experience, may affect the individual's performance. One should also be aware that the accuracy of inferences concerning intelligence, necessarily based upon the belief that the "slice of life" being observed is a relatively accurate sample of the person's behavior, must be constantly reappraised. As will be discussed later, the problem of accurate sampling of behavior may be a particularly acute one with middle-aged and aged individuals.

According to Hunt, psychologists, in their attempts to understand the nature of intelligence, have until recently been guided by two principles [19]. One of these is the notion of "fixed intelligence"; the other is "predetermined development." These beliefs together lead to the assumption that intelligence is primarily a genetically programmed dimension of human personality which fixes the capacity of an individual in relation to his peers and which is played out during the life-span in a predetermined sequence of development and decline. Thus a measurement at any point in time would be predictive of an individual's position throughout life. A peculiar leap of logic has also led to the acceptance of data from cross-sectional studies, representing time slices across the age-span from many individuals, to reflect the pattern of changes in intelligence with age after maturity has been reached. In view of these factors, the influence of the methodology used to obtain data in this area needs to be examined.

## RESEARCH STRATEGIES

In the examination of intellectual function in adults and the aged three different research strategies have been employed: the cross-sectional, the longitudinal, and the cross-sequential approach. Group as well as individually administered tests have been used, each with a built-in bias. Sampling problems have cropped up persistently. Not only is there a selectivity in survivorship into old age, but education, employment status and history, physical health, test experience, and attitude toward examinations are only a few of the relevant variables that require more precise control.

Most of the studies of age-related changes in intelligence have involved the cross-sectional approach. This paradigm, which has the twin advantages of requiring only a single measurement from each age group and of rapid availability of data, has characteristically not controlled for educational level, cultural differences between age cohorts, and other such factors.

Age cohorts thus may differ on a number of variables which have profound effects on intellectual functioning. The advantage of longitudinal research is that repeated measurements are obtained on the same individual. This is time-consuming and cumbersome; it involves the added complication of creating a test-wise population. In addition, it may become difficult to hold a team of scientists and subjects together for the necessary length of time to complete the study.

Schaie in 1965 suggested an alternative model to the traditional cross-sectional and longitudinal designs for studying changes across time [32]. The cross-sequential model involves repeated measurements on a population of subjects of various ages sampled at the same time. It serves to shorten the duration of the study, to minimize possible environmental effects, and hopefully to reflect a more valid picture of the aging process.

## MEASUREMENT OF INTELLIGENCE

Numerous problems are encountered in the measurement of intellectual changes, not the least of which is the paucity of equivalent test-retest materials, and the inappropriateness of many of the tests to the aging condition. Ideally, in studying human development it would be well to proceed through a variety of tests purporting to measure the same phenomenon, but shifting focus as one goes from one test to another, from one age to another [21, 27].

Examining the aged is a specialized problem. Most of the testing materials are geared to the young, not only in that they appeal to the young, but also in that they measure knowledge and abilities which are a function of temporal proximity to the academic situation. Many of the tasks on the typical test of intelligence may be seen, therefore, as uninteresting or dull or more typically "silly" by aging individuals. The elderly may also be more apprehensive because they lack recent exposure to testing situations and because there is in them an undercurrent of fear that they may be losing intellectual ability.

Older people tend to withhold answers, particuarly on timed tests. They respond more frequently and with better results when they are given additional time, although, in fact, they may not need the additional time [12]. Thus, in the testing situation, it is necessary to give the average older person more time to answer questions and to attempt to control for any anxiety the test situation causes. Familarizing the older person with the laboratory situation prior to the actual testing will often help to alleviate heightened arousal levels [38, 39]. Rosenfelt has suggested that the investigator must use whatever data possible and develop new ways of looking at the results when there is a minimum output of data. He also suggests that new methods and interpretations must be found for behavior that does not fit the standard, particularly when dealing with the physically and mentally handicapped aged individuals [31].

Among the techniques used to appraise individual adult intelligence, the tests designed by Wechsler have been the most widely used in the United States. In fact, Wechsler, using the 1955 standardization of the Wechsler Adult Intelligence Scale (WAIS), and using a cross-sectional design, generated a curve depicting intellectual change with age [41]. The highest level of "mental ability" was found at approximately age 24, with a decline beginning after age 30, and continuing virtually as a straight line function into old age. A comparison was also made between the standardization curves for the Wechsler Bellevue test of 1939 and the WAIS of 1955. The WAIS scores showed a higher peak, and there was a slight age shift in the ability level, favoring older persons. Wechsler attributes this shift to better sampling, particularly to better control of educational level.

On the basis of his data Wechsler has also suggested that, with aging, more rapid losses occur on performance-type tests of the WAIS (Digit Symbol, Picture Completion, Block Design, Picture Arrangement, and Object Assembly subtests) than on tests of verbal performance (Information, Comprehension, Arithmetic, Similarities, Digit Span, and Vocabulary subtests). Thus, while the ability to manipulate words may seem to hold up moderately well with increasing age, the ability to manipulate symbols on the basis of coordinated perceptual motor skills appears to be somewhat compromised. These data are supported in part by Horn and Cattell [17] and Jones and Conrad [22], using other measures of intelligence in a cross-sectional paradigm.

Jarvik, Kallman, and Falek performed a nine-year follow-up of subjects past age 60, using the Wechsler Bellevue test, and suggested that intelligence might be stable for the aged across that period [20]. The authors did note, however, that among persons who died before the end of the nine-year follow-up period, there had been a drop in the Similarities and Vocabulary subtests, as well as in three of the performance measures.

Eisdorfer, in a three- to four-year follow-up study of the Duke longitudinal sample, found no demonstrable decline in his group of subjects aged 60 to 94, and suggested that there was a regression to the mean [9]. This finding has been supported by Rhudick [30]. In addition, Eisdorfer and Wilkie (1968) in a ten-year follow-up study of the survivors of the original Duke group found that the decade from age 62 to 72 is not associated with rapid intellectual decline and that changes in the 74 to 86 age range were not overly striking [15]. While it is difficult to evaluate the effects of test repetition, the findings, coupled with the works of others, suggests the need for re-appraisal of our concept of a "normal" age-related loss of intellectual function.

Eichorn, speaking for one of the Berkeley Longitudinal Studies at the Institute on Human Development, reported in 1968 that mental ability is incremental during adulthood, with an overall increase for both sexes between the ages of 16 and 36, beyond which there is some deceleration [8]. It is interesting to note that while the females started out at a higher level, they tended to peak by age 26 and subsequently showed only slight improvement in certain subtests (i.e., Vocabulary and Information), while the males continued to improve achieving equality with the females at age 36. While the females past age 36 continued to exceed the males on the vocabulary and information subtests, the males were superior on arithmetic.

Basing their views on a somewhat different longitudinal approach, Bayley and Oden suggested that intellectual decline in the aging population might be affected by the initial level of intelligence [3]. They contended that brighter individuals showed less decline than normal or below-average persons. Owens, in a 31-year follow-up study using the Army Alpha score for World War I inductees, found that there was no appreciable difference in rate of decline between those individuals who were initially more mentally able and those who were initially less able [25]. However, his data do support the notion that age-related decline is not nearly so dramatic as might have been supposed from Wechsler's curves [41]. Eisdorfer and Service have suggested that high IQ individuals may have a greater propensity to respond than their average counterparts, this in turn serving to contaminate the interpretation of their test performance [14]. Schaie and Strother studied a stratified random sample of 500 subjects ranging in age from 20 to 70 years and found that, while there were significant age cohort differences cross-sectionally, only performance on the tasks emphasizing speed declined appreciably over time [33].

A suggestion which may emerge from such findings is that age differences in intelligence reported in cross-sectional studies may be a function of a variety of factors which have affected the intelligence of the subject in earlier stages of his development, but which may not be consistent from one age group to the next. Numerous variables in addition to age act upon intelligence level: amount of education, recency of education, occupation, character pattern, test responsiveness, familarity with tests, and a variety of sociological and biological influences which may have affected different age cohorts, e.g., the possibility of radiation damage or malnutrition in certain groups of children. Schaie's cross-sequential model, combining the cross-sectional and the longitudinal methods within the framework of a single design, may give a more valid picture of the aging process [32]. If this is so, "a major portion of the variance attributed to age differences in past cross-sectional studies would be more properly assigned to differences in ability between successive generations."

## HEALTH AND INTELLECTUAL PERFORMANCE

Botwinick and Birren have reported that among a group of elderly men pre-selected for good health, those who showed "mild" and "asymptomatic" abnormalities performed less well on the WAIS and on a number of other cognitive tasks than did their extremely healthy peers [6]. Birren and Spieth [4] and Spieth [34] have indicated that individuals with cardiovascular disease perform poorly on psychomotor and intellectual tasks. In another study Spieth found that a group of highly intelligent adults who manifested untreated hypertension performed significantly more poorly than did their disease-free peers or a group of medically managed hypertensives [35]. The latter did as well as did healthy individuals.

Szafran, studying decision-making in pilots, reported that cardiac output was related to age and was negatively correlated with speed of decision-making, but this was not noticeable until information "overload" was achieved [36]. After the information "overload" point had been reached, intelligence test performance was significantly impaired among pilots with reduced cardiac output. Short-term memory was particularly affected. Szafran also demonstrated that pilots had greater difficulty in handling information overload material when they showed early indices of cardiovascular decline [37]. Kedzi and his colleagues found among a group of cardiovascular patients that a significant decrement in performance occurred only when there was a significant history of cardiac failure [23]. Reitan and Shipley showed that reversal of elevated cholesterol levels in the blood could be associated with improved performance on the Halstead-Reitan battery of tests, with this improvement being proportionately greater for the group past the fourth and fifth decades of life [29].

Apter, using the Halstead Impairment Index, found that hypertensive individuals showed marked signs of organic brain impairment [1], while Reitan found signs of intellectual impairment on the Rorschach [28]. Eisdorfer reported WAIS differences among subjects in the Duke longitudinal project on the basis of cardiovascular functioning [11]. Wilkie and Eisdorfer found that in the Duke sample hypertensive individuals, as defined by elevated diastolic pressures and associated left ventricular hypertrophy, had lower initial intelligence test scores than did normal or borderline subjects [43]. In a ten-year follow-up study of a group of subjects who were in the 60 to 69 age range at the start of the study, there was a significant correlation between blood pressure level and the amount of intellectual decline that occurred in both the verbal and performance area. In a group of subjects who were in the 70 to 79 age range at the start of the study, none of the hypertensives lived long enough to complete the ten-year study. Nevertheless there was a significant correlation between the initial blood pressure level and the amount of decline in verbal subtests. All subjects, regardless of blood pressure level, at this older age had some decrement on performance subtests. The results of the study suggest that, during the ten-year period of the study, intellectual decrement was highly associated with elevated blood pressure levels. The data also support the contention that the intellectual decline among the aged found in many cross-sectional studies may be related to the fact that at older ages more persons with cardiovascular or cerebrovascular disease are included.

## LEARNING

Another approach to the study of behavioral deficits in the aged has been through experimental learning studies. The idea that older individuals cannot profit from experience has been seriously put into question by the work of Canestrari [7], Eisdorfer, Axelrod, and Wilkie [13], Hulicka [18], Arenberg [2], and others. These studies have also resulted in some new insights into the learning process. Canestrari [7] and Eisdorfer *et al.* [13] have demonstrated, using the paired associate and the serial rote learning model respectively, that older individuals with average IQ do better at more slowly paced (or self-paced) tasks than at more rapidly paced learning situations. This is reminiscent of Welford's earlier observations that the older worker is less efficient in an assembly line situation than he is at tasks which are untimed and require a higher degree of craftsmanship [42]. The work of a number of authors thus seems to suggest that, with more time available, there is a greater probability that the older person will learn. This appears to be primarily related to the fact that, given enough time, the older individual is more likely to make a response, thus indicating that learning has taken place. In summarizing much of his own work, Eisdorfer has suggested that response inhibition may be a crucial variable in the apparent learning difficulty of older persons. This inhibition of responses, with consequent absence of reinforcement and apparent failure, may be related to a characteristic on the part of older individuals which might best be termed "fear of failure."

Both Canestrari [7] and Eisdorfer *et al.* [13] demonstrated that the improvement of learning which resulted when older people were given more time to respond involved an increase in the total number of responses. Eisdorfer also demonstrated that the time taken by older subjects for making a response was, in fact, short enough so that the response could have been made under the rapidly paced conditions [10]. When the pace was rapid, however, responses were withheld.

Wallach and Kogan [40] and Botwinick [5] have demonstrated that older individuals are less prone to a risk-taking behavior. This might serve as an appropriate explanation for the failure of older persons to respond in a learning or cognitive task situation. Thus the inhibition on the part of the aged may be seen as a fear of being wrong, and as such as a fear of failure. The possibility that "fear of failure" replaces the "need to achieve" as a motivating force in older individuals cannot be ignored. It has fairly dramatic implications for the general behavior patterns of older individuals. If an achievement-oriented motivation characterizes much of middle and upper-middle class Western behavior, then it might be expected that in older individuals, when positive reinforcement begins to be replaced by negative feedback (through loss of abilities, social change, displacement of the job by younger, better-trained persons, or whatever), a shift from a more aggressive posture to a more defensive posture might result. Thus, in a doubtful situation, the tendency might be to defensively limit the response in order to avoid failure rather than to respond in the hope of being successful.

To the extent that older persons inhibit their responses they may fail to develop appropriate stimulus-response reinforcers. Eisdorfer and Wilkie have indicated that aged individuals probably learn through a combined stimulus-response and cognitive approach [16]. It would seem clear that responsiveness is needed in order to obtain appropriate environmental reinforcements which then provide further motivation to continue the learning process. A vicious spiral of withdrawal, negative feedback, and atrophy of function, followed by more withdrawal, might then be postulated. The relationships between initial withdrawal, subsequent withdrawal, and a declining physical condition are obviously very complex.

## CONCLUSION

It would appear that in studies of cognition we are faced with the need to assess a host of social, psychological, behavioral, and physiological variables. Patterns of response may in large measure be influenced by socially and psychologically mediated interaction with the environment. These in turn may lead to physiological changes which may make the effort of responding to new situations more difficult. However, nothing presented in this chapter should be construed to indicate that there are no truly age-related changes in intellectual and cognitive functioning. Loss of neuronal tissue, change in the metabolic rate of the brain, loss of circulatory capacity, all lead to a level of primary change. The fact remains, however, that we know little about many of these phenomena, and how much they would affect behavior in the absence of other complicating social and psychological variables.

## REFERENCES

1. Apter, N.S., Halstead, W. C., and Heimburger, R. F. Impaired cerebral functions in essential hypertension. *Amer. J. Psychiat.* 107:808–813, 1951.
2. Arenberg, D. Anticipation interval and age differences in verbal learning. *J. Abnorm. Psychol.* 70:419–425, 1965.

3. Bayley, N., and Oden, M. H.   The maintenance of intellectual ability in gifted adults. *J. Geront.* 10:91–107, 1955.
4. Birren, J. E. and Spieth, W.   Age, response speed, and cardiovascular functions. *J. Geront.* 17:390–391, 1962.
5. Botwinick, J.   Cautiousness in advanced age. *J. Geront.* 21:347–353, 1966.
6. Botwinick, J., and Birren, J. E.   Cognitive Processes: Mental Abilities and Psychomotor Responses in Healthy Aged Men. In J. E. Birren (Ed.), *Human Aging: A Biological and Behavioral Study.* Washington, D.C.: U.S. Government Printing Office, 1963.
7. Canestrari, R. E.   Paced and self-paced learning in young and elderly adults. *J. Geront.* 18:165–168, 1963.
8. Eichorn, D.   Follow-up of the Berkeley Growth Study. Paper presented as part of the Symposium on "Longitudinal Changes With Advancing Age" at the annual meeting of the American Psychological Association, San Francisco, Calif. August-September, 1968.
9. Eisdorfer, C.   The WAIS performance of the aged: A retest evaluation. *J. Geront.* 18:172–192, 1963.
10. Eisdorfer, C.   Verbal learning and response time in the aged. *J. Genet. Psychol.* 107:15–22, 1965.
11. Eisdorfer, C.   Psychologic reaction to cardiovascular change in the aged. *Mayo Clin. Proc.* 42:620–636, 1967.
12. Eisdorfer, C.   Discussion of the paper: R. E. Canestrari, Age differences in verbal learning and verbal behavior. In K. Riegel (Ed.), *Interdisciplinary Topics Gerontology,* vol. I. New York: Karger, 1968.
13. Eisdorfer, C., Axelrod, S., and Wilkie, F.   Stimulus exposure time as a factor in serial learning in an aged sample. *J. Abnorm. Soc. Psychol.* 67:594–600, 1963.
14. Eisdorfer, C., and Service, C.   Verbal rote learning and superior intelligence in the aged. *J. Geront.* 22:158–161, 1967.
15. Eisdorfer, C., and Wilkie, F.   Intellectual changes with advancing age: A 10 year follow-up of the Duke sample. Paper presented at the Symposium on "Longitudinal Changes with Advancing Age" at the annual meeting of the American Psychological Association, San Francisco, Calif., August–September, 1968.
16. Eisdorfer, C., and Wilkie, F.   Components of verbal learning in the aged: Position learning and sequential associations. *J. Geront.* In press.
17. Horn, J. L., and Cattel, R. B.   Age differences in primary mental ability factors. *J. Geront.* 21:210–220, 1966.

18. Hulicka, I. M., and Weiss, R. L. Age differences in retention as a function of learning. *J. Consult. Psychol.* 29:125–129, 1965.
19. Hunt, J. McV. *Intelligence and Experience.* New York: Ronald, 1961.
20. Jarvik, L. F., Kallman, F. J., and Falek, A. Intellectual changes in aged twins. *J. Geront.* 17:289–294, 1962.
21. Jones, H. E. Intelligence and Problem-Solving. In J. E. Birren (Ed.), *Handbook of Aging and the Individual: Psychological and Biological Aspects.* Chicago: University of Chicago Press, 1959. Pp. 700–738.
22. Jones, H. E., and Conrad, H. S. The growth and decline of intelligence: A study of homogeneous population between the ages of ten and sixty. *Genet. Psychol. Monogr.* 13:233–298, 1933.
23. Kedzi, P., Zaks, M. S., Costello, H. J., and Boshes, B. The impact of chronic circulatory impairment on functioning of central nervous system. *Ann. Intern. Med.* 62:67–77, 1965.
24. Owens, W. A. Age and mental abilities: A longitudinal study. *Genet. Psychol. Monogr.* 48:3–54, 1953.
25. Owens, W. A. Is age kinder to the initially more able? *International Symposium on Medical-Social Aspects of Senile Nervous Diseases.* Venezia (Italia) 20–21, July 1957.
26. Owens, W. A. Age and mental abilities: A second adult follow-up. *J. Educ. Psych.* 57:311–325, 1966.
27. Pressy, S. L. Viewpoint: Not all decline. *Gerontologist* 6:66, 1966.
28. Reitan, R. M. Intellectual and affective changes in essential hypertension. *Amer. J. Psychiat.* 110:817–824, 1954.
29. Reitan, R. M., and Shipley, R.E. The relationship of serum cholesterol changes in psychological abilities. *J. Geront.* 18:350–357, 1963.
30. Rhudick, P. J., and Gordon, C. Intellectual changes: Report of a follow-up study. Paper presented at the symposium on "Longitudinal Changes With Advancing Age" at the annual meeting of the American Psychological Association, San Francisco, Calif., August–September, 1968.
31. Rosenfelt, R. H., Kastenbaum, R., and Kempler, B. The untestables: Methodological problems in drug research with the aged. *Gerontologist* 4:72–74, 1964.
32. Schaie, K. W. A general model for the study of developmental problems. *Psychol. Bull.* 64:92–107, 1965.
33. Schaie, K. W., and Strother, C. R. A cross-sequential study of age changes in cognitive behavior. Paper presented at the meet-

ing of the Midwestern Psychological Association, St. Louis, Mo., April, 1964.

34. Spieth, W. Abnormally slow perceptual motor task performance in individuals with stable mild to moderate heart disease. *Aerospace Med.* 33:370, 1962.

35. Spieth, W. Cardiovascular health status, age, and psychological performance. *J. Geront.* 19:277–284, 1964.

36. Szafran, J. Age differences in choice reaction time and cardiovascular status among pilots. *Nature* (London) 200:904–906, 1963.

37. Szafran, J. Age differences: The rate of gain of information, signal detection strategy and cardiovascular status among pilots. Read before the 73rd annual convention of the American Psychological Association, Chicago, Ill., September, 1965.

38. Troyer, W. G., Eisdorfer, C., Bogdonoff, M.D., and Wilkie, F. Experimental stress and learning in the aged. *J. Abnorm. Psychol.* 72:65–70, 1967.

39. Troyer, W. G., Eisdorfer, C., Wilkie, F., and Bogdonoff, M. D. Free fatty acid responses in the aged individual during performance of learning tasks. *J. Geront.* 21:415–419, 1966.

40. Wallach, M. A., and Kogan, N. *Modes of Thinking in Young Children.* New York: Holt, Rinehart and Winston, 1965.

41. Wechsler, D. *The Measurement and Appraisal of Adult Intelligence* (4th ed.). Baltimore: Williams & Wilkins, 1958.

42. Welford, A. T. *Skill and Age.* London: Oxford University Press, 1951.

43. Wilkie, F., and Eisdorfer, C. Hypertension and intelligence in the aged. Read before the symposium on "Somatic-psychic Effects and the Aging Process" at the annual meeting of the American Psychological Association, San Francisco, Calif., August–September, 1968.

# 12

# The Brain and Time

F. STEPHEN VOGEL

It is customary for the biologist to equate life with living matter and to characterize the latter structurally as a composite of morphological units or cells, and functionally, as an unending interplay between anabolic and catabolic processes. Needless to say, all somatic cells have a finite life span. As part of a complex organism, most are replaced by cell proliferation, but some, notably the neurons, are incapable of mitotic division. The flaws in cellular replacement, and cell depletion, ultimately lead to impaired function, and this compromises the biological potentials of an organism. To the biologist, this is aging.

By necessity, these events occur in time and thus time is a constituent of the ecology of all biological systems. It is convenient, therefore, to employ time as a quantitative index or marker of age. But time is not truly the essence of aging, for the aging phenomena can be accelerated or delayed. Actually neither aging nor death results from the burden of time alone. It is then the prospective of this chapter to characterize those biological features of the nervous system that render it prone to progressive dysfunction, for herein lies its vulnerability to aging.

## NEURAL DEVELOPMENT

There are several important biological principles that prevail in the embryonic and postnatal developmental period. This stage of neural development is dynamic and is characterized by orderly sequences of structural events. These occur chronologically, the latter usually dependent for fulfillment upon the former. For example, both the neurons and the glia take origin from a common population of primitive cells. These stem cells occupy the subependymal region about the lateral ventricles in the cerebral hemispheres, and also in the margins of the central canal in the spinal cord. The subependymal region, termed the *germinal mantle*, is truly the breeding ground of the embryonic nervous system [11]. It is only here and only during embryonic development that neurons manifest the propensity for mitotic division. As neurons differentiate and migrate into the cortex, they acquire certain advantageous functional properties, notably stability of structure and longevity, but at the same time they relinquish a cardinal attribute of other somatic cells, the potential for self-replication. This characteristic is germane to most neurological disorders, and in it is inherent the progressive loss of function that accompanies the neuronal depopulation of the central nervous system. This loss invariably occurs with time and is therefore a concomitant of age. It is also significant that this population of cells, the neurons, experience and reflect the accumulative effects of repetitive insults that might occur throughout life.

Thus it is that any adverse situation, whether it be inborn or an insult arising out of the environment of the cell, such as anoxia, bacterial toxins, and physical compression, can have but one quantitative or numerical influence upon these functional units. Clearly, this depopulation of cells occurs at different rates in different individuals, but it is an inescapable phenomenon and it reaches a significant magnitude in the aged brain. This feature of neurons stands in sharp contrast to other somatic cells; partial hepatectomy is followed promptly by a regeneration of liver mass and a reestablishment of full hepatic function, and unilateral nephrectomy, when performed early in life, initiates hypertrophy of the contralateral kidney, again with a restoration of tissue mass and function.

The glial cells, similar to the neurons, are on a well-established timetable of differentiation and cytologic activity. They, like neurons, take origin from primitive stem cells in the germinal mantle of the subependymal region, and, as undifferentiated spongioblasts, they migrate outward into the white matter during the latter phase of embyronic development and also throughout the first several years of postnatal life [9]. It is the mission of these cells, now in the white matter, to participate in a major fashion in myelinogenesis. A structural change occurs in these cells after myelinization is completed. They lose cytoplasm and assume the morphology characteristic of the oligodendroglial cells of the adult nervous system. These latter cells, in mature form, maintain a close anatomical relationship to the myelin sheath and ostensibly contribute, in an unending fashion, to the metabolic integrity of these lipid-protein membranes. However, again, cell maturation has extracted a decrement in functional capacity, for it is clear that in the adult nervous system oligodendroglial cells cannot remyelinate to any significant degree. Thus, as the neurons have lost the propensity for mitotic division with differentiation, so too the glial cells have lost the capacity for remyelinization.

This is seemingly the price of cell maturation. The phenomenon, as evidenced in the human, may not be fully manifested in lower animals, for it was demonstrated by Bunge, Bunge, and Ris that under very select experimental conditions the glial cells of the spinal cord in the cat can reassume the morphology of spongioblasts and, more importantly, can then reconstitute myelin [2]. The precise role of myelin as a contributor to neuronal function is not clear. There is much evidence to indicate that with myelinization the conduction speed through axons is accelerated. Disturbed neuronal function is cardinal to the leucodystrophies and also the demyelinating states. However, one cannot accurately attribute this dysfunction to a deficiency of myelin, rather than to Wallerian degeneration. Although myelin is clearly sensitive to ischemia, a feature common to most aged brains, alterations in myelin have not been accurately assessed as participants in the neural dysfunctions that characterize the aged brain.

Since the peripheral and central nervous systems take origin together from the neural tube and neural crest, the differences in the biological properties of these two portions of the nervous system are of particular interest [7]. For example, Wallerian degeneration in the peripheral nervous system is a two-phase phenomenon wherein the axon beyond a point of transection first degenerates and then, in the second phase, regenerates as an outgrowth from the cell body, and is subsequently remyelinated by Schwann cells [1]. There is overwhelming evidence to indicate that the neurons in the adult human central nervous system, by contrast, do not manifest the capacity for regeneration of their axons to any significant degree. Ostensibly then, a biological limitation has been imposed upon these central neurons. Thus a patient with a degenerative disease such as tabes dorsalis does not regenerate a posterior column even after the spirochetes have been destroyed by penicillin. Nor is an area of infarction in the internal capsule bridged by regrowth of pyramidal fibers, no matter how slender the line of transection. This seemingly is a severe penalty that the host has paid to gain a system of cells that through differentiation has acquired a high degree of stability. The major price has been the loss of potentiality for cell replication and for even the regeneration of an important cell constituent, the axon.

The price has not been paid, however, without benefit. For perhaps the most important single feature of the nervous system is the establishment of a stable, complex network of synapses. By these anatomical connections, the central nervous system becomes a confederation of neurons, a concert of functional activity. The integration acquired through synapses is germane to the high cortical functions, such as intelligence. Synapses are established during the latter period of embryonic life and throughout the first year or so of the postnatal period. It is likely that disturbances in their formation and in their function underlie many metabolic disorders that occur during this early period of life. A common metabolic disorder which may be manifested by alterations in neural metabolism, including synapse formation, is phenylketonuria [3, 5]. Perhaps a more illustrative example is to be found in cretinism. In contrast to phenylketonuria, in this condition the central nervous system has a more clearly manifest potential for proper maturation and function. Until birth its development has been proper and has been supported by the transplacental passage of maternal thyroxin. However, during the first year of life, when this hormone is deficient because of hypothyroidism, the nervous system does not acquire more than a fraction of its functional potential.

The genesis of this phenomenon is not well understood. If one examines the central nervous system during this period or at a later interval in life, it is to be noted that the neurons are present in approximately normal number and generally with normal architectonics. Also, myelin is present in normal amounts. If thyroxin is administered to such a patient early in the first year of life, the central nervous system attains its full functional capacity. However, if the hormone is withheld the decrement in function increases progressively and after one year is essentially irreversible. These observations illuminate the timetable of cellular maturation as it pertains to high cortical function. It is to be suggested that disorders in synaptic formation may be cardinal to the problem of cretinism.

Thus the normal evolution of cortical function is dependent in part upon factors outside the brain—in the case of cretinism, upon a hormone. Clearly, many metabolites need to reach the central nervous system in an unending flow. This establishes a critical dependency upon the integrity of the circulation. Thus cerebral vascular occlusive disorders, such as atherosclerosis, manifest themselves in cerebral dysfunction. They cut deeper and deeper inroads into the metabolic reserves of the neural tissue. A point of no return is reached when the sensitive structures of the nervous system, the neurons and the myelin sheaths, undergo ischemic necrosis. Neither structure nor function is regained. Thus vascular problems are frequent in the aged. Indeed, cerebral atherosclerosis is a hallmark of this segment of our population. Many patients manifest, in their ever increasing neurological decrement, the progressive nature of the occlusive disorders of the cerebral vasculature. However, the dependency of neural tissue upon an adequate circulation has its onset early in the embryonic period, at the moment when the cerebral vessels, which are formed *in situ* within the neural tissues, are incorporated into the systemic circulation. This is accomplished through union with the circle of Willis. It occurs during the sixth week of fetal life. There is much evidence to indicate that anomalous development of the neural tissues can be a manifestation of abnormal angiogenesis. Such a pathogenesis has been proposed for such lesions as anencephaly, hydranencephaly, and hemiatrophy of the brain. Thus the mechanism of tissue damage is the same whether it occurs in the embyro or the adult brain. It is a response of the sensitive neural parenchyma to ischemia. In the embryonic tissues this response is manifested by delays and errors in cell maturation. These responses occur principally in the densely cellular regions of the germinal mantle where metabolic activity is greatest.

## NEURONAL DEPOPULATION

It is characteristic of all nonreplicating neurons to die, as individuals, and thus for depopulation to occur. This phenomenon has even been demonstrated in the honey bee [10]. It has been estimated that the human central nervous system contains approximately $2 \times 10^{10}$ neurons at age 30 and that a decrement of approximately 0.8 percent per year occurs thereafter. Is there a cause and effect relationship between the state of the vasculature and this decrement in neurons? During their transition from embryonic to adult form, neurons have lost the capability for anaerobic glycolysis; thus they are rendered critically sensitive to anoxia. The ubiquitous phenomenon of neuronal depopulation is unquestionably accelerated by occlusive vascular disease. The relationship, however, is not easily quantitated, since the impediment in the vasculature is most critical at the level of the capillary bed; yet it has been rarely examined beyond the caliber of the major cerebral vessels. Cortical atrophy accompanies those disorders which affect the arterioles and capillaries, such as hypertensive encephalopathy, and is less well correlated with the obstructive disorders of the major cerebral vessels, as by cerebral atherosclerosis. One might logically conclude that the depopulation of neurons is un-doubtedly accelerated by occlusive vascular disease, but yet it pro-ceeds independent of this disorder, and plainly, the "aged brain" is not synonymous with cerebral atherosclerosis.

While the importance of the cerebral circulation to brain cell survival cannot be denied, other factors are also worthy of con-sideration. Thus it is a truism that longevity comes to him who carefully selects his ancestors. This is to say that we are physical and functional expressions of our deoxyribonucleic acid (DNA). Clearly, the human species is far from homogeneous in this regard. No two individuals are endowed with the same genetic informa-tion nor, for this reason, with the same biological potential. One concept suggests that all biological systems are driven as by a main spring (DNA) which is wound at birth and thus energizes life and establishes its timetable. Such a concept would suggest that longev-ity is predetermined solely by inherent genetic characteristics. In-deed, it would be unwise to underestimate the contributions of DNA. However, it would be equally unrealistic to forget that the human organism exists in a generally adverse ecology, to which neurons are responsive. The effects of the ecology are generally detrimental.

In this light, the term *abiotrophy* holds interesting connota-tions [4]. The concept is best exemplified by the condition of Huntington's chorea. This disorder is clearly an inborn genetic error present at birth but generally not manifested in dysfunction until the early adult period. The evidence suggests that the neu-rons of the caudate nucleus function properly for these many years but then undergo degeneration and die at a disproportion-ately rapid rate, as compared with neurons elsewhere in the same nervous system. This disorder is seemingly a direct manifestation of the genetic composition of the individual neurons of the caudate nucleus, and to a lesser extent those in the cortex and elsewhere. An analogy might be drawn between this human biological event and the tree upon which an individual branch has died, quite in-dependent of the vigor of the remaining limbs. The genetic back-ground of Huntington's chorea singles out DNA as the prime offender. The pathogenesis has been ascribed to exhaustion or depletion of intracellular metabolic processes. It is tempting, though perhaps not universally correct, to conclude that the structural integrity and the longevity of neurons are dependent in major fashion upon the quality of their DNA.

A further documentation of the importance of this constituent to the cell, both functionally and structurally, is to be found in Down's syndrome. Here the disturbance in chromosomal composition is so gross as to be clearly visualized in a karyotype. There is not a satisfactory explanation of the pathogenesis of the mental deficiency which accompanies this condition. Most certainly there are imbalances in protein synthesis as expressions of the altered chromosomal composition. Examination of the central nervous system from patients with Down's syndrome, however, rarely discloses cytological abnormalities, and the morphology of this condition remains obscure.

Germane to the problem of aging, nevertheless, is a phenomenon which occurs with regularity in Down's syndrome. Neurofibrillary degeneration, senile plaques, and granulovacuolar degeneration make their appearance precociously in these individuals [6]. The lesions are identical to those which characterize Alzheimer's disease. This latter entity occurs rather rarely in the general population, most frequently after the age of 50, and by definition before 65. Identical lesions are also found, with increasing incidence, as the years accumulate beyond 65. Unfortunately, the term *Alzheimer's disease* is no longer applicable; instead, the term *senile dementia* is now employed. Clearly, the morphological changes are precisely the same in all three instances, namely, Down's syndrome, Alzheimer's disease, and senile dementia. It appears unlikely that the morphological and functional changes in Alzheimer's disease and in senile dementia are expressions of disordered genetic composition, as they are in Down's syndrome. But in each instance there is seemingly a progressive alteration in intracellular metabolism. Thus it is tempting to ascribe a causative role to the passage of time *per se*. However, the supreme importance of time is denied by the absence of lesion in many individuals who have lived considerable years beyond their three score and ten.

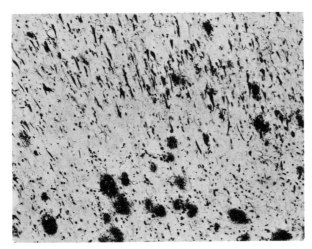

FIGURE 1. *The cerebral cortex in the frontal lobe of a patient with Down's syndrome, age 55 years. Advanced neurofibrillary degeneration characterizes most neurons. They appear contracted and argentophilic. In addition, there are numerous senile plaques in various stages of development. Lester-King stain, ×100, before 30% reduction.*

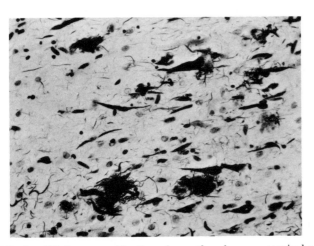

FIGURE 2. *Higher magnification shows the close anatomical relationship between neurons with neurofibrillary degeneration and the senile plaque. It is questioned whether the former plays a role in the genesis of the latter. The senile plaques are composed of a tangle of glial processes. Appropriate stains would disclose amyloid, mucopolysaccharide, and glycoproteins within the core of each plaque. Lester-King stain, ×250, before 30% reduction.*

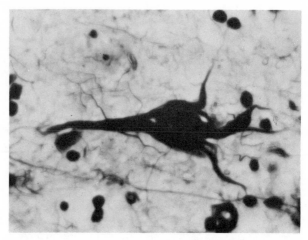

**FIGURE 3.** *A neuron with advanced neurofibrillary degeneration. Normally the perikaryon contains delicate neurofibrils. These increase in mass and coalesce until they occupy most of the neuronal cytoplasm. The alterations extend into the axons and dendrites, as in this neuron, with extreme advancement of the process. Lester-King stain, ×1,000, before 30% reduction.*

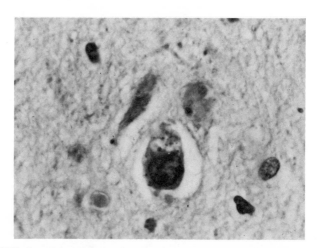

**FIGURE 4.** *Granulovacuolar degeneration is characterized by a foamy appearance of the cytoplasm and by dense particulate granules within individual vacuoles. The triad, neurofibrillary degeneration, senile plaque, and granulovacuolar degeneration characterize Alzheimer's disease and senile dementia. They are precocious features in the central nervous system in patients with Down's syndrome. Luxol Fast Blue stain, ×1,000, before 30% reduction.*

Denying then that time is a direct causative factor, it is of considerable interest that the morphology of the lesions, their biochemical composition, and the profound functional effect are uniform, whereas ostensibly the causation is multiform. The unity of the lesions is underscored by the common biochemical composition of the senile plaque. Regularly, they are structured with a central core of amyloid, with surrounding zones rich in mucopolysaccharides and glycoproteins, and with a background structure of astrocytes and glial processes [8] (Figs. 1–4). In these conditions lipofuscin pigment accumulates in neurons throughout the brain. Actually this is a feature of all aged brains; it is viewed as a disturbance of lysosomal metabolism. In conclusion we can say that time alone is not likely to be the catalyst for such sophisticated and complex biochemical events. Yet there is no single metabolic alteration that is synonymous with senescence.

Perhaps we should seek a simple lesson from the lowly planaria. This flatworm is capable, after bisection, of regenerating either a head or a hind part from the respective counterpart. The lesson is embodied in the phenomenon that the life-span of the planaria, caused to regenerate a new head from a hind part, is significantly shorter than that of its half brother, which has regenerated a hind part from a normal head. Thus we are instructed to keep our heads if we cherish longevity.

## REFERENCES

1. Barton, A. A.   An electron microscopic study of degeneration and regeneration of nerve. *Brain* 85:799, 1962.
2. Bunge, M. B., Bunge, R. T., and Ris, H.   Ultrastructural study of remyelinization in an experimental lesion in adult cat spinal cord. *J. Biophys. Biochem. Cytol.* 10:67, 1961.
3. Chrome, L., and Pare, G. M. B.   Phenylketonuria. A review and report of the pathological findings in four cases. *J. Ment. Sci.* 106:862, 1960.
4. Gowers, W. R.   A lecture on abiotrophy. *Lancet* 1:1003, 1902.
5. Jervis, G. A.   Phenylpyruvic oligophrenia. *Arch. Neurol. Psychiat.* 38:944, 1937.

6. Jervis, G. A. Early senile dementia in mongoloid idiocy. *Amer. J. Psychiat.* 105:102, 1948.

7. Johnston, M. C. A radioautographic study of the migration and fate of cranial neural crest cells in the chick embryo. *Anat. Rec.* 156:143, 1966.

8. Margolis, G. Observations on senile cerebral deposits using the periodic acid–Schiff's technique. *Amer. J. Path.* 29:588, 1953.

9. Roback, H. U., and Scherer, H. J. Über die feinere Morphologie des frühkindlichen Gehirns unter besonderer Berücksichtiguing der Gliaentwicklung. *Virchow Arch. Path. Anat.* 294:365, 1935.

10. Rockstein, M. The relation of cholinesterase activity to change in cell number with age in the brain of the adult worker honeybee. *J. Cell. Comp. Physiol.* 35:1023, 1950.

11. Yakovlev, P. I. Pathoarchitectonic studies of cerebral malformations. *J. Neuropath. Exp. Neurol.* 28:22, 1959.

# 13
# Organic Brain Syndromes

H . - S H A N   W A N G

The *Diagnostic and Statistical Manual of Mental Disorders,* published by the American Psychiatric Association, defines as organic brain syndrome "basic mental condition characteristically resulting from diffuse impairment of brain tissue function from whatever cause" [1]. Although such brain syndromes are known to be very common among old persons, much remains to be learned about the exact dimensions of the clinical problem they present. We do not know just how prevalent they are, and our methods of diagnosing and treating them are far from satisfactory.

## PREVALENCE OF ORGANIC BRAIN SYNDROMES IN OLD AGE

The fragmentary information that we have concerning the prevalence of organic brain syndromes among the elderly is based largely on statistical data derived from psychiatric hospitals, both public and private [46, 47]. It has been estimated that the number of resident patients in all psychiatric hospitals in the United States at the end of the year 1966 totaled 466,147. During that year, 214,493 patients were admitted to a psychiatric facility for the first time. The proportion of individuals 65 years of age or over was 29.5 percent among the resident patients and 16.8 percent among the first admissions (Table 1). It is calculated, according to the estimated population for that year [43], that the incidence of psychiatric disorders requiring psychiatric hospitalization was 941 per 100,000 among the

TABLE 1. *Estimated number of patients living in or admitted to psychiatric hospitals in the United States during 1966*

| Age | Patients in Residence | | | First Admissions | | | | |
|---|---|---|---|---|---|---|---|---|
| | Public | Private | Subtotal | Public | Private | Subtotal | Total | Rate[a] |
| Under 65 | 317,379 | 11,115 | 328,494 | 131,715 | 46,814 | 178,529 | 507,023 | 284.2 |
| 65 and over | 134,710 | 2,943 | 137,653 | 30,771 | 5,193 | 35,964 | 173,617 | 940.7 |
| Total | 452,089 | 14,058 | 466,147 | 162,486 | 52,007 | 214,493 | 680,640 | 345.8 |

[a] Per 100,000 population of corresponding age group.
Sources: [50, 51].

elderly population—3.3 times higher than the rate of 284 per 100,000 for those under 65 years old.

The diagnosis made most commonly in these elderly patients was organic brain syndromes. Among the 35,964 geriatric patients admitted to a psychiatric institution for the first time, 77.7 percent were given this diagnosis (Table 2). In contrast, only 47.6 percent of the

TABLE 2. *Diagnoses made in persons age 65 and over living in or admitted to psychiatric hospitals in the United States in 1966*

| | Resident Patients | First Admissions | Total | Percent | Rate[a] |
|---|---|---|---|---|---|
| Organic brain syndromes | 65,449 | 27,935 | 93,384 | 53.8 | 506.00 |
| Psychoses | 61,779 | 2,793 | 64,572 | 37.2 | 349.90 |
| Neuroses | 1,655 | 1,932 | 3,587 | 2.1 | 19.40 |
| Personality disorders | 1,172 | 962 | 2,134 | 1.2 | 11.60 |
| Psychophysiological disorders | 60 | 19 | 79 | 0.1 | 0.42 |
| Transient situational disturbances | 187 | 227 | 414 | 0.2 | 2.20 |
| Others | 7,351 | 2,096 | 9,447 | 5.4 | 51.20 |
| Subtotal | 137,653 | 35,964 | 173,617 | 100.0 | 940.72 |

[a] Per 100,000 elderly population (65 years or over).
Sources: [50, 51].

137,653 elderly patients already in residence had this diagnosis. The incidence of functional psychoses was only 7.8 percent among the first admissions, as compared with 44.6 percent among the resident patients. This difference was probably due in large part to the fact that many of the resident patients were hospitalized initially with functional psychoses and had grown old in the institution. It is probable that the incidence of organic brain syndromes in these resident patients was underestimated.

In 1964 a survey was made on the prevalence of chronic conditions and impairments among residents of nursing and personal care homes in the United States. Of the total number of residents in these homes (estimated at 554,000), 88 percent (487,800) were over 64 [44]. Brain disorders were extremely common among these geriatric residents: 36.0 percent were considered to have vascular lesions affecting the central nervous system and 29.7 percent to have a disorder attributable to senility.

Many old persons with organic brain syndromes are admitted to psychiatric services of general hospitals or in various types of psychiatric outpatient facilities. According to reports from 650 general hospitals (out of a total of 888 known institutions of this type), 11.7 percent of all psychiatric patients discharged from these hospitals were over 64 [47]. In 46.5 percent of these elderly patients, the discharge diagnosis was an organic brain syndrome; in another 15.4 percent, it was functional psychosis. Only 2 percent of the patients seen in psychiatric outpatient clinics were over 64 [45]. Among all elderly patients discharged from such clinics, a diagnosis of organic brain syndromes was made in 43.9 percent and a diagnosis of functional psychosis in 22.3 percent.

With few exceptions, patients discharged from the psychiatric service of a general hospital or from a psychiatric outpatient clinic can be considered as belonging to one of two possible categories: (1) those having mild or temporary disorders who will probably remain in the community and lead a relatively normal life; (2) those with more chronic and severe disorders who will likely be admitted to one of the institutions that provide long-term and intensive care. Admission to a psychiatric hospital or a facility that provides nursing or personal care usually indicates that the condition of the patient is such that he is no longer capable of leading an independent life or of being cared for in the average family or the average community. When the data from psychiatric hospitals are combined with those from nursing and personal-care homes, it appears that approximately 3,700 out of every 100,000 old persons in the population require such institutional care. Of these geriatric patients, 62.6 percent had organic brain syndromes or conditions in which such brain syndromes are almost invariably present. This percentage suggests that the rate of organic brain syndromes of moderate to severe degree among the elderly population is at least 2,300 per 100,000.

The reliability of this estimate is obviously questionable, since the data from which it is derived were collected through different procedures from diverse sources, and were based on a variety of criteria evaluated by persons of diverse training and experience. Another factor that tends to obscure the true prevalence of organic brain syndromes is the lack of objective, reliable, and practical means for routine evaluation of the cerebral status.

## EVALUATION OF ELDERLY PATIENTS WITH SYMPTOMS SUGGESTING AN ORGANIC BRAIN SYNDROME

Any impairment of the brain tissue is usually accompanied by impairment of those cognitive functions that are directly dependent on the activity of the brain tissue involved. *Disorientation, memory loss,* and *impairment of intellectual function* and *judgment* are, therefore, considered the primary characteristics of organic brain syndromes [1]. These symptoms may be the only manifestations present, or they may be accompanied by behavioral disturbances or psychotic symptoms that may or may not be related to the brain impairment. When several or all of the primary characteristics of an organic brain syndrome are present, this is the diagnosis usually made, regardless of the presence of other behavioral or psychotic symptoms. When the syndrome is temporary, it is called *acute,* and the underlying brain disorder is assumed to be reversible. When the syndrome is permanent, it is called *chronic,* and the underlying brain damage is considered irreversible. This concept of organic brain syndromes clearly reflects the current tendency in psychiatry to divide mental disorders into *organic* and *functional* (or psychogenic) categories. The current diagnostic approach, in fact, overemphasizes the role of the organic factor, while it neglects environmental factors and the patient's underlying personality. The diagnosis of organic brain syndromes implies an understanding of the structural or functional status of the brain and its relationship to clinical manifestations (whether cognitive impairment, behavioral disturbance, or psychotic symptoms). Actually, we have very few reliable means for evaluating the brain *in vivo*. Most of those available are traumatic and involve considerable risk, and hence are usually reserved for highly selected cases. The clinical diagnosis is usually based on observation and interpretation of the patient's behaviors and responses, both verbal and nonverbal, during an interview or during some simple test designed to reveal the presence of the primary characteristics of an organic brain syndrome. When the brain is moderately or severely impaired, the detection of such characteristics is not too difficult. At this late stage, however, the probability that any therapeutic intervention will be effective is remote.

The prevalence of a fatalistic attitude among psychiatrists working with old persons can, to a great extent, be attributed to the organicistic orientation of the current diagnostic approach, combined with the lack of effective treatment for organic brain syndromes. Consequently, the emphasis has been on the differential diagnosis of organic and functional disorders.

It is well established that the brain undergoes considerable alterations during senescence (see Chapter 12). The structural changes include a loss of neurons and other tissue, and an increase in the number of senile plaques and in the amount of neurofibrillary degeneration. Functionally, there is a reduction in the metabolic activity of the brain tissue involved. Some of these changes are probably associated with chronological aging; others are due to pathological processes in the brain or elsewhere in the body.

The relationship between the status of the brain and the clinical manifestation of organic brain syndromes has long been a matter of controversy. A review of the literature indicates that the cognitive functions of old persons do depend, though not consistently, on the structural and functional status of the brain [48]. It is well known, however, that many variables other than age (sex, race, socioeconomic background, and education, for example) can affect the cognitive function and its assessment [4]. The same variables can also affect such measurements of cerebral activity as the EEG [49]. A relationship between cerebral status and cognitive function is more likely to be demonstrable in elderly people with various brain disorders than in those whose health is good and who show little evidence of mental deterioration. In the latter group, such a relationship can be demonstrated clearly only by controlling the sociocultural factors known to affect the assessment of these parameters and by employing methods that assess a specific psychological or physiological function of one particular region of the brain [50].

The discrepancies observed between brain status and cognitive function, and between these two parameters and the clinical symptoms, suggest that other factors too may be involved in determining how well an old person can function or adjust in a particular setting.

The adjustment of a person, whether young or old, to a particular environment, can be viewed as the outcome of the ego's functioning —its capability and efficiency in meeting demands from the id or superego in coping with environmental situations and in resolving conflicts that arise from all these demands. Cerebral impairment inevitably has an adverse effect on many functions of the ego (perception, comprehension, learning, reality-testing, and the like). The ability of the impaired ego to carry out its functions is, however, relative rather than absolute, being dependent on the types of defensive mechanisms that are available on the one hand, and on the intensity and the nature of the environmental stresses or intrapsychic demands or conflicts on the other hand. Consider, for example, two elderly persons with the same quantity and quality of brain impairment or cognitive deficit—one, a 60-year-old man, compulsive and competitive, who is still active in his business, the other, an easy-going, self-content man of 80 who is retired. The clinical manifestations—that is, the degree of difficulty manifested by these two men in adjusting to their environment and in coping with the problems of their situation—will be quite different.

Few, if any, of the psychiatric disorders in old age can be viewed as either exclusively organic or exclusively psychogenic. Even the so-called organic brain syndromes should be regarded as *sociopsychosomatic* in origin, although it is true that one or more components may be more conspicuous in some disorders than in others. Any old person with whatever psychiatric disorder, particularly if it is of recent onset, should be thoroughly evaluated with respect to:

1. Psychological factors (personality traits, defense mechanisms, intrapsychic conflicts).

2. Environmental factors (interpersonal and family relationships, socioeconomic factors).

3. Somatic factors, both cerebral and extracerebral.

The social and psychological evaluations have always been emphasized in the management of patients of all ages with so-called functional or psychogenic psychiatric disorders. These evaluations are equally as important for old persons with varying degrees of brain impairment and will depend on the same standard clinical approaches: interviews, examinations to determine the patient's mental status, social history, and psychological tests. Some of the social and psychological problems commonly associated with old age as well as their evaluation and treatment are discussed in other chapters in this book. In the present chapter, some of the methods available for evaluating the status of the brain and some considerations in treating persons with brain impairment will be discussed.

## EVALUATING THE STATUS OF THE BRAIN

### Evaluation of Behavioral Manifestations

Although clinical neuropsychiatric examinations have long been the standard procedure for evaluating the behavioral manifestations of the cerebral status, the reliability and sensitivity of this approach are open to question. With relatively severe brain damage, the primary characteristics of organic brain syndromes—memory loss, disorientation, and impairment in intellectual functions and judgment—are easily recognized, and it is possible to obtain a rough estimate of the degree of brain impairment on the basis of such a clinical examination. With some exceptions, the clinical diagnosis of dementia and clinical estimates of the degree of dementia correlate well with the postmortem histopathological findings [3, 8]. In certain cases it is even possible to make a differential diagnosis between various types of brain impairment (cerebral degenerative disease and cerebrovascular disease, for example) on the basis of the history and the neuropsychiatric examination [35]. The usefulness and effectiveness of this clinical approach become more uncertain in patients with mild to moderate brain impairment. Such patients usually present no clear-cut neurological signs, and their cognitive function, although impaired, may still remain within the normal range of variation that may be expected in healthy old people. Since the examiner is required to make interpretations and judgments during this clinical procedure, the results of such an examination tend to be biased by his training, experience, and personal interest. Attempts have been made to standardize the interview and mental-status examination [20, 40]. Some of these are too simple or are applicable only to cases of severe dementia; others still need validation.

Many psychological tests have been developed to evaluate various aspects of cognitive behavior [2, 5]. In these tests clearly defined stimuli, questions, or tasks are presented in a structured manner to the individual in a well-controlled setting. They are usually designed so that responses are simple and unequivocal and therefore can be measured readily. The responses are usually standardized further according to the many factors known to affect the results of testing: age, sex, education, socioeconomic background, and so on.

Psychological testing is generally agreed to be more objective than the clinical examination. In certain cases it is probably more reliable and sensitive in demonstrating evidence of intellectual impairment, whether general or specific (reasoning, problem-solving, memory, perception). While these impairments can be considered as evidence of brain damage, they cannot be directly related to the location, intensity, or extent of the cerebral impairment. The relationship between behavioral and cerebral impairment is neither simple nor specific. Impairment in an intellectual function may result from any one of a number of structural or functional abnormalities in the brain [2, 5, 29].

The limitations of psychological testing are the same as those of the clinical neuropsychiatric examination. Both evaluate essentially the individual's performance or behavior, which depends not only upon the brain but upon many other factors, such as motivation, attention, anxiety, and the individual's psychological reaction toward the testing or toward his cognitive deficit. The results of psychological testing must therefore be interpreted in the light of all other findings available from the clinical history, the neuropsychiatric examination, and the laboratory findings.

*Histopathological Examination*

The common feature of insults to the brain, from whatever cause, is a loss of neurons and a decline in neuronal function. The only direct method of evaluating the brain is to make a biopsy of brain tissue and examine it by histopathological techniques. Such an approach, even if it were not so obviously impractical, is not as informative as one would expect. Smith and his co-workers [37] encountered considerable difficulty in interpreting cerebral biopsies from patients with presenile dementia. Out of 59 biopsies, 17 were classified as nonspecific because they showed only changes due to operative trauma or mild unclassifiable atrophic change or no relevant changes at all. The biopsy diagnosis of Pick's disease was particularly difficult because of the artifactual neuronal changes and the inaccessibility of the maximally affected areas.

*Measurement of Cerebral Atrophy*

An alternative to the histopathological approach is to evaluate the degree of cerebral atrophy resulting from the loss of neurons or other tissues of the brain. Although the presence of cerebral atrophy can be inferred from clinical symptoms and signs, psychological tests, the EEG, or measurements of cerebral metabolic activity or cerebral blood flow, the diagnosis can be confirmed only by pneumoencephalographic demonstration of cortical atrophy or ventricular dilatation. Definite evidence of cerebral atrophy is present in almost all patients with senile or presenile dementia [15, 17]. As the degree of cerebral atrophy increases, impairment of intellectual functioning or adaptive capacity also increases [23, 52]. The intellectual impairment is more closely correlated with cortical atrophy, particularly that of the frontal region, than with ventricular dilatation [52].

Intellectual impairment associated with a given degree of cerebral atrophy varies considerably among different individuals. As a rule, the same degree of atrophy produces greater intellectual impairment in elderly persons than in the young [52]. The explanation may lie in the fact that the cerebral blood flow and the compensatory capacity of the remaining brain tissue are usually reduced in old age. Premorbid personality also contributes to the individual variation; it has been shown that patients who, before their illness, demonstrated a high order of adaptive versatility, had less intellectual impairment in relation to loss of brain tissue than those who had for some time exhibited difficulties in overall adaptation, with much anxiety [23]. The individual variations in the degree of impairment were more striking when cerebral tissue loss was small and less evident when it was great.

Because of its traumatic nature and the danger of aggravating the patient's condition, pneumoencephalography is used only in selected cases. Echoencephalography, which does not have these disadvantages, has long been used to demonstrate the midline shift resulting from the pressure of a mass lesion in the brain or from marked unilateral cerebral edema. According to recent reports, this technique can also be used to measure the ventricular size [11, 13]. It has been shown [12] that the width of the third ventricle, as measured by echoencephalography, is significantly greater in persons aged 70 or over than in young adults (6 to 11 mm. with a mean of 7.2, as compared with 4 to 7 mm. with a mean of 5.0).

*Measurements of Cerebral Metabolism and Cerebral Blood Flow* [22, 25, 38]

The brain derives its energy almost exclusively from the aerobic oxidation of glucose; hence the cerebral metabolic activity is represented by the rate at which oxygen and glucose are utilized by the brain. Oxygen consumption is probably a more reliable indicator of cerebral metabolism than the utilization of glucose, for two reasons:

(1) the stores of glucose in the brain, though small, are still much greater than those of oxygen; and (2) the analytical method used in the determination of glucose is not specific and includes other reducing substances present in the blood.

The cerebral metabolic rate of oxygen (oxygen consumption) can be calculated by multiplying the cerebral oxygen uptake during a given unit of time by the amount of blood flowing through the brain during this interval (cerebral blood flow). It has been estimated that, in healthy young adults, each 100 Gm. of brain tissue consumes about 3.5 ml. of oxygen per minute. Because of a unique compensatory mechanism in the brain, the cerebral oxygen consumption, under normal conditions, is more or less independent of the supply of blood to the brain and of the oxygen content of the blood. A reduction in the oxygen content of the blood (hypoxia) is usually compensated for by an increase in blood flow; a reduction of blood flow, by an increase in the brain's uptake of oxygen. Consequently, the cerebral metabolic rate remains constant under a wide range of changes in cerebral blood flow or in the oxygen content of the blood.

The cerebral uptake of oxygen, which is represented by the difference between the amount of oxygen in the blood of any artery and that in blood taken from the superior bulb of the internal jugular vein, is sometimes used as a measurement of cerebral metabolism. Only when the cerebral blood flow is constant, however, is the oxygen *uptake* directly proportional to, and hence useful as an indicator of, the *utilization* of oxygen by the brain.

The cerebral blood flow, under normal circumstances, is unable to affect the cerebral metabolic rate, but is dependent on it. This is because the most important metabolites produced by the aerobic oxidation of glucose are water and carbon dioxide, a potent vasodilator. Any changes in the cerebral blood flow, although not always proportional to changes in the cerebral metabolic rate, are as a rule in the same direction. The former can therefore be used as an indicator of the latter.

Of the many methods being developed for estimating cerebral blood flow, only a very few are capable of providing quantitative information [16, 28]. All these quantitative methods depend upon a diffusible indicator, usually an inert gas, which is administered intra-arterially, intravenously, or by inhalation. The uptake of this indicator by the brain or its clearance from the brain is then determined by measuring the amount contained in samples of arterial blood and of blood from the internal jugular vein, or by monitoring extracranially when a radioactive indicator is employed. Some methods, such as the nitrous oxide or [85]Kr inhalation method, give only an estimate of the average blood flow of the whole brain; others, such as the intracarotid injection method using [133]xenon, can also estimate separately blood flow through the gray matter and the white matter in a small region of the brain. All these methods require a puncture of the artery and/or of the internal jugular vein, and thus involve considerable trauma and risk. The inhalation method using [133]xenon [32] avoids these hazards but is not as sensitive or reliable as the other methods, because of the problems of recirculation and extracerebral loading.

Although the cerebral metabolic rate of oxygen is by far the most reliable and accurate measure of cerebral metabolism, it does not provide any quantitative information regarding the metabolic rates of various components of the brain. These are known to differ considerably under normal conditions, and one would expect them to be affected differently by various pathological processes of the brain. Measurements of the regional cerebral blood flow, such as can be obtained by the carotid injection or inhalation of a radioactive inert gas, probably correlate well the local metabolic rate. They, however, provide no morphological information about the brain or the vascular system. The localization of the mass lesions in the brain can be helped by brain scans or cerebral angiograms. The latter is particularly valuable in demonstrating vascular lesions.

The decline in the cerebral metabolic rate and cerebral blood flow usually observed in senescent patients is believed to be due principally to pathological conditions rather than to chronological age per se. Dastur and his co-workers showed that, in old persons who are in excellent health and have no apparent mental deterioration, the cerebral oxygen consumption and blood flow do not differ greatly from those of healthy young adults [9].

Cerebral atherosclerosis is accompanied by an increase in peripheral vascular resistance and an impairment of the compensatory mechanism by which cerebral blood flow is maintained constant in spite of changes in blood pressure or changes in peripheral vascular resistance. Cerebral atherosclerosis is one possible factor in the reduction of cerebral blood flow that often occurs in senescence. Another possible factor is depression of cerebral metabolic activity secondary to functional or structural impairment of the brain. Such impairment may result from degenerative diseases primarily involving the brain or from metabolic disorders arising from conditions outside the brain (hypoxemia, ischemia, anemia, uremia, drug effect). The reduction in cerebral blood flow or metabolic rate is, therefore, not specific for any particular pathological process. It only indicates the presence of functional or structural impairment of the brain.

Among elderly persons with various psychiatric or neurological disorders it has been repeatedly observed that a reduction of cerebral oxygen consumption and cerebral blood flow is associated with an impairment in intellectual function [7, 18, 24, 26]. In a recent study, the [133]xenon inhalation method was used to measure the cortical blood flow of the left parietal region in a group of aged community volunteers (mean age, 79 years) having relatively good health and in a group of healthy young adults [32, 50]. Values for the elderly subjects were significantly lower than those obtained in the younger ones (33 to 72 ml. per 100 Gm. of brain tissue per minute in the former group, as compared with 57 to 92 ml. in the latter). In elderly subjects of comparable educational status and socioeconomic background, there was significant correlation between cerebral blood flow and intellectual functioning, as indicated by scaled scores on the WAIS test, administered both at the time of the blood flow study and prior to the blood flow study [50].

*Electroencephalographic Study*

The electroencephalograph (EEG) has long been employed to study electrocortical activity of the brain *in vivo*. A review of the literature [6] shows that EEG abnormalities are extremely common among hospitalized psychiatric patients over 60 years of age. The incidence of abnormal EEGs is significantly higher (75 percent or more) in elderly persons with brain disorders of various types than in old people with so-called functional or psychogenic disorders. These abnormalities are not specific for any type of brain disorder; they consist almost exclusively of *diffuse slow activity in the theta or delta range,* whether the brain impairment is caused by cerebral degenerative disease or by a metabolic disturbance secondary to systemic disease. Several studies [19, 31] have shown a good correlation between the dominant frequency in the EEG and cerebral oxygen consumption or cerebral blood flow. It is very likely that the slowing of dominant frequency so often observed in old persons is due to depression of cerebral metabolic activity—a common feature of almost all brain disorders associated with old age.

As a rule, the EEG abnormalities, particularly the degree of slowing, correlate well with the degree of intellectual deterioration or with the clinical evidence of organicity found on psychiatric examinations or psychological tests [6, 48]. It is also possible to demonstrate a relationship between the EEG findings and the prognosis. Patients with diffuse slowing in their EEG tracings are more likely to remain hospitalized and have a shorter life expectancy than those with normal EEG tracings [6]. Exceptions do occur, however. The EEG may be negative or unremarkable even in the presence of definite brain disease or severe dementia, while psychologically well-preserved persons may have abnormal tracings.

The interpretation of the senescent EEG is made more difficult by the fact that similar, though less marked, slowing of the dominant rhythm is frequently observed in elderly persons with excellent health. A longitudinal study on a group of elderly community volunteers whose good health was maintained for at least three years after they entered the study showed an inverse relationship between age and the frequency of the dominant rhythm [49]. The mean frequency declined, at an almost steady rate of 0.08 c.p.s. per year, from 10.3 c.p.s. at age 60 to 9.5 at 70 and 8.7 at 80. Subjects with the slowest dominant frequencies on the first examination functioned initially at an intellectual level that was not much different from that of volunteers with faster frequencies; but the decline in their performance ability during the next three to four years was significantly greater than that in the subjects whose dominant frequencies were initially higher [50].

Other EEG findings that are common in senescence are *focal disturbances* and *diffuse fast activities in the beta range;* the clinical significance of these patterns is not clear [6]. Focal disturbances seem to appear first in middle age and to increase in incidence with advancing age. They usually consist in slow activity of theta or delta frequency; less frequently, in marked amplitude asymmetry and localized sharp waves or spikes. In almost all cases these foci occur predominantly or exclusively over the left anterior temporal region. Although similar focal disturbances are also not uncommon in patients with cerebrovascular insufficiency or with intratentorial or deep subcortical neoplasms, longitudinal studies have shown that such foci may be present for several years without the development of clinical symptoms. The EEG finding has not been correlated with any particular psychological or physical factors [6], although there is evidence suggesting that subjects with such foci showed a significantly greater decline in verbal ability over three to four years than those without such foci [50].

In about half the elderly population, fast activities of the beta range are present in one or more EEG tracings; this finding is inversely related to the occurrence of diffuse slowing. These fast waves appear to be related to age and mental status; they become less common after the age of 80 and in the presence of mental deterioration [6]. It has also been shown that elderly subjects who did well in verbal learning had significantly more beta waves during eye opening and photic stimulation than those who did poorly in such learning [41].

Because the EEG changes associated with various conditions common in senescence are neither specific nor pathognomonic and because of the wide variations found among old persons of compatible age and health status, the diagnostic value of single EEG tracings is somewhat limited, especially in cases in which the findings deviate only slightly or moderately from the standards for healthy young adults. Serial EEG tracings, on the other hand, are of great value, particularly in following the course of a patient suspected of having a brain disorder.

## THERAPEUTIC CONSIDERATIONS

The ultimate goal of evaluating the brain is to uncover any conditions in which causative or contributory factors can be corrected or at least alleviated before the brain tissue is permanently damaged. The many conditions included in this category [10, 27] can be divided into two groups:

1. Those in which there is an insufficient *supply* of the two nutrients that are essential for normal brain function—oxygen and glucose. The brain's supply of *oxygen* may be decreased by low ambient oxygen or by respiratory depression or various pulmonary diseases that lower the oxygen content of the blood (hypoxic hypoxia); by anemia of various types (anemic hypoxia); or by ischemia secondary to hypotension or to cerebrovascular insufficiency (ischemic hypoxia). The amount of *glucose* available to the brain may be decreased in essential hypoglycemia or by certain drugs such as insulin.

2. Those in which there is inefficient *utilization* of the nutrients that are essential for normal brain function. The brain's consumption of oxygen and glucose may be impaired or depressed by certain drugs such as barbiturates; by a deficiency of vitamins such as $B_{12}$; or by various metabolic and electrolyte disturbances such as diabetes mellitus, uremia, hyperammonemia, hypothyroidism, dehydration, and acidosis.

Unfortunately, the causative or contributory factors in many brain disorders—for example, senile or presenile dementia—are not yet recognized. Other types of cerebral impairment are due to factors that are recognized but cannot be effectively controlled or treated—for example, cerebral atherosclerosis. Several drugs are capable of increasing the cerebral blood flow under normal conditions but have little or no effect on the blood flow or brain function when cerebral atherosclerosis is present.

Brain tissue, once damaged, cannot be restored. In many cases, therefore, the most important part of treatment is to prevent any complication or aggravating factors that may cause further impairment of cerebral function. Drugs that are known to depress the cerebral function (barbiturates, for example) should be avoided if possible. Drugs that may reduce the blood pressure, such as phenothiazines, should be used with the utmost caution. A fall in blood pressure which would hardly be noticeable to persons with normal vessels may significantly affect the cerebral hemodynamics in persons with cerebral atherosclerosis. Because this condition increases the peripheral vascular resistance and impairs the compensatory mechanism of the cerebral vascular system, a relatively high blood pressure is required to maintain the normal supply of blood to the brain.

The tendency to cerebral hypoxia is also greater in old persons than in young adults [30, 36, 39]. Conditions that cause hypoxia—for example, low ambient oxygen and certain anesthetics, surgical procedures, medications, or postures [30, 33, 51]—should be avoided if possible. If hypoxia occurs, it should be corrected as soon as possible in order to avoid further insult to the already impaired brain.

Among the positive steps that can be taken to help old people with brain impairment are any measures—drugs, activities, psychotherapy, environmental manipulation—that can alleviate the social and psychological stresses contributing to their problems of adjustment.

## PROGNOSIS

It is generally agreed that psychiatric disorders of later life have a particularly poor prognosis when evidence of brain impairment is present. Because of the high mortality and long periods of institutionalization that are characteristic of elderly psychiatric patients who show evidence of dementia or organic brain disease on clinical examination [21, 34, 42], the differential diagnosis between organic and psychogenic disorders has been emphasized. All too frequently, aggressive therapeutic approaches are reserved for patients with disorders of the latter type.

From the clinical point of view, such a categorical differentiation and the fatalistic attitude often adopted toward elderly persons with organic disorders are unjustified, particularly in the treatment of an *individual* patient. First of all, the clinical differentiation between these two diagnostic categories is not reliable. Secondly, most psychiatric disorders in old age are neither exclusively organic nor exclusively psychogenic. Thirdly, even if it were possible to differentiate clinically between these two groups, the belief that organic disorders have a poor prognosis is true only when they are viewed as a *group* and are compared with psychogenic disorders as a *group*. There are considerable individual variations within each diagnostic category, and hence overlapping between them. Two separate studies made on elderly patients two years after their admission to a psychiatric institution [34, 42] showed that almost 10 percent of those having so-called organic disorders were living in the community, and an even larger proportion (11 to 33 percent) were still alive in the institution. Among those having so-called psychogenic disorders, more than 25 percent were dead and another 25 percent had remained institutionalized during these two years.

To predict the outcome of a psychiatric illness for an individual patient on the basis of the clinical diagnosis is extremely difficult and unreliable [21]. It has been demonstrated that, among aged institutionalized patients, predictions by psychiatrists or internists that death would occur within a specified period after admission were correct in only one-third of the cases; usually the prediction was more pessimistic than the actual outcome [14]. The prognosis for each individual elderly patient with whatever psychiatric disorder cannot safely be based on his age, the diagnostic classification, or any single variable. It must be based on the *total* condition of the individual, including his sociocultural background and premorbid personality, current environmental and psychological stresses to which he is subject, his physical health, and the structural and functional status of his brain. Another factor in the prognosis—perhaps the most important of all—is the result of vigorous intervention and treatment designed to alleviate or improve all the above-mentioned factors.

## SUMMARY AND CONCLUSION

Senescence is commonly associated with many adaptational or behavioral problems, and even psychotic symptoms. These conditions may or may not be related directly to the structural or functional impairments that are expected to develop sooner or later in all senile brains.

The primary characteristics of a diffuse brain disorder are impairments of those cognitive functions that depend directly on the activity of the brain tissue involved. These impairments are readily recognized when the disorder is severe. When the disorder is mild, however, its manifestations may be completely masked by other clinical problems resulting from environmental stresses, intrapsychic conflicts, or both. For this reason, a thorough evaluation of the brain is as important for old persons with so-called functional or psychogenic psychiatric disorders as for those in whom a brain syndrome is obvious. Such an evaluation, in addition to determining whether or not a brain disorder is present, should ideally be able to reveal also its severity and its relationship to other concurrent clinical manifestations.

Unfortunately, there are very few safe, effective, and practical clinical procedures that throw much light on the status of the brain. The electroencephalography, the xenon-inhalation method of measuring cerebral blood flow, and the echoencephalography are the only methods that are completely nontraumatic and safe enough to be used for routine screening of the brain. Electroencephalography is by far the most practical diagnostic procedure; the value of serial electroencephalograms is well recognized. The xenon-inhalation method and the echoencephalography are still under development and need further validation.

In some cases it seems wise to employ more specific evaluative procedures, in spite of the trauma and risk involved. Although the biopsy is the only procedure that offers an opportunity to study the brain tissue directly, the pneumoencephalogram may provide considerable morphological information about the brain and is the only sure method of determining the presence and degree of cerebral atrophy. The cerebral metabolic rate can be determined by measuring both the oxygen uptake of the brain and the cerebral blood flow. Brain scans and cerebral angiograms help to localize mass lesions in the brain, and the latter is particularly valuable in demonstrating vascular lesions.

It is obvious that no single procedure can provide complete information regarding the status of the brain. To evaluate even a limited aspect of the brain, more than one use of a particular procedure will be necessary. Because of the considerable variation found among individuals with much the same condition, the *change* observed in a variable over a period of time is much more informative than a single reading. This is particularly true of brain disorders in their early stages.

When a complete evaluation of an elderly person with slight, moderate, or marked brain disorder uncovers any causative or contributory factor that is amenable to treatment, everything possible should be done to eliminate, or at least alleviate, the underlying problem. Where the brain disorder is due to factors that cannot be controlled, the therapeutic effort should be directed toward preventing further insults to the impaired brain and alleviating environmental and intrapsychic stresses that may be contributing to the patient's problem.

## REFERENCES

1. American Psychiatric Association. *Diagnostic and Statistical Manual of Mental Disorders* (2d ed.). Washington, D.C.: American Psychiatric Association, 1968.
2. Benton, A. Psychological Tests for Brain Damage. In A. M. Freedman and H. I. Kaplan (Eds.), *Comprehensive Textbook of Psychiatry*. Baltimore: Williams & Wilkins, 1967.
3. Blessed, G., Tomlinson, B. E., and Roth, M. The association

between quantitative measures of dementia and of senile change in the cerebral grey matter of elderly subjects. *Brit. J. Psychiat.* 114:797–811, 1968.

4. Botwinick, J.   *Cognitive Processes in Maturity and Old Age.* New York: Springer, 1967.

5. Burgemeister, B. B.   *Psychological Techniques in Neurological Diagnosis.* New York: Harper, 1962.

6. Busse, E. W., and Wang, H.- S.   The value of electroencephalography in geriatrics. *Geriatrics* 20:906–924, 1965.

7. Butler, R. H., Dastur, D. K., and Perlin, S.   Relationships of senile manifestations and chronic brain syndromes to cerebral circulation and metabolism. *J. Psychiat. Res.* 3:229–238, 1965.

8. Corsellis, J. A. N.   *Mental Illness and the Aging Brain.* London: Oxford University Press, 1962.

9. Dastur, D. K., Lane, M. H., Hansen, D. B., Kety, S. S., Perlin, S., Butler, R., and Sokoloff, L.   Effects of Aging on Cerebral Circulation and Metabolism in Man. In J. E. Birren, R. N. Butler, S. W., Greenhouse, L. Sokoloff, and M. R. Yarrow (Eds.), *Human Aging: A Biological and Behavioral Study.* Washington, D.C.: U.S. Government Printing Office, 1963.

10. Dewan, J. G., and Spaulding, W. B.   *The Organic Psychoses, A Guide To Diagnosis.* Toronto: University of Toronto Press, 1958.

11. Erba, G., and Lombroso, C. T.   Detection of ventricular landmarks by two dimensional ultrasonography. *J. Neurol. Neurosurg. Psychiat.* 31:232–244, 1968.

12. Feuerlein, W., and Dillin, H.   The Echo-encephalogram of the Third Ventricle in Different Age Groups. In E. Kazner, W. Schiefer, and K. J. Zulch (Eds.), *Proceedings in Echo-encephalography.* New York: Springer, 1968.

13. Garg, A. G., and Taylor, A. R.   A-Scan echoencephalography in measurement of the cerebral ventricles. *J. Neurol. Neurosurg. Psychiat.* 31:245–249, 1968.

14. Goldfarb, A. I., Fisch, M., and Gerber, I. E.   Predictors of mortality in the institutionalized aged. *Dis. Nerv. Syst.* 27:21–29, 1966.

15. Gosling, R. H.   The association of dementia with radiologically demonstrated cerebral atrophy. *J. Neurol. Neurosurg. Psychiat.* 18:129–133, 1955.

16. Harper, A. M.   Measurement of cerebral blood flow in man. *Scot. Med. J.* 12:349–360, 1967.

17. Haug, J. O.   Pneumoencephalographic studies in mental disease. *Acta Psychiat. Scand.* (Suppl. 38) 165:1–104, 1962.

18. Hedland, S., Köhler, V., Nylin, G., Olsson, R., Regnström, O., Rothström, E., and Åström, E. Cerebral blood circulation in dementia. *Acta Psychiat. Scand.* 40:77–106, 1964.

19. Ingvar, D. H., Baldy-Moulinier, M., Sulg, I., and Horman, S. Regional cerebral blood flow related to EEG. *Acta Neurol. Scand.* (Suppl. 14) 179–182, 1965.

20. Kahn, R. L., Goldfarb, A. I., Pollack M., and Peck, A. Brief objective measures for the determinations of mental status in the aged. *Amer. J. Psychiat.* 117:326–328, 1960.

21. Kay, D. W. K., Norris, V., and Post, F. Prognosis in psychiatric disorders of the elderly, an attempt to define indicators of early death and early recovery. *J. Ment. Sci.* 102:129–140, 1956.

22. Kety, S. S. The Cerebral Circulation. In J. Field (Ed.), *Handbook of Physiology, Section I, Neurophysiology,* vol. III. Washington, D.C.: American Physiological Society, 1960.

23. Kiev, A., Chapman, L. F., Guthrie, T. C., and Wolff, G. The highest integrative functions and diffuse cerebral atrophy. *Neurology* (Minneap.) 12:363–385, 1962.

24. Klee, A. The relationship between clinical evaluation of mental deterioration, psychological test results, and the cerebral metabolic rate of oxygen. *Acta Neurol. Scand.* 40:337–345, 1964.

25. Lassen, N. A. Cerebral blood flow and oxygen consumption in man. *Physiol. Rev.* 39:183–238, 1959.

26. Lassen, N. A., Munck, O., and Tottey, E. R. Mental function and cerebral oxygen consumption in organic dementia. *Arch. Neurol. Psychiat.* 77:126–133, 1957.

27. McCarron, M. M., and McCormick, R. A. *Acute Organic Disorder Accompanied by Mental Symptoms.* Sacramento: California Department of Mental Hygiene, 1967.

28. McHenry, L. C., Jr. Cerebral blood flow. *New Eng. J. Med.* 274:82–91, 1966.

29. Meyer, V. Critique of psychological approaches to brain damage. *J. Ment. Sci.* 103:80–109, 1957.

30. Nunn, J. F. Influence of age and other factors on hypoxemia in the postoperative period. *Lancet* 2:466–468, 1965.

31. Obrist, W. D., Sokoloff, L., Lassen, N. A., Lane, M. H., Butler, R. N., and Feinberg, I. Relation of EEG to cerebral blood flow and metabolism in old age. *Electroenceph. Clin. Neurophysiol.* 15:610–619, 1963.

32. Obrist, W. D., Thompson, H. K., Jr., King, C. H., and Wang, H.- S. Determination of regional cerebral blood flow by inhalation by 133-xenon. *Circ. Res.* 20:124–135, 1967.

33. Payne, J. P., and Conway, C. M.   Hypoxemia after surgery and anesthesia. *Postgrad. Med. J.* 42:341–350, 1966.

34. Roth, M.   The natural history of mental disorder in old age. *J. Ment. Sci.* 101:281–301, 1955.

35. Rothschild, D.   The clinical differentiation of senile and arteriosclerotic psychosis. *Amer. J. Psychiat.* 98:324–333, 1941.

36. Simonson, E.   Experimental hypoxemia in older and younger healthy men. *J. Appl. Physiol.* 16:639–640, 1961.

37. Smith, W. T., Turner, E., and Sim, M.   Cerebral biopsy in the investigation of presenile dementia: II. *Brit. J. Psychiat.* 112: 127–133, 1966.

38. Sokoloff, L.   Metabolism of the Central Nervous System in Vivo. In J. Field (Ed.), *Handbook of Physiology, Section I, Neurophysiology*, vol. III. Washington, D.C.: American Physiological Society, 1960.

39. Sorbini, C. A., Grassi, V., Solinas, E., and Muiesan, G.   Arterial oxygen tension in relation to age in healthy subjects. *Respiration* 25:1–11, 1968.

40. Spitzer, R. L., Fleiss, J. L., Endicott, J., and Cohen, J.   Mental status schedule. *Arch. Gen. Psychiat.* (Chicago) 16:479–493, 1967.

41. Thompson, L. W., and Wilson, S.   Electrocortical reactivity and learning in the elderly. *J. Geront.* 21:45–51, 1966.

42. Trier, T. R.   Characteristics of mentally ill aged: A comparison of patients with psychogenic disorders and patients with organic brain syndromes. *J. Geront.* 21:354–364, 1966.

43. U.S. Bureau of the Census. *Current Population Reports.* Series P-25, No. 352. Washington, D.C.: U.S. Government Printing Office, 1966.

44. U.S. National Center For Health Statistics. *Prevalence of Chronic Conditions and Impairments Among Residents of Nursing and Personal Care Homes—United States, May–June, 1964.* P.H.S. Publication No. 1000, Series 12, No. 8. Washington, D.C.: U.S. Government Printing Office, 1967.

45. U.S. National Institute of Mental Health. *Outpatient Psychiatric Clinics, Special Statistical Report, Old Adult Patient, 1964, State and Total United States.* P.H.S. Publication No. 1553. Washington, D.C.: U.S. Government Printing Office, 1967.

46. U.S. National Institute of Mental Health. *Patients in Mental Institutions, 1966, Part II. State and County Hospitals.* P.H.S. Publication No. 1818. Washington, D.C.: U.S. Government Printing Office, 1968.

47. U.S. National Institute of Mental Health. *Patients in Men-*

*tal Institutions, 1966, Part III. Private Mental Hospitals and General Hospitals with Psychiatric Service.* P.H.S. Publication No. 1818. Washington, D.C.: U.S. Government Printing Office, 1968.

48. Wang, H.- S. The brain and intellectual function in senescence. Presented at the American Psychological Association Meeting, San Francisco, Calif., 1968.
49. Wang, H.- S., and Busse, E. W. EEG of healthy old persons, a longitudinal study: I. Dominant background activity and occipital rhythm. In press.
50. Wang, H.- S., Obrist, W. D., and Busse, E. W. Neurophysiological correlates of the intellectual function of community elderly. Presented at the American Psychiatric Association Annual Meeting, Bal Harbour, Fla., 1969.
51. Ward, R. J., Tolas, A. G., Benveniste, R. J., Hansen, J. M., and Bonica, J. J. Effect of posture on normal arterial blood gas tensions in the aged. *Geriatrics* 21:139–143, February 1966.
52. Willanger, R., Thygesen, P., Nielsen, R., and Petersen, O. Intellectual impairment and cerebral atrophy—a psychological, neurological, and radiological investigation. *Danish Med. Bull.* 15:65–93, 1968.

# 14

# Institutional Care of the Aged

ALVIN I. GOLDFARB

Approximately one million of the nearly 20 million elderly persons in the United States are now in institutions. Many more need protective care in hospitals, "homes," and well-regulated congregate living arrangements. This actual and potential institutional population is heterogeneous. It includes persons from 65 to well over 90 years of age, of varied ethnic, religious, cultural, occupational, and socioeconomic backgrounds, who differ in family, friends, personal resources, energy, interests, and illnesses, as well as in physical and emotional state. Their psychiatric conditions also span a wide range. In some, disorders are brought into old age from youth, while in others depressive and paranoid reactions develop or first emerge as significant in old age; organic mental syndromes, very often complicated by disorder of affect or thought, are present in the predominant number.

There has been much discussion, both lay and professional, about how the needs of this varied population of aged persons can best be met. Personal prejudices, the bias of vested interests, misconceptions about society, underestimation of the number of afflicted individuals and of their needs for comprehensive health care, and—not least—widespread reluctance to finance expensive services have influenced or blocked the development of institutions and their patterns of care.

## STATE HOSPITALS

Prior to 1950 the burden of care of old persons with combined psychiatric and physical illness was carried in large part by state hospitals and was shared to some extent by homes for the aged and chronic disease hospitals. Overcrowding in state hospitals and the medical demands made by a large number of acutely ill first admissions, whose death rate soon after entrance to the hospital was extremely high, led to protests, surveys, and claims that state hospitals were being used as dumping grounds for the incurably ill aged and poor, that medically ill were being misdirected, and that large numbers of relatively well, aged individuals were kept in state hospitals simply because they had no place to go. In the 1940's there was much talk about excluding aged homeless persons, and among other efforts to decrease the state hospital burden was the passage, in one state, of a law forbidding state hospital admission or retention of dotards; this was soon rescinded.

The claims that state hospitals were being abused as a site of care for aged persons were actually exaggerated. For example, the examination of patients in Connecticut state hospitals by Schindell [15] at the time the furor about "mistaken admissions" was at its height revealed that very few could justifiably be transferred to other types of facilities, not to speak of private homes. Furthermore an examination of the categories of hospitalized old persons reveals that first admissions in old age constitute only 12 pecent of the total hospital population; and, despite the fact that they might have constituted 30 to 40 percent of all first admissions in a given year, they are only one-fourth to one-third of the hospital geriatric population. It is patients who have aged in the hospital who constitute by far the largest number of old persons in state hospitals. They are chiefly schizophrenics. A relatively small proportion entered with affective disorder, drug dependence, or organic mental syndromes of relatively early occurrence. Many have proved resistant to therapy or have become withdrawn examples of the "hospitalization syndrome" which emerges with relative neglect. Others are relatively well adjusted within the protective hospital setting [2, 5].

Recently there has been renewed agitation to reduce the number of old persons in state hospitals. This has been attempted in several ways: (1) by transfer of chronologically old persons—predominantly the well adjusted, the chemically restrained, or the relatively meek and submissive members of the aged-in-the-hospital group—to nursing homes, boarding homes, lodgings or foster homes; and (2) by exclusion "at the gate" of chronologically old persons who appear to be physically acutely ill, who appear likely to become permanent residents, or who appear to be free of gross affective disorder.

In the 1950's the growth of proprietary nursing homes burgeoned; regional overbuilding and empty beds led, in part, to the recruitment of "improved or well" or "well-adjusted" state hospital patients to fill them. This was accepted as a solution to hospital overcrowding and was welcomed as a means of decreasing direct financial responsibility by many state hospital systems. Also, it was heralded as a humane "return of aged patients to the community." The wholesale transfer of patients to nursing homes was advocated as the preferred alternative to state hospital care. In fact the predominant number of transferred persons was from those who had aged in the hospital and not from the group of persons first admitted in their old age. Moreover, the change of institutions was the equivalent of transfer from one inadequate, poorly staffed backward to another where space, medical and general care, helpful personnel, and community life either within or outside were less rather than more available. Through the use of preadmission screening teams prior to state hospital admission, nursing homes as alternatives to the state hospital have been recommended and implemented for selected patients. This is especially true recently, since Medicare and Medicaid have increased available funds.

## NURSING HOMES AND HOMES FOR THE AGED

Even well before these efforts to use alternatives to state hospitals, old persons with psychiatric disorders were found in a variety of institutions. These are variously and confusingly named. Two general types in addition to the state hospital can be more or less clearly identified: homes for the aged and nursing homes. Each of these types of facility is at present in an accelerated transitional state because of Medicare and Medicaid financing. Therefore the type and quality of functioning of institutions of the same general type tend to vary from place to place and time to time. There are wide variations in size, staffing, programs, and quality of care, as well as in cost to the consumer.

Table 1 (on page 294) attempts to define these two chief non-hospital categories. It should be noted that small (for example, 8- to 15-bed) old-age homes as well as lodging houses, "senior citizen hotels," residential hotels, housing projects for the old, or foster homes that are not clearly affiliated with homes for the aged, are not considered to be institutions in the sense of this discussion. Unfortunately these miscellaneous residences for the aged house many persons who actually need and would benefit from the use of the more formally titled institutions; in general they are make-shifts which have arisen because of social attitudes that discourage the use of hospitals and homes for the aged as well as because of their relatively low cost [14].

As noted in Table 1, now that Medicare provides money to old persons for a three- to four-month period of posthospital care in specified nursing homes, there have been changes in the selection of patients by many of the homes. In an attempt to raise and maintain standards of nursing home care, Medicare reimbursement has become predicated upon a nursing home's rehabilitative, re-storative efforts, and its staff and facilities, thus giving rise to the "extended care facility." While praiseworthy in their intent to ele-vate standards of care, these rulings have had considerable but not entirely desirable influence upon patient selection and care.

By making large numbers of persons eligible for relatively short-term care in nursing homes which improve their staffs and pro-grams—or appear to do so—Medicare has created a large popula-tion of affluent consumers. They are preferable to persons who must pay their own way on limited personal resources or welfare aid because they are below Medicare age or have exhausted its benefits. Although persons appear to be selected on the basis of potential for rehabilitation as suggested by Medicare, the individual's financial resources affect his acceptability. Thus, admitted freely are the rich and sick, or the poor and well; the rich "well" are also acceptable, but the poor and sick are largely unwelcome. This is a matter of common sense—a move from Medicare payment to full payment for continued care by a rich patient provides a stable population making for economic security of the institution. The poor "well" can be discharged within a reasonable period before the expiration of Medicare reimbursements, making the place "look good." The relatively well rich similarly speak well for the restorative function of the home but contribute to troublesome turnover. As for the poor sick, they, unfortunately, present a problem of disposition unless the home is willing to continue them at a considerable reduction of rate.

Proprietary nursing home discrimination against persons with long-term needs for protective care, unless they have personal resources, is further evidence that facilities develop in accordance with financing; "the patient goes the way the money flows." Poor persons who need care because of varying degrees of organic mental syndrome, with or without physical functional impairment, have no place to go. They are not welcome in state hospitals, have a limited appeal to extended care facilities, and are now faced with a scarcity of low-cost nursing home beds and old-age homes, as well as the discriminatory, selective practices of the latter.

A second problem arising from the creation of the extended care facility concept of classification has been its effect on homes for the aged—especially the large, urban, well-staffed quasihospitals, which contain the highest proportion of beds. These homes, for purposes of reimbursement under Medicare provisions, are being categorized as extended care facilities and accredited as such rather than as hospitals. In actuality such homes now receive few or no patients on a Medicare reimbursable basis because such admissions must be within a ten-day period after discharge from a general hospital, and old-age home waiting periods must exceed this by far because of their low turnover—about 18 percent or 90 possible admissions, to a 500-bed facility a year. Thus, unless methods of processing applicants are changed, the applicants are relegated to

TABLE 1. *Comparison of old-age homes and nursing homes*

| | Old-Age Homes (OAH) | Nursing Homes (NH) | Comment |
|---|---|---|---|
| Auspices | Nonprofit, voluntary, usually sectarian. The private (nonsubsidized) divisions may resemble NH in admission policy and patient population | Proprietary, with few exceptions | A few nonprofit voluntary NH are comparable to OAH. Some "homestead" wards of general hospitals are comparable to NH |
| Supervision or licensure | Social services departments (residential areas), department of health (state), (infirmary and hospital areas) | State and municipal departments of hospitals, social welfare or health | Welfare department supervision usually occurs because 50 to 80 percent of NH residents are welfare supported. Also for most OAH this is true |
| Medical care | Varies from minimal to almost complete, exclusive of major surgery and radiotherapy. Care in outside hospitals paid for by Medicare, in most instances | None. Must be obtained from private physician or one assigned by welfare agency through group, hospital, panel or team or, for acute illness, by transfer to local hospital | OAH are permitted to employ physicians, NH are not |
| Nursing care | Varies from fair to excellent. Patients may be required to have special nurses and/or aides if family wishes or patient requires care in excess of institution norm, and if patient or family can afford the care | Very limited, often on paper but not in fact. "Specials" frequently required | Extended Care Facilities (ECF), like voluntary or private hospitals, may require family to pay for special nurses if patient to remain |

| | | | |
|---|---|---|---|
| Social services | Variable, but often considerable. Applicant screening, continuing liaison work with family is customary | Rare, usually none | NH may encourage family counseling. At times this is a means of increasing reimbursement otherwise restricted by law |
| Length of residence | For remainder of life | Usually for remainder of life, but transfers are frequent from home to home and to hospitals, rarely to OAH | Length of stay decreasing (see Admissions policies) as NH are converting to ECF |
| Size (beds) | 20 to 500 or more. Wide range of services: occupational therapy, recreational therapy, sheltered workshops, physiatry, podiatry, barbers and hairdressers, shops, chapel, clinics, dentistry, clubs, activities, library, music rooms, etc. | 15 to 300 or more. Services usually limited. No library, shops, hairdressers, etc.; podiatry and other services by special arrangement only | Adequate range of services is rare in small homes (under 100 beds). Services for which Medicare reimburses are often encouraged by ECF |
| Admissions policies | Variable, usually highly selective: patients in crisis, acutely ill, mentally ill excluded. Donations may be invited. Waiting periods variable, e.g., 3 to 6 months for the relatively well and 2 to 3 years for the ill, impaired, or disabled. "List hopping" for various reasons is not uncommon, e.g., donations, suitability as roommates in vacancy area, connections with important persons | Until recently, "anything goes"—if adjustment not made, patient transferred, often to state hospital. In past usually no waiting period. Availability of patients with Medicare money has resulted in waiting periods which vary from time to time, and has permitted selection of residents | Recently with ECF label, many NH are converting to . . . 100-day . . . type facilities which select those "who can profit from rehabilitation". Many small selective homes have shorter waiting periods because of the paucity of eligible persons |

TABLE 1 (cont'd.)

|  | Old-Age Homes (OAH) | Nursing Homes (NH) | Comment |
|---|---|---|---|
| Socioeconomic, cultural and religious affiliations of residents | Population usually homogeneous | Population is less homogeneous than in OAH | ... "100-day" ... Medicare policy encourages ECF admission of rich and sick, or poor and well, in preference to the poor and sick |
| Race | Few homes for Negro population | Negro population is over-represented | Changes due to Medicare, and restrictions in Medicaid money now presses many OAH toward becoming ECF and/or NH with decreased medical services and generally lowered standards of care |
| Financial arrangements | Patients' own funds—savings and income from Social Security and/or other pensions—used for maintenance. Referral to department of social services for Old Age Assistance or Medical Aid for the Aged, upon exhaustion of own funds or to make up difference between patient's monthly income and the monthly rate (set by department of health and/or department of social services). Rates for domiciliary care much lower than for infirmary care. Since 1965 amendments to Social Security Act doing away with filial responsibility, maintenance rarely paid for by families<br><br>Contributions to institution *must* be from families—not out of patient's funds—and are for capital, not mainte- | 60 to 80 percent are recipients of Old Age Assistance; proprietary homes are, in effect, subcontractors to government for the care of sick or impaired aged poor |  |

the lower Medicaid or welfare reimbursement on the same basis as nonextended care proprietary homes even though they provide far more facilities, staff, and restorative programs than the extended care facilities. Old-age homes, which now provide good care, are not adequately reimbursed, while extended care facilities are being well reimbursed for doing far less for only selected groups and for limited periods. From this present, somewhat confused picture it is difficult to predict future developments.

In the future there may be a decrease of staffing and facilities in old-age homes. Or, to state it conversely, more patients will be crowded into the same space or programs. If Medicare funds are not available to them and Medicaid payments are kept low, even the best of old-age homes may be forced to lower their standards of care. Old-age homes may then fall to the level of the type of nursing homes which do not qualify as extended care facilities and together with them will provide for the long-term housing—one can scarcely call it care—of chronically impaired old persons. Simultaneously, the number of available beds for such care may decrease because of the lack of economic incentive on the part of nursing homes to provide such beds. At the same time abuses of Medicare may lead to curtailment of extended care facility reimbursement and of its own usefulness to the aged poor. There may also be escalation of costs of care which may not be reversible. It is to be hoped that, as this problem of welfare and public health becomes more pressing, legislative or other public action will cause changes in the allocation of funds, in state hospital policies, and in the regulation or implementation of Medicare and Medicaid which will improve matters. In many states there have already been moves toward the strengthening and expansion of state hospital systems despite talk which indicates the converse.

The differences between old-age homes and nursing homes, somewhat dogmatically stated in the accompanying tables, are not well known and lead to misunderstandings. These misunderstandings tend to be reinforced by the misleading names which confuse the types. Doctors and nurses in general hospitals, for example, often overrate the functional and care-taking potential of residences whose names include the term *nursing* and underestimate the severity of impairment found in residents of old-age homes. Also, there is inadequate understanding of the complex admission procedures and the variety of plans for financing care. Mistaken ideas may lead to unreasonable demands upon families to make arrangements for a patient's care. These misconceptions are all too often shared by social workers who, despite their presumed training in welfare matters, often have scant knowledge about nursing home or old-age facilities, staffing, or procedures in general, and little or no knowledge about local institutions.

INSTITUTIONAL POPULATIONS

Contrary to popular beliefs old persons do not reach old-age homes for social reasons, nursing homes for medical reasons, and state hospitals for psychiatric reasons alone. A number of factors contribute to overlapping characteristics in these groups [3, 4, 11]. In Table 2 are seen some of the characteristics of persons at the time of their admission to the three types of institutions.

A comparison of the findings obtained in 1957–58 with a similar study performed in selected homes of the northeast United States by the Council of Jewish Federation and Welfare Funds in cooperation with the National Institute of Mental Health in 1966 indicates that for old-age homes the age at admission and the age of residents are slightly more advanced. The prevalence of brain syndrome is now somewhat greater, and the proportion of severely impaired persons in the old-age homes is higher. There is no significant change with respect to marital state at the time of admission, or to number of living children. A higher proportion of those in the more recent sample was dependent upon welfare aid, at admission and at the time of the study [10, 16]. This appears to reflect primarily a change in the law which now relieves children of legal responsibility for the support of aged indigent parents.

It can be seen from these data and from other studies that the sampled 1957–58

| | Percent in Old-Age Homes | Percent in Nursing Homes | Percent in State Hospitals | Percent in All Institutions |
|---|---|---|---|---|
| Age at admission: 65–74 | 44 | 33 | 44 | 40 |
| 75–84 | 47 | 48 | 44 | 37 |
| 84 + | 9 | 18 | 11 | 13 |
| (*Average admission age*) | (76) | (79) | (76) | (—) |
| Marital state: Married | 12 | 9 | 22 | 12 |
| Widowed | 67 | 60 | 60 | 64 |
| Divorced/separated | 6 | 2 | 5 | 4 |
| Single | 15 | 23 | 12 | 18 |
| Number of living children: None | 35 | 43 | 34 | 36 |
| One | 14 | 22 | 26 | 18 |
| Two | 16 | 14 | 12 | 15 |
| Three + | 35 | 11 | 23 | 26 |
| Sources of income at admission: Welfare | 28 | 73 | 22 | 43 |
| Family aid | 32 | 18 | 21 | 27 |
| Personal income | 72 | 29 | 9 | 58 |
| Admitted from: Own home | 61 | 25 | 41 | 45 |
| Relative's home | 26 | 8 | 31 | 19 |
| Nursing home | 8 | 8 | 7 | 8 |
| General hospital | 3 | 56 | 15 | 21 |
| Other | 4 | 3 | 4 | 2 |
| Years of schooling: 0–7 | 33 | 70 | 54 | 55 |
| 8 + | 67 | 30 | 46 | 45 |

Note: Where categories add to less than 100 percent, the remainder represents "unknown." "Sources of income" adds to over 100 percent because of multiple sources per individual.

These figures gathered in 1958, and representative of the New York metropolitan area, are a fairly accurate reflection of the present situation throughout the urban United States, except that patients (or residents), both on admission and on a sampling of the population at any given time, are older and more impaired—physically and mentally—and except that, as described in the text, all institutions are now in a transitional state.

majority of those who come to live in the institutions as first admissions in their chronological old age do so when in their late seventies or eighties [12, 13]. The presence of protective, caretaking persons such as a mate or children favors chances of the aged's admission to an old-age home as does the existence of a good personal or family income; many aged persons, even if extremely incapacitated or disturbed, can wait out the time required. Years of schooling are a fair index of socioeconomic status and are illustrative of the same point—the better off one is socioeconomically, the less one is apt to use a nursing home or state hospital. This is now changing as nursing homes that have moved toward extended care facility status are developing areas of long-term old-age home type of care in response to prompt admission of rich aged ill on a Medicare basis and extension of their care on a personal payment basis.

While immediate factors leading to institutional care include advanced age and debility or multiple impairments—of sight, hearing, ambulation, mentation, and self-care ability—together with a need for care, these are usually joined by an absence of available resources, such as money or family, sufficient to provide a "one-bed nursing home" (or hospital) in their own home. The proportion of men and women may vary greatly from one institution to another. It may be based upon facilities available, but in general women tend to outnumber men by at least two to one; in some homes for the aged the ratio is as high as seven to one. This is because they live longer than men and outlive their usually older spouses, thus providing a large population at risk of institutionalization on account of age and the absence of a protective mate. Conversely men of considerable disability may be maintained at home by younger and functionally more capable wives. Persons of either sex, more often women, are frequently maintained outside of institutions by children who thus provide protection against institutionalization. Nursing homes and old-age homes have been, almost invariably, permanent residences; for state hospital patients the existence of a spouse or children increases the chances of leaving the hospital, at times for home, at others for an alternative institution. The better educated and socioeconomically advantaged tend to reach an institution later than their poorer counterparts. It then is more likely to be a home for the aged, except for the very old who, because of a severe mental state, find their way to a state hospital. Men who have never married appear to make use of institutional protection earlier than equally disabled married men or widowers. The youngest and oldest of old people are admitted to state hospitals. These ends of the age spectrum are represented, respectively, by functional disorders, and by severe brain syndrome in the presence of relatively sound body. Admission to old-age homes and state hospitals is usually directly from home, whereas admission to nursing homes is most frequently from general hospitals.

Symptoms of disturbed behavior such as suicidal attempts, attacks on others, dangerous wandering, or confused and dangerous misuse of household appliances frequently lead to psychiatric hospitalization. The loss of protective persons by death, or the loss of accommodations or changes in neighborhoods, as well as needs for protective care, often lead to application to old-age homes on the part of persons who can foresee waiting the three months to three years required. Crises such as accentuation of preexisting impairment by acute illness, accidents, or a sudden shift in social circumstances frequently lead to nursing home care by way of the general hospital or, less frequently, directly from home.

Auspices, admission and retention policies and procedures, and modes of financing result, then, in a mutual selection of patients and institutions not based strictly upon personal needs or institutional abilities to meet them. This results in institutionalized groups which overlap in their physical, mental, and social characteristics. This is contrary to the common impression that each of the three types serves a separate segment of the older population. Some of the similarities, as well as differences, in characteristics of residents in the three types of institutions are shown in Table 3.

As shown in Table 3, old-age homes do not serve only social and retirement needs. Over 50 percent of their beds are of the infirmary type, caring for grossly impaired and disabled aged persons. Nurs-

TABLE 3. *Selected characteristics in three types of institution by percentage of persons, 1957–58*

|  | Percent in Old-Age Homes | Percent in Nursing Homes | Percent in State Hospitals | Percent in All Institutions |
|---|---|---|---|---|
| Age distribution of residents: | | | | |
| 65–74 | 23 | 21 | 44 | 25 |
| 75–84 | 49 | 43 | 43 | 46 |
| 85 + | 24 | 24 | 13 | 23 |
| All mental disorders | 90 | 93 | 100 | 90 |
| Chronic brain syndrome: | | | | |
| Mild | 37 | 24 | 9 | 27 |
| Moderate | 28 | 35 | 32 | 31 |
| Severe | 15 | 29 | 53 | 27 |
| Total | 80 | 88 | 94 | 85 |
| Physical functional status: | | | | |
| Fair | 51 | 21 | 30 | 36 |
| Poor | 37 | 36 | 38 | 36 |
| Very poor | 13 | 43 | 32 | 27 |
| Bedfast | 10 | 33 | 27 | — |
| Incontinent | 10 | 37 | 29 | — |
| Physical dependency: *Cannot* | | | | |
| Bathe self | 33 | 77 | 57 | 50 |
| Dress self | 13 | 40 | 36 | 24 |
| Walk alone | 11 | 37 | 28 | 22 |
| Mobility poor | 7 | 26 | 13 | 14 |

ing homes serve a large number of relatively ambulatory, energetic, and physically well but moderately to severely mentally impaired aged. State hospital populations of persons first admitted in old age include a few relatively "young-old" persons (60 to 70) with functional disorders, and some with organic mental syndromes (chronic brain syndromes—CBS) related to cerebral arteriosclerosis (presenile brain disease); a very large number of "middle-aged-old" (70 to 80), most of whom have CBS of the senium, often in association with disorders of affect or thought content; and a substantial number of the very old with relatively uncomplicated severe CBS.

Persons with CBS are found in each setting. The proportion of the severely afflicted, however, is less in old-age homes than in nursing homes, and is highest in state hospitals. Also, persons with disorders of mood and content associated with brain syndromes are found in all, but there are fewest in old-age homes and more in state hospitals than in nursing homes. Also, persons with poor physical functional status (PFS) and multiple impairments or chronic illnesses are found in each type of institution—the highest proportion being found in nursing homes, fewest in state hospitals. It should be noted that until recently less than 10 percent of persons coming to state hospitals in their old age had a disorder of affect or thought in the absence of CBS. On the other hand, in private psychiatric hospitals, prior to Medicare, the majority of persons admitted in old age suffered from disorders of affect (depressive reactions), a few were paranoid, and the rest had CBS. Now that general hospital psychiatric wards have been developed, the largest number of old persons with affective disorder will go (admission policies permitting) to such units, although the state hospitals, because of their commitment to developing as intensive care centers, would welcome them. A further reason for state hospital competition for these patients is their value as payers via Medicare.

In sum, with advancing age an increasingly high proportion of old persons reaches institutions. When found in the institutions, over 30 percent are bedridden, about 25 percent are incontinent, and the majority are constantly disoriented for time, place, and person, have gross memory defects, obvious difficulties in doing the simplest of calculations, as well as dearth of general information. The PFS of these persons is usually poor, active disease is the rule, and most are depressed in some degree; many are paranoid. For all such patients—whatever the name of the institution or its categorical type—because of the vulnerability of old persons with even minimal brain syndrome to confusional states, disorganized behavior, agitation, depression, and angry outbursts, psychiatrically oriented care is a requirement. Whatever the institution, the patient's needs are such that it can be said: "If medical care is good, psychiatric care should be improved; if both are good, social services should be improved; if all are good, all should be improved."

## ATTITUDES TOWARD INSTITUTIONAL USE

Old persons in general are opposed to the use of institutions; this is more the rule than the exception, and is most obvious in the clearly mentally ill, the subtly mentally disturbed, and in the oldest and the most impaired. Thus it is that those who need protective care the most want it the least and may oppose it the most vigorously, whereas those who may need it the least are less resistive to accepting the change in residence. This makes it obvious that one reason aged persons who need protective institutions also need psychiatric assistance is the intensity of their feelings that institutional use constitutes rejection by family and friends and a loss of independence.

Unfortunately, the low quality of institutional care, however attractive the physical plant, tends to reinforce such beliefs and attitudes. Institutions are for the most part so poorly equipped, staffed, and organized that the resistance of families of aged persons to making use of them is more frequently related to realistic appraisal of the site of care and anger against "the system" than to guilt based upon giving the care of the parent over to others or, as is so often asserted, upon unconscious hostility.

Institutional care is usually regarded as a prelude to death by applicants and their families rather than as a new, useful experience in community living, such as it can be in the best old-age homes and could be in many state hospitals that attempt to become communities in themselves as well as to remain related to the outside world. Unfortunately, most homes, especially proprietary nursing homes, do not have the potential for becoming self-contained communities and are by no means a part of the large community. Therefore, they do become places in which old persons with little or nothing to do, their senses, minds, and emotions blunted by drugs, simply wait for death.

Entrance into residences of such poor quality tends to downgrade the individual's image of himself; his disability may become greater, and there may be development or exaggeration of psychological and emotional disorder. Institutional deterioration can be counteracted by the provision of community type activities: sheltered workshops in hospitals or homes, recreational therapy, hotel type accommodations, and the contagion of high morale in well-motivated staff. These improve concept of self, improve behavior, and help decrease objections to entrance into homes as well as to continued residence in them.

## THERAPEUTIC EFFORTS

Patients generally do better if they have opportunities for privacy. For sufficiently well persons, social interaction and good interpersonal relationships are favored by residential accommodation in private, unshared rooms. Cultural differences, however, exist, and many old persons prefer to share rooms because they have never lived alone. Other reasons for a desire or need to share living space are extremely severe impairment and fear of becoming ill and not being able to signal for help, or simply of being alone, which may be continuation of a lifelong anxiety. Eating facilities, however, should not be in the patient's room but in a common dining room. Atmosphere should be homelike and it should not be clinical, even in units where medical care is intensive, because this is the patient's home. Rugs are useful and should be wall to wall, nonskid, washable, and not so soft as to impede walking or interfere with balance. Rugs of any type, however, prove to be unsatisfactory where incontinence is uncontrollable. Lamps, homelike fixtures, and individual, easily accessible, yet personally safeguarded storage places are essential.

The beds should be low for the sake of the patient, although this may mean some extra effort for the nurse. Side rails generally cause more falls and fractures than they prevent, in addition to being personally humiliating; furthermore, in the absence of additional restraints they are rarely effective in limitation of wandering. The best restraints for confused and agitated patients are properly motivated alert personnel, minimum amounts of the proper medications, and "seduction" into activity. A useful way to restrain wandering patients is to build in the round so that the wanderer is never further from the centrally stationed nurse than he is when in his own room no matter how far he walks. Necessary in all institutions that care for the aged is psychiatrically oriented supervision of residents based on recognition that most behavior can be understood as motivated.

Basically, the establishment of relationships with personnel, not physical restraints nor chemical restraints, is a patient's greatest safeguard and reassurance. Optimal care of the frightened and confused aged is consequently expensive under the best of conditions.

Encouraging social interests in old persons with CBS requires leadership. As in military groups, relationships are established first with the leader and later, if at all, with peers through this common bond.

Staff morale, in turn, is favorably influenced by vertical and horizontal staff conferences about patient problems, in which a framework for the selection and collection of information is provided and guidelines for care and management are offered and freely discussed. Such conferences are best led by psychiatrists or psychologists experienced in the care of the aged. In general, institutional staffs have too little an appreciation of their importance as psychotherapists and of the importance of their nonpsychiatric skills and duties as vehicles for psychotherapy; they need psychiatric consultations and conferences to educate them to these factors, to maintain morale, and for periodic reinforcement. They respond with optimism to the interest of a psychiatrist and react favorably to his policing function with respect to human transactions. Staff attitude, interest, and care of aged mentally-impaired persons, the severely physically disabled, and the slowly dying or terminally ill are improved by the introduction of psychiatric assistance.

Aged institutional residents tend to respond favorably to a structured but flexible program which leads them to exploitation of their assets without unduly subjecting them to failure or confrontation of their deficits—physical or mental. In this, even skilled staff may need considerable aid so that patients may not be wrongly assessed. For example, behavioral disturbance should not be mistaken for dementia, or mild and cooperative behavior be taken as evidence of cerebral competence. In a recent survey staffs of unsophisticated old-age homes grossly underestimated the number of persons in their charge who had CBS; the disorder was recognized only if severe.

Staff members often need assistance in reaching decisions about the specific types of activity which can have maximal restorative or remotivational influence. The fear that patients will lose self-sufficiency if permitted to become emotionally dependent, or that they may be vulnerable to grief at the loss of personnel by staff turnover, must be vigorously countered. Personnel on all levels need much instruction about the value of transference, rapport, "parentification," or the interest of the "significant other," found in the guise of a staff member, in promoting self-sufficiency or optimal function. The nuclear importance of a dependency relationship, as a means of helping the patient toward optimal functioning and least vulnerability to personal losses, is a paradox with which institutional staff must become well acquainted.

The importance of sheltered workshops, music rooms and music therapy, but most of all of physiotherapy as vehicles for psychotherapy cannot be overrated. Each of these, like the provision of good basic medical care and the establishment of a relationship with the physician or the medical department of the institution, has extremely important reassuring and supportive influence on the patient. Individual differences must be grasped and their implications heeded. For example, many old persons gain a sense of worth and confidence from "work for pay," while to others this is objectionable: they feel they have worked long enough; for some, any such work for pay is felt to be humiliatingly childlike, especially if patronizingly led by children or rich volunteers [1].

## MORTALITY

Mortality is higher in institutional populations than in the general population [9]. Taken as a group and excluding those acutely ill persons who die in the first three months after admission to a psychiatric hospital, about 25 percent are dead within the first year, over 40 percent by the end of the second year, over 50 percent by the end of the third year, and the percent dead after four, five, six, and seven years is 65, 73, 79 and 82 percent, respectively. The death rate is higher for males than females and is exceptionally high for persons who have severe CBS as determined by psychiatric or psychological test or by a high degree of physical functional impairment or incontinence [7]. See Table 4.

TABLE 4.  *Comparative percentages of deaths by year in old-age homes, nursing homes, and state hospitals*

|  | Total | | Percent Died Within: | | | | | | |
|---|---|---|---|---|---|---|---|---|---|
|  | No. | % | 1 yr. | 2 yrs. | 3 yrs. | 4 yrs. | 5 yrs. | 6 yrs. | 7 yrs. |
| OAH | 454 | 100 | 17 | 32 | 46 | 58 | 69 | 74 | 78 |
| NH | 396 | 100 | 26 | 45 | 58 | 71 | 79 | 86 | 89 |
| [a]SH | 166 | 100 | 35 | 48 | 63 | 69 | 75 | 80 | 83 |
| Total | 1016 | 100 | 24 | 40 | 53 | 65 | 74 | 80 | 83 |

[a] Survivors of at least three months in the hospital.

The high mortality of state hospital patients in the first year and especially in the first few months after admission is undoubtedly due to their moribund or preterminal condition. Many aged persons in their last few months of life become extremely difficult problems of management: noisy, destructive, impulsive, assaultive, or self-damaging to degrees that endanger others as well as themselves. When medicated they may become more disorganized or comatose. Their nursing needs tend to exceed the available facilities in general hospitals. In desperation they are sent to the psychiatric hospital. The latter, unfortunately, has not always been well enough equipped or staffed to manage the multiple medical problems of these patients. Despite the likelihood that the best of medical care would make little difference to most, might prolong the lives of a few for a short time, and of an exceptional patient for longer, there has been criticism of state hospitals for their high death rate.

Perhaps it is partly in reaction to this that state hospital systems have tended to declare themselves out of bounds to the medically acutely ill aged patient, whatever his mental status. Studies have demonstrated that mortality is high even for aged persons who are not acutely ill and who have reached nonhospital institutions. Presently available data obtained by evaluation of nonhospital institutions, following the course of transferred patients, and by longitudinal study of institutionalized persons, point to the relation of mortality to the basic condition of the patient rather than to the facility, program, or transfer. In general the data suggest that, given adequate shelter, food, and general medical care, the life-span of severely impaired and disabled aged persons in the three major types of institution is related to their physical condition or viability. It seems doubtful that the provision of extra services greatly prolongs life in the very ill, although it may add immeasurably to comfort. Conversely, the relatively well may live somewhat longer in shelters which have programs and services which contribute to pleasure and the maintenance of dignity. The relatively robust also may react favorably to shift or change in domicile, whereas for the severely functionally impaired shifts appear to make demands or lead to relative neglect which may shorten life.

## CONCLUSION

There are a number of commonly held beliefs about persons who have reached, or appear to need, institutional care in their old age. Some of these ideas can be summarized as follows:

Aged persons in our society are rejected and neglected and discriminated against. They are discarded by selfish, callous families and are relegated to loneliness and discomfort which affects their mental and emotional well-being. When they become ill, they are quickly dumped into state hospitals, nursing homes, or old-age homes where many of them die from the shock of transfer or from humiliation. Large numbers of them are forced to remain in institutions simply because they have no place to go, and this is largely because their place in the community has been permitted to close in behind them. The children of this generation lack estimable character and virtue—they make one wonder how it is that "while one parent can take care of twelve children, twelve children cannot take care of one parent."

Such seemingly compassionate remarks appear to be exhortative toward improving the sorry lot of the aged. They are actually misstatements which tend to confuse thought and to block social action. They tend to turn one away from social organization aimed at ameliorating a major public health and welfare problem [6].

Thoughtful review of the general conditions noted above supports the contention that only persons with great need for institutional aid reach such points of care. There is no evidence that families "dump" troublesome old persons into an institution, state hospital, or whatever. On the contrary, the presence of family tends to be a major protection against institutional care, often to the disadvantage of the patient and contrary to his needs. It is more the rule that families wait too long for and fight against the use of institutions than that they make unnecessary use of them. Individual capacity for self-maintenance or the existence of personal and familial resources helps impaired persons avoid institutionalization; an absence of family, the presence of excess disability favored by ignorance, psychological or emotional disorder, or alcoholism, increases an individual's chances of institutional use.

The question "Is institutionalization really necessary?" for those found in these facilities can best be answered by the research findings which have demonstrated that it is usually a last resort—and a late solution—on the part of persons helping the aged, rather than a properly-timed search for assistance [8].

## REFERENCES

1. Goldfarb, A. I. Contributions of psychiatry to the institutional care of aged and chronically ill persons. *J. Chronic Dis.* 6:438–496, 1957.
2. Goldfarb, A. I. Current Trends in the Management of Psychiatrically Ill Aged. In P. Hoch and J. Zubin (Eds.), *Psychopathology of Aging.* New York: Grune & Stratton, 1961. Pp. 248–265.
3. Goldfarb, A. I. Mental health in the institution. *Gerontologist* 1:178–184, 1961.
4. Goldfarb, A. I. Prevalence of psychiatric disorder in metropolitan old age and nursing homes. *J. Amer. Geriat. Soc.* 10:77–84, 1962.
5. Goldfarb, A. I. An exploration of research findings. In *Research Utilization in Aging,* P.H.S. Publication No. 1211. Washington, D.C.: U.S. Department of Health, Education, and Welfare, 1964. Pp. 24–38.
6. Goldfarb, A. I. Responsibilities to our aged. *Amer. J. Nurs.* 11:78–82, 1964.
7. Goldfarb, A. I. Predicting mortality in the institutionalized aged. *Arch. Gen. Psychiat.* (Chicago) 21:172–176, 1969.
8. Goldfarb, A. I. Intimacy, loneliness and boredom in the older patient. Paper presented at the annual meeting of the American Psychiatric Association, Miami Beach, Fla., May, 1969. To be published.
9. Goldfarb, A. I., Fisch, M., and Gerber, I. Predictions of mortality in the institutionalized aged. *Dis. Nerv. Syst.* 27:21–29, 1966.
10. Goldfarb, A. I., Zelditch, M., and Burr, H. *Mental Impairment in Homes for the Aged.* New York: Council of Jewish Federations and Welfare Funds, 1969.
11. Pollack, M., Kahn, R., Gerber, I., and Goldfarb, A. I. The

relationship of mental and physical status in institutionalized aged persons. *Amer. J. Psychiat.* 117:120–124, 1960.
12. Pollack, E., Locke, B., and Kramer, M.   Trends in Hospitalization and Patterns of Care of the Aged Mentally Ill. In P. Hock and J. Zubin (Eds.), *Psychopathology of Aging.* New York: Grune & Stratton, 1961. Pp. 21–56.
13. Riley, M., Foner, A., et al.  *An Inventory of Research Findings.* Aging and Society, vol. I. New York: Russell Sage Foundation, 1968.
14. Rogin, M., Goldfarb, A. I., and Turner, H.  Institutional care facilities of older people in New York City. *J. Mount Sinai Hosp.* 35:358–370, 1968.
15. Shindell, S., and Cornfield, E.  Aged in Connecticut state mental hospitals. *J.A.M.A.* 160:1121–1125, 1956.
16. Wolk, R., Karp, E., and Goldfarb, A. I.   Mental impairment in residents of homes for the aged. Research project on mental impairment in the aged. Council of Jewish Federation and Welfare Funds and Office of the Consultant for the Aged, New York State Department of Mental Hygiene. Abstract in *Gerontologist* 7:24, 1967.

# 15

# Nursing of Older People

VIRGINIA STONE

Nursing of older people has gone through three distinct evolutionary stages since the turn of the century. Originally such nursing was provided by "kind hearty souls" who supplied sheltered care. As the older population increased, the demand for trained nurses to provide nursing care increased. Within the profession, the care of older people had low priority, and the nursing care provided was limited in scope. These conditions prevailed because of the paucity of knowledge in the field, as well as the lack of role models in the clinical setting. The first textbook in the field, *Geriatric Nursing*, did not appear until 1950. Research in the field was nonexistent at mid-century. The development of the nursing home movement accentuated the need for nurses to care for older patients. However, among nurses there was a lack of interest in this field of nursing, partially because they had received little training in it. As late as 1966 it was reported that the curriculum of most baccalaureate nursing programs did not include courses that emphasized geriatric nursing.

The nursing profession has concern for the upgrading of care for this age group. There is interest in moving from practice based on imitation and intuition (the second phase in this evolution) to practice supported by scientific theory. One means of improving practice is to develop a specialized area of practice, built on specific knowledge transmittable through various types of educational programs. A specialty arises in a profession when there is a body of knowledge dealing with the specific, and a large group of individuals whose care depends on the use of that specific knowledge. With the growing body of knowledge in gerontology and nursing, and with the increases in the older age population, it seems timely that the specialty, gerontological nursing, developed as the third stage in the evolutionary process.

The individual prepared as a gerontological nurse functions in such a way as to assist the aged person to regain or maintain his functional capacities, both physical and mental. She must, therefore, have knowledge of the psychosocial and physiological changes related to the process of aging.


## PSYCHOLOGICAL KNOWLEDGE INFLUENCING NURSING PRACTICE

Research findings, as well as clinical experience, strongly suggest that the nursing approach to the aged needs to be different from that directed toward other age groups. The slowing-down processes accompanying aging demand that the nurse adjust her own behavior to that of her patient. It is difficult for a young, energetic individual to move at a rate less than her usual speed. Yet if a correct response to a stimulus is desired, timing on the part of both the sender and the receiver of the message must be considered.

To determine an effective nursing approach, the nurse has a responsibility to assess the older person's capacities. This includes an assessment of the thought processes, as well as of physical capacity. Speed of perception is considered an important factor in the thought process of the aged. Two important areas of perception which the nurse can aid to some extent are vision and hearing. These can be grossly evaluated on initial contact. Because of the prevalence of hearing loss in old age, the nurse should assume the patient may have difficulty in hearing. She therefore tests the pitch and level of her voice to that of the gerist to determine the level of hearing for meaningful dialogue. This is done in such a way that the questions posed require a declarative sentence response. The nurse in her evaluation also determines if there is a problem in speech discrimination. Various patterns of speech spacing are presented and responses evaluated to determine the most effective pattern for the individual patient. Provisions should be made for some background sounds, for as Busse [1] has indicated, the older person is often unaware that he is missing background noises, but is aware of a feeling of loss and a sensation that the world is dead. Thus, hearing ability, speech discrimination, and background noise in relation to the strength of communicational stimuli all influence the effectiveness of the reception of these stimuli.

To determine the correct nursing approach, visual acuity needs to be similarly assessed. Because of changes in the visual pathway, lighting intensity needs to be increased with age. As the nurse considers the changes in dark adaptation, side vision, color matching, and contrast discrimination, she can assess the vision potential. She can then make environmental adjustments as necessary, such as the use of light bulbs with high wattage and the use of contrasting colors. In generally dark areas, such as bathrooms, there should be constant low lights for safety.

Aged persons often have difficulty perceiving the outlines of objects, especially if they are small and lack color contrast. Therefore they may require the assistance of another person in handling such things as a glass of water. Because of the translucence of both water and many drinking glasses, the perception of the object is difficult. Therefore the patient needs assistance and time to identify the glass of water and the rim as separate from the whole. Otherwise he may spill the contents to his embarrassment. Adaptations to visual difficulties can be made when the nurse realizes their influences on patient behavior.

Though efforts are made to improve the distinctness of the input in the nursing approach, the processing of information has some influence on the response. The stage of research in this area gives limited direction to nursing the older person. However, it is known that processing seems to be influenced by the number of message units presented at one time. It is believed that when the nurse is interacting there should be a presentation of one thought at a time with time allowance between each thought for a response. This is of major importance when teaching the older person about self-care or instructing him about a procedure such as using a walker.

The nurse, more than any other professional health worker, has a more intimate and sustained relationship with the older person. Because of her assessment and evaluation of her own nursing action, she may have a better understanding of the patient's behavior. Acting as interpreter to members of the health team, she can assist in the diagnosing and understanding of the patient by others. Correct interpretation of behavior can sometimes prevent false classifications of patients as "uncooperative," "disoriented," or even "senile." When a fast-moving entourage of a health team approaches an elderly person, its pace and numbers are such that the older person often behaves inappropriately at the moment. It is in this situation that the gerontological nurse has the obligation to be a clarifier of patient behavior. Summarizing what has been said thus far, the nurse, using research findings from other disciplines, realizes the need to pace her behavior to match that of the older patient so that the patient has an opportunity to perform at his level. As Welford [8] has stated in relation to performance:

> . . . pacing, in relation to age, illustrates an important general point about the relation between environmental demand and individual capacity. If the pace is slow enough, the effects of age, or any other factor which slows performance, will make little or no difference at first; all the necessary decisions will be made in the available time, . . .

## PHYSIOLOGICAL KNOWLEDGE INFLUENCING NURSING PRACTICE

The foregoing has emphasized psychological data, especially as they affect communication processes. But the nurse must also consider physiological changes as they influence physical care.

In providing care for patients of any age, the nurse needs to assist in the maintenance of homeostasis. This becomes difficult when caring for older people because of differences in physiological reactions. As an example, it may be more difficult to stabilize temperature in old people in that their bodily response to changes in environmental temperature is less effective than that of younger people. Hypothermia is not uncommon. Protection from extreme temperatures becomes an important nursing responsibility.

Decreases in oxygen utilization and the amount of blood pumped by the heart under resting conditions occur in aging. Cerebral anoxia or hypoxia is a common occurrence in the aged caused by such conditions as pneumonia or chronic emphysema. Because of the relationship between anoxia and confusion, the nurse is aware of those factors which may contribute to the lowering of blood pressure, such as rapid movement from a reclining position to a standing position, or a sudden neck movement which may cause a kinking and occlusion of the vertebral arteries.

Another common nursing act that needs special attention is that of bathing of the older person; for if the water is too hot, the blood vessels in the skin and muscles dilate and may cause temporary slowing of blood to the brain, which may cause a temporary confusional state.

Difficulty in physical movement is influenced by muscular wasting and weakness as well as by joint discomfort from arthritis and rheumatism. Sensory changes, such as sensitivity to temperature changes, the lowering of pain threshold with age, and olfactory alterations, are physiological modifications that require modification of nursing intervention.

This limited enumeration of physiological changes does indicate that the nurse needs to use a more protective approach when dealing with the aged. She must rely many times on covert rather than overt behavior to determine the older patient's needs. Some older persons can fracture a bone without being aware of such an accident. The alert nurse may discover this fracture when bathing the individual. It is not uncommon for the aged patient to have an extended bladder without feeling discomfort. Therefore the nurse has to depend on her observations rather than on expressions of discomfort by the patient.

As the nurse intervenes, regardless of the simplicity of the act, she uses the psychophysiological knowledge available to determine her nursing approach. This is illustrated in the simple act of assisting the patient to sit on the side of the bed. The nurse has to consider muscular weakness, she has to time the movement, and then evaluate the patient's behavior as to its appropriateness. The act could be simplified if there were color contrast between the sheets and the furniture. Should the patient become confused while carrying out the act, this could have been caused by faulty communicational input and/or by the rapidity of movement from the reclining to the sitting position.

## OTHER INFLUENCES

In the care of older people, the nurse has to consider not only the psychological and physiological influences but also the physical environment of the individual. The environmental needs of older patients can be determined by examination of life-style, life-space, and functional capacity from the physical and psychological point of view. If one is to understand the needs, motivations, and anxieties of the individual, understanding of his life-space is of paramount importance, keeping in mind that his psychological present is influenced by his past and future. Illness, especially that of a debilitating nature, tends to narrow life-space. Therefore, the nurse attempts to prevent the shrinking of the space and seeks ways to enlarge it. Institutionalization causes some isolation. Isolation can produce physiological and psychological disturbances. By finding ways of maintaining life-space, the nurse is assisting in the prevention of such disturbances.

Since it is stated that "each life-style has its characteristic structural property, especially in relation to orientation to interaction and types of social relationships" [9], the life-style needs to be identified and support provided to maintain the style, even in an institutional setting. The correlation of life-space, life-style, and functional capacity would provide the nurse a broad frame of reference for determining the sociological, psychological, and physiological needs of the elderly patient.

## GERONTOLOGICAL NURSING RESEARCH

Though gerontological nursing practice has been based on knowledge from other fields, nurse researchers are beginning to test such knowledge in clinical settings to determine applicability to nursing. Several nurse investigators have examined the influence of nursing intervention on orientation status. Thomas [6], exploring the effects of individualized nursing intervention on senile status, found that when individualized care was administered positive trends were observed in the achievement of self-care and in the alteration of senile status.

Tyler [7], in studying the effects of individualized nursing intervention upon orientation status, found that the state of orientation did not change, but that functional capacity improved. Both studies indicate a change in behavior, in that elderly individuals improved in the area of self-care when nursing intervention took into account psychophysiological alterations in old age.

A group of nurses, realizing the need for communication with the elderly, conducted a study on the use of expanded speech and self-pacing in communication with the aged. They concluded [5]: "The comfort and reassurance that the elderly person derives by the slowing of the pace of the situation and by communication at a slower rate of speed is invaluable."

Still another research project dealt with the environment. It was hypothesized that the psychosocial atrophy common to institutionalized older patients might be reversible through the medium of skilled nursing intervention. It was found that it was possible for older people to be involved in meaningful human relationships. For the purpose of the study nurse-patient dyads were organized, with special emphasis on continuing verbal communication. It was found that enriched environments generally fostered positively bio-psychosocial change whereas deprived environments inhibited the development. The introduction of skilled nursing care produced the greatest impact in those environments in which the prior level of active interactional involvement of patients was lowest [10].

Lowery [3] was interested in the relationship of patient life-style and gerontological nursing. Using a nursing home as the locus of her study she concluded that: (1) patients adjust differently to confinement, and as they adjust, they alter their life-styles; (2) nursing intervention should vary for each patient because of the different adjustment patterns, the alterations in life-style, and the uniqueness of the individual; and (3) nursing intervention can be planned so that life-style is partially restored.

One nurse, using the operant conditioning theory, attempted to modify incontinence in neuropsychiatric geriatric patients using an experimental and a control group. The hypothesis that incontinence could be significantly decreased by the introduction of social and/or material reinforcement and that the decrease would be greater in experimental subjects was not confirmed in his study [2].

These are examples to illustrate that nurses are attempting to explore the effects of nursing intervention on patient behavior. To carry on this exploration, theory from other disciplines is utilized to build a body of knowledge concerning the nursing practice relating to the care of older people. As this body of knowledge is extended, gerontological nursing practice will be based mainly on scientific knowledge rather than on imitation and intuition. As the body of knowledge increases, and the level of practice rises, better qualified personnel will be attracted and the quality of care improved.

## REFERENCES

1. Busse, E. W.  Geriatrics today—An overview. *Amer. J. Psychiat.* 123:1231, 1967.
2. Grosick, J.  Effect of operant conditioning on modification of incontinence in neuropsychiatric geriatric patients. *Nurs. Res.* 17:304–311, 1968.
3. Lowery, P.  *Patient Life Style and Gerontological Nursing.* Durham, N.C.: Duke University, 1968. Unpublished thesis.

4. Moses, D. V., and Lake, C. S. Geriatrics in the baccalaureate nursing curriculum. *Nurs. Outlook* 16:41, 1968.
5. Panicucci, C. L., et al. Expanded Speech and Self-Pacing in Communication with the Aged. *A.N.A. Regional Clinical Conferences.* New York: Appleton-Century-Crofts, 1968. Pp. 95–101.
6. Thomas, F. J. Effects of Individualized Nursing Intervention on Senile Status and Self Care Achievement on Institutionalized Senile Patients. *A.N.A. Regional Clinical Conferences.* New York: Appleton-Century-Crofts, 1968. Pp. 152–162.
7. Tyler, C. *The Effect of Individualized Nursing upon the Orientation Status of the Elderly Patient in a Long Term Setting.* Durham, N.C.: Duke University, 1968. Unpublished thesis.
8. Welford, A. T. Social, Psychological, and Physiological Gerontology—An Experimental Psychologist's Approach. In R. H. Williams et al. (Eds.), *Processes of Aging,* vol. I. New York: Atherton, 1963. P. 119.
9. Williams, R. H., and Wirths, C. G. *Lives Through the Years.* New York: Atherton, 1965. P. 13.
10. Weiss, J. M. (Ed.). *Nurses, Patients, and Social Systems.* Columbia, Mo.: University of Missouri Press, 1968.

# 16

# Social Casework and Community Services for the Aged

DOROTHY K. HEYMAN AND
GRACE H. POLANSKY

In many communities there is a growing awareness of the needs of the elderly and a new willingness to take responsibility for more adequate services to these citizens. Welfare agencies provide basic financial assistance to those in need in all areas of the country. In addition, other social services are expanding, in local communities as well as on state and national levels. While the medical needs of the elderly have been properly emphasized, it must also be made clear that their needs are far more extensive than for medical assistance alone. For the bedridden are only a small fraction of the total older population [14]. Most older people continue to live active and independent lives [8]. They continue to function in their accustomed ways until a crisis or change occurs profound enough to challenge their equilibrium. The crises of old age may take various forms, and they are usually multiple in nature. At such times of distress older persons are turning increasingly to social workers for help.

This chapter will be concerned first with social casework as it attempts to help individuals and their families with: problems of social functioning and maintenance of optimum emotional and physical health in the older person's usual setting, as long as this is possible; and with the same problems in a new setting when this becomes necessary. Second, a variety of other community services will be discussed which also seek to maintain or improve the level of adaptation in older people.

## SOCIAL CASEWORK WITH OLDER PERSONS

The basic problems of the aged are in the areas of emotional and physical health, retirement and finances, physical living arrangements, marital and family relationships, relationships between generations, and problems connected with the use of leisure time, all of which relate to a sense of worth and belonging. Many older persons struggling with these problems, singly or in combination, can use social casework help. Interestingly, some of these problems do not require intensive intervention but respond to assistance of a fairly superficial nature. Unfortunately, the aged are often unaware of the resources available to them. For this reason it is extremely important that information about such resources be widely disseminated to the aged themselves and to those in contact with them. Applications for help may be received by agencies from older persons themselves, from immediate family or other relatives, from friends and neighbors. Referrals are frequently made by physicians, ministers, nurses, and other professional persons. Usually only a simple telephone call is needed to initiate the process of obtaining assistance for a troubled elderly person.

*Goals*

Social casework has as its goals helping the older person in his adaptation, in his social functioning, and in maintaining or re-establishing psychic equilibrium. Old age is a time when crises involving losses and changes coincide with diminishing strength and energy. The impact of multiple losses may result in a depletion of personal resources, and a supportive relationship and other restitutive measures may be needed. Casework tries to aid the person in adapting his environment to his diminishing functional abilities, or in lessening external stress. If these adjustments are not possible or sufficient, he is then assisted in moving to a new setting in which physical, emotional, and social needs can be met more adequately [16]. At all points the older person is helped to maintain or regain his self-image, to maintain a sense of mastery and control over his environment, and to be relieved of immobilizing fears and anxieties.

Casework frequently involves not only the older person but the spouse, adult children, grandchildren, and other relatives, as well as interested friends. Professionals such as the physician, nurse, attorney, clergyman, banker, and other social workers may participate in planning and treatment. Landlords, neighbors, staffs of institutions and home care facilities, paramedical personnel, and others are additional resources. The individual may need the help of an increasing variety of people. At the same time the emotional involvements of some of these people, particularly of family and friends, need to be taken into account.

## Settings

The setting for social casework may be in a counseling service for older persons, a sectarian or nonsectarian family agency, a public welfare department, an institution for the aged, or a general, geriatric, or psychiatric hospital. Other settings are senior centers, community centers, and housing projects or other locations easily accessible to older persons. Agencies such as public welfare departments which perform many supportive functions also use casework concepts and techniques. Here, at the frequently painful point of applying for help, dignity and sense of self-worth can be maintained or increased while a determination is made as to what services are needed. Continued individualized interest in the person and the experience of a positive relationship can be as helpful as the concrete financial or other assistance provided.

## Problems

The specific focus of counseling and the specific services to be provided are generally determined by multiple, interrelated needs. For example, personal adjustment to actual and threatened changes and losses, as well as marital and extended family relationships, are areas in which help is frequently requested. These problems are often accompanied by inadequate income and by the necessity to change physical living arrangements. At other times, physical and mental disability, or retirement, with its possible loss of social and economic roles, may necessitate treatment intervention by a caseworker. A brief case history may serve to illustrate the problem:

Mr. B., age 82, and his wife, who was six years younger, each were experiencing difficulties because of Mr. B.'s progressive brain disease. He was showing memory loss, increasing suspiciousness, disorientation, and lack of judgment. His increasing dependence on Mrs. B. was becoming intolerable to her, especially as it represented a reversal of their previous roles. She herself was feeling vigorous and full of plans and activities but was prevented from carrying them out because of Mr. B.'s unwillingness or inability to participate. Although depressed with her "babysitting" role, Mrs. B. felt guilty about her thoughts of placing her husband in a home for the aged. Friends, too, reinforced her guilt by hinting that he would die sooner if placed in an institution. Her husband clearly opposed any discussion of such placement, and their son obviously was uneasy with the idea of having his father in a home for the aged. Mrs. B. was clearly conflicted in her feelings about the problem. She and her husband had gotten along well during 53 years of marriage. She was afraid she would miss him greatly if he were to leave. In fact, she hardly knew whether the present situation was not better than the guilt she might feel if she placed him in an institution.

A caseworker met with Mrs. B. and her son over a period of time. On one occasion the psychiatrist who had evaluated Mr. B. joined them. In these sessions Mrs. B. and her son were given emotional support and guided toward realistic planning. The caseworker suggested the possibility of hiring an attendant who could relieve Mrs. B. from time to time, thus freeing her for her own activities and interests and for an occasional vacation. This plan was more acceptable, and the caseworker told them of the resources for such help.

For his part, Mr. B. was experiencing fears of abandonment which he expressed through concerns that his wife might die before him. He said that he regretted being such a "burden" to her. His past occupational success and his previous sexual prowess became important elements in his conversation. At one point he made a sudden attempt to have sexual relations with his wife, after 15 years of inactivity. This proved upsetting to Mrs. B., and she retaliated at first with threats of proceeding to institutionalize him. In casework Mrs. B. was helped to see the meaning of these developments and to be more understanding. She was also helped to anticipate her own emotional reactions to having someone else caring for her husband for periods of time, and she also grew somewhat more comfortable with the idea of temporary or permanent placement of her husband if the present plan did not work out. She was able to make good use of professional support. The son, too, became freer to look at the needs of each parent without over-identifying with his father's wishes.

## Clients

A study of the whole person, with concern for his individual physical, emotional, and social needs, is the basis for treatment. The older person may be identified as the primary client, or he may be seen as part of a family unit which can then be considered "the client," with the needs of each family member taken into account. Thus, treatment can be client-centered or family-centered.

## Casework Treatment

Identification of the problem is followed by treatment planning. Goals of treatment may be limited to helping the person deal with the immediately stressful situation. On the other hand, increased self-awareness and self-understanding, with consequent behavior modification, may be sought [16]. Treatment is basically ego-supportive, with the caseworker sustaining and developing the healthy personality aspects and useful defenses of the client. The essential ingredient is the relationship between caseworker and client. Past achievements and present strengths are given recognition. Physical and emotional supports within the family and the community are utilized to promote self-mobilization and independence. Depending on the ego strength of the client, confrontation, clarification, and interpretation may also be used on a selective basis. Sometimes role shifts occur in old age which require the establishment of new or changed relationships and a redefinition of social identity.

Casework continues as long as it is needed. It may be resumed at any time when a new crisis arises. For the elderly, need, rather than motivation for behavioral change, is the primary indication for intervention. Prompt response to requests for service is essential for the older person whose self-esteem may be depleted. Caseworkers cannot expect to see all of their elderly clients in the customary office settings; many will have to be visited in their own homes, or in hospitals and nursing homes. Interviews cannot be hurried, and repeated contacts may be needed to accomplish what might be accomplished in a single sitting with a young individual. Personal warmth and positive affect are essential [16].

Among specific problems often referred for treatment are marital problems. Possible causes for disruption in the marriage are many, for instance, retirement and new uses of leisure, or changing financial and health situations. Primary family roles often shift from a focus on child care to mutual nurturance between the two marriage partners. If the marriage has been essentially sound it can become even more satisfying in old age. If there have been deficiencies in closeness, perhaps camouflaged by the presence of children in the household, these tend to increase when children move out and family roles change. Casework assistance may then be needed to reestablish a satisfactory balance [16].

A second area for casework help is the relationship between the aged parent and his adult child. Old problems between parents and children may be reactivated as help from adult children is needed. Because disabilities in old age often progress at an uneven pace the adult children may themselves become confused and require help in modifying their own roles and changing relationships to their parents. On the part of the older person alternate feelings of dependency and hostility are not uncommon responses.

A poignant and possibly traumatic situation requiring casework intervention occurs when a decision must be made about a change in living arrangements or placement of an older person in a rest home, nursing home, or other institutions. Careful evaluation is made of the desirability and necessity of placement, along with its meaning to the older person and those close to him. Caseworkers must be aware of all the alternative placement possibilities in a given community in order to best match the specific services required by the aged person to the services available in specific institutions. Sometimes a seemingly intolerable home situation can be ameliorated and the aged person maintained in his own home, with the provision of added supports, such as skilled home nursing care.

The most common reason for relocating an individual is the development of mental deterioration in the absence of adequate supervision in his own home. Organic brain changes may result in severe memory loss and disorientation; the older person may wander away from home, forget to turn off the stove, thereby creating a fire hazard, or become offensive in his personal hygiene. Dramatic personality changes may take place, with loss of inhibitions, irritability, or paranoid ideation. A rest home may provide adequate care in some instances; in others, admission to a psychiatric hospital may be required.

A second common reason for considering placement is the presence of a physical disability requiring extensive care. The individual who has suffered a stroke or is for some other reason bed-ridden, who may require special medication or is in need of physical assistance which cannot be provided at home, may need to be admitted to a nursing home or extended care facility. There are some elderly who are not significantly deteriorated either mentally or physically but who are socially isolated and require an environment in which social interaction is again possible. A day care center or a rest home may provide enough satisfaction to prevent or reverse emotional problems. As of this writing not all of the types of facilities mentioned are available in all communities. But it is hoped that eventually each community will be able to provide a full range of coordinated alternatives to serve the elderly.

Older persons often find the change to completely new settings very disturbing. The older person as well as members of his family may experience feelings of ambivalence, anger, rejection, depression, and guilt. A caseworker can often be of help with these feelings not only in the planning of the move but also after the aged person has moved to a new setting.

Thus casework helps the older person and his family to handle as comfortably and effectively as possible changes resulting from those internal aging processes which effect each one at different rates and in different areas of functioning. For those elderly persons who are not in need of the kinds of services described above there exist many valuable supportive structures in the community which may be used as tools to bolster the drive to remain independent and to maintain a continuing role in society.


## COMMUNITY SERVICES FOR THE AGED

As Shanas has pointed out, it is often assumed that the community, through the provision of social services and voluntary organizations, has supplanted the family and its functions, providing the elderly with a "kind of comfortable seclusion. The evidence suggests [however] that the social services tend to complement rather than replace informal community and family associations and that they tend to reach those in genuine need" [15]. Through gerontological research new concepts of aging have become accepted, and have brought about the establishment of a different type of agency for the elderly, integrating new and traditional services.


*Comprehensive Services by a Single Agency*

Probably the most important element in a community program for older persons is to have available those resources which enable older people to remain independent with a maximum degree of self-determination. . . . Of great importance is the central referral service with caseworkers able to work with the older person on his own terms, going into the home if necessary [12].

The Information and Counseling Service for Older Persons at Duke University was established to respond to the needs of the elderly, with the idea in mind that the multiple nature of an older person's problems often requires an interdisciplinary approach to a solution. This service is unusually comprehensive in its organization and includes professional personnel in psychiatry, social work, psychiatric nursing, physical therapy, psychology, pastoral counseling, occupational therapy, and medicine. It objectives, according to the agency, are:

. . . to provide a variety of approaches to counseling and therapy for the problems of the aged, including intergenerational family crises; to assist in the coordination of services in such areas as housing, finance, employment, medical assistance, home safety, nutrition and exercise; to cooperate with professional personnel in community agencies to encourage high quality care for the aged persons and to build training, research and evaluation procedures into its structure [9].

The Information and Counseling Service, located in a medical center, has many cases referred which involve medical and psychiatric problems. However, the services of this agency are available to the entire community. Counseling is provided regarding legal help, recreation, financial assistance, rest home, nursing home, or other placement. Help is also given in making discharge plans from the hospital. Close cooperation with a family agency is maintained in providing simultaneous casework services. In one disturbed family situation in which Family Service was working with the children, Information and Counseling Service was asked to help the divorced father and his own mother arrive at a mutually acceptable arrangement which would permit his forthcoming remarriage to take place without destroying the three-generational family ties.

The Information and Counseling Service has cooperated with other community projects: cosponsorship of a Hearing Aid Bank with the Junior Woman's Club; presentation of an Institute on Pre-Retirement Counseling for personnel managers in labor, industry, and business; consultation with the Comprehensive Community Mental Health Center; supervision of Friendly Visitors to Information and Counseling Service clients; consultation in an Earned Income for Older Workers Program; and active participation in a Senior Center in which a caseworker provides individual counseling and conducts a discussion group.

While most referrals are made by physicians on the hospital staff and in community private practice, many other referrals are initiated by adult children, grandchildren, or siblings, rather than by spouse of the older person. There are few self-referrals, implying probably that in this age group there is either little awareness of the service or there is resistance to applying for professional help.

A unique feature of this service is the training opportunity afforded professional persons such as psychologists, ministers, physical therapists, caseworkers, and others to work with the elderly within a multidisciplinary setting.

## Project Outreach

An interesting example of another effort to assist the aged is "Project Outreach" established by the Central Utah Resource Development Association [13]. Because applicants often "become lost in the process of referrals and re-referrals" and despair of being helped, an expediter has been appointed whose chief responsibility is to locate the service needed by his client. The expediter is "employed to represent the client's interests against all the tendencies in all the agencies that may delay or deprive the client of the agencies' services." He may act in a variety of roles: negotiator, advocate, teacher, and helper.

## Retirement Planning

Services for the aging are concerned in a major way with the problems of retirees, i.e., those facing a readjustment which "involves filling the gap in social relations, the day-to-day or hour-by-hour contact with other persons which was provided by the work situation" [5]. In recognition of the fact that retirement can be problematical, widespread efforts are being made by industry, labor, and communities to prepare the preretiree to accept and enjoy his post-65 years. Classes are held, sometimes years before a man is scheduled to retire, to help him face the implications of retirement with its possible financial, social, personal, and family problems. Typical preretirement courses may include management of financial resources, budgeting, and health information along with adult education classes, hobby shops, and a variety of other subjects.

The role of the wife of a retiree is often overlooked. Although retirement is a different experience for the wife than the husband and although she may feel herself less deeply involved [10], her attitudes undoubtedly will affect the satisfactions which both derive from the retirement years [7]. Wives must be included in planning for retirement.

## Homemaker Services

Although "most of the older people continue to live in environments that permit them to be independent" [14], many of the aged, particularly the widowed, single, and divorced, live in isolated and lonely circumstances. Provision of specialized services to these as well as to elderly couples may enable them to live independently in the community. To keep the elderly functioning in their own homes, homemaker services are available in some communities from the public welfare or private social agencies.

The trained homemaker assigned by the caseworker as the need arises is usually responsible for the general housework, shopping, and cooking. She also gives some personal care, such as helping with bathing, hairwashing, and dressing. This is a fairly expensive service, and it is therefore generally used only on a part-time basis. When necessary, this service may be supplemented by visits of the public health nurse.

## Meals-on-Wheels

Many of the elderly living and eating alone lack motivation for proper meal planning and preparation. They soon deteriorate in energy and in interest, and continued poor nutrition can lead to illness. Some communities have therefore established programs which deliver appetizing and balanced meals to the homes of individuals at modest cost. The program must be subsidized even though much of the food preparation and delivery is done by volunteers. Arrangements are sometimes made to have meals prepared in the kitchen of an institution such as an old-age home or in a church kitchen and are then delivered before noon. Two meals are provided, one to be eaten hot and one cold.

*Physical Therapy*

While many hospitals now include physical therapy departments with extensive exercise and retraining programs, these hospital services are not often available to the homebound elderly. County health departments often have graduate physical therapists on their staff who will make regular visits for evaluation and treatment. There are also a number of therapists in private practice who accept patients upon referral by a physician.

The physical therapist, after an evaluation of the facilities of the home, devises an individualized program to help the handicapped adapt to his setting and to maintain or regain maximal functioning. Often equipment is improvised with whatever resources the home setting provides. All the prescribed exercises and planned activities are oriented toward achieving physical independence. The physical therapy program which aims at preventing chronic invalidism may begin with simple instructions on transferring from bed to chair, the use of a walker, or techniques for self-care.

The aged confined to the home can be helped to move out into the community by learning simple methods of managing steps and curbs and entering a taxi or a bus. Progress in self-help, even when measured by small achievements, leads to a sense of independence and is valuable in combating depression and self-devaluation.

*Occupational Therapy*

Although there are not enough trained occupational therapists to maintain a home visiting program, the skills of this discipline are appropriate to services in the home. Self-maintenance can be taught to the partially disabled so that meals may be prepared and other chores carried out satisfactorily. The goals are not to teach arts and crafts per se or to provide entertainment, although these are often pleasurable by-products. Through individually designed occupational therapy programs, the aged may be assisted in regaining their physical and emotional strengths while learning to adjust to their limitations and disabilities.

*Home Nursing Care*

County health departments in many areas maintain a staff of registered nurses to make home visits and evaluations, to perform nursing duties, and to educate the patient and family in nursing care procedures. There are also private organizations, religious and secular, which provide visiting nurse services at modest fees. The Visiting Nurses Association of America, nursing services of Metropolitan Life and other insurance companies, as well as Catholic nursing orders, are all established in some large cities.

*Protective Services*

Older persons, without close and interested relatives or friends, are often in need of protective services since they are not capable, physically and/or mentally, of either planning or caring for themselves or of protecting whatever resources they may have. Serious legal and financial problems may be involved and require the services of experts.

The nature of protective services for the elderly is not generally understood, and responsibility for protecting those in need of such services has not as yet been clearly allocated. "To date, the person generally considered to need protective services from some agency is the one who is mentally disordered to a degree that prevents his making rational decisions, who is seriously limited in his ability to care for himself physically and financially, who is dangerous to himself or others, or whose behavior is a grave disturbance . . ." [16].

In many states the Department of Public Welfare assumes legal responsibilities. Professional persons working with older people recognize the deficiencies in this field. There is also a need to establish protective devices for the elderly person who may not be irrational or totally incompetent, but is nevertheless helpless in the face of complex problems.

A study of a group of cases of persons requiring protective services revealed that: (1) old persons in need of such services often do not or cannot seek the help of an agency; (2) service must continue for a long time, possibly the balance of the client's lifetime; and (3) the client's helplessness, his demands, and needs may require that the caseworker assume a preponderant amount of responsibility. "Resources of many kinds must be readily available, to be used immediately and flexibly. . . . Among these resources are medical and psychiatric care, legal services, nursing care, hospital and nursing home care, family home care, housekeeper and homemaker services, drugs, ambulance service, and funds for immediate needs such as rent, clothing and food" [6].

## Extended Care Facilities

In spite of strenuous efforts to maintain independence many elderly face the necessity of giving up their homes. The available choices may be limited by lack of money, family problems, or poor health. While for some the only possible resource is a nursing home or chronic disease hospital, for others suitable arrangements may be made in a boarding or a family care home where membership in a "family" provides some protection and concern on the part of interested nonrelatives, yet permits some degree of independent living. This arrangement would benefit the isolated man or woman who is not able or willing to prepare adequate meals or is in need of some assistance with medications.

Intermediate care, between a boarding home and a nursing home, is provided by the rest home which accepts ambulatory persons who need a protected environment and some supervision, including minor nursing care. Nursing homes will accept bed care patients and offer a full range of nursing and medical care.

## Volunteer Services

A central volunteer bureau staffed by older persons is needed in many communities. Elderly persons who are in good health should be encouraged to serve as volunteers; as friendly visitors to other elderly at home or in institutions; as Girl Scout or Boy Scout leaders or assistant leaders; or as hospital auxiliary or ward aides, helping to write letters and passing out books.

Programs designed specifically to encourage intergenerational contacts have been established. Children's wards in hospitals or custodial institutions have foster grandparents programs with regular visits of the elderly to read and play with the youngsters, thus providing love and individual attention.

Young people on some college campuses have established programs in which visits are made to homes for the aged or to individuals in their own homes at regular intervals. Often a grandparent is "adopted." Birthday parties are held, entertainment provided, and trips outside the home arranged. Both of these programs appear to provide mutually shared satisfactions.

Another volunteer program is that of the Friendly Visitor. Open to individuals of all ages, this activity offers opportunities for older well persons to be of service. It can provide much satisfaction to both the visitor and to the persons visited. A friendly visit with a contemporary may be especially enjoyable. Activities should be mutually satisfying and may include table games, gardening, sewing, knitting, reading, crafts, going for rides, shopping, movies, lectures, or any interests which appeal to both.

Friendly Visitors, either to institutions or to individuals in their own homes, should operate under the supervision of a social agency for the protection of both the person visited and the Friendly Visitor. Although the volunteer is anxious to be helpful, this quality is not necessarily innate. Thus the volunteer should be carefully selected, trained, and supervised. Perhaps the most satisfying results are obtained when there is not too great a difference in educational or intellectual level, socioeconomic status, and interests.

A Friendly Visitor assumes certain minimum responsibilities. He obligates himself to serve the client's needs rather than his own, to be dependable in making regular visits, to be a good listener and interested in the client as a person, to refrain from comments which may be upsetting or depressing, and in general to be one who is welcomed with pleasure in another's home. He has a very worthwhile goal and together with the social worker and other professionals can help in bringing satisfaction and meaning to an isolated or unhappy older person.

### Centers for Older Persons

It has been amply shown that social interaction and activity improve the morale of the elderly. "Social structure constraints which limit or deny contacts with the environment tend to be demoralizing and alienating and to be associated with withdrawal or various forms of aggressive behavior" [11].

Organized activity for the elderly exists in many places and in many forms. The fundamental questions are not only what older people need but what they want and how their wants and needs can be combined. Experience in working with older people has demonstrated that to be successful the programs offered to older people must meet their needs and interests, and must be sufficiently varied to satisfy differences. It is also important that some of the older people participate in the planning of these programs [2]. Too often activities are planned for the elderly by the middle-aged and are consequently poorly attended since they do not relate to the needs and interests of the group.

As Wickenden has pointed out, "Most successful social programs for older people appear to meet all or at least a combination of certain needs": a sense of usefulness, the opportunity to learn, as well as to create something, the desire for recognition, an environment in which to establish social relationships with others as well as to find oneself in relaxing preoccupations [17].

Community centers for the aging, with their varied and well-planned programs, offer these opportunities. Centers usually provide recreational activities and entertainment, are often equipped with game rooms, craft shops, sheltered workshops, and cooking and dining facilities. The staffing of centers varies, but many have professional group workers, a public health nurse, a case worker, and a part-time physician.

Programs reflect the interests of the members. Films, lectures, discussion groups, and other intellectual activities are available. Summer camp programs are occasionally sponsored. A few centers contain such auxiliary services as a barber shop, mending shop, swap-shop, and mimeographed newspaper published by center members.

It cannot be assumed that the establishment of a center will automatically attract older people. Lifelong characteristics persist into old age, and while the gregarious will probably turn up promptly, the shy, timid, or those who feel themselves handicapped by inadequate education or by social awkwardness will need to be encouraged to participate.

Public welfare workers who have frequent contact with the elderly have in many places made a special effort to stimulate the interest of their clients, especially the isolated ones, by preparing mimeographed lists of social organizations with neighborhood locations, interests, meeting times, and places, or lists of specific projects such as hobby shows or lectures. Volunteer groups have printed directories containing information on community resources which may be of particular interest to the elderly. The Durham, North Carolina, Golden Age Society, for instance, has developed an attractive pamphlet listing social and educational organizations, public health facilities, nursing and rest homes, and legal aid and public health resources in that community.

The housebound elderly are, of course, more limited in their opportunities for organizational participation but need not be forgotten. Regular visits by a bookmobile are provided in some communities.

### Involvement of Community in Program Planning

At a meeting, organizational leaders concerned with programs for the aging were asked which activities sponsored by their organizations had been considered most successful by their members. Listed as successful were (1) classes on information pertaining to wills,

property, Social Security benefits and similar matters; (2) classes on
personal grooming as well as volunteer services of hairdressers to the
bedridden; (3) transportation to meetings, clinics, church, and Sun-
day school; (4) Red Cross-sponsored courses on "Fitness for the
Future" which emphasized exercises appropriate for the elderly;
(5) classes dealing with diet, health care, and health problems;
(6) bird watching groups and nature walks; (7) parties, suppers, and
picnics in which three generations participated; and (8) classes in
which members not only made items to take to hospitals or to shut-
ins but taught each other skills in knitting, woodworking, or some
other craft.

*Adult Education*

In planning ahead, it should be recognized that the elderly of the
future not only may expect to live longer but they may maintain
reasonably good health for a longer period of time, be better educated, and have more intellectual interests. Adult education programs, although not new, will need to expand if the interests of
the elderly are to be met. This challenge has been accepted by
many churches, clubs, and schools which sponsor afternoon or
evening courses. The necessary equipment is usually already in the
building, and staff is not difficult to recruit.

Interesting examples of such activity are the Institutes of Lifetime
Learning, sponsored jointly by chapters of the American Association
of Retired Persons, local teachers associations, universities, and colleges. The pilot project in Washington, D.C., offers classes for a
ten-week period, at the college level, of over 51 different subjects,
including refresher courses in commercial subjects, painting, lip-
reading, music, and many more [3].

Too often the activities of older persons are thought of purely in
terms of leisure, recreation, or entertainment. "Work substitutes
[should] do psychologically for the person what work [did] for him
in his period of maturity. . . . What is needed is a type of interaction
between the person and the task in which the task brings out the

person's resources and in so doing permits the person to feel that he is growing or developing" [1].

## Vocational Rehabilitation

The Vocational Rehabilitation Agency, while geared primarily to the needs of the handicapped "of working age," may be of assistance in rehabilitating older persons. In North Carolina 111 persons over the age of 65 at the time of referral were rehabilitated during the fiscal year 1966-67, according to a report of the state Division of Vocational Rehabilitation. Disabled housewives have been accepted for help and assisted in learning better ways of managing a household [4]. Older persons who cannot be retrained for employment in the open labor market may find employment in sheltered workshops utilized by this agency.

## Employment Opportunities

Although many older people retire from work with a sense of relief, others in good health would enjoy continued employment for many reasons, including financial reasons, a continued sense of usefulness, and of participation in the mainstream of life. Older people cannot easily find jobs in the open market, but employment opportunities can be located or even created by a skilled employment counselor matching the job opportunity to a selected individual. The North Carolina State Employment Service includes a department that concerns itself entirely with placement of older persons. Employers often have opportunities available which do not appeal to younger people and yet are suited to the capacities or interests of the older man or woman. Jobs offering only part-time or seasonal work or unusual hours may be more appealing or more acceptable to the older person, particularly with the existence of social security limitations on yearly earnings. The value of hiring older persons in appropriate positions must often be interpreted to employers and the importance of experience, stability, and reliability emphasized.

Vocational guidance is a helpful adjunct to job placement even with older persons.

## CONCLUSIONS

Although the services described above are many and varied, few communities now provide all of them to their elderly populations. Funding new programs is always difficult, as is providing them in adequate numbers to accommodate the demand. Accessibility to the facilities is also a problem in that some of the elderly do not like or are not physically able to travel to various centers or offices. The meagerness of programs in some locations may be due to community inertia or lack of awareness but, hopefully, not to disinterest. When communities are small or unable to offer much financial support, strong volunteer efforts are needed, or else, the resources of several communities may be combined into regional programs.

Future planning for the needs of older persons should envision the extension of comprehensive and coordinated services to ever increasing numbers. It is important to help not only those whose needs are critical but also those in somewhat less difficult circumstances. For them the availability of these programs would serve to enhance the quality of life; it would help to reintegrate them into the larger society, and avoid in them a painful sense of marginality.

## REFERENCES

1. Anderson, J. E.   Psychological Aspects of the Use of Free Time. In W. Donahue, W. Hunter, D. Coons, and H. Maurice (Eds.), *Free Time: Challenge to Later Maturity*. Ann Arbor: University of Michigan Press, 1958.
2. Burgess, E.W.   The Retired Person and Organizational Activities. In W. Donahue, W. Hunter, D. Coons, and H. Maurice (Eds.), *Free Time: Challenge to Later Maturity*. Ann Arbor: University of Michigan Press, 1958.
3. Fitch, W. C.   The new look in aging. *Wilson Library Bull.* May, 1966.

4. *For the Disabled: Help through vocational rehabilition.* Washington, D.C.: U.S. Department of Health, Education, and Welfare. Vocational Rehabilitation Department, 1967.
5. Friedman, E. A., and Havighurst, R. J. *Meanings of Work and Retirement.* Chicago: University of Chicago Press, 1954.
6. Hemmy, M., and Farrar, M. Protective services for older people. *Social Casework* 42:16–20, 1961.
7. Heyman, D. K., and Jeffers, F. C. Wives and retirement: A pilot study. *J. Geront.* 23:488–496, 1968.
8. Hobson, W., and Pemberton, J. *Health of the Elderly at Home.* Toronto: Butterworth, 1955.
9. Jeffers, F. C., and Polansky, G. H. Initiation in a university medical center of an information and counseling program for older people. Paper presented to annual meeting of the Gerontological Society, Denver, Colo., November 1968.
10. Kerckhoff, A. C. Husband-Wife Expectations and Reactions to Retirement. In I. H. Simpson and J. C. McKinney (Eds.), *Social Aspects of Aging.* Durham, N.C.: Duke University Press, 1966.
11. Maddox, G. L. Activity and morale. Paper presented to meeting of Gerontological Society, Washington, D.C., 1962.
12. Mathiesen, G. Current Status of Services to the Aging. In J. L. Gorn (Ed.), *Social Work Education for Better Services to the Aging.* Proceedings of seminar on the aging, Aspen, Colo., 1958. New York: Council on Social Work Education, 1959.
13. Personal communication from the Central Utah Resources Board, March 1968.
14. Shanas, E. *Family Relationships of Older People.* (Health Information Foundation Research Series, Number 20.) New York: Health Information Foundation, 1961.
15. Shanas, E., Townsend, P., Wedderburn, D., Friis, H., Milhoj, P., and Stehouwer, J. *Old People in Three Industrial Societies.* New York: Atherton, 1968.
16. Wasser, E. *Creative Approaches in Casework with the Aging.* New York: Family Service Association of America, 1966.
17. Wickenden, E. *The Needs of Older People.* Chicago: American Public Welfare Association, 1953.

# 17

# Training in Geropsychiatry

ADRIAAN VERWOERDT

*Geropsychiatry* is the psychiatry of late life. It encompasses the behavioral sciences, psychodynamic concepts, and psychiatric practice with reference to the aging personality and to the mental disorders of late life. The term *geriatrics* usually denotes medical practice in the care of the aged which yet remains within the purview of a given medical or surgical specialty. Similarly, *gerontologists* tend to identify themselves primarily as biologists, psychologists, or sociologists who happen to be studying the aging process [7, 14]. Since geriatrics is not clearly defined with regard to its position in medicine [18], the question has been raised if something can be gained from organizing geriatrics into a structured speciality [2]. This same question has been raised with respect to geropsychiatry. Whether psychiatric work with the elderly will develop into a more or less distinct subspecialty in the field of general psychiatry will depend on whether a need for skilled practitioners in this area can be demonstrated, whether special problems exist in psychiatric practice with the elderly, and whether a body of knowledge characteristic of geropsychiatry can be identified.

## PERSONNEL NEEDS

Although at the present time no meaningful quantitative estimate of the need for personnel can be made [17, 22], there does seem to be a consensus that the personnel now serving the aged (e.g., psychiatrists, nurses, social workers, hospital aides) is insufficient, and that additional training for existing personnel is desirable. There are several reasons for the discrepancy between the magnitude of the problems and the adequacy of available solutions. (1) The number and proportion of aged individuals has increased. (2) Elderly individuals are beginning to express greater demands for treatment. (3) Although mental illness among the aged continues to present major problems with regard to etiology, diagnosis, and treatment, comparatively little attention has been given to the psychiatry of senescence [8]. Child, adolescent, and adult psychiatry continue to attract the majority of practitioners. (4) Difficulties in personnel recruitment exist on all levels. When manpower shortage leads to an emphasis on "custodial" care, morale problems and therapeutic pessimism among geriatric personnel may develop. This, in turn, makes it more difficult to recruit competent and well-motivated individuals. Also, the existing geriatric personnel are hard-pressed for time so that it becomes difficult to take time out for training. Thus, a vicious cycle develops which is self-perpetuating and may be very difficult to reverse.

## SPECIAL PROBLEMS IN WORKING WITH
## AGED PATIENTS

Zinberg points out that psychiatric therapy of the aged involves an unusually large number of emergency situations. Furthermore, there are problems of scheduling, problems related to the patient often being dependent on other family members, the typically multigenerational nature of the problem, and the frequent coexistence of organic brain disease, psychogenic trauma, and physical illness [28].

When the older patient "lives in the past," the therapist may be seen as a person in the patient's past. The patient may not be able to distinguish the therapist as a real person from the therapist as a transference figure. In therapy with younger adults the transference can be analyzed, but this is less feasible in the aged.

Countertransference may present serious problems, too. For the therapist who has "gerophobic" attitudes or unresolved fears of aging and death, it will be difficult to approach disorders in the aged with enlightened detachment and rational compassion. The therapist has to be content with accepting limited therapeutic goals. He will often be frustrated by his inability to modify life-long behavior patterns in aged patients. In addition, our cultural emphasis on youth and attractiveness may be a further burden to the therapist dealing with the aged or chronically ill. Finally, early emotional conflicts between the therapist and his own parents may be reactivated, causing specific countertransference attitudes.

Communication with psychiatrically ill elderly persons may be disturbed not only by psychogenic factors but also by organic impairment. Aged patients with a decrement in cognitive and abstract capacity present unique problems. Although there are analogies to these problems in dealing with the mentally retarded, the difference lies in the fact that the aged have experienced losses of capacities which were once present.

The need for frequent contacts with relatives makes it imperative for the geropsychiatrist to be skilled in the diagnosis of disturbed family interactions, in counseling, and in family therapy. Such approaches can be compared with the pattern of practice found in child psychiatry. However, there are differences. The nature of the transference and of the identifications observed between the child patient and his parents is the reverse of that observed between the child and the parent patient.

Social geropsychiatry includes cooperation with community agencies, consultation with nursing homes, environmental planning, and programs of releasing hospitalized patients into the community [26]. It also includes retirement counseling. Since the psychopathology of retirement often reflects the psychopathology of work, the geropsychiatrist needs to be acquainted with the meaning of work, leisure, and recreation.

In addition to these clinical concerns, there is a need for research. One of the major challenges is the prevention and treatment of senile regression. Age-related personality changes, psychological reactions to loss, and the effect of aging on psychiatric disorders are other areas in which more investigation is needed. To some extent the senium has remained *terra incognita,* and an understanding of this life phase is essential for a comprehensive theory of human behavior. Information about the final step in human development can provide additional insights into earlier developmental periods and their impact on the total personality.

When we speak of the psychodynamics of the last phase of life, the emphasis is on the word *last.* The movement toward a final end distinguishes old age from foregoing life phases. The latter have a beginning and an end which are, at the same time, a new beginning. The question comes up, if old age, too, can be viewed as a developmental phase, what are its goals? Psychodynamic development is a process in which physiological factors and the psychological processes stimulated by them are integrated in such a way that one is enabled to master further environmental stimulations [5]. Such an intrapersonal reorganization during senescence may entail a reappraisal of one's values. Thus in old age leisure and intellectual activities may be more highly valued than the expansive activities characteristic of earlier years.

The phenomena of senescence revolve around the central issue of involutional change and grief [27]. A progressive series of object losses may lead to contraction of the self, with death in the end constituting the total loss of self. True acceptance of one's past life as it has been lived includes acceptance of one's own death as the appropriate outcome of one's life. This active acceptance is probably essential to the capacity to experience old age as the consummatory phase of life [21]. In this sense, then, we can identify a developmental task which calls for completion. But this implies that there is also a risk of failure and the possibility of resultant psychopathology.

The psychopathology of senescence can be either age specific or age-nonspecific. Nonspecific psychopathology is that which can be found among individuals of any age. When present in the senium, it may be a carry-over from earlier life phases. For example, a schizophrenic individual who reaches the senium is not suffering from specifically senescent pathology. Examples of specific psychopathology are the maladaptive reactions to the aging experience itself, the depressive reactions to object losses, and the manifestations of failure in achieving a sense of integrity. The physical decline of the aging organism may be so severe as to preclude attempts to cope effectively with interpersonal losses and to achieve "integrity" [12]. A major therapeutic goal, therefore, is to assist the aged patient in actualizing his potential—to free him sufficiently from illness so that he will be able to attain specific goals: a sense of integrity, the maintenance of personal dignity, and the creative capacity to experience the last years as the consummation of life. Psychotherapy is often aimed at "adjusting" the individual for future mastery. In the case of geropsychiatry, however, this aim might well be replaced by an accent on consolidation: mastery of the past as a basis for adapting to the present [13].

## TRAINEE CATEGORIES AND CHARACTERISTICS

Having outlined the field of geropsychiatry and the special problems encountered in working with aged patients, we can now go on to consideration of the diverse types of persons in need of training. On all levels, there appears to be a shortage of professional personnel working with elderly patients. In addition, there is a need to increase the skills of semiprofessional persons and volunteers already active in the field of aging and to train new ones. As has already been pointed out, an accurate quantitative assessment of the manpower shortage is not possible at the present time. Kleemeier and Birren [17] attribute this to the fact that the majority of workers in the field of aging spend only part of their time with the aged while their basic professional identity remains rooted in other disciplines. It is from these other medical disciplines and allied health professions that candidates for training in aging may be drawn.

The fact that the majority of workers have only a partial commitment to the field of aging does not negate the need for a core group of professional individuals who spend most of their time in this area. This core group may regard itself as a group of "specialists" in aging, with their professional identity being closely related to their expertise in a particular gerontological or geriatric area. Without a minimum number of such specialists little effective training could take place in the various branches of aging. A medical student, for example, may take certain courses in aging, but these are not necessarily sufficient for geriatric clinical work later on. Rather, the medical student should learn how the "being-old" of his patient can cause age-related impairments and disabilities; how these determine the patient's reactions to therapy; and how they influence the doctor-patient relationship. He should also have the opportunity to apply this knowledge in a variety of clinical situations, under close supervision and with opportunities to observe his instructor perform clinically with geriatric patients. Similar considerations apply to other fields and professions. In the area of occupational therapy it is clear that elderly patients with mental disorders require a spectrum of therapeutic activities that is quite different from those for patients of other age groups. This is especially true for senile, withdrawn, or apathetic patients, or those who have lost the capacity for abstract thought. In the field of nutrition the need for specialized knowledge is underscored by the fact that many elderly patients present a host of peculiarities related to loss of teeth, diminution of taste and smell sense, altered gastro-intestinal functioning, as well as a great variety of psychological, social, and economic factors. Thus it would seem that geriatric medicine, geriatric occupational therapy, and geriatric dietetics are sufficiently unique and complex so as to require special training experiences organized by experts in these respective areas. The same can be said, of course, for many other areas, such as geriatric dentistry, recreation, and social work.

It follows that, in general, two types of training activities are needed: (1) staff and teacher development and training, productive of specialists with a major commitment both to education and to the field of aging; and (2) training of personnel in the medical specialties and in the allied health profession whose work involves, to a lesser or greater extent, the rendering of services and care to aged patients. Four occupational groupings to which training activities are to be directed have been outlined in a report from the U.S. Department of Health, Education, and Welfare [24]:

1. *Health and medical services,* including the professions of clinical psychologist, dietition, dentist, health educator, nursing home operator, nutritionist, occupational therapist, physical therapist, physician, podiatrist, practical nurse, professional nurse, rehabilitation counselor, social worker, and speech therapist.

2. *Social work,* embracing the tasks of financial planning with older people; casework, personnel work; family counseling; providing intake services and assisting in adjustment in institutions; planning hospital discharges; arranging for guardianships; organizing and administering home social services; providing information, referral and placement services; conducting group programs for older people; and participating in community planning.

3. *Educational, religious, and recreational services,* covering needs for program planners, teachers in the fine arts and art crafts, vocational and avocational counselors, librarians, club leaders, administrators of senior activity centers, group workers, religious counselors, and pastors with specialized knowledge of older people.

4. *Environmental planning and administration,* including needs relative to architecture, community organization, federal and state planning, institutional administration, and staffing for housing developments for older people.

To these may be added semiprofessional personnel (e.g., hospital attendants) and others (e.g., "Friendly Visitors").

Geropsychiatry can make contributions to the training of many of these professional service fields, as illustrated by the following examples. The rehabilitation counselor needs to know how psychological factors influence motivation, and how mental impairment affects performance. The nursing home operator can be more effective when he is aware of the high incidence of psychiatric symptomatology among nursing home residents [23] and has a working knowledge with regard to the implications for the institution's treatment programs, and for planning an optimal physical and social environment. The family counselor needs to be well informed about the psychopathology of senescence, as well as the possible effects of the presence of an aging person on other members of the family. Group workers, religious counselors, and recreationists can benefit in their work with the aged from a knowledge of the psychodynamic aspects of normal and pathological personality functioning in late life. Specialists in architecture and human engineering are better equipped to create specific types of optimal environments (retirement villages, recreation centers) when their basic expertise is supplemented by a comprehension of the particular needs of elderly persons. Such complicated tasks as balancing the need for privacy against the risk of psychological withdrawal and social isolation, the need for stimulation and activity against the risk of undue passivity, the need for peer contact against the risk of alienation from younger people, can be more easily carried out if the persons assigned these tasks have had training in geropsychiatry.

## METHODS OF TRAINING

Teaching methods depend, among other factors, on the training objectives, the curriculum contents, and on the type and level of professionality of the trainees. Trainees pursue specific goals which fit into their individual career patterns. Thus the training focus may be on clinical therapeutic skills, on principles and tactics of basic or clinical research, or on teaching techniques. These objectives are further modified by the nature of the setting in which the trainee ultimately expects to work (e.g., academic career, private practice, institutional work, solo or group work, full-time or part-time work). Teaching methods should be closely attuned to the subject matter to be taught. For example, it is not really possible to master the science and art of psychotherapy without doing psychotherapy under close supervision. Nor can one learn to teach without the actual experience of instructing different types of students, or without proper feedback from an experienced teacher. Such a matching of course contents to practical experience is feasible, however, only in training programs of reasonable duration. It is a drawback of conferences, workshops, and short courses that they do not provide the time-consuming but crucial element of "experience."

Finally, methods of training are also determined by the type of professional to be trained, and by the level of his education (e.g., physicians, clergymen, social workers, nurses, physical therapists, hospital aids, community volunteers). The differences in characteristics between these groups and levels will necessitate corresponding differences in focus and depth of content. The process of transmitting to others one's own personal knowledge requires that it be transformed into objective information that can be received and assimilated. The greater the "professional distance" between teacher and trainee (e.g., psychiatrists who are teaching hospital aides) the greater are the potential difficulties in communication. It then is essential that the teacher has thoroughly understood, and clearly conceptualized for himself, what he is about to teach and that he find the kind of language that is appropriate for transmitting the information to his audience.

Types of teaching used in the field of aging include conferences, workshops, or institutes; regular consultations; formal courses; or full-time professional training programs.

*Conferences, workshops, and institutes* are a rather common and popular means of disseminating information. This format usually involves a series of presentations by authorities in the field, the use of discussion groups, and panel discussions. The program may last from one to several days and usually has a fairly substantial attendance. The advantages of this approach are strategic (e.g., alerting a relatively large group of professionals to particular aspects of aging, creating attitudes of good will and enthusiasm); economic (e.g., little expenditure of time and money on the part of the participants); and social (e.g., the fringe benefits of conventioneering). The disadvantages include the relatively high teaching cost per individual participant, the risk of superficiality of the learning experience, and the difficulty in evaluating accurately the effectiveness of the training effort. Institutes and workshops are most effective when participants are carefully selected; when the number of participants is small enough to permit group discussion; when the conference lasts long enough to allow for assimilation and integration of the information presented; and when the proceedings are later made available to the participants. Examples of institutes that meet these criteria are the Institutes in Administration of Extended Care Facilities organized by the Veterans Administration for selected personnel of its chronic care units [15].

*Consultation programs* represent a format less clearly defined than other training programs. The approach is usually less systematic, without a structured curriculum. Consultation programs may take the form of problem-centered seminars or of individual and group supervision. Typically, the latter is requested by the consultee, in contrast to educational programs which are often initiated "from above." Consultations vary in duration and frequency; when they are on a short-term basis, their scope is somewhat limited compared with formal educational methods. The consultant, who may be of a different professional background than the consultee, usually functions in an advisory role and tends to avoid recommending solutions based on his own experience [6].

Because of the relatively unstructured nature of the consultation process, special difficulties may arise, such as disillusionment on the part of the consultees when they discover that the consultations do not answer all of their questions [20]. Kaufman emphasizes the need for clearly defining the roles and expectations of consultant and consultees, respectively [16]. It would appear that learning cannot proceed without a certain degree of structure, either in terms of role-definition or by way of introducing a formal, didactic element. As an illustration of some of these issues, brief mention will be made of a consultation program for caseworkers dealing with the aged in the framework of a state welfare department [11].

This two-year program was developed jointly by the staff of the Section on Aging of the North Carolina Department of Public Welfare and the Duke Geropsychiatry Training Program.

The goals of the Geropsychiatry Consultation Program were to broaden the caseworker's knowledge of the biological and psychological changes, psychodynamic aspects, and sociocultural influences during senescence; to increase comprehension of the multifaceted problems of individual cases through the case consultation method; to increase familiarity with appropriate therapeutic techniques; and to increase the caseworker's skill in recognizing mental disorders and making appropriate referrals to psychiatrists.

Staff members of the Duke Geropsychiatry Training Program conducted daylong sessions at quarterly intervals throughout the state of North Carolina. The consultation day was divided into two periods. During the morning session didactic material was presented by the geropsychiatric consultant. The lectures dealt with the normal psychology of aging; psychopathology of aging; symptoms and signs of psychiatric disorders; mental disorders in the aged; psychosomatic disorders; environmental planning and rehabilitation; techniques of interviewing and counseling; and family dynamics. In the afternoon two case presentations, previously submitted by caseworkers and distributed to the participants, were discussed in depth. The case discussions provided useful opportunities for practical application of concepts presented in the lectures. In addition, films or videotapes were shown depicting certain features of the psychopathology of senescence. Several months after the initial discussions follow-ups were presented to evaluate the effectiveness of any new approaches that had been suggested.

In order to make the material presented to the caseworkers as relevant as possible, the lectures or films for a forthcoming session were "tried out" on the staff of the Section on Aging. Since these staff members were regularly involved at the county level with the individual caseworker they could reflect the strengths, deficiencies, and needs of the caseworkers toward whom the program was geared. Clarification of the consultant's role was facilitated and many pitfalls were avoided through these regular planning conferences.

During the two years of the program, there was a steady rise in participants, from 140 caseworkers during the first round of consultations to 295 during the final round. Using the above described format, it was found that the consultant could work effectively with as many as 40 group members at a time, provided the group was relatively homogeneous in professional background and interest.

*Courses* are usually offered as part of a larger curriculum, such as continuing education programs, or as part of in-service training programs. It should be noted that courses in geriatric medicine or psychiatry are not currently a regular feature of medical school curricula, nor are they a regular part of residency training programs in the various medical specialties. Donahue mentions that student demand for training in aging has been minimal [10]. Krauss, however, states that medical students do evince some interest, in contrast to the medical school faculty [18]. This observation has been confirmed by others [3].

This apparent lack of interest in geriatrics is further illustrated by an analysis of continuing education courses for physicians [4]. During the period from September 1, 1967 to August 31, 1968, a total of 1,830 continuing education courses for physicians were offered. Only eight of these contained any specific reference to geriatrics. In the field of psychiatry, a total of 333 courses were offered; only two of these referred to aging problems, while 41 of the courses in psychiatry dealt with problems of children or adolescents. Thus, specific attention to age-related problems is reserved, by and large, for the phase of growing up, but not for that of growing old. Likewise, it is significant that in the curriculum outline for the new specialty of family practice little mention is made of geriatrics [1]. This is all the more surprising since one would expect family practitioners to deal with a substantial number of geriatric patients, and with family problems related to the presence of an aging family member.

On the other hand one gets the impression that many physicians, especially after some years of clinical practice, are aware of the need for additional training in geriatrics and geropsychiatry and would welcome such training. In this connection the curriculum project of the Gerontology Society deserves to be mentioned. Its purpose is to provide teaching materials that can be used in workshops or institutes [13]. According to Donahue, there will eventually be more interest in aging if more gerontology courses are included in undergraduate and graduate curricula [10]. Dawson emphasizes the need for a more intensive didactic approach in training young physicians for geriatric practice. As clinical exposure and education are broadened, investigation in geriatric diseases will become more intense [9]. Krauss stresses the importance of geriatric medicine as part of the medical school curricula for a number of reasons. The clinical interpretation of structural, physiological, and pathological changes in the elderly requires great understanding for modern medical care. More emphasis should be placed upon basic needs of the aging, such as housing, employment, retirement, and use of leisure time. The increasingly important role of the medical profession in the preventive and curative aspects of aging should also lead to the development of a closer working relationship with paramedical disciplines. Geriatric research deserves more attention in the overall study of the process of aging [19].

Courses in the medical and psychiatric aspects of aging have special relevance for persons already working with elderly patients. Among these groups there is usually substantial interest in additional training opportunities. The largest number of persons engaged in the care of geriatric patients are probably the nursing aides and practical nurses employed by chronic care facilities. These persons appear to receive little in the way of formal training in topics that are specifically geriatric. For example, mental hospital aides usually receive a general course orienting them to work with psychiatric patients. Topics related to aging constitute only a small part of the curriculum. When these aides are placed on a geriatric unit, on-the-job training is expected to supplement their limited knowledge. It is questionable, however, if these circumstances foster a reasonable sense of confidence and an optimal degree of clinical know-how.

In-service training programs for this type of personnel are not without problems. First, there is the problem of finding staff with competence in specific content areas as well as in teaching methods, who are willing to teach, and who have sufficient time. Second, additional personnel must be available to carry on patient care while the trainees are in class. Third, mental hospital aides represent a heterogeneous group with regard to age, intelligence, and motivation. By and large, they are more interested in learning practical know-how than in theoretical concepts.

With these considerations in mind, an in-service training program for aides on the geriatric units of a mental hospital was organized (John Umstead Hospital, Butner, N.C.). The training faculty consisted of staff members and fellows of the Duke Geropsychiatry Training Program and members of the hospital nursing staff. The latter had received prior training with regard to content areas, teaching techniques, and course organization. An occupational and physical therapist also participated in the program. The training program lasts 12 weeks, with 15 hours of lectures and conferences per week. Eight to 10 aides make up a class. The course covers topics which are relevant for nursing care primarily. Practical application to patient management is continually stressed. Open-ended discussion sessions are held regularly for the purpose of getting feedback from the trainees. Tests administered toward the end of the course have indicated a noticeable increase in knowledge concerning the content areas of the curriculum.

A few comments on the evaluation of training programs may be in order here. Several methodological problems exist. (1) The accuracy and usefulness of the assessment data depend on pretraining determination of trainee knowledge and skills. (2) Knowledge and information can be more easily and accurately tested than the level of clinical skills. (3) Improved morale, self-confidence, and job satisfaction in the trainees, which can be a definite fringe benefit of the training experiences, are even more difficult to measure. These subjective phenomena may be evaluated on the basis of personal reports expressed by the trainees. (4) Occasionally a somewhat paradoxical observation can be made: Some trainees seem to know less upon completion of training than at the start. One possible explanation is that these are individuals who, as a result of the training experiences, have begun to ask themselves questions about phenomena previously taken for granted. The evaluation test catches them at a time when they have more questions than answers.

In-service training staffs tend to develop their own course materials: texts, reprints, bibliographies, edited lectures, illustrative clinical case write-ups, and so on. These materials can eventually be put together in the form of a compendium or manual. Once such course materials are available, they can facilitate extension of the training program to other institutions.

One type of teaching technique which the author has found particularly useful deserves separate mention. This is the use of edited or unedited videotapes. The Duke Geropsychiatry Training Program has made rather extensive use of television for the purpose of clinical instruction and demonstration. Closed circuit television enables an audience of varying size to follow closely an actual interview and permits the instructor to make ongoing comments on the behavior and communication of physician and patient. Playback of previously recorded videotapes offers the advantage that, at any time, the audience or instructor can have the videotape stopped to discuss specific behavioral phenomena, or to replay parts of particular importance. A third major use of audiovisual materials is the development of a library of videotapes on such topics as psychopathology of senescence, techniques of interviewing elderly patients, family dynamics, and intergenerational conflict. From the videotapes instructional films can be made.

*Formal training programs* in aging requiring full-time participation on the part of the trainee apparently are more commonly found in the disciplines of psychology and sociology than in the medical disciplines. Furthermore, existing programs are usually oriented more toward training in research than in applied gerontology or geriatrics. This trend is not surprising because a professional orientation toward research in aging promises the rewards of prestige; and too, the scientific, intellectual detachment needed in research may be preferable to the personal anxieties and professional frustrations with which the clinician has to come to grips. But, at the same time, this particular trend suggests that, in order to recruit young, bright and well-motivated persons for clinical work with the aged, part-time research may need to be emphasized. In fact, diversification generally is a wise choice: The investigator may get new hunches from clinical work, and the clinician may improve his professional effectiveness by participation in research. Examples of programs with a major emphasis on training for clinical work are the Geropsychiatric Nursing Training Program of the Duke School of Nursing and the Duke Geropsychiatry Training Program.

The Duke Geropsychiatry Training Program has been in existence since 1966 and is aimed primarily at physicians who have completed two or three years of psychiatric residency. The objectives of the program are to increase skills in the practice of geropsychiatry, to stimulate clinical research, and to develop teaching skills in geropsychiatry. The two-year program includes training in biological, psychological, and social gerontology, as well as training in geriatrics and in geropsychiatry proper.

The areas outlined in Tables 1 and 2 represent the core curriculum of the program. They are covered in weekly seminars which feature assigned readings, case presentations, and occasional visiting lecturers. Clinical training includes case studies and supervised therapy of ambulatory aged patients in the Duke Information and Counseling Service for Older Persons, of patients hospitalized at Duke Medical Center and at two nearby state mental hospitals, as well as of residents of a retirement home. Liaison with the North Carolina Department of Mental Health provides opportunities for training experiences in social gerontology and community geropsychiatry. Research training in the field of aging is offered in the form of supervised participation in basic research projects in the laboratory, as well as in applied research in clinical settings, such as the Duke Cerebral Diagnostic Unit.

TABLE 1. *Duke Geropsychiatry Training Program (curriculum)*

---

*Geropsychiatry*

Psychodynamics of senescence (patterns of successful aging, coping in crisis, etc.)
Psychopathology and psychiatric syndromes of senescence
Psychotherapy (individual and group therapy, family therapy, etc.)
Psychopharmacology and other somatic therapies
Environmental planning (milieu therapy, reality orientation, etc.)

*Geriatrics*

Geriatric medicine and neurology
Somatopsychology (changes in body image, psychological reactions to chronic illness and disability, etc.)
Psychosomatic approach (the sick role, psychosocial factors in organic brain syndrome, rehabilitation techniques, management of hypochondriasis and regression, etc.)

*Psychosocial Gerontology*

The human life cycle
Ecology of senescence; sociocultural determinants
Social attitudes toward aging and mental illness
Work and retirement (career patterns, psychopathology of work and retirement, leisure and recreation, etc.)
Family dynamics and conflict
Programs of care for the aged and chronically ill

*Psychological Gerontology*

Age-related changes and measurement techniques (of cognition and intelligence, perception, psychomotor skills, learning and memory)
Neuropsychological deficits in neurological and psychiatric syndromes of senium (clinical and laboratory techniques)

*Biological Gerontology*

Psychophysiology (autonomous conditioning in the aged, autonomous nervous system aspects of learning in the aged, etc.)
Neurophysiology (senescent EEG, cerebral blood flow studies, EEG correlates of learning and memory in the aged, etc.)
Neurochemistry and neuropharmacology
Genetics and biology and aging

---

Each of the members of the Geropsychiatry Training Faculty is a specialist in one of the five basic content areas of the training program outlined above. In addition, many qualified faculty members associated with the Duke Center for the Study of Aging and

TABLE 2. *Duke Geropsychiatry Training Program (activities and resources)*

| Training Activities | Resources |
|---|---|
| *Geropsychiatry* | |
| Diagnostic studies<br>Individual and group therapy<br>Drug therapy<br>Ward milieu techniques<br>Clinical research projects | —Duke Cerebral Diagnostic Unit<br>—Duke Info. & Couns. Serv. for<br>    Older Persons<br>—Geropsychiatry Services of John<br>    Umstead Hospital and Doro-<br>    thea Dix Hospital |
| *Geriatrics* | |
| Psychosomatic aspects<br>Neurological aspects (stroke)<br>Rehabilitative techniques<br>Therapy in chronic illness | —Duke Psychosomatic Service<br>—Duke Dept. of Neurology<br>—Duke Dept. of Phys. Med. and<br>    Rehab.<br>—Nursing Homes |
| *Social Gerontology* | |
| Retirement counseling<br>Family counseling<br>Agency consultations<br>Environmental planning<br>Research projects | —Duke Dept. of Med. Sociology<br>—N. C. Dept. of Welfare (Section<br>    on Aging)<br>—Durham Mental Health Center<br>—Duke Center for Study of Aging<br>    and Human Development |
| *Psychological Gerontology* | |
| Neuropsychological tests for<br>    CNS deficits<br>Measurement of cognitive,<br>    perceptual, learning and<br>    memory, and psychomotor<br>    functions<br>Basic and clinical research<br>    projects (in the above) | —Duke Gerontol. Research<br>    Laboratories<br>—Duke Gerontol. Research Train-<br>    ing Program<br>—Duke Center for Study of Aging<br>    and Human Development |
| *Biological Gerontology* | |
| Electrophysiology, bioelectric<br>    techniques in clinical<br>    diagnosis<br>EEG, cerebral blood flow | —Duke Psychophysiology Labora-<br>    tory<br>—Duke Gerontol. Research<br>    Laboratories<br>—University Courses |

Human Development are available for training and supervision. A personal advisor helps the trainee in formulating his specific career plans; these are then implemented with the assistance of an advisory committee. The latter is composed of faculty members whose interests parallel those of the trainee.

Since it is impossible to become well versed in all phases of the program, the trainee is encouraged to select those training experiences that will best fit his career plans. Thus the curriculum of the program is flexible and adaptable to the needs of individual trainees. Because the program is designed for the training of psychiatrists, primary emphasis is placed upon geropsychiatry proper, including the psychodynamics and psychopathology of senescence, relevant therapeutic techniques, and the like. Next in importance is the area of geriatrics with special focus on the psychosomatic approach, which involves an understanding of psychophysiological and somatopsychic reactions. Thorough acquaintance with geriatric pathophysiology and an understanding of general psychodynamics must be supplemented by, and integrated with, clinical experience. Only then can the practitioner develop the skills needed to implement the principles of a comprehensive treatment approach.

An important element of this program is teacher training. Experiences in the techniques of transmitting knowledge to other individuals and groups can be gained in such settings as nursing homes and the geriatric units of mental hospitals. Certain community programs in aging on the state or county level (e.g., the Division of Services to the Aged of the North Carolina Department of Public Welfare) present unique opportunities for training in the techniques of consultation and in the organization of workshops.

REFERENCES

1. American Academy of General Practice (Commission on Education). *Graduate Training for Family Practice.* Kansas City: American Academy of General Practice, September 1967.

2. American Geriatrics Society Seminar. Distinguishing the health care needs of the aging. *J. Amer. Geriat. Soc.* 16:159, 1968.
3. *Ibid.,* p. 161.
4. American Medical Association Department of Continuing Medical Education. Continuing education courses for physicians. *J.A.M.A.* 201:379–473, 1967.
5. Benedek, T. Climacterium: A developmental phase. *Psychoanal. Quart.* 19:1–27, 1950.
6. Bindman, A. J. Mental health consultation: Theory in practice. *J. Consult. Psychol.* 23:473–482, 1959.
7. Blumenthal, H. T. The shape of the gerontological society. *Gerontologist* 5:2, 1965.
8. Clausen, J. A. Conceptual and Methodologic Issues in the Assessment of Mental Health in the Aged. In A. Simon and L. J. Epstein (Eds.), *Aging in Modern Society.* Psychiatric Research Report No. 23. Washington, D.C.: American Psychiatric Association, 1968.
9. Dawson, D. Orienting the young physician to the geriatric age group and its problems. *J. Amer. Geriat. Soc.* 13:843–844, 1965.
10. Donahue, W. Development and Current Status of University Instruction in Social Gerontology. In R. E. Kushner and M. E. Bunch (Eds.), *Graduate Education in Aging Within the Social Sciences.* Ann Arbor: University of Michigan Press, 1967.
11. Elmore, J. L., and Verwoerdt, A. Geropsychiatric training for case workers. *Gerontologist* 8:291–294, 1968.
12. Erikson, E. H. The problem of ego identity. *J. Amer. Psychoanal. Ass.* 4:56–121, 1956.
13. Gerontological Society. *The Practitioner and the Elderly.* Working With Older People, vol. I. Washington, D.C.: U.S. Department of Health, Education, and Welfare (Division of Chronic Diseases, Gerontology Branch), 1966.
14. Gitman, L. Is the gerontological society necessary? *Gerontologist* 3:98–99, 1963.
15. Institute in Administration of Extended Care Facilities. Conference of the Education Service and Extended Care Service of the V.A. Department of Medicine and Surgery. Los Angeles: Veterans Administration Center, January 20–30, 1969.
16. Kaufman, I. Role of psychiatric consultation. In S. L. Green

(Ed.), Use of the Consultant, Workshop, 1955. *Amer. J. Orthopsychiat.* 26:223–251, 1956.

17. Kleemeier, R. W., and Birren, J. E.  Society and the Study of Aging. In R. E. Kushner and M. E. Bunch (Eds.), *Graduate Education in Aging Within the Social Sciences.* Ann Arbor: University of Michigan Press, 1967. P. 8.

18. Krauss, T. C.  Indoctrination of medical students in principles of geriatrics. *Gerontologist* 3:152–154, 1963.

19. Krauss, T. C.  The role of geriatrics and gerontology in medical education. *J. Amer. Geriat. Soc.* 13:699–707, 1965.

20. Maddux, J. F.  Psychiatric consultation in a rural setting. *Amer. J. Orthopsychiat.* 23:775–784, 1953.

21. Parsons, T.  Old age as consummatory phase. *Gerontologist* 3:53, 1963.

22. Smyth, V. M., and Cole, W. E.  *A Pilot Survey of Personnel Training Needs in the Field of Aging.* Atlanta: U.S. Department of Health, Education, and Welfare, 1963. Pp. 1–41.

23. Stotsky, B. A.  Allegedly non-psychiatric patients in nursing homes. *J. Amer. Geriat. Soc.* 15:535–545, 1967.

24. Unsigned.  The role and training of professional personnel in the field of aging. In *Reports and Guidelines from the White House Conference on Aging.* Washington, D.C.: U.S. Department of Health, Education, and Welfare, 1961. No. 8. Pp. 8–9.

25. Verwoerdt, A., and Eisdorfer, C.  Geropsychiatry: The psychiatry of senescence. *Geriatrics* 22:139–149, 1967.

26. Weinberg, J.  Implications of increasing population of the aged for community mental health services—The psychiatrist's responsibility. *Gerontologist* 5:74–77, 1965.

27. Zetzel, E. R.  Dynamics of the Metapsychology of the Aging Process. In M. A. Berezin and S. H. Cath (Eds.), *Geriatric Psychiatry.* New York: International Universities Press, 1965. Pp. 109–119.

28. Zinberg, N. E. Geriatric psychiatry: Need and problems. *Gerontologist* 4:130–135, 1964.

# 18

# The Aged and Public Policy

JOSEPH J. SPENGLER

> Seventy is not a sin.
> —Golda Meir, *Time*, March 14, 1969

> Let's take the instant by the forward top;
> For we are old, and on our quick'st decrees
> Th' inaudible and noiseless foot of Time
> Steals ere we can effect them.
> —Shakespeare, *All's Well That Ends Well*

> Nothing 'gainst Time's scythe can make defence.
> —Shakespeare, "Sonnet XII"

> To live is to struggle.
> René Dubos, *So Human an Animal*

Over the past 40 years increasing public provision has been made for the aged. The concern in this last chapter is with some of the forces giving rise to this increase in public provision and with prospective future trends.

The prospect for increase in longevity will not be considered.* Note may be taken in passing, however, of recent gains in longevity and of the effect of eliminating the leading causes of mortality after

---

* While man may complete a larger fraction of his life-span, the life-span itself is limited by the deterioration and loss of cells and physiological function. See N. W. Shock, The Physiology of Aging, *Sci. Amer.* 206:100–110, Jan. 1962; L. Hayflick, Human Cells and Aging, *Sci. Amer.* 218:32–37, March 1968; B. L. Strehler and A. S. Mildvan, General Theory of Mortality and Aging, *Science* 132:14, July 1960; H. J. Curtis, Biological Mechanisms Underlying the Aging Process, *Science* 141:686–694, Aug. 1963. R. W. Prehoda believes, however, that man's life-span may approximate 200 years within three to four decades and eventually 1,000 years. R. W. Prehoda, *Extended Youth: The Promise of Gerontology* (New York: G. P. Putnam's Sons, 1968).

age 45. Over the past 25 years the expectation of life at age 45 has increased about 1½ years for men and 4 years for women. Mainly responsible for post-45 mortality are cardiovascular-renal diseases and malignant neoplasms. If mortality from these two sets of diseases were reduced by 30 percent, expectation of life at ages 45 and 65 would increase only about 3 and 2.4 years, respectively, for males; the corresponding gains for females would be about 2.9 and 2.45 years. If mortality from all causes were reduced by 30 percent, expectation at age 65 would increase by 2.94 years for males and 2.88 years for females. These extensions would raise life expectancy at age 65 to about 15.9 years for males and 19 years for females.*

## FORCES OPERATIVE IN THE RECENT PAST

When one seeks to identify the forces giving rise to legislation economically favorable to the aged, one may look at immediate antecedents or at longer-run forces. It is the latter, however, that are overriding in the longer run. It is these, therefore, that we shall discuss.†

The long-run forces are divisible into the ideological and the real. At least three somewhat distinct *ideological* forces are recognizable. First, already in the early part of this century a kind of collectivistic, redistributive ideology was coming into being, only to be smothered during World War I and its immediate aftermath. Yet, like the fabled phoenix, it began again to take on life in the 1920's and lent passive support to actual demands for various kinds of public assistance for the aged (as well as for others). After 1929 the havoc-spreading Great Depression triggered this support off into something more

* Future Gains in Longevity After Age 45. *Statistical Bulletin* of the Metropolitan Life Insurance Co. 48:8–9, March 1967; B. L. Strehler (Ed.), *Advances in Gerontological Research.* (New York: Academic Press, 1964); A. M. Brues and G. A. Sacher, *Aging and Levels of Biological Organization* (Chicago: University of Chicago Press, 1965).

† On relatively recent aspects of the genesis of the so-called war on poverty, including poverty of the aged, see the symposium, Antipoverty Programs, *Law and Contemporary Problems* 31, No. 1, 1966.

active and gave it manifold organizational form (e.g., the Townsend Movement).

Second, with the secularization of values and the dissipation of conduct-determining religious belief, the ancient religious obligation to be charitable gradually metamorphosed into a politically and economically oriented poverty ideology. This ideology is now current among those (many of whom are economically untutored) presently in charge of critical and strategic channels of communication and engaged in the dissemination of "information" to college students and other well-meaning receivers of "information," most of whom are also economically untutored. These opinion-dispensers have helped propagate a distorted, value-ridden picture of the poor (among them the aged) which, as Walter Miller observes, is at variance with both the judgments of the poor themselves and that subculture of poverty which affords the relatively poor a "coherent way of life geared to the circumstances of lower-class labor."* Poverty, in other words, has two dimensions, one objective, the other subjective and reflective of the interpretation and self-image which one who is objectively defined to be poor puts upon his own status and condition. The image which a person defined to be poor forms of his objective poverty, even though self-protective, may be modified by exposing him to subjective influences, propagandistic and otherwise. Usually he is made to feel poor even though he originally did not view his plane of living as falling within an objectively defined category of poverty. In the United States many who were not aware of being poor have learned, after the manner of characters in a Molière play, that they had always been poor.

Third, a kind of ideological rationale for many kinds of public spending was canonized in the later 1930's as a result of the writings of Lord Keynes and his disciples. Arguments in support of public spending were not, of course, new, having long found utterance; but never before had so persuasive a case been made for the alleged

* See summary of Seminar on Poverty, *Bull. Amer. Acad. Sci.* 22:4–8, Dec. 1967; C. A. Valentine, *Culture and Poverty* (Chicago: University of Chicago Press, 1968); E. D. Canham (Ed.), *The Concept of Poverty* (Washington, D.C., U.S. Chamber of Commerce, 1965).

social costlessness of a great deal of public spending. This rationale was to prove useful to both advocates of public welfare and their political spokesmen. Presumably the progressive inflation to which these programs might give rise would not materialize until after the programs had gotten wedged into the essentially uncontrolled and uncontrollable bureaucratic structure of modern democratic governments. The rationale was useful also in that it had to do only with the elastic pecuniary dimension of welfare and not with its real dimension which tends to be inelastic. For example, when Medicare was being developed, emphasis was upon monetary support and not upon increasing the supply of medical, paramedical, and service personnel in keeping with the necessarily augmented monetary demand for this personnel. As a result, many prices have risen notably, and the capacity of Medicare to support care of the aged has been reduced.*

The *real* conditions, of which six may be considered, are interrelated. Historically first is the Great Depression, together with the resulting massive unemployment of the 1930's. Unemployment rose from 3.2 percent of the civilian labor force in 1929 to 8.7 percent in 1930 and thereafter to annual levels from 1931 to 1940 varying between a low of 14.3 percent in 1937 and 24.9 percent in 1933. Moreover, not until after two years of defense spending and the country's entry into World War II did unemployment fall below the 5 percent level, in 1942. This long-continuing unemployment reduced the capacity of many households to make provision for their support after retirement. Moreover, such provision as was made underwent dissipation through inflation, with prices rising 71 percent between

---

* On these issues, see W. F. Berry and J. C. Daugherty, A Closer Look at Rising Medical Costs, *Monthly Labor Rev.* 91:1–8, Nov. 1968. What is needed is careful economic analysis of the supply and allocation of medical services. J. C. Brackett, A New Budget for a Retired Couple, *Monthly Labor Rev.* 91:33–40, June 1968 puts the annual cost of medical care of a couple with an annual income of around $4,000 at 7 to 8 percent of this income. Between 1950 and 1967, despite the prospect of Medicare, etc., physicians per 100,000 population increased only 6 percent. See *Health Resources Statistics* (Washington, D.C.: U.S. Department of Health, Education, and Welfare, Dec. 1968), p. 123; also R. Fein, *The Doctor Shortage* (Washington, D.C.: Brookings Institution, 1967).

1938 and 1948, 20 percent between 1948 and 1958, and 144 percent over the whole period 1938 to 1968.

Second, already by 1930 the number of aged persons was increasing more rapidly than the population mainly because gross reproduction had been falling. Natality and the excess of births over deaths did not begin to rise until in the late 1930's and not notably until after the war and then only until the later 1950's after which natality again fell. Those aged 65 and over formed only 5.3 percent of the population in 1929, but this fraction had risen to 9.5 percent by 1968 and may rise to about 10 percent by 1985 or earlier. It will rise significantly above 10 percent, however, only if gross reproduction falls appreciably, or if the expectation of life at birth rises notably above 70 years.

This aging trend gave greater visibility to the aged, even though it was not at first accompanied by a marked increase in their political power. Those of an age anticipatory of the advent of, say, age 65 are likely to have interests more in common with those aged 65 and over than with those aged only 21 to 44 years. Suppose, at least for sake of exposition, that we include in this anticipatory category persons aged 45 to 64 but without supposing their consciousness of kind to be as intense as that of persons aged 65 and over. Not until recent years, however, have the aged, together with persons of similar interests, formed close to a majority of the voting population. This near preponderance is, of course, a variable one and must be taken advantage of when it exists, if the aged would improve their position through political means.*

Third, steady decrease in the number of persons living in rural areas had increased the number of persons exposed to economic disabilities of the sort to which older persons are especially prone

---

* Around 1930 the population 45 or more years old formed only four-tenths of the population of voting age, then 21 years and older. This fraction had risen to about 43 percent by 1950, 49 percent by 1960, and about 50 percent by 1968. On prospective changes in age composition, see below. In the text above it is supposed, though without establishing the fact for present and future, that around age 45 individuals become concerned about retirement and begin to develop an identity of interests with those already retired.

(e.g., loss of job, inability to find employment, decrease in monetary income, large medical expenses). Today, of course, the risk of poverty, objectively defined, is greater in rural than in urban areas. In the past and often even today, however, a given plane of living is less expensive in rural than in urban areas. Moreover, the threshold of consciousness of being poor is associated with lower income levels in nonrural than in rural areas. Accordingly, as the nonrural population increased absolutely and relatively,* its increase must have been accompanied by increase in the awareness of poverty, and in some measure also by an increase in demands for public assistance. After all, city populations probably are more collectivistically inclined, as a rule, than are rural populations.

Fourth, per capita real disposable income has been growing since 1940, by which time it had finally returned to the 1929 level from which it had declined with the advent of the Great Depression. Between 1940 and 1968, it grew about 2.5 percent per year. National income per capita grew at about the same rate. This steady increase in real income per capita, combined with the progressive nature of income-based tax revenue, suggested that use of the income-tax apparatus to redistribute income somewhat (in part to older persons) might be acceptable. The Social Security system also had a redistributive impact, especially after additional burdens were placed upon it— justifiable, it was believed, by the lesser ability to pay of many of its beneficiaries. The steady increase in posttax income must have made requests for some redistribution of income attractive to those who stood to benefit eventually and/or were uncertain about their security in retirement. It must also have fed that "revolution of expectations" which for several or more decades has been causing

---

* The farm population continued to decline after 1920 except for a temporary farmward movement in the economically depressed early 1930's. By 1950 the farm population formed only 15.3 percent of the total population, half what it had been in 1920; by 1966 it amounted to only 5.9 percent of the nation's population. While the farm population has continued to decline, the rural population has not changed greatly in absolute size since 1910; it has, however, formed a declining fraction of the total population, falling from 54.3 percent in 1910 to 43.8 percent in 1930 and 40.4 percent in 1950.

the potential demands of many persons for goods and services to increase much faster than their posttax earnings.

Fifth, with the development of poverty bench-marks, albeit arbitrary and subject to variable definition, it was found that households headed by older persons predominated among those with incomes deemed below the poverty level. This condition reflected the inability of many persons to find steady and fairly remunerative employment as well as their earlier inability to accumulate adequate savings for old age. The incidence of unemployment has tended to be somewhat higher among workers over 55 years of age than among those aged 21 to 54; it would be higher still were not many older workers protected by rules of seniority. Indeed, in 1967, unemployment among those aged 55 or over was below the national level and compared favorably with that found among persons aged 21 to 54.* When older workers become unemployed, however, they find it much harder than younger workers to obtain new employment. They are sometimes handicapped, furthermore, by their being less mobile than younger workers.† It is not surprising, therefore, that the income status of the older population has been inferior to that of younger persons for a number of decades.‡

Sixth, older persons have become increasingly conscious of the income-eroding effects of inflation, effects which Congress has several

* As late as 1968 between one-fifth and one-fourth of all families with head over age 64 received incomes below the poverty level, whereas in 1963 two-thirds of those over age 64 and not in institutions were described as "subject to poverty." See U.S. Bureau of the Census, *Current Population Reports,* Series P–60, No. 55, Aug. 1968; and on poverty and unemployment, M. Orshansky, Counting the Poor, *Social Security Bull.* 28:16–25, Jan. 1965, and report of P. M. Ryscavage and H. M. Williams, in *Monthly Labor Rev.* 91:15–21, Aug. 1968.

† The role of immobility probably is exaggerated. See S. Goldstein, Socio-Economics and Migration Differentials Between the Aged in the Labor Force and in the Reserve, *Gerontologist* 7:37–40, March 1967.

‡ In 1949, for example, median income for white nonfarm males 65 years and over was only 40 percent as high as that for those aged 45 to 54; the corresponding percentage for nonwhite males was 38. The corresponding percentages in the farm population were 46 and 60. Even for those with a high school or a college education, median income after age 65 was very much lower than that for persons in the 45 to 54 age group. See H. P. Miller, *Income of the American People* (New York: Wiley, 1955), chap. 6.

times sought to counterbalance by increasing social security benefits. Periodic counterbalancing legislation on the part of Congress is
an inferior means of offsetting the income-dissipating effects of inflation. It is preferable to prevent inflation altogether, or, failing in
this, to attach an inflation-offsetting escalator clause to social security
benefits. Inflation has, of course, long been under way. It is true
that between 1930 and 1940 the Bureau of Labor Statistics consumer
price index declined from 58.2 to 48.8. But thereafter it rose, to 83.8
by 1948, 100.7 by 1958, and 120.9 by 1968. It rose nearly 5 percent
in 1968 and over 22 percent from 1960 to 1968, a period notable for
the introduction by the Kennedy-Johnson administrations of the so-
called New Economics. Today a consumer needs about $1.50 to
buy what cost a dollar in 1949 and about $1.20 to buy what cost only
a dollar in 1960.

What has been said boils down to this: In and after the 1930's
demand for assistance to the aged and for measures suited to improve their situation increased markedly. This trend was reenforced
by ideological changes. At the same time the capacity of the state
to provide this assistance increased, especially after the late 1930's.
Given these conditions it was possible for political spokesmen for
the aged to set up arrangements providing some income security in
old age, together with relatively free access to medical care and related forms of assistance. But what does the future hold in store for
the aged?

## THE FUTURE OF THE AGED

While the lot of the younger aged in the United States should
prove attractive in the near future, this future is not so attractive
for most older aged persons, especially not for those beyond their late
seventies. After all, as Democritus wrote about 2½ millenia ago,
"Old age is a general mutilation. It has all the limbs and organs, but
they each lack something." The advent of this stage of aging may
be put off for many if not most persons until late in the seventies,
but it cannot be put off much longer, even under highly favorable

circumstances. Even the supposedly salutary medication of King David of old loses its vaunted curative powers.* Given a more rational and less superstition-ridden view of life than now prevails, therefore, euthanasia may be given more serious consideration than at present. Otherwise, given further prolongation of life without corresponding prolongation of use of faculties, the lot of many aged could resemble that of mythological Tithonus, or that of residents in the Republic of the Half Dead portrayed in Kipling's "Strange Ride of Morrowbie Jukes," or that of Jonathan Swift's "Struldbrugs" whose very appearance weakened the appetite for living.†

Let us now consider some of the reasons that could make the emerging future of the aged bleak, certainly in a relative if not in an absolute sense. Notice will be taken mainly of real circumstances, though several ideological factors may be mentioned. The ideological factors differ from the real ones, of course, in that, being mental in character, they may be more susceptible of change.

1. It is highly probable that the society of the future, even more than that of the present, will be a society of so-called secular values (in reality, often merely new superstitions in place of the old), one bereft of the beliefs and values which in the past have enabled an adaptive mankind to cushion the impact of hardship, even when in the guise of aging. In the past when people were much less mobile than now, familial care reenforced whatever public care was conferred upon the aged; and familial care was likely to include some love and affection—far less than was accorded to children, it is true—but much more than is likely to be bestowed even by kindly hirelings skilled at simulating affection. In one respect, however, the aged of today are better off: They lose fewer of their temporal associates. Writing in 1623, John Donne, the English poet, observed

---

* "Let there be sought for my lord the king a young virgin; and let her stand before the king, and cherish him; and let her lie in thy bosom, that my lord the king may get heat . . . and the damsel . . . ministered to him; but the king knew her not." 1 Kings 1:2–4.

† "I am a hulk—only breathing and excreting," declared Sir Winston Churchill in 1953 as he watched himself becoming helpless and senile. *Time*, p. 31, May 6, 1966. See also on the plight of the aged, J. Henry, *Culture Against Man* (New York: Random House, 1963).

that when the bell tolls for friend or acquaintance, it also "tolls for thee"; for "no man is an Iland, entire of selfe," but one whose reality consists in his being part of the furniture of the minds of others. At that time only about 84 in 1,000 females aged 20 reached the age of 80, whereas in 1900 about 194 in 1,000 white females aged 20 reached age 80. Today the corresponding figure is 479. We may say, therefore, that today the chances of an octogenerian's having surviving friends of one's own age are twice as good as they were in 1900 and nearly six times as good as they were in 1623.

Ideology, or the content of people's minds, helps to determine the degree of support provided for the aged under given income conditions, for it affects the decisions of both legislatures and the public at large. How ideology will affect the future lot of the aged is not clear, however. It is not certain that secular ideological trends will continue in directions favorable to increasing and diversified support of measures designed to afford material aid to the aged. Should an upward trend continue, the impact of favorable material trends will be accentuated. Should a downward ideological trend develop, however, the impact of favorable material trends will be reduced somewhat.

2. The age composition of the American population will be less favorable to productivity in the course of the next 40 years than it was for 1930 to 1960.* It is possible, therefore, that employment opportunities for persons aged 65 and over will be slightly better over the next 30 years than they were from 1930 to 1950. Even should this prospect materialize, it will fluctuate somewhat insofar as there is variation in the ratio of entries into the labor market to departures from that market. In a stable population this ratio is highly correlated with the gross rate of reproduction.† Employment

---

* In 1930 about 56 percent of the population was of working age defined as persons aged 20 to 64 years; in 1950 about 58 percent were of this age. Between 1960 and 1968, however, only about 52 percent were aged 20 to 64 years. This fraction will rise slightly in the future, to nearly 54 percent by 1980 and then, after falling nearly to 53 percent in 1990, rise nearly to 55 percent by 2015.

† E.g., see *The Aging of Populations and Its Economic and Social Implications*, Population Study No. 26 (New York: United Nations, 1956), pp. 55–59.

opportunities for the aged will probably be less satisfactory from 1970 to 2000 than in 1960, though they will be better later in the century.*

Should the American population grow according to the Bureau of the Census Series C projections (released Dec. 18, 1967, and March 14, 1968), the political position of the aged may be expected to deteriorate in the present century. Indeed, between 1970 and early in the next century, the potential political power of the aged will be less favorable than it was in the decade now ending. Whence one may say that if the aged would profit politically by their current but transitory strength they must act now.†

It is evident from these data that the political power of the aged would be greatly reduced should their representatives in Congress and state legislatures confer the vote upon all persons attaining the age of 18. Should this take place, the fraction which persons age 45 and over would form of the then population aged 18 and over would decline from 45.6 percent in 1970 to about 40 percent in 1990; thereafter it would rise slowly, to nearly 49 percent by the year 2015. It seems likely that at the hands of these younger people, if they were to become voters, the cause of the aged would receive little political support.

3. The aged may continue to count upon inflation to erode the purchasing power of their fixed incomes, whether these flow from pensions, government bonds, annuities, or other fixed sources. The economic disciplines formerly counted upon to prevent both un-

---

The ratio of entries to departures varies greatly from industry to industry because of interindustry differences in growth of output, technology, etc. See A. J. Jaffé and J. Froomkin, *Technology and Jobs* (New York: Praeger, 1968).

* We may use as a crude index of change in the ratio of entries to departures the ratio of persons aged 15 to 19 to those aged 65 to 69. This ratio, 2.14 in 1960, rises to about 2.77 by 1970 and thus, given *ceteris paribus*, reduces employment opportunities for the aged below what they were in 1960. The ratio is expected to approximate 2.55 in 1980, 2.33 in 1990, and 2.29 in 2015.

† From 1960 to 1970 the population aged 45 and over approximated one-half of the population of voting age, 21 and over. This fraction will decline after 1970, however, to just below 46 percent in 1980 and about 43 percent in 1990, thereafter rising slightly above 45 percent by the year 2000 and slightly above 52 percent by 2015.

warranted price increases and a rising price level have disappeared along with the old prescription for curing a dog of killing sheep: "cut off his tail, just behind the ears" [3]. Barriers to the upward movement of prices have been relaxed, with trade union and corporate czars increasing asked-prices faster than warranted by increases in productivity, and with the government standing by to increase the money supply commensurately if essential to prevent unemployment. An ideology in support of rising prices has come into being and infiltrated the minds of some economists, among others.

At least six specific forces may strengthen the upward drift of prices bearing upon the aged. (a) Outstanding is the decline in the relative political power of the aged, since ultimately whether we have inflation or not turns on whether congressmen who might acquiesce in inflation are permitted by the voters to endorse or pursue inflationary policies. (b) The amount of tax revenue slated to be collected by federal, state, and local governments is likely to exceed 35 percent of the national income, a ratio in excess of that which some believe compatible with the avoidance of inflation. The tendency toward inflation is intensified by the fact that so much of governmental expenditure is upon objectives which amount to little more than governmental potlatch and which contribute little or nothing to man's welfare or to the progress of economic development. (c) Governmental and trade union wage policy contributes to inflation in several ways. On the one hand it causes unemployment by elevating wages to unemployment-fostering levels and thereby increasing the cost of governmental support for the unemployed. On the other hand trade union and business leaders, by agreeing to wage increases in excess of increases in productivity, not only prevent price decreases but also give rise to price increases and thereby strengthen inflation-generating forces. Even if wages in more productive industries merely keep pace with increases in output, their doing so fosters excessive wage and price increases in industries experiencing lower advances in output per man-hour (e.g., in some of the services, the whole of which now employ more than half the labor force).*

* For a description of the price-increasing mechanism see J. J. Spengler and J. M. Kreps, Equity and Social Credit for the Retired. In J. M. Kreps (Ed.), *Em-*

(d) No New Politics has been brought into existence to complement the so-called New Economics. In other words, no new set of political institutions has been established to put the so-called new "full-employment," "growth-fostering" fiscal policy into effect in such wise as to accomplish the objectives of this policy without at the same time generating continuing inflation. Hence, even as some economists warned years ago, when they advised that the annual rate of growth of the national money supply be kept at the 3 or 4 percent level, inflation has become the hallmark of recent American administrations and is likely to remain so as long as a soft administration is combined with a prodigal Congress.* (e) It seems now to be assumed that, when employment is less than "full," deficit spending should be resorted to even though most unemployment is of short duration, at least two-fifths of households with an unemployed head have a breadwinner, and considerable unemployment is not imputable to a "deficiency" of "aggregate demand." Moreover, if "full" employment is defined as equivalent to less than, say, 4 to 5 percent unemployment, inflation is assured, particularly when many of the unemployed lack skills and experience in demand.† Should such a guideline be operative and produce inflation, the demand of the aged for assistance will be intensified. (f) Premature retirement also tends to strengthen the forces making for inflation, whether that retirement is voluntary or is in effect imposed on a worker by a combination of trade union and corporate czars. For, in proportion as the ratio of a man's years in retirement to his years in the labor

---

*ployment, Income, and Retirement Problems of the Aged* (Durham: Duke University Press, 1963), chap. 6, esp. pp. 213–219; and on services, J. J. Spengler, Services and the Future of the American Economy, *South Atlantic Quart.* 76:105–115, Winter 1967.

* On sources of inflation see Kreps, *op. cit.,* p. 228, and R. T. Elson, How the Old Politics Swamped the New Economics, *Fortune* 75ff, Sept. 1968, and *Studies by the Staff of the Cabinet Committee on Price Stability* (Washington, D.C.: U.S. Government Printing Office, Jan. 1969), esp. chaps. 2, 4.

† On the original goal of the 1946 Employment Act see E. G. Nourse, Defining Our Employment Goal Under the 1946 Act, *Rev. Econ. Stat.* 38:193–204, May 1956; also I. H. Siegel, *Fuller Employment with Less Inflation* (Upjohn Institute Staff Paper) (Kalamazoo: Jan. 1969); S. W. Stahl, The Phillips Curve: A Dilemma for Public Policy, Inflation versus Unemployment, *Bus. Rev.* (Federal Reserve Bank of Philadelphia), pp. 11–17, Jan. 1969.

force increase, the ratio of his retirement income to his preretirement income diminishes.* This in turn leads to pressure upon Congress to increase social security and other benefits, probably through recourse to general revenue or to deficit financing instead of to increase in social security "taxes."

4. Attention may be drawn to Clarence D. Long's theory of "creeping unemployment," a companion effect of the process referred to in (c) under (3), just preceding. When all wages increase at the same pace as wages of the most productive workers, it becomes increasingly uneconomic to employ infra-average workers at these supra-average wage levels. The unemployment of infra-average workers therefore increases, and so does that of older workers insofar as they are members of infra-average categories [4: pp. 397–398]. Here again uneconomic arrangements price older and other workers out of the market and augment their need of public assistance and hence intensify inflation-generating forces.

5. The need as well as the demand of the aged for greater assistance will be intensified by deterioration of the employment opportunities open to the aged, together with relatively early retirement imposed upon older workers by trade union, corporate, and governmental bureaucracies. Given a relatively low ratio of years worked to years in retirement, a worker cannot earn enough to enjoy a comfortable income in retirement, nor can or will the federal government supplement retirement incomes enough to make them comfortable under prospective conditions. Yet this ratio has been falling even though most workers can continue in their employments until age 70, given good health and refresher training, the cost of which could be met by cutting down the cost of high school and college education, perhaps by one-fourth, as suggested by Machlup

* See reports in *U.S. News & World Report,* pp. 99–100, Nov. 8, 1965, pp. 72–73, Oct. 16, 1967; E. K. Faltermayer, The Drift to Early Retirement, *Fortune,* pp. 112ff., May 1965. A man's pension is reduced by something like 6 to 7 percent for each year he retires prior to his normal retirement age. *Ibid.* p. 113. See also M. S. Gordon, National Retirement Policies and the Displaced Older Worker, reprinted from *Age with a Future* (Copenhagen: Munksgaard, 1964).

[4: pp. 133–134]. Indeed, the ratio could easily be kept at five or six work years to one year in retirement.*

6. One may divide the labor force in various ways, analytical or descriptive. For purposes of lay exposition one may divide it into *job makers* and *job takers*. One may also assume that the amount of employment of job takers depends very roughly upon the number of job makers. If this be true, then whatever forces (e.g., excessive taxation) diminish the number or prevent the growth in number of job makers will affect job takers adversely, particularly job takers near the margin of employment, as a good many older workers are likely to be.

7. As Kreps has shown in chapter 4, the average real income of older persons may increase over time, but probably not fast enough to keep pace with the average real income of the population. A retired worker's income, being fixed, not only is not augmented by economic progress, but is subject to erosion through both inflation and the inability of many corporations to pay the pensions they are pledged to pay [6]. Not surprisingly, the incomes of many aged are below the poverty level and may be kept there if the poverty level is adjusted upward. Even so, given a prospective 2 percent per year increase in average output, the prospective need of the aged for governmental supplements can be met.†

8. The continuing employability of older workers, as shown elsewhere, depends upon their meeting minimal health standards and hence *inter alia* upon their having adequate access to medical and

---

* Between 1900 and 1960 the number of years at work per year in retirement on relatively low retirement income fell from 14.1 to 6.1. Should a worker typically enter the labor force at age 20, retire at 60, and die at 80, he would work two years for every one in retirement. Within these two years he would have to earn enough to support himself comfortably and at the same time set aside enough to give rise to a comfortable retirement income. It would appear preferable under the assumed circumstances that he work at least 50 years to age 70 and thus raise the number of work years per retirement year at least to five (a ratio anticipated by the year 2000).

† On some of the issues, see C. T. Brehm and T. R. Saving, The Demand for General Assistance Payments, *Amer. Econ. Rev.* 54:1002–1018, Dec. 1964; J. Conlisk, Simple Dynamic Effects in Work-Leisure Choice: A Skeptical Comment on the Static Theory, *J. Hum. Resources* 3:324–326, 1968.

paramedical service, now in short supply because of the uneconomic manner in which medical service is produced and supplied [5]. Man's health problems are being intensified also, as René Dubos points out, by "slowly developing injurious effects" of man's "technological environment and the new ways of life" [2]. His whole environment is undergoing pollution—one might almost say that pollution is a form of entropy, a kind of perverse miracle of "loaves and fishes" whereunder when man consumes $x$ of something it gives rise to $3x$ of pollutants of one sort or another. To these conditions external to the worker must be added such body-weakening practices as overnutrition and the substitution of spectatorial for participative recreation. In sum, despite the improvements achieved in the field of medicine, the sum total of changes in the circumstances surrounding and animating man may eventually decrease man's employability in later years. After all, in the end the functioning of a body may reflect adverse events much as a tree's rings reflect adverse seasons.

## CONCLUSION

The need older people feel for public assistance will remain high in the future and will probably be intensified as well. On the one hand the purchasing power of their income streams will be gradually reduced by the inflationary pressures built into the American economy. On the other hand there will probably be increasing pressure to throw older workers out of the labor force as control of industry and access to employment becomes still more bureaucratized. Meanwhile, for at least several decades the potential political power of the older members of the population is likely to be diminished. The prognosis, therefore, is for increasing public satisfaction of the material requirements of the aged, but not in an amount sufficient to correct the current tendency toward increase in the relative deprivation of the aged. Only effective organization and leadership of the Townsend sort would be likely to reverse this tendency.

The older population's requirement of public assistance will turn in large part upon the extent to which its disengagement from involvement in community socioeconomic activities parallels its physical and mental capacity for such involvement. Of overriding importance is its being kept engaged in economically gainful activity, since its involvement in other forms of activity depends largely upon its remaining engaged in gainful activity. Such engagement depends in turn upon the maintenance of physical and mental health at least into the early seventies and upon the prevention of enforced disengagement of older persons either by trade union and corporate czars or by essentially autonomous bureaucrats. Flexibility and differentials in remuneration in keeping with differences in ability to perform are also essential. Some older persons may prefer disengagement. This they should be permitted, but with the right of an individual to reverse a decision to disengage within, say, 6 to 12 months should they find disengagement unsatisfying and be capable of reengagement [1].

## REFERENCES

1. Clark, F. L. *Work, Age and Leisure.* London: Michael Joseph, 1966.
2. Dubos, R. *So Human an Animal.* New York: Scribner, 1968.
3. Eastburn, D. P. Economic discipline and the middle generation. *Business Review* of Federal Reserve Bank of Philadelphia. No. 3, July, 1968.
4. Machlup, F. *The Production and Distribution of Knowledge in the United States.* Princeton: Princeton University Press, 1962.
5. The plight of the U.S. patient. *Time,* pp. 53–58, Feb. 21, 1969.
6. Wise, T. A. Those uncertain actuaries: II. *Fortune,* p. 164, Jan. 1966.

# Index

Abiotrophy, 257
    morale and, 59
    satisfaction and, 59
    stereotypes concerning, 50–51
    theory of aging, 27–28, 30
Activity(ies)
    disengagement vs., 57–60
Adaptation
    determinants of, 183–185
    task of, in old age, 185–186
Adjustment to retirement, 108
Adult education, 340–341
Age
    differences
        of aged, 41–43
        in living arrangements, 131
    pensionable. See Pensionable age
    retirement
        job discrimination and, 103
        pensionable age and, 79–81
    specific death rates by cause, 120
    unions and, 102
Aged
    "aged brain," 257
    in agricultural societies, 36–39
    analysis of, 226–227
    cognitive changes in, 237–250
    community services for. See Community services
    definitions of, 6, 13
    economic differences among, 41–47
    employment and, 53–55
    free time of, 109–111
    future of, 374–382
    future society and, 60–64
    health care. See Health, care, of aged, constraints to
    health experience of, 115–128
    illness patterns of, 115–118
    income of, 72
    in industrial societies, 39–41
    institutional care of, 289–312

intellectual changes in, 237–250
    interests of, basic, 35
    as a minority group, 2–3, 47–57
    mortality of, 118–119
    needs of, basic, 35
    nursing of, See Nursing
    older, definition of, 6
    population, estimates of, 2
    psychiatric disorders. See Psychiatric disorders
    public policy and, 367–383
        forces operative in recent past, 368–374
    religion and, 45–47
    roles, in the future, 63
    sexual behavior of. See Sexual behavior
    social casework. See Social casework
    social differences among, 41–47
    stereotypes of, 47–52
    subculture of, 55–57
        increase in future, 62
    younger, definition of, 6
Aging
    body components and, 17–18
    brain and time, 251–262
    cross-cultural differences in, 34–41
    definitions of, 12–13
    genetic determinants of, 24–25
    primary, 12–13
    process, as deliberate biological programming, 18
    secondary, 13
    sociological aspects of, 33–69
    in somatic cells, 22
    space travelers and, 26
    theories. See Theories, of aging
Agricultural societies, aged in, 36–39
Alcohol and death awareness, 176
Alzheimer's disease, 258
Amitriptyline for severe depression, 213

Anencephaly, 256
Angiogenesis, abnormal, 256
Anoxia, 252
    cerebral, 317
Anxiety
    bodily manifestations of, 196–197
    death, 163
    definition of, 196
    experience of, in aged, 196–199
    psychophysiological manifestations of,
        197
    tranquilizers for, 198–199
Apartments, high-rise, for aged, 144–
    145
Army Alpha score, 242
Arteriosclerotic heart disease, 119–122
Arthritis, 117
Aspirin, 124
Atherosclerosis, 255
    cerebral, 256, 275–276
        measurement of, 272–273
    cortical, 256
Atrophy-of-disuse theory, 30
Attitudes
    health care of aged and, 127
    toward institutional use, 304–305
Autobiography and awareness of death,
    177
Autoimmune mechanisms, stimulation
    during senescence, 24
Aventyl for severe depression, 213
Awareness of death, 164–167
    emotional reactions to, 169–171
    preconscious, of impending death,
        165
    Rosow Death Awareness Scale, 173–
        174

Bacterial toxins, 252
Balinese culture, 36
Barbiturates, 124
    sleep and, 201
Bathing and nursing care, 317
Behavior, risk-taking, and learning, 246
Benefits
    old age, in selected countries, 77
    retirement, 87
Berkeley Longitudinal Studies and
    mental ability, 242
Blood flow, cerebral, measurements,
    273–276

Body components and aging, 17–18
Brain
    "aged," 257
    damage, and brief psychotherapy,
        228
    hemiatrophy of, 256
    impairment, and psychiatric disorder
        prognosis, 280
    status
        cognitive function and, 269
        evaluation of, 270–279
            behavioral manifestations, 270–
                272
            cerebral atrophy measurement,
                272–273
            cerebral metabolism and blood
                flow measurements, 273–276
            EEG study, 276–279
            histopathologic examination, 272
    syndrome
        organic. *See* Organic brain syn-
            dromes
    paranoid reactions and, 220
    time and aging, 251–262

Cardiac output and intellectual per-
    formance, 244
Cardiovascular disease and intellectual
    performance, 244
Catholic tradition and aging, 44–45
Cells
    animal, faults in, 20
    glial, 252–253
    HeLa, 17
    immortality and, 16
    maturation of, 253
    renewal of, 19
    somatic, aging in, 22
Centers for older persons, 338–339
Cephalization, index of, 24
Cerebrum
    anoxia, 317
    atherosclerosis, 255, 256, 275–276
    atrophy, measurement of, 272–273
    cortex, in Down's syndrome, 259
    hypoxia, 280, 317
    metabolism and blood flow measure-
        ments, 273–276
    thrombosis, and hemorrhage, 122–
        123

Children
proximity to, and living arrangements, 134–136
roles of, and living arrangements, 133–137
Chlordiazepoxide and anxiety, 198–199
Chlorpromazine in paranoid reactions, 220
Cholesterol levels and intellectual performance, 244
Chorea, Huntington's, 257
Class differences of aged, 43
Cognitive changes in aged, 237–250
Cognitive function and brain status, 269
Community involvement in program planning for aged, 339–340
Community, planned, for aged, 144
Community services, 330–342
adult education, 340–341
centers for older persons, 338–339
community involvement in program planning, 339–340
comprehensive services by single agency, 330–332
employment opportunities, 341–342
extended care facilities, 336
homemaker services, 333
home nursing care, 335
meals-on-wheels, 333
occupational therapy, 334
physical therapy, 334
protective services, 335–336
retirement planning and, 332–333
vocational rehabilitation, 341
volunteer services, 336–338
Composite theory, 21–22
Conferences and geropsychiatry, 353–354
Congregate living arrangements, 142
Consultation programs and geropsychiatry, 354–356
Coronary artery disease, 117
Counterphobic mechanisms and death awareness, 176
Countertransference in geropsychiatry, 347
Courses in geropsychiatry, 356–359. *See also* Geropsychiatry
Credits, deferred retirement, 80
"Creeping unemployment," 380
Cretinism, 254, 255

Crime, 224–225
Cross-cultural differences in aging, 34–41
Cross-linkage theory, 23–24
Cybernetic theory, 30

Deafness and paranoid reactions, 217–218
Death
anxiety, 163
awareness of, 164–167
emotional reactions to, 169–171
Rosow Death-Awareness Scale, 173–174
concerns about, 167
coping with the prospect of, 171–179
defense mechanisms and, 171–172
denial of, 175
facing death, 163–181
fear of, 169–170
impending, preconscious awareness of, 165
life after, belief in, 172–173
personal meanings of, 167–169
the anticipated or the unknown, 168
continuation or cessation of life, 167–168
death as the enemy, 168
reunion or isolation, 168
reward or punishment, 168
rates, age-specific, by cause, 120
satisfaction with past and, 172
taboo on open discussion of, 174
thoughts, frequency of, 165–167
Defense mechanisms
death and, 171–172
primitive, 199
Dementia, senile, 258
prognosis, 280
Demographic factors in retirement in industrial societies, 97
Denial of death, 175
Deoxyribonucleic acid (DNA), 257
Depression, 209–214
dynamics of, 209–210
milder, treatment of, 210
severe
drug therapy of, 213
electroconvulsive therapy, 214
psychotherapy, 212–213
treatment, 212–214

Desipramine for severe depression, 213
Diagnosis. *See* Psychiatric diagnosis
Discrimination in employment of aged,
    53–55
Disease. *See* Illness
Disengagement
    vs. activity, 57–60
    death awareness and, 175, 176
    theory, 27
Disorientation in organic brain syn-
    dromes, 267
DNA (deoxyribonucleic acid), 257
Down's syndrome, 258
    cerebral cortex in, 259
Drug(s)
    death awareness and, 176
    therapy of severe depression, 213
Duke Longitudinal Studies, 6–8
    findings on sexual behavior of aged,
        157–160
    sample of, 7
Duke University Information and
    Counseling Service, 330–331

Earnings
    average hourly, international com-
        parisons, 76
    pension ratios, 79
Economic differences among the aged,
    41–47
Economic factors
    in health care of aged, 126–127
    in retirement in industrial societies,
        97–98
Economic retirement, 95–97
Economic unit size and retirement in
    industrial societies, 98–99
Economics of retirement, 71–91
Economies, advanced, income and lei-
    sure in, 72–84
Education, adult, 340–341
Ego strength of aged, 227
Elavil for severe depression, 213
Elderly. *See* Aged
Electroconvulsive therapy for severe
    depression, 214
Electroencephalographic study of brain
    status, 276–279
Employment
    of aged, discrimination in, 53–55
    opportunities, and community ser-
        vices, 341–342

Encephalopathy, hypertensive, 256
England
    international comparisons of income,
        76–78
    social insurance in, 101–102
English Poor Law, 101
Epidemiology of psychiatric disorders
    of old age, 190–193
Equation, Gompertz's, 14–15
Error theory, 22–23
Erythrocyte, absence of nucleus in, 19
Euthanasia, 61–63
    acceptance of, 62
    definition, 61–62
Eversion theory, 23–24
Exhaustion theory, 18
Extended care facility, 292
    as community service, 336

Facilities, medical, and health care of
    aged, 125–126
Failure, fear of, and learning, 246
Faults in animal cells, 20
Fear
    of death, 169–170
    of failure, and learning, 246
Fountain of Youth, 12
Free time, 109–111
Friendly Visitors, 337
Future of aged, 374–382
Future societies and aged, 60–64

Genetic determinants of aging, 24–25
Geriatrics. *See also* Aged
    definition, 345
Germany
    international comparisons, of in-
        come, 76–78
    pensionable age in, 82
    social insurance in, 101
Germinal mantle, 252
Gerocomy, 12
Gerontologists, definitions, 345
Gerontophobia, 5
Geropsychiatry, 345–365
    conferences, workshops, and insti-
        tutes, 353–354
    consultation programs, 354–356
    courses, 356–359
    definition, 345
    personnel needs, 345–346
    social, 347

special problems in working with aged, 346–349
trainee categories and characteristics, 349–352
training methods, 352–363
training programs
at Duke, 360–363
activities and resources, 362
curriculum, 361
formal, 359–363
Glial cells, 252–253
Glucose, determination of, 274
Glycolysis, anaerobic, 256
Gompertz's equation, 14–15
Gompertz's plot, 15
"Grab bars," 144
Grandparent generation of the future, 147
Granulovacuolar degeneration, 258
characteristics of, 260
Great Britain. *See* England
Group
identification, 57
minority
aged as, 2–3, 47–57
nature of, 3–4
pride, 56
research, 1
therapy, 228–229

Haldol in paranoid reactions, 220
Haloperidol in paranoid reactions, 220
Halstead Impairment Index, 244
Happiness, study of, 50
Health
care, of aged, constraints to, 124–127
attitudinal factors in, 127
economic factors in, 126–127
experience, in aged, 115–128
intellectual performance and, 243–245
Hearing and nursing care, 314
Heart
disease, 117
arteriosclerotic, 119–122
output, and intellectual performance, 244
Heart block, complete, 122
HeLa cells, 17
Hemiatrophy of brain, 256
Hemorrhage, cerebral, 122–123

Hepatectomy, partial, and regeneration, 252
Hit in stochastic theories, 20
Home(s)
nursing care, 335
old-age compared with nursing, 294–296
ownership, 140
Homemaker services, 333
Hospital(s)
for institutional living, 137
independence and, 142
psychiatric, patients living in or admitted to, in U.S., 264
state, 289-291
"Hospitalization syndrome," 290
Hotels, retirement, 143, 145
Housing, 129–130, 138–148
characteristics of, 140–141
future trends, 146–148
new forms of, 143–146
population distribution, 139–140
rental, 140
shortages, and living arrangements, 133
Huntington's chorea, 257
Hydranencephaly, 256
Hyperactivity and death awareness, 176
Hypertension and intellectual performance, 244
Hypochondriasis, 202–209
dynamics of, 202–204
surgery and, 205
treatment of, 204–208
effective techniques, 205–208
handling of interviews, 207–208
handling of relatives, 206–207
placebos, 205–206
Hypothyroidism, 255
Hypoxia, cerebral, 280, 317

Identification, group, 57
Illness
acute, 115–117
days of restricted activity due to, 116
incidence of, by age, 116
chronic, 117–118
incidence of, 118
patterns in aged, 115–118
stereotypes of, 47–49

Imipramine for severe depression, 213
Immortality
  animals and, 16
  cells and, 16
  survival and, 15–17
Income
  in advanced economies, 72–84
  of aged, 72
  as basis for status, 56
  fixed, and inflation, 377–378
  international comparisons of, 74–79
  inverse relation to work, 73–75
  levels, and work of aged, 75–79
  maintenance, in U.S., 84–91
  national, in selected countries, 76
  real, increase in, 84
  retirement, 86–89
  temporal distribution of, 89–91
Independence and housing, 141–143
Index of cephalization, 24
Industrial societies
  aged in, 39–41
  retirement in, 93, 97–99
    demographic factors influencing,
      97
    economic factors influencing, 97–
      98
    economic unit size and, 98–99
    segregation of work and leisure
      and, 99
    skills required and, 98
Infarction
  ischemic, 123
  myocardial, 121
Inflation and fixed incomes, 377–378
Information and Counseling Service
      for Older Persons at Duke
      University, 330–331
Insomnia, chronic, 201
Institutes and geropsychiatry, 353–354
Institution(s)
  admissions to, and socioeconomic
      factors, 299
  care of aged in, 289–312
    therapeutic efforts and, 305–308
    nonhospital, 291–298
    use of, attitudes toward, 304–305
    populations of, 298–304
    mortality and, 308–309
Institutional living, 132–133
  function of the institution, 137–138
Insurance. See Social insurance

Intellectual changes in aged, 237–250
Intellectual function impairment in
      organic brain syndrome, 267
Intellectual performance and health,
      243–245
Intellectualization and death aware-
      ness, 176
Intelligence
  concept of, 238–239
  measurement of, 240–243
  research strategies, 239–240
    cross-sectional approach, 239
    cross-sequential approach, 239, 240
    longitudinal approach, 239
Interdisciplinary, discussion of term, 1
Interests
  basic, of aged, 35
  stereotypes concerning, 49
International comparisons of income
      and work, 74–79
Ionizing radiation, exposure to, 21
Ischemia
  infarction and, 123
  myelin and, 253
Isolation, stereotypes concerning, 51–52

Jewish tradition and aging, 44
Job
  discrimination, and retirement age,
      103
  makers and takers, 381
Judeo-Christian tradition and aging,
      44
Judgment impairment in organic brain
      syndromes, 267

Kafir culture, 36
Kinsey's findings on sexual behavior in
      aged, 154–155
85Kr inhalation method of blood flow
      estimation, 275

Labor force participation of aged in
      selected countries, 78
Learning, 245–247
Legislation, retirement, 101
Leisure
  in advanced economies, 72–84
  growth in U.S., 85
  segregation from work, and retire-
      ment in industrial societies, 99
  temporal distribution of, 89–91

Librium and anxiety, 198–199
Life
after death, belief in, 172–173
expectancy, 14
increase in, 61
review
death awareness and, 177
self image and, 183–184
-span, factors influencing, 25–26
-style, 318
Lithium carbonate in mania, 214
Living arrangements, 129–138
changes, and social casework, 328–330
congregate, 142
distribution by sex and age, 131
future trends, 146–148
proximity to children, 134–136
roles of children, relatives, and neighbors, 133–137
Loneliness, 188–190
schizophrenia and, 188
Longevity, 13–15
Looking-glass self, 34

Mania, 214–215
lithium carbonate in, 214–215
phenothiazine in, 215
Manpower
medical, and health care of aged, 125–126
needs, and retirement policy, 81–84
Marital problems and social casework, 328
"Martin" method of psychotherapy, 226
Masters and Johnson's findings on sexual behavior of aged, 155–157
Meals-on-wheels, 333
Mean time to failure concept, 20
Meanings of death. *See* Death, personal meanings of
Medical manpower and facilities, and health care of aged, 125–126
Medicare
coverage, of psychiatric treatment, 195–196
institutional care and, 292
quasihospitals and, 293
Mellaril in paranoid reactions, 220
Memory loss in organic brain syndromes, 267

Men. *See* Sex differences
Mental abilities, stereotypes concerning, 49–50
Mental disorders. *See* Psychiatric disorders
Metabolism, cerebral, measurements, 273–276
Methyprylon and sleep, 201
Middle-class workers and adjustment to retirement, 108
Minnesota Multiphasic Personality Inventory Study, 50
Minority groups
aged as, 2–3, 47–57
nature of, 3–4
Mobile home parks for aged, 145
Morale
activity and, 59
stereotypes concerning, 50
Mortality
age-specific death rates by cause, 120
in aged, 118–119
institutional populations and, 308–309
rate, as function of age, in U.S., 15
Multidisciplinary, discussion of term, 1
Mutation theory, 23
Myelin and ischemia, 253
Myelinization, 253
Myelinogenesis, 253
Myocardial infarction, 121

Needs, basic, of aged, 35
Negroes, aged, 43–44
Neighbors, roles of, and living arrangements, 133–137
Nephrectomy, unilateral, and regeneration, 252
Nervous system
synapses of, 254
Wallerian degeneration in, 254
Neural development, 251–256
Neurofibrillary degeneration, 258
neuron with, 260
neurons and senile plaque, 259
Neuron
depopulation, 256–261
neurofibrillary degeneration and, 259, 260
regeneration of, 254
senile plaque and, 259

Neurosis
  hypochondriacal, 202
  incidence, 191
Nitrous oxide method of blood flow
    estimation, 275
Noludar and sleep, 201
Normative reactions to old age, 186–
    188
Norpramine for severe depression, 213
Nortriptyline for severe depression, 213
Nursing, 313–321
  home nursing care, 335
  homes, 137
    comparison with old-age homes,
      294–296
    independence and, 142
  practice
    environmental needs of aged and,
      318
    physiological knowledge influenc-
      ing, 316–318
    psychological knowledge influenc-
      ing, 314–316
  research, gerontological, 319–320

Obligation to retire, 99–100
Occlusive vascular disease, 256
Occupational therapy, 334
Old-age benefits, in selected countries,
    77
Old-age homes, comparison with nur-
    sing homes, 294–296
Organic brain syndromes, 263–287
  characteristics of, 267
  evaluating brain status. *See* Brain,
    status, evaluation of
  evaluation of age with symptoms
    suggesting, 267–270
  permanent, 267
  prevalence in old age, 263–267
  prognosis, 280–282
  as sociopsychosomatic in origin, 269
  temporary, 267
  therapy, 279–280
Osteoarthritis, 117–118
Osteoporosis, 123–124
Oxygen consumption, 273–277

Palaung of North Burma, 36
Paraldehyde and sleep, 201
Paranoid reactions, 215–220
  chlorpromazine in, 220

deafness and, 217–218
  haloperidol in, 220
  psychotic, 218–219
  symptoms, 215–216
    in other psychiatric disorders, 220
  thioridazine in, 220
  treatment, 219–220
Patriarchal family of nineteenth cen-
    tury, American, 36–37
Paying for psychiatric care, 194–196
Pension
  plans
    private, proportion of workers
      covered by, 95
    savings and, 106
  ratios of, to earnings, 79
Pensionable age
  age of retirement and, 79–81
  in Germany, 82
  in selected countries, 77
Personality disorders. *See* Psychiatric
    disorders
Pertofrane for severe depression, 213
Phenothiazine
  mania and, 215
  paranoid reactions and, 220
Phenylketonuria, 254
Physical therapy, 334
Physician shortage and health care of
    aged, 125–126
Placebos and hypochondriasis, 205–206
Plaque, senile, 258
  neurons and neurofibrillary degen-
    eration, 259
Political power, 56–57
Population, elderly, estimates of, 2
Poverty, 72
Power, social and political, 56–57
Prejudice, nature of, 4–5
Presbycardia, 122
Pride, group, 56
Privilege to retire, 99–100
Productivity, stereotypes concerning, 51
Project Outreach, 332
Protective services, 335–336
Protestant attitudes toward aging, 45
Psychiatric care, paying for, 194–196
Psychiatric diagnosis
  in aged living in or admitted to psy-
    chiatric hospitals in U.S., 265
  suicide and, 222–223

Psychiatric disorders
epidemiology, 190–193
functional (psychogenic), 183–235, 267
incidence, 191
organic, 267
Psychiatric hospitals, patients living in or admitted to, in U.S., 264
Psychiatry
geropsychiatry. *See* Geropsychiatry
preventive, in old age, 193–194
Psychoanalysis of the aged, 226–227
Psychopathology, incidence, 191, 192
Psychosis
affective, 211
paranoid symptoms in, 220
depressive, 211–212
incidence, 191
paranoid, 218–219
Psychotherapy, 225–228
brief, and brain damage, 228
of depression, severe, 212–213
group, 228–229
insight-oriented, 227
"Martin" method, 226
supportive, 227
Public policy and aged, 367–383
forces operative in recent past, 368–374

Quasihospitals, 293

Race differences of aged, 43–44
Radiation, ionizing, exposure to, 21
Ratios, pension/earnings, 79
Regression and death awareness, 175
Relatives, roles of, and living arrangements, 133–137
Religion, importance for aged, 45–47
Religious differences of aged, 44–45
REM sleep, 200, 201
Rental housing, 140
Research
multidisciplinary, 1
nursing, gerontological, 319–320
"Retired" workers, 95
Retirement
acceptance by society, 105
adjustment to, 108
age
job discrimination and, 103

pensionable age and, 79–81
unions and, 102
ambiguity of, 93–114
individual facing, 104–111
society creating the ambiguity, 99–104
benefits, 87
changing meaning of, 93–99
credits, deferred, 80
early, 90
economic, 95–97
economics of, 71–91
free time and, 109–111
hotels, 143, 145
income, 86–89
in industrial society. *See* Industrial societies
legislation, 101
obligation and, 99–100
planning, and community services, 332–333
policy
development of, 100–104
manpower needs and, 81–84
prevalence in U.S., 94–95
privilege of, 99–100
process of, 105–107
as crisis, 106
regarded as achievement but actually dreaded, 100
social, 95–97
society's attitudes toward, 101
sociopsychological problem of, 100
status changes in, kinds of, 104
type of society and, 93–94
villages, 143
work status and, 107–109
Risk-taking behavior and learning, 246
Roles of aged in the future, 63
Rosow Death-Awareness Scale, 173–174

Satisfaction
activity and, 59
study of, 50
Savings and pension plans, 106
Schizophrenia and loneliness, 188
Segregation of aged, 52–53
Self-hatred, mixed group, 56
Self image and life review, 183–184
Self, looking-glass, 34
Senile dementia, 258

Senile plaque, 258
  neurons and neurofibrillary degeneration, 259
Sex differences
  of aged, 41–43
  in living arrangements, 131
  in retirement in U.S., 94–95, 96
Sexual behavior, 151–162
  Duke Longitudinal Study findings, 157–160
  implications of findings, 160–161
  Kinsey's findings, 154–155
  Masters and Johnson's findings, 155–157
  stereotypes concerning, 49
  taboo against sex in old age, 152–153
    nature of taboo, 153–154
Sick role, 202–203
Skills and retirement in industrial societies, 98
Sleep
  barbiturates and, 201
  disturbances, 199–202
  methyprylon and, 201
  paraldehyde and, 201
  pattern changes in aged, 200–201
  REM, 200, 201
Sleeping pills, prevalence of usage, 201
Social casework, 323–330
  client, definitions, 327
  goals, 324–325
  problems, 325–327
  settings, 325
  treatment, 327–330
    living arrangement changes, 328–330
    marital problems, 328
    relationship between aged parent and adult child, 328
Social deprivation, pathological effects of, 28
Social differences among the aged, 41–47
Social insurance, 101
  in England, 101–102
  in Germany, 101
Social power, 56–57
Social psychological problem of retirement, 100
Social security, 87
  proportion of workers covered by, 95

Society(ies)
  acceptance of retirement by, 105
  agricultural, aged in, 36–39
  attitudes toward retirement, 101
  creating the ambiguity of retirement, 99–104
  industrial. *See* Industrial societies
  type of, and retirement, 93–94
Socioeconomic factors and institutional admission, 299
Sociological aspects of aging, 33–69
Somatic complaints in nonmedical settings, 208–209
Space travelers and aging, 26
Spongioblasts, 253
Spouse, loss of, 188
State hospitals, 289–291
Status
  change, retirement process as, 105
  changes, and retirement, 104
  as a minority group, 2–3
  work, and retirement, 107–109
Stereotypes of aged, 47–52
Stochastic theories, 20
Subculture of aged, 55–57
  growth of, reason for, 55
  increase in future, 62
Sublimation and death awareness, 176
Suicide, 221–224
  attempted, 223–224
  death awareness and, 175
  prevention of, 224
  psychiatric diagnoses of persons committing, 222–223
  rates of, in U.S., 221
Surgery and hypochondriasis, 205
Survival
  of the fittest, 15–16
  immortality and, 15–17
Sweden, international comparisons of income, 76–78
Switzerland, international comparisons of income, 76–78

Tabes dorsalis and cell regeneration, 254
Taboo
  against sex in old age, 152–153
    nature of taboo, 153–154
  on open discussion of death, 174
Theories
  of aging, 11–32

accumulation of deleterious material and, 18
activity, 27–28, 30, 57
  biological, selected, 18–27
  combined, 29–30
  mean time to failure concept and, 20
  psychological, 29–30
  sociological, 27–29
atrophy-of-disuse, 30
composite, 21–22
cross-linkage, 23–24
cybernetic, 30
disengagement, 27, 57
error, 22–23
eversion, 23–24
exhaustion, 18
mutation, 23
stochastic, 20
Thioridazine in paranoid reactions, 220
Thorazine in paranoid reactions, 220
Thrombosis, cerebral, 122–123
Time
  brain and aging, 251–262
  free, 109–111
Tofranil for severe depression, 213
Toxins, bacterial, 252
Tranquilizers and anxiety, 198–199
Traumatic life experiences and life-span, 25–26

Unconscious mind and prejudice, 5
Unemployment, 75
  "creeping," 380
Unions and retirement age, 102
United Kingdom. *See* England
United States
  income maintenance in, 84–91
  international comparisons of income, 76–78

leisure in, 85
prevalence of retirement in, 94–95
Vascular occlusive disease, 256
Villages, retirement, 143
Vision and nursing care, 314
Vocational rehabilitation, 341
Volunteer services, 336–338

WAIS (Wechsler Adult Intelligence Scale), 241
Wallerian degeneration in nervous system, 254
Wealth as basis for status, 56
Wechsler Adult Intelligence Scale (WAIS), 241
Wechsler Bellevue test, 242
Widowhood, prevalence of, 132
Withdrawal and death awareness, 175, 176
Women. *See* Sex differences
Work
  of aged, and income levels, 75–79
  international comparisons of, 74–79
  inverse relation to income, 73–75
  meaning of, 111
  segregation from leisure, and retirement in industrial societies, 99
  status, and retirement, 107–109
Workers
  middle-class, and adjustment to retirement, 108
  "retired," 95
Working age population in selected countries, 83
Workshops and geropsychiatry, 353–354

133Xenon method of blood flow estimation, 275, 276

Youth
  Fountain of, 12
  prolonged, 11–12